THE
FAST &
FRESH
COOKBOOK

drawings by **Ruth Bornschlegel**

THE
FAST &
FRESH
Cookbook

Julie Dannenbaum

Galahad Books • New York

Previously published in two separate volumes as
FAST AND FRESH Copyright © 1981 by Julie Dannenbaum.
MORE FAST AND FRESH Copyright © 1983 by Julie Dannenbaum.

Published in 1994 by
Galahad Books
A division of Budget Book Service, Inc.
386 Park Avenue South
New York, NY 10016

Galahad Books is a registered trademark of Budget Book Service, Inc.
Published by arrangement with Harper Collins Publishers, Inc.

Library of Congress Catalog Card Number: 93-80403
ISBN: 0-88365-847-X

Printed in the United States of America.

CONTENTS

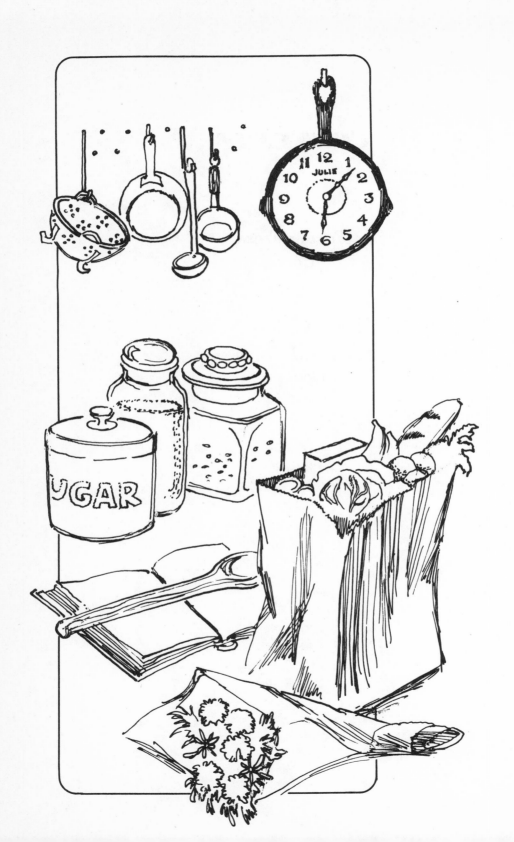

FAST & FRESH

Menus

CONTENTS

11. IMPROVISING FOR DROP-INS   199

12. COME FOR CASSE-CROÛTE!   217

13. CHEERS: DRINKS HOMEMADE AND OTHERWISE   221

14. WEEKENDS AND COOKING DAYS: SAUCES, STOCKS, AND OTHER INDISPENSABLES   232

15. FOOD HAS FEELINGS, TOO: METHODS AND TECHNIQUES   249

16. TOOLS OF THE TRADE: UTENSILS AND APPLIANCES   257

17. THOUGHTS FROM A COOKING TEACHER   261

To the memory of Dione Lucas
and to Jim Beard and Richard Olney

I would like to thank all my students and helpers in my cooking school for their support and enthusiasm. I especially would like to thank Bill Brodsky and Charles de Grasse. Barbara Graybeal deserves a thank-you from me as she admits she had fun in helping me with this book. Thanks, too, to my family for eating all the mistakes!

J.D.

1 INTRODUCTION

I've spent my day preparing such soul-satisfying creations as glazed poached chicken with a satiny chaudfroid sauce, brioche, *coulibiac*, and an ultra-rich cold Grand Marnier soufflé. Now comes the big question: *What are we having for dinner tonight?*

What with teaching at my cooking school (where the students promptly eat my masterworks), demonstrating, testing, and creating new recipes, I am completely involved with food during most of my waking hours. Food has become my career, and I love it! The tempo of my life, however, has dictated that it's time to come to terms with the truth: complicated recipes and lengthy menus just will not fit into my schedule all the time.

My pilgrimage in cooking began in my own home. Never would I serve my family and friends anything but food that is fresh, retains great flavor, and is as delicious as I can make it look and taste. While my ideas about time-saving meals were incubating I gradually developed recipes and menus for family only. Their enthusiastic reaction fired my journey onto the sidepaths of classic cuisine. Not only did they fully savor the meals, but they appreciated the time I saved, to spend with them.

Next I invited some friends to join us for a dinner prepared, from start to serving time, in one hour. These friends know I can cook, and they know good food. That evening, we all decided that while we adore lengthy, complicated, and wickedly rich foods, elaborate meals should be reserved for times, such as weekends, holidays, and special occasions, when we are not rushed.

I do not mean in any way to call classic cuisine trite: nothing is more fulfilling to me than teaching classes of students the most intricate recipes and techniques, then having them report back to me about a magnificent meal they've produced. It also pleases me that respect for good cooking is now part of American life. It means we are enjoying life more! The proliferation of cooking schools, pot and pan shops, spice and cheese shops, and marvelous takeout shops— along with books, magazines, newspaper sections, and television programs devoted to food—proves that knowing how to prepare a *beurre blanc*, a *choucroute garni*, a crown of lamb Béarnaise, or perhaps a puff pastry has become to the American psyche an accomplishment on par with playing tennis.

These recipes and menus are not meant to replace your collection of classics, but to enhance your repertoire and preserve your time. I wouldn't consider depriving you, or myself, of the satisfaction of preparing a wonderful meal, worth every day it requires to produce, a treasure to store in the memory box of great culinary experiences that everyone should possess.

Once you are accustomed to fine cooking, moreover, you can't revert to ordinary fare. But fast, fresh, and simple does not mean commonplace or pedestrian. After these menus passed a series of tests in my home, I initiated a "Fast and Fresh" course at my cooking school in Philadelphia, Pennsylvania. The response was amazing, an instant sellout. What surprised me even more, it included a number of my former students who had long since been graduated into the stratosphere of classic cuisine. "What are *you* doing here?" I asked. The answer from each was, "I love to cook, but don't have time for the full works every day."

I've worked out these menus so that each meal should take about an hour to create. This is not a stopwatch book, and you will not feel that I'm standing over you barking away the seconds. It is compiled in pace with an average cook, not a robot or a professional chef. If you are at ease with cooking techniques, you can follow each recipe straight through. If you need a few notes to help you understand what to do or how to do it, or if your memory needs a little nudge, notes are keyed into the basic recipes for instant reference. The recipes and menus can be interpolated to suit your pleasure, and to take advantage of fresh foods in season.

As for your own individual needs, be they low-calorie or low-cholesterol, listen to your doctor! While I cannot be responsible for any flops you might produce by altering my recipes, I can urge you to explore your own cooking talent, and I applaud you in your triumphs. I would not, for example, consider using a substitute for butter in my recipes, though perhaps I could change my mind if it climbs to ninety-five dollars a pound. You have the right, of course, to follow your own choices. In my cooking classes, in all my work, I encourage imagination and experimentation. I've learned a lot from my own failures, and you can, too. Besides, it's great when you pull off a winner!

If you are concerned about calories, I sympathize and have included some menus that will linger in your memory but not around your middle. My recipe for Scallops Minceur tastes so rich you'll feel guilty when you eat it. When I invented this dish, on a New Year's

Eve my husband and I spent alone at home, he said, "I'd love to take seconds, but I daren't. It's too fattening." "Not to worry," I smiled, doling out another portion for him, "this is extremely lo-cal and you can eat all you want."

"How do you stay so slim when you spend all your time cooking?" When people ask me this question, I feel proud to answer that I weigh the same now as I did thirty years ago. The reason is that I have come to terms with balancing days of eating very rich foods with days of eating lightly—and I try to abstain from snacking, the true culprit and figure-killer. Both classic cooking and simple, low-calorie food are enjoyable and I alternate styles without apology.

Indulge me, please, while I philosophize for a moment. There was a time when I believed no self-respecting meal could include any dish that was not a conversation piece. Now wiser and more mellow, I think one show-stopper accompanied by a simple but attractive cast is enough to make a meal a hit on most occasions. While once I served huge portions as a kind of way of telling my family and friends how much I love them, I have learned otherwise during my frequent travels abroad. We Americans serve entirely too much food, and this is not necessary or kind! Not that I believe in stinginess; I'm still American enough to think that a very tiny portion reveals mean spirit in the host or hostess. Your guests, nonetheless, should leave the table satisfied, not satiated.

Simplicity is the keynote throughout this book, and in simplicity there is an elegance, an integrity that makes natural, fresh food shine in its own light—beautiful. Many of these recipes suggest a garnish, a finishing touch, to show you care.

What if one of your creations zigs when it should zag? Don't stand there weeping or apologizing. Sometimes an imperfection enchants, proves that you did not buy everything from a shop. (Remember that the people who run those elegant takeout shops sometimes flaw their professional masterpieces just a bit to make them look homemade.)

Several decades of cooking have led me to an exciting life; great food is woven into the tapestry of interesting living. I think I have learned enough to know that being rigid is a mistake, in the kitchen or anywhere else. I do, however, have one cooking rule about which I'm inflexible. Plan your time! Control your menu rather than the other way around. Nothing is more uncomfortable for guests than an uptight host or hostess who makes them feel as though they've been invited to an anxiety attack instead of a delightsome meal. Plan, then relax and enjoy! This book is my way of helping you make the planning and the preparation of good food a tribute to your taste as well as to your time.

2 WHAT'S FOR DINNER?

When I commenced to design the menus for this chapter, I sorted them into "family" and "company" categories. Then that division seemed ridiculous to me: the most special company I will ever have is my own family, and anything I'd serve to them I'd proudly serve to guests.

As promised, any menu here can be prepared in about 60 minutes if you are an average cook. No meal features more than one dish with a sauce; on principle, I have decided that one sauce is almost always quite enough.

I've given careful thought to dinners that are delicious, varied, and interesting because I sincerely believe dinnertime should be sacrosanct in everyone's house. Sometimes, of course, we must rush, but as a general rule the dinner hour (and I mean hour) is privileged, a time to enjoy not only food, but each other.

Long before medical experts advised against stress-generating conversation at mealtime, arguments at the table were a no-no in our house. This tradition is one I grew up with and perhaps explains why good food, properly served and enjoyed, is a part of life to me. My mother was a gifted cook, the daughter of a professional chef; my college-professor father insisted that we grow our own vegetables. Mealtime for me means an ambience, a completeness of good food, love, security, people talking and sharing their lives day by day.

Today's pace, whereby kids race in, clutch whatever fast food is handy, and head for the television set seems to me a contrived and cruel trauma to family life and taste. When my daughter went off to college, she found that some of her classmates had never eaten one of life's great treasures—from-scratch mashed potatoes. Some of them are now imparting the grim legacy of instant mashed potatoes to their own children.

If I didn't know that most of us are too busy for leisurely dining all the time, I would not be writing this book. No one is going to convince me, however, that any family cannot share dinner once each week, delicious, served on the good china and with an hour's worth of good conversation interspersed. How else can children learn civilized table manners, or understand the sublime pleasure of *dining?*

I believe it's wrong to insist that anyone clean up the plate, but I also believe it's silly to cater to picky eaters. Even if it's just a soupçon, a tiny taste, each person should sample everything on the table unless there is a compelling excuse, such as a medically certified allergy. When another mother warned me that her child ate only peanut butter sandwiches, I battened down the peanut butter jar. It worked, and the child ate what I served to all the other kids. One of my own children disliked cheese of any kind, but through family custom she ate a sliver anyway. In time she made verbal music for her mother's ears by saying, "I don't know if I like French Port Salut better, or the Danish Port Salut."

I plan menus for flexible eaters. It's a mistake to prepare extra dishes in case someone does not like your meal, and if a guest has a doctor-ordered special diet, it is that person's responsibility to let you know. When an adult fusses and picks and complains about not liking this or that, I am reminded of the little kid whose mother let him stick to peanut butter sandwiches!

Some of the following menus call for made-ahead sauces and stocks, which you can find in the "Weekends and Cooking Days" chapter. These are so basic they should be in everyone's repertoire, like homemade mashed potatoes. Read them, please, so you won't waste precious bones and juices they require.

A number of the dinners suggest an attitude, a mood, an occasion. That's part of the fun of planning a meal, and it's an outlet for flair, showmanship, the theatrical touch that is in the fingertips of every creative cook.

A Dinner for 6 Hungry People

MENU   **Ham and Cabbage Roll, Piquant Mustard Sauce
Boiled Red-Skin Potatoes
Fresh Crisp Apples with Warm Spice Cookies**

BEVERAGE: Beer

WORK ORDER: *Ham and Cabbage Roll, Potatoes, Cookies (unless you
must start from scratch, in which case make cookie dough and keep
in freezer 40 minutes before slicing)*

Ham and Cabbage Roll

☆ Leftover ham works fine;
any cooked ham will do.

□ See p. 240. The amount
you need will depend on
size of pan.

1 cabbage, 2–3 pounds
6 tablespoons butter
1 onion, finely chopped
1 pound ham, finely diced☆
Salt and freshly cracked
black pepper to taste

Few grains of freshly
grated nutmeg
4 eggs
½ cup dry bread crumbs
2 tablespoons finely
chopped fresh parsley
6–8 cups chicken stock□

1. Trim away outer leaves of the cabbage, then carefully remove 12 leaves.

2. On a double thickness of cheesecloth or utterly clean kitchen towel, approximately 17 by 24 inches, overlap the cabbage leaves. If they should tear, patch by tearing off, from the remaining cabbage, pieces to fit.

3. Cut rest of cabbage into four wedges and remove the core. Chop finely by hand or in food processor with shredding disk.

4. Put the butter into a large sauté pan or skillet. Heat but do not brown. When foam subsides, add finely chopped onion and the shredded cabbage. Stirring with a wooden spatula, cook about 10 minutes or until the cabbage and onion are soft.

5. Transfer this mixture to a large bowl. Mix in ham. Add salt, pepper, and nutmeg. Beat eggs and add. Put in bread crumbs and parsley; mix well. Spread this filling evenly over the bed of cabbage leaves.

6. Roll up tightly as possible, as for a jelly roll. Use the towel as an aid, but make sure you don't roll it up with the cabbage. Twist the 3-inch ends of the towel, which now is a casing for the roll, and tie ends tightly with clean string. Tie about every 2 inches along the roll.

7. Place roll in a fish poacher or roasting pan. Add simmering chicken stock to cover the roll by ¾ inch.

8. Cook at a fast simmer for 45 minutes.○

○ Roll can be cooked ahead for 30 minutes, left in chicken stock, and reheated.

9. Remove roll and allow to drain. Reserve the stock. Remove strings and let the roll amble onto a long, narrow platter. Cut into slices and serve with the following mustard sauce. Serves 6.

Piquant Mustard Sauce

3 tablespoons butter
3 tablespoons flour
2 tablespoons good sharp mustard

2½ cups of stock you cooked the cabbage roll in
Salt and freshly cracked black pepper to taste

1. Make a roux in a small saucepan by melting the butter, which you are careful not to burn, and adding the flour.

2. Add mustard and cook another minute.

3. Add the stock, switch from the wooden spatula to a whisk, and cook until smooth. Season with salt and pepper and continue to cook 5–6 minutes. Serve over slices of cabbage roll.

Boiled Red-Skin Potatoes

□ Eight red-skin potatoes weigh approximately a pound. If you cook more than you need, they will not be wasted, since leftovers can be used for a salad tomorrow.

✧ Or cook potatoes separately by boiling or steaming them.

2 or 3 potatoes per person.□
4 tablespoons melted butter, if desired

Salt and freshly cracked black pepper

Wash potatoes and drop them into the pot where the cabbage roll is simmering in chicken stock.✧ Allow about 15 minutes, or until potatoes can be pierced with a little knife tip and offer slight resistance—do not overcook! Pour the melted butter over them, if you like; the potatoes will pick up flavor anyway from the ham and cabbage. Season with salt and pepper.

Warm Spice Cookies

¾ cup soft butter
⅓ cup sugar
1 egg

1 cup flour
1 tablespoon rum
1 tablespoon ground allspice

1. Put all ingredients in food processor fitted with a steel blade and spin for about 10 seconds, or until all ingredients are blended. Or mix in order, using electric mixer.

2. Remove batter (which may be on the thin side) from processor and place on a piece of heavy aluminum foil. Roll into sausage shape, twist ends of foil, and shape roll with hands to form a solid cylinder.

3. Place in freezer—it will keep for 3 months.

4. Unwrap foil and use a warm knife to slice off as many cookies as you'll need. Slices should be about ⅛ inch thick.

5. Lay on a baking sheet greased with 2 tablespoons melted butter or lined with baking parchment. Bake in a preheated 375° oven for 9–12 minutes or until edges are a lush brown. Makes about 2 dozen.

An Elegant Dinner for 4

MENU　**Baby Lamb Chops with Mint Butter**
Shredded Zucchini
Stuffed Baked Tomatoes
Fresh Strawberries with Grand Marnier

WINE SUGGESTION: A Beaujolais such as Moulin à Vent

WORK ORDER: *Stuffed Baked Tomatoes, Mint Butter, Shredded Zucchini, Strawberries, Lamb Chops*

Baby Lamb Chops with Mint Butter

☆ If you can't get baby chops, use larger ones and allow 2 per person.

4 tablespoons softened butter
12 baby lamb chops, well trimmed, ¾ inch thick☆

Salt and freshly cracked black pepper to taste
Watercress for garnish

1. Rub the softened butter over the lamb chops, both sides. Sprinkle chops with salt and pepper.

2. Place chops on broiler rack 3 inches from broiler. Broil 3 minutes, turn, and broil 2–3 minutes more for pink chops, or 4–6 minutes for medium done.

3. Place chops on a platter garnished with watercress.

4. Dollop a spoonful of mint butter (see following recipe) on each chop just before serving. Serves 4.

Mint Butter

8 tablespoons softened butter
¼ cup finely chopped fresh mint

1 tablespoon fresh lemon juice

□ See p. 255.

1. Put butter into a bowl. Add the chopped mint and squeeze in lemon juice.□ Mix with a wooden spatula until creamy, about 2–3 minutes.

2. Set in freezer to harden for 5–10 minutes before serving over the chops. Makes a bit more than ½ cup.

Stuffed Baked Tomatoes

△ See p. 236.

4 medium-sized tomatoes
4 tablespoons butter
¼ cup finely chopped shallots
½ cup dried bread crumbs△
Salt and freshly cracked black pepper

2 tablespoons freshly grated imported Parmesan cheese, if desired
2 tablespoons chopped fresh parsley
2 tablespoons melted butter
1 tablespoon vegetable oil

1. Slice off stem ends of tomatoes and discard. Squeeze tomatoes gently over a bowl, then place them upside down on a paper towel to drain.

2. Melt, but do not brown, 4 tablespoons butter in a small sauté pan. Add shallots and cook, stirring with a wooden spatula, for 3 minutes.

3. Add shallots and butter to the tomato pulp in bowl. Add bread crumbs and salt and pepper to taste; mix well. Add Parmesan cheese if desired. Mixture should have consistency of wet sand. Add chopped parsley.

☆ You can slice off a tiny bit from the bottom of each tomato so it will stand proud in the pan.

4. Fill tomatoes☆ with mixture. Drizzle the melted butter over them.

5. Place on oiled baking sheet and set in a 350° preheated oven. Bake 20 minutes. Serves 4.

Shredded Zucchini

✧ If you have time, put shredded zucchini in a bowl and scatter a tablespoon of salt over it to make it give up its liquid. Let stand 15 minutes, squeeze through your fingers, and cook.

○ If you opt for garlic, add it now. Cook but do not brown for 1 minute, before adding zucchini.

4–6 small zucchini, washed but not peeled
4 tablespoons butter
1 clove finely chopped fresh garlic, if you wish

Salt and freshly cracked black pepper to taste
1 tablespoon chopped fresh parsley

1. Shred zucchini, using shredding disk of food processor, a hand grater, or the shredding side of a four-sided grater.✧
2. Melt, but don't brown, the butter in a sauté pan.○ Add zucchini and toss over high heat for 4–5 minutes, until tender crisp.
3. Season with salt and pepper, add chopped parsley, and serve. Serves 4.

Fresh Strawberries with Grand Marnier

□ Depending on sweetness of berries. You may not need any sugar.

✧ Strawberries demand very quick rinsing, else they will give off too much juice and become watery.

○ Be careful not to bruise the berries.

1 quart large ripe strawberries, hulls removed
4 tablespoons Grand Marnier

2–3 tablespoons confectioners' sugar□

1. Quickly rinse berries.✧ Dry on paper towels or shake in a sieve. Place in a crystal serving bowl.
2. Add the Grand Marnier and turn berries over gently with wooden spatulas.○ Set bowl with berries to macerate in refrigerator for at least 20 minutes. Check for sweetness and add sugar if needed. Serves 4.

Simply Stupendous Dinner for 4

MENU   **Pork Chops with Apple Calvados Cream**
           Grated Red Cabbage and Caraway
           Chocolate Sponge

WINE SUGGESTION: Riesling

WORK ORDER: *Sponge, Chops, Cabbage*

Pork Chops with Apple Calvados Cream

4 tablespoons butter
4 one-inch-thick pork chops
2 tablespoons Calvados
2 garlic cloves, chopped
½ cup chopped shallots
2 celery ribs, chopped
1 apple, peeled, cored, and chopped
½ teaspoon fresh thyme

1 tablespoon flour
2 tablespoons Dijon mustard
½ cup chicken stock
1 cup sour cream
1 tablespoon finely chopped fresh parsley
Salt and freshly cracked black pepper to taste

1. Melt 2 tablespoons of the butter in a sauté pan. Over fairly high heat, sauté the chops, 3 minutes to a side. Remove chops and keep them warm.

2. Pour off fat from pan, and deglaze the juices with flaming Calvados.△

△ See page 251.

3. Add 2 remaining tablespoons butter, the garlic and shallots. Cook 3 minutes.

4. Add celery and apple and cook 5 minutes, or until soft.

5. Sprinkle in the thyme, flour, and mustard. Stir with a wooden spatula and cook for 2 minutes.

6. Add the chicken stock and bring to a boil.

7. Remove contents of pan to a blender and purée.

8. Return to pan and whisk in the sour cream, parsley, salt, and pepper.

9. Return chops to sauce and simmer 15-20 minutes or until chops are cooked through. Serves 4.

Grated Red Cabbage and Caraway

4 tablespoons butter
1 head (1½ pounds) red cabbage, core removed, grated
1 tablespoon caraway seeds
¼ teaspoon freshly grated nutmeg

Salt and freshly cracked black pepper to taste
½ cup dry white wine
1 tablespoon finely chopped fresh parsley

1. Melt the butter in a skillet. When it is foaming, add the cabbage. Stir around and add the caraway, nutmeg, salt, pepper, and wine. Mix well. Cover and cook over medium heat for 5 minutes.

2. Remove lid, raise heat, and cook 8–10 minutes longer, or until tender crisp. Toss on the parsley and serve. Serves 4–6.

Chocolate Sponge

1½ squares unsweetened chocolate
¾ cup milk
3 tablespoons butter
1 tablespoon cornstarch
½ teaspoon salt
1 teaspoon vanilla extract
4 eggs
½ cup sugar
Butter and sugar for coating the baking dish
Whipped cream, if desired

1. Melt the chocolate in a custard cup placed in a skillet of simmering water.

2. Scald milk.

3. In a separate pan, melt the 3 tablespoons butter. Blend in the cornstarch and salt. Remove from fire, and slowly stir in the scalded milk. Return to medium heat, and stir until thickened.

4. Again remove the butter mixture from heat, and blend in the vanilla and melted chocolate.

5. Separate the eggs. Beat yolks with the sugar until thick. Add this mixture gradually to the chocolate base. Cook over very low heat for 1 minute, stirring constantly. Let cool about 10–20 minutes.

6. Beat egg whites until stiff but not dry. Fold into the chocolate mixture.

7. Butter a 1-quart soufflé dish and dust it with sugar. Place the chocolate mixture in it, and put in a bain-marie with very hot water one-fourth the depth of the soufflé dish. Bake in a preheated 350° oven 45–50 minutes. Can be served with whipped cream, if desired. Serves 6.

Stay-for-Dinner Menu for 3

MENU Julie's 15-Minute Chicken
Puffed Potato Wedges
Shredded Carrots with Oil and Vinegar
Sabayon over Sliced Bananas

WINE SUGGESTION: A California Hearty Burgundy

WORK ORDER: *Carrots, Potatoes, Sabayon, Chicken*

Julie's 15-Minute Chicken

With this dish, serving a fabulous wine is folly. The vinegar will only overwhelm it.

2 chicken breasts, skinned, boned, and cut into finger-size pieces about 3 inches long
¼ cup flour
¼ cup butter
Salt and freshly cracked white pepper to taste

1 tablespoon crushed fresh rosemary
3 tablespoons raspberry vinegar, lemon or orange juice, Madeira, sherry, or white or red wine
1 tablespoon finely chopped fresh parsley

1. Roll chicken pieces, a few at a time, in the flour. Pat off excess.
2. In a large skillet, melt butter until it sizzles. Add chicken, and toss or stir over high heat 3–5 minutes or until chicken is no longer pink.
3. Stir in salt, pepper, and rosemary. Add the vinegar, or one of the alternative ingredients, to deglaze the pan. Sprinkle the parsley on top. Serves 6.

Puffed Potato Wedges

☆ Or 6 little red-skin potatoes, cut in half.

3 Idaho☆ potatoes
Bacon fat or oil to coat skins of potatoes

Salt for dipping

1. Wash potatoes, dry with a paper towel, and rub with fat. Cut each potato into 8 wedges. Do *not* let water touch the cut part of the potatoes.
2. Put salt on wax paper and dip cut sides of each wedge.
3. Arrange wedges on a cake rack. Let stand 10 minutes.
4. Put into a 425° oven, on the rack only—no baking sheet— and bake 15–20 minutes or until potatoes are brown, crusty, and puffed. Serves 3.

Shredded Carrots with Oil and Vinegar

2 large carrots
Salt and freshly cracked white pepper to taste

¼ cup oil
2 tablespoons vinegar

Peel carrots and shred in food processor or on a hand grater. Place in a bowl and add salt, pepper, oil, and vinegar. Adjust seasonings. Serves 4.

Sabayon over Sliced Bananas

Sabayon can be served over any fruit; let the season make your decision. Remember to adjust the liqueur so that it complements the fruit—kirsch with strawberries, framboise with raspberries, and so forth.

3 bananas
 Juice of ½ medium lemon
3 egg yolks

1 egg
⅓ cup sugar
2 tablespoons rum

1. Slice bananas into a bowl. Sprinkle with lemon juice.
2. Put egg yolks, egg, sugar, and rum in a bowl and stand it in a pan of hot water over medium heat. Whisk constantly for 10–15 minutes, until mixture becomes thick and creamy.
3. Pour over bananas and serve immediately. Serves 3.

Dinner for 6 Before the Hockey Game

MENU   **Ham Steak in Mustard Cream**
Diagonal Asparagus
Pineapple Doused with Rum

WINE SUGGESTION: A California Chardonnay, or a Rosé or Beaujolais-Villages

WORK ORDER: *Pineapple, Ham, Asparagus*

Ham Steak in Mustard Cream

2 tablespoons butter
1 large precooked ham steak, 2 inches thick (about 3 pounds)
2 tablespoons finely chopped shallots
2 tablespoons chopped fresh tarragon

1 tablespoon Dijon mustard
 Salt and freshly cracked black pepper
2 tablespoons Madeira wine
¾ cup heavy cream
1 tablespoon finely chopped fresh parsley

1. Melt butter in a skillet until it sizzles. Add the ham and cook 3–4 minutes on each side. Remove ham, transfer to a baking sheet, and place in a 300° oven to keep warm.

2. To the butter in the pan add the shallots, tarragon, mustard, salt and pepper. Stir around with a wooden spatula for a minute or so, then add the Madeira and cream. Cook over medium heat until cream reduces and coats a metal spoon— about 5–7 minutes, depending on richness of cream.

3. Carve ham into thin strips and arrange on a platter. Pour the sauce over and garnish with parsley. Serves 6.

Diagonal Asparagus

30 stalks fairly thin asparagus	Salt and freshly cracked black pepper to taste
4 tablespoons butter	

1. Thoroughly wash asparagus and cut off the tough ends. Lay each piece on a cutting board and cut on the diagonal into 1-inch pieces.

2. Melt the butter in a skillet until it foams. Throw in the asparagus, salt, and pepper. Toss or stir with a wooden spatula for 5–7 minutes until tender crisp. Serves 6.

Pineapple Doused with Rum

1 ripe pineapple, large as possible, or 2 medium ones	6 teaspoons sugar
	6 tablespoons dark rum

1. Cut the pineapple by standing the fruit up straight and slicing through the leaves to the base. (If you use a large pineapple, cut 6 sections; with 2 medium ones, cut each into thirds.) Remove the core from each piece.

2. Use a sharp serrated knife to cut the fruit from the skin, then cut meat across into bite-size pieces and replace in the shell.

3. Sprinkle each "boat" with a teaspoon of sugar and a tablespoon of rum. Serves 6.

Dinner for a Quartet of Vegetarians

MENU   **Celery with Coarse Salt**
          Eggplant Bake
          Wheat Germ Muffins
          Oranges with Fresh Coconut

WINE SUGGESTION: California Mountain White

WORK ORDER: *Eggplant, Muffins, Celery, Oranges and Coconut*

Celery with Coarse Salt

1. Neatly trim 1 large bunch of celery. Wash and cut into pieces 2 to 3 inches long. Place in a bowl of ice water and set in refrigerator 15 minutes.

2. At serving time, drain the celery but do not dry it; it should be a bit moist to hold the dipping salt.

Eggplant Bake

1 small eggplant, peeled or unpeeled, cut into ½-inch slices
4 tablespoons olive oil
1 clove garlic, finely chopped
1 small green pepper, seeded and cut into strips
1 medium onion, sliced
1 large tomato, about ½ pound, peeled and sliced

3 or 4 fresh basil leaves, finely chopped
6 or 8 thin strips Fontina cheese
3 eggs
¾ cup light cream
Salt and freshly cracked black pepper to taste

1. Preheat oven to 400°.

2. Cook eggplant in 2 tablespoons of the oil in a skillet until tender and lightly browned, about 5–7 minutes. Remove with a slotted spoon and drain on absorbent paper.

3. Add the remaining 2 tablespoons of oil to the same skillet, then add the garlic and cook 1 minute. Next add the green

pepper and onion and cook until barely tender, about 5 minutes.

4. Arrange vegetables in a 9-inch shallow baking dish and put sliced tomatoes on top of vegetables. Sprinkle chopped basil leaves over top.

5. Place cheese strips over the vegetable mixture in a pattern like that of the spokes in a wheel.

6. Combine eggs, cream, salt, and pepper and mix well. Pour over ingredients in baking dish.

7. Bake 30 minutes, or until set. Serves 4.

Wheat Germ Muffins

1½ cups flour
¼ cup sugar
2 teaspoons baking powder
1 teaspoon salt
1 cup wheat germ

¾ cup milk
¼ cup dark molasses
¼ cup melted butter
1 egg, well beaten

1. Preheat oven to 400°. Lightly butter 12 muffin cups.

2. In a bowl, mix together flour, sugar, baking powder, and salt. Stir in wheat germ.

3. Combine remaining ingredients and add, all at once, to the dry ingredients. Stir just enough to moisten them (batter should be lumpy).

4. Fill each muffin cup about two-thirds full and bake 15 minutes, or until brown on top. Makes 12 muffins.

Oranges with Fresh Coconut□

□ See page 254 for instructions for handling coconut.

4–6 large oranges, peeled and sectioned
1 fresh papaya, peeled and sliced (optional)

½ cup freshly grated coconut

Place orange sections (and sliced papaya, if you like) in a serving bowl. Sprinkle the fresh coconut on top and serve. Serves 4.

Trump Dinner for 4 Bridge Players and 2 Kibbitzers

MENU   **Corn Chowder**
Romaine Salad with Lemon Vinaigrette
Rolled Soufflé
Fudge Nut Ring

WINE SUGGESTION: Zinfandel

WORK ORDER: *Nut Ring, Soufflé, Chowder, Salad*

Corn Chowder

In summer, this can be served as a velvety cold soup, if you omit the bacon and substitute 4 tablespoons vegetable oil or butter. Purée the finished chowder in the blender, chill, and serve with a dollop of sour cream and chopped chives.

½ cup chopped celery
1 medium onion, chopped
½ leaf fresh sage, if available
6 slices bacon, cut up
2 cups chicken stock
½ pound potatoes, diced

3 cups fresh corn
1 large bay leaf
Salt and freshly cracked
white pepper to taste
1 tablespoon flour
2 cups light cream

1. In a large saucepan, cook celery and onion with sage and bacon until bacon is cooked, but not crisp, and vegetables are tender. Blend in flour with wooden spatula.
2. Add stock, potatoes, corn, bay leaf, salt, and pepper. Cover and bring to a boil. Then reduce heat, cover, and cook until vegetables are tender (10–15 minutes). Remove bay leaf.
3. Add cream all at once. Cook and stir until mixture thickens. Serves 6–8.

Romaine Salad with Lemon Vinaigrette

◇ I never tear lettuce. See page 102.

○ See page 245.

2 medium heads romaine lettuce, cut◇ into bite-size pieces

1 cup vinaigrette dressing○ made with lemon juice

Place greens in any bowl but a wooden one. Pour the vinaigrette on top, toss, and serve. Makes 6–8 servings.

Rolled Soufflé This soufflé also makes a beautiful entrée for Sunday night supper, brunch, or luncheon.

Oil and flour for pan
2 tablespoons chopped shallots
¼ cup butter
½ cup flour
Salt and freshly cracked black pepper to taste

½ teaspoon Dijon mustard
2 cups milk
6 eggs, separated
2 cups grated sharp Cheddar cheese

1. Preheat oven to 350°. Oil sides and bottom of a 10-by-15-by-1-inch jelly-roll pan and line with aluminum foil. Then oil foil generously, dust sides and bottom with flour, and tap to remove excess.

2. In a saucepan, sauté shallots in butter. Remove from heat; blend in flour, salt, pepper, and mustard. Cook 3–5 minutes. Gradually whisk in milk until smooth. Return to heat and cook, stirring constantly, until mixture thickens.

3. Meanwhile, in a large bowl, beat egg yolks until they become thick and lemon-colored (about 3 minutes).

4. Gradually whisk the beaten yolks into the sauce and cook 1–2 minutes, to cook the egg.

5. Remove from heat and pour into a bowl to cool slightly.

6. Using a clean bowl and clean beaters, beat egg whites until stiff but not dry. Add a small amount to yolk mixture and mix until smooth. Then quickly but gently fold in remaining egg whites.

7. Spread evenly in the prepared pan; bake 25 minutes.

8. Remove from oven and invert onto wax paper. Sprinkle with Cheddar cheese. Using wax paper as a guide and starting at the narrow end of the roll, roll it up tightly, like a jelly roll. Let stand a few minutes to melt cheese slightly. Makes 8–10 thin slices or 6–8 thick slices.

Fudge Nut Ring☆

☆ If you like, you can serve this with whipped cream, but it is a rich, chewy, and fudgy dessert that really does not need embellishment.

TOPPING

2 tablespoons butter
2 tablespoons brown sugar
2 tablespoons light corn syrup
2 tablespoons light cream
⅓ cup finely chopped walnuts

CAKE

¼ cup softened butter
¾ cup granulated sugar
1 egg, separated
2 ounces melted unsweetened chocolate
1 teaspoon vanilla extract
1 cup cake flour
1 teaspoon baking powder
Pinch of salt
1 cup milk

1. Grease a 6-cup ring mold.
2. In a saucepan, combine all ingredients listed for the topping, except the nuts. Bring to a boil. Now add the nuts, and spoon into the ring mold.
3. In a bowl, cream the softened butter. Add sugar and beat until light and fluffy. Mix in egg yolk, chocolate, and vanilla.
4. Combine flour, baking powder, and salt. Add to creamed mixture alternately with milk.
5. Beat egg white until stiff peaks form; fold into batter.
6. Carefully spoon this batter over the topping which you previously placed in the pan. Put in a preheated 350° oven and bake about 30 minutes.
7. Remove cake from oven. Gently loosen from edges of pan. Invert onto a serving platter. Scoop out any topping clinging to the pan and spread it over the cake. Serves 8–10.

Inflation Fighter Dinner for 4 or 6

MENU **Spinach with Ham Florentine**
Shredded Beets with Orange
Poached Pears

BEVERAGE: Iced Tea or Rosé Wine

WORK ORDER: *Spinach, Pears, Beets*

Spinach with Ham Florentine

1 tablespoon butter
10-ounce package fresh
  spinach
1½ cups light cream
3 eggs, well beaten
½ cup cooked rice
½ cup diced cooked ham
¾ cup grated Cheddar
  cheese

½ teaspoon freshly grated
  nutmeg
Salt and freshly cracked
  black pepper to taste
2 tablespoons grated
  Parmesan cheese

1. Preheat oven to 350°. Butter a 1-quart shallow baking dish.

2. Wash spinach and remove stems. Place, undrained, in a large pan so that the spinach will cook in the water that clings to its leaves. Cover and cook over high heat until steam forms. Reduce heat and simmer 5–6 minutes, or until tender. Drain well.

3. In a bowl, combine spinach with remaining ingredients, except Parmesan cheese. Pour the mixture into the baking dish and sprinkle Parmesan over the top.

✧ See page 251.

4. Fill a bain-marie✧ with hot water to a depth of 1 inch. Place spinach casserole in this water bath and bake 30 minutes, or until set. Serves 4–6.

Shredded Beets with Orange

If you'd prefer a raw vegetable salad, shredded beets can be tossed with vinaigrette△ and used with this meal.

△ See page 245.

☆ Save the tops for a later
meal. Cook them as you
would spinach.

2 pounds young beets, peeled
  and trimmed☆
6 tablespoons butter
Salt and freshly cracked
  black pepper to taste

4 tablespoons orange juice
1 tablespoon grated orange
  rind

1. Shred the beets in food processor or on a four-sided grater.

2. Melt butter in a skillet. When hot, add beets, salt, and pepper. Toss or stir with a wooden spatula for 5 minutes.

3. Add orange juice and rind, and simmer 10 minutes longer. Beets should be tender crisp. Serves 6.

Poached Pears

1 cup sugar
1 cup water
2 cups red or white wine
1 inch piece vanilla bean or
    4–6 whole cloves

4–6 medium pears, peeled,
    halved, and cored

1. Bring sugar, water, wine, and vanilla or cloves to a boil in a saucepan. Boil 5 minutes; turn to simmer.

2. Add pears, cover, and simmer, turning pears over carefully, for 10–20 minutes or until pears can be pierced with the tip of a sharp knife. Do not overcook; time depends on ripeness of pears.

3. If time permits, remove pears from pan and reduce the poaching liquid by half, then spoon it over the pears at serving time. If you haven't time to reduce the liquid, store the surplus in a covered jar and refrigerate; it will keep for 1 month.

4. Pears can be served warm or cold, depending on time and preference. Serves 4–6.

Day-Before-Payday Supper for 4

> **MENU** Cabbage Soup
>   **Swiss Baked Eggs**
>   **Cupcakes**
>
> **BEVERAGE:** Iced Tea or Coffee
>
> **WORK ORDER:** *Cupcakes, Soup, Eggs*

Cabbage Soup

4 slices bacon
4 cups shredded cabbage
    (about 1 pound)
2 medium onions, sliced
1 teaspoon caraway seeds
6 cups chicken stock, or
    enough to cover cabbage in
    pot

½ cup vermouth
Salt and freshly cracked
    black pepper to taste
Sour cream

1. In a heavy pot, cook bacon until crisp. Remove, crumble, and set aside.

2. Add cabbage, onions, and caraway seeds to bacon fat. Cook and stir until cabbage is *just barely* tender, about 10 minutes.

3. Add stock and vermouth; bring to a boil. Cover, reduce heat, and simmer 25 minutes. Add bacon. Season with salt and pepper.

4. Serve garnished with a dollop of sour cream. Makes 8 cups.

Swiss Baked Eggs

3 tablespoons butter
8 eggs, slightly beaten
2 tablespoons minced green
    pepper

½ cup light cream
Salt and freshly cracked
    black pepper to taste
2 slices imported Swiss
    cheese

1. Preheat oven to 400°. Lightly butter four individual ramekins. You'll need about a tablespoon of butter for this.

2. Combine eggs, green pepper, cream, salt, and pepper.

3. Melt the remaining 2 tablespoons butter in a skillet. When butter becomes foamy, pour egg mixture into skillet and cook, stirring occasionally and only until eggs are soft (they will finish cooking in the oven).

4. Divide eggs among the 4 ramekins. Top with strips of cheese. Bake 5 minutes, or until cheese melts. Serves 4.

Cupcakes

1 cup sugar
⅓ cup butter
1 egg
2 cups cake flour

2 teaspoons baking powder
½ teaspoon salt
¾ cup milk
2 teaspoons vanilla extract

1. Preheat oven to 400°. Line 2½-inch muffin pans with fluted paper liners.

2. In a large bowl, cream the sugar with the butter. Add egg; beat until light and fluffy.

3. Mix together the flour, baking powder, and salt. Combine milk and vanilla.

4. Add dry ingredients and liquid alternately to the butter mixture, beginning and ending with the dry ingredients. After each addition, beat *just until smooth.*

(continued)

5. Spoon a scant ¼ cup batter into each cup. Bake 25 minutes. Makes 12 two-and-one-half-inch cupcakes.

Nut Cupcakes: Mix in ½ cup chopped nuts before spooning batter into cups. Makes 14 cupcakes.

Spice Cupcakes: Add 2 teaspoons ground cinnamon, 1 teaspoon ground nutmeg, and ½ teaspoon ground allspice to dry ingredients. Proceed as above. This makes 12 cupcakes. (You can also add nuts to these.)

Chocolate Cupcakes: Reduce sugar to ¾ cup, flour to 1¾ cups, and baking powder to 1 teaspoon. Add ¼ cup cocoa and 1 teaspoon baking soda to dry ingredients. Substitute buttermilk for the regular milk; proceed as above. Makes 12 cupcakes.

Spring Meal for a Single

For most of us, it's too much of a hassle to cook dinner for one. But I have friends who live alone and make a habit of cooking a proper dinner each night and setting the table with best china, linen, crystal, and silver. The boost to one's spirit is well worth the extra time.

MENU   **Shad Roe Poached in Butter**
Asparagus Vinaigrette
Herbed New Potatoes
Fresh Strawberries

WINE SUGGESTION: Muscadet

WORK ORDER: *Vinaigrette, Asparagus, Potatoes, Berries, Roe*

Shad Roe   1 small set (pair) of shad roe   Juice of 1 lemon
A little bit of flour   Salt and freshly cracked
8 tablespoons butter   black pepper to taste

1. Dry the roe well and dredge in flour. Pat off excess.

2. In a saucepan, heat the butter until it foams, then add the shad roe. Cook 5–10 minutes, turning once.

3. Remove to a platter. To the butter in the pan, add lemon juice to taste, salt, and pepper. Pour this over the roe. Serves 1.

Asparagus Vinaigrette

□ See page 245.

6 medium stalks asparagus, trimmed and peeled
Salt

2–3 tablespoons vinaigrette dressing□

1. Bring enough water to barely cover asparagus to a boil in a skillet. Add a generous pinch of salt. Add asparagus and cook, uncovered, for 7–10 minutes, or until tender crisp.

2. Drain and plunge into ice water to refresh (to set color) and stop the cooking.

3. Add the vinaigrette dressing. Serve warm or at room temperature. Serves 1.

Herbed New Potatoes

As many unpeeled new potatoes as you'd like for dinner
Salt and freshly cracked black pepper to taste

1 tablespoon finely chopped fresh dill, chives, parsley, or *any* fresh herb available

Boil potatoes in salted water 5–10 minutes, until tender crisp—or longer if you like them very soft. Sprinkle with salt and pepper and the finely chopped herb. Serves 1.

Fresh Strawberries

8–10 large strawberries
Confectioners' sugar for dipping, if desired

I like to eat strawberries out of hand, with the stems on. When I dip them in confectioners' sugar, I rinse the berries just before eating so the sugar will stick.

Superb Little Dinner for 4

MENU   **Curried Crabmeat**
Libby Warner's Black Bananas
Green Rice
Melon Spiked with Lime

BOISSON: Pale Indian Ale

WORK ORDER: *Bananas, Crabmeat, Rice, Melon*

Curried Crabmeat

1 tablespoon butter
¼ cup chopped green pepper
4 shallots, chopped
1–2 tablespoons curry powder✧
¼ cup butter
¼ cup flour

2½ cups light cream
Salt and freshly cracked white pepper to taste
1 pound (3 cups) crabmeat
2 hard-cooked eggs, chopped
1 large apple, cored and coarsely chopped

✧ The amount you need depends on the curry and your affinity for spicy food.

1. Preheat oven to 350°. With the tablespoon of butter, grease a 1½-quart casserole.

2. In a large saucepan, cook green peppers and shallots with curry in ¼ cup butter, stirring with a wooden spatula until tender.

3. Stir in flour; cook and stir 2 minutes.

4. Remove from heat; gradually whisk in cream, salt, and pepper.

5. Return to stove and cook, whisking constantly, until mixture thickens.

6. Gently fold in crabmeat, chopped egg, and apple. Spoon into prepared casserole and bake 25–30 minutes. Serves 4.

Libby Warner's Black Bananas

My friend Libby Warner, niece of Clare Booth Luce, served these bananas at a dinner, and everyone was deliciously mystified: no one could guess what they were. They look like shiny eggplant and do not taste like fruit. When you serve them, ask each guest to split a banana open lengthwise and eat it from the skin. Black bananas are also good served with curry-and-honey-glazed squabs or duck.

1 banana in its skin per serving

1 tablespoon fat (butter, bacon, or oil) for each banana

1. Rub skin of each banana with the fat.
2. Lay bananas on a baking sheet and bake at 350° for 45–60 minutes, or until they are absolutely black and shiny.
3. Serve 1 to each guest, and don't tell anybody what they are.

Green Rice Make certain that this rice is cooked in a heavy pan with a lid. I use an iron or enamel casserole. Leftover rice can be turned into a rice salad.

4 tablespoons butter
½ cup finely chopped onion
1½ cups rice
3 cups chicken stock
1 teaspoon salt

½ teaspoon freshly cracked white pepper
½ cup finely chopped fresh parsley

1. Melt butter, but do not brown it, in a saucepan. Stir in the onions and cook for 5 minutes; do not brown them. With a wooden spatula, stir in rice to coat it well with butter.
2. Add chicken stock, salt, and pepper and bring to a boil.
3. Reduce heat to simmer, cover, and cook for 23 minutes without lifting lid.
4. Fold chopped parsley into rice and serve. Serves 4 generously.

Melon Spiked with Lime

1 large or 2 small cantaloupes

1 lime, cut into quarters

Cut cantaloupe in halves or quarters, depending on size. Remove seeds and fiber. Place on a glass serving dish. Garnish each piece of fruit with lime quarter. (You may want to pass more lime.) Serves 4.

Dinner for the New Club President and 4 Well-Wishers

MENU　Scalloped Oysters
　　　　　Sweet-and-Sour Broccoli
　　　　　Frosted Fudge Squares

WINE SUGGESTION: Muscadet

WORK ORDER: *Fudge Squares, Oysters, Broccoli*

Scalloped Oysters

This dish has excellent flavor, with a consistency like that of bread pudding.

4 tablespoons butter
6–8 slices bread, dried and cubed (3 cups cubes)
30 oysters, freshly opened, juice saved

Salt and freshly cracked white pepper to taste
1 teaspoon finely chopped fresh thyme
¾ cup light cream

1. Preheat oven to 375°. Generously grease a 1½-quart shallow baking dish with 2 tablespoons butter.
2. Place 1 cup of the bread cubes in baking dish.
3. Drain oysters and reserve ½ cup of their liquor.
4. Place 15 oysters over bread, and season with salt, pepper, and thyme. Top with a cup of bread cubes and dot with 1 tablespoon butter. Repeat to make the second layer.
5. Combine oyster liquor and cream. Pour over mixture in casserole. Bake 20–30 minutes or until bread begins to brown. Serves 5.

Sweet-and-Sour Broccoli

Whether or not you like broccoli, you'll like this: it doesn't really taste like broccoli.

2 pounds broccoli
¼ cup minced shallots
8 slices bacon, cut up
1 tablespoon brown sugar

2 tablespoons vinegar
Salt and freshly cracked black pepper to taste
⅛ teaspoon dry mustard

1. Wash broccoli well and trim off stem ends. Cut into bite-size pieces and cook in boiling salted water until *just barely* tender, about 10 minutes.

2. Meanwhile, in small skillet, cook the shallots with bacon until bacon is barely crisp. Stir in brown sugar, vinegar, salt, pepper and dry mustard; heat.

3. Pour the shallot-bacon mixture over the broccoli. Serve at once, if you want a hot vegetable, or serve at room temperature as a delicious salad. Serves 5.

Frosted Fudge Squares

These have excellent flavor, volume, and texture, and the frosting tastes like fudge. They also go well at kids' parties.

FUDGE SQUARES

1 tablespoon butter for greasing pan
¼ cup cocoa
¼ cup butter
1 cup water
2 cups all-purpose flour
2 cups sugar
1 teaspoon baking soda
½ cup milk
2 eggs
1 teaspoon vanilla extract

FROSTING

½ cup butter
⅓ cup milk
¼ cup cocoa
1 pound confectioners' sugar
1 teaspoon vanilla extract
1 cup nuts (optional)

1. *To make the fudge squares:* Preheat oven to 400°. With the tablespoon of butter, lightly grease a 10-by-15-by-2-inch jelly-roll pan.

2. In a saucepan, combine the ingredients for fudge squares: cocoa, butter, and water; bring to a boil.

3. In a large bowl, combine flour, sugar, and baking soda. Add chocolate mixture and mix well.

4. Add milk, eggs, and vanilla; beat until smooth.

5. Pour into the prepared pan and bake 20 minutes. Cool 10 minutes and frost.

6. *To make the frosting:* In a saucepan, combine frosting ingredients: butter, milk, and cocoa. Bring to a boil.

7. In a small bowl, combine confectioners' sugar, chocolate mixture, and vanilla. Beat until smooth. Spread over cake and sprinkle with chopped nuts if desired. Makes 24 squares—plenty for leftovers.

Too-Hot-to-Cook Dinner for 4 or 6

> **MENU**   Crabmeat with Lemon and Oil
> Beefsteak Tomatoes
> Cucumbers, Sour Cream, and Chives
> Frozen Watermelon Slices
>
> **WINE SUGGESTION:** Sancerre
>
> **WORK ORDER:** *Watermelon, Crab, Cucumbers, Tomatoes*

Crabmeat with Lemon and Oil

○ Try to purchase really fresh crabmeat, not the pasteurized kind, which I find slimy.

1½ pounds large lump crabmeat○
4 tablespoons lemon juice
Good olive oil, just enough to bind the crabmeat (about ½ cup)
Salt and freshly cracked white pepper to taste

1 tablespoon drained capers, if desired
1 tablespoon finely chopped fresh parsley
4 beefsteak tomatoes
Watercress sprigs

1. Place the crabmeat in a bowl; discard any cartilage from the crabmeat, but be careful not to break the meat up too much.
2. Drizzle over the lemon juice and (careful here! don't over-do) the oil; add salt and pepper. Add the capers, if you wish, and the parsley.
3. Place mixture in the center of a chilled platter. Peel and slice tomatoes, which have been kept at room temperature, and place them around the platter so that the slices overlap. Tuck in a few sprigs of watercress. Serves 4–6.

Cucumbers, Sour Cream, and Chives

This fresh, light dish goes well with any kind of fish.

3 medium cucumbers, peeled, seeds removed with tip of a spoon
1 tablespoon salt
½ cup sour cream

Freshly cracked black pepper
2–3 tablespoons freshly snipped chives (or dill, parsley, or mint)

1. Slice the cucumbers as thinly as possible with a knife, on a mandoline, or in a food processor.

2. Put into a bowl and sprinkle the cucumbers with salt. Let stand 10 minutes, time enough for them to give off their juices. Squeeze gently with your hands, and place in a bowl.

3. Add sour cream, pepper to taste, and chives (or other herb) and transfer to another clean bowl before serving. Serves 4–6.

Frozen Watermelon Slices

Cut a piece of really ripe watermelon 1½ inches thick for each person. Tightly cover each wedge or slice with plastic wrap and place flat on a shelf in freezer. Turn the pieces over after 30 minutes. Leave in freezer until ready to eat. Remove wrap before serving. These taste like sherbet.

Valentine's Day Orgy for 2

MENU   A Dozen Oysters on the Half Shell Each
Honey-Glazed Squabs
Angel Cake Roll

WINE: Champagne

WORK ORDER: *Cake, Squabs, Oysters*

Oysters on the Half Shell

In the opulent Victorian days, it wasn't unusual for a Diamond Jim and his lady to pack away three dozen oysters each. A single dozen per person in our more subdued era suggests a splendid self-indulgence.

○ I ask the fishmonger to open these.

24 very fresh oysters○
Seaweed, if possible, for garnish

Freshly cracked black pepper
Lemon wedges

1. Order the oysters already opened by your fishmonger.
2. Bed 12 oysters firmly on each of two plates of crushed ice.
3. Garnish with seaweed, and serve with pepper and lemon wedges.

Honey-Glazed Squabs

2 squabs (about 14–16 ounces each)
Salt and freshly cracked black pepper
½ cup honey
3 tablespoons soy sauce
1 tablespoon vegetable oil
Watercress sprigs

1. Wash and dry squabs. Truss with string. Sprinkle with salt and pepper.
2. Combine honey, soy sauce, and oil in a small bowl. Brush this mixture over the squabs.
3. Set the birds on a rack in a small roasting pan and bake at 375°. Every 10–15 minutes, brush with the glaze. Birds should require 45 minutes, more or less, depending on size and desired doneness. To check, prick leg with a skewer. Juices should not be pink, but squab is better undercooked a bit. Skin should be shiny.
4. Serve with watercress. Makes 2 portions.

Angel Cake Roll

1 tablespoon oil
8 egg whites
¼ teaspoon salt
½ teaspoon cream of tartar
½ teaspoon vanilla extract
½ teaspoon almond extract
1 cup granulated sugar
⅔ cup cake flour
Confectioners' sugar
1½ cups heavy cream
1 tablespoon kirsch or framboise, if desired
1½ cups sliced strawberries

1. Preheat oven to 300°. Oil a jelly-roll pan (10 by 15 by 1 inch), line with wax paper, and oil the paper generously.
2. In a large bowl, beat egg whites until foamy. Add salt, cream of tartar, vanilla, and almond extract. Continue beating at high speed until soft peaks form. Gradually add ¾ cup of the granulated sugar, a tablespoon at a time, beating until stiff but not dry.
3. Combine remaining ¼ cup granulated sugar and flour. Gently fold a small amount of this mixture at a time into the beaten egg whites. Spread in pan and bake 20–25 minutes.
4. Place wax paper on 2 overlapping cake racks. Sprinkle with confectioners' sugar. Invert cake onto paper and cool flat for 15 minutes.
5. Make filling by beating heavy cream until soft peaks form. Add 2 tablespoons confectioners' sugar, along with kirsch or framboise if you like.

6. Spread filling over cake, right out to the edges. Top with strawberries. Using waxed paper as a guide, roll tightly from the long edge as for a jelly roll. Ordinarily this makes 8–10 servings, but this is an orgy! Besides, you'll want some tomorrow.

One-Dish Light Supper for 6

MENU   **Gazpacho Pasta**
Toasted Bread Sticks
Fresh Fruit with Gorgonzola Cheese

WINE SUGGESTION: Verdicchio

WORK ORDER: *Pasta, Vegetables, Fruit, Bread Sticks*

Gazpacho Pasta   This is an adaptation of my original recipe, which first appeared in *House and Garden* in 1976. Prepare and cook the pasta according to the directions on page 94.

1½ pounds homemade pasta	½ cup unpeeled, seeded, and chopped cucumber
½ cup olive oil	½ cup unpeeled, finely chopped tiny zucchini
1 cup peeled, seeded, and diced fresh tomato	2 tablespoons finely chopped fresh basil
½ cup chopped red onion	Salt to taste
½ cup chopped celery	A cruet of good olive oil
¼ cup peeled and chopped carrot	Pepper mill with black pepper
½ cup seeded and chopped green pepper	

1. Drain the cooked pasta and place on a large platter. Toss with ½ cup olive oil.

2. Sprinkle all the vegetables over the pasta—but save the basil for last. Toss, and season with salt.

3. Serve at room temperature with a cruet of good olive oil, and pass the pepper mill. Serves 6.

Dinner for 4 Celebrating Springtime

MENU   **Lamb Patties with Rosemary**
Baked Potato Slices
Rhubarb Crisp

WINE SUGGESTION: Cabernet-Sauvignon or a Beaujolais such as
Fleurie

WORK ORDER: *Rhubarb, Potatoes, Lamb*

Lamb Patties with Rosemary

1 pound coarsely ground lamb
¼ pound bacon
1 teaspoon crushed rosemary

Salt and freshly cracked black pepper to taste
2 tablespoons port wine
¾ cup heavy cream

1. Place the ground lamb in a bowl.
2. Partially cook the bacon; crumble it. Mix bacon, rosemary, salt, and pepper into lamb. Form into four patties.
3. Pour off all but 2 tablespoons of the bacon fat. Sauté in this the lamb patties, allowing about 3 minutes on each side. Remove the patties from the pan.
4. Pour off fat in pan, and add the port and cream. Reduce the sauce by about half; stir all the while. Serve with lamb. Serves 4.

Baked Potato Slices

2 large baking potatoes, washed and dried but not peeled
¼ cup butter

¼ cup vegetable oil
Salt and freshly cracked black pepper to taste
½ teaspoon chopped fresh thyme

1. Slice the potatoes ¼ inch thick; there should be about 32 slices.
2. Melt the butter and pour it and the oil into a shallow baking dish (I use an 8-by-8-by-2-inch dish). Lay the potatoes in the dish and add salt, pepper, and thyme. Turn potatoes over to coat them well in the oil-butter mixture.

3. Place in a preheated 400° oven 20–30 minutes, or until cooked through. Stir them around once in a while so they will cook evenly. Serves 4.

Rhubarb Crisp

6 cups rhubarb, cut in
  1-inch pieces
1 cup brown sugar
½ cup flour

1 teaspoon ground
  cinnamon
1 teaspoon freshly grated
  nutmeg
⅓ cup softened butter
Cream, if desired

1. Preheat oven to 350°. Place rhubarb in a 1½-quart casserole.

2. Combine sugar, flour, cinnamon, and nutmeg. Mix into this the butter; blend until mixture is crumbly. Sprinkle it over the rhubarb.

3. Bake 30–35 minutes, or until rhubarb is tender but not mushy. Serve with cream to make it extra good. Makes 1 quart.

By-the-Seaside Dinner for 6

MENU   **Clams and Oysters on the Half Shell**
Baked Lobster
Matchstick Potatoes
Shredded Cabbage with Vinaigrette
Pears Baked with Ginger

WINE SUGGESTION: Muscadet or Pouilly Fuissé

WORK ORDER: *Pears, Cabbage, Potatoes, Lobster, Shellfish*

Clams and Oysters on the Half Shell

○ I ask the fishmonger to open these.

18 oysters and 18 clams○
  (3 per person)

3 lemons, cut into halves
Pepper in a mill

Place cracked ice on individual plates and arrange the shellfish over it. Serve a lemon half with each portion, and pass the pepper mill. Serves 6.

Baked Lobster   This is my favorite way to cook lobster. It comes out juicy, never dry.

6 lobsters, 1–1½ pounds each	3 lemons, halved
½ pound butter	¾ pound melted butter for dipping
Juice of 2 lemons	

1. If the fishmonger can prepare the lobsters for you, so much the better. Otherwise, split them lengthwise from the center of the cross at the back of the lobster's head. (Make certain the claws are plugged.) Remove the little sack of gravel from behind the eyes, and pull out the long thin black intestinal tract. Open lobsters flat and lay on baking sheets, cut side up.

△ If you have only one oven, you may need to do this in shifts.

2. Divide the ½ pound butter into chips and distribute evenly over the 12 lobster halves. Squeeze lemon juice over the lobsters and place in a 350°oven△ for 30 minutes. Lobsters will turn red when done.

3. Serve on long platters with lemon halves and little cups of melted butter.

Matchstick Potatoes

4 large Idaho potatoes	Salt to taste
2 cups solid shortening or peanut oil	

1. Wash and peel the potatoes. Slice them very thin lengthwise on the mandoline, then cut into julienne strips as fine as possib'e. (This, too, can be done on the mandoline.)

2. Drop strips into cold water, then drain and dry thoroughly.

3. Melt the fat in a large skillet—about 10 inches if possible—to the point of smoking.

4. Drop in the potato sticks, two handfuls at a time.

5. With a slotted spoon, keep moving them or they will stick together. As they turn light brown, as for French fried potatoes, remove with a slotted spoon.

6. Drain on paper towels or a brown paper bag.

7. Salt just before serving. Serves 6 (4 potatoes are more than enough if you slice them very, very thin).

Shredded Cabbage with Vinaigrette

☆ See page 245.

1 medium head firm white cabbage
2 tablespoons finely chopped fresh parsley

Salt and freshly cracked black pepper to taste
1 cup vinaigrette☆

1. Cut the cabbage into quarters and remove the core. Shred in the food processor or on a four-sided cutter.
2. Place in a salad bowl. Add the parsley, salt, and pepper and pour the vinaigrette over. Let marinate until serving time. (This can be prepared the day before.) Serves 6.

Pears Baked with Ginger

2 tablespoons butter
6 pears, large, but not too ripe
2 cups brown sugar
½ cup brandy

¾ cup chopped crystallized ginger
8 tablespoons melted butter
1 cup sour cream

□ Cooking time depends on ripeness of the pears.

1. Grease a shallow 2½-quart baking dish with 2 tablespoons butter.
2. Peel, core, and halve the pears. Lay them rounded side up in the dish.
3. Combine the brown sugar, brandy, and ½ cup of the chopped crystallized ginger in a bowl. Sprinkle over the pears, and pour the melted butter over all.
4. Bake at 350° for 30–60 minutes, □basting occasionally.
5. Serve with a topping made of the sour cream mixed with the remaining ¼ cup ginger. Serves 6, with luscious leftovers if the pears are large.

Gussied-Up Ham 'n' Yams for 6

MENU	**Rosy Ham Gateau with Mustard Sauce** **French Fried Yams** **Glazed Baked Apples**

WINE SUGGESTION: Tavel Rosé

WORK ORDER: *Apples, Gateau, Yams, Mustard Sauce*

Rosy Ham△
Gateau

△ If you're in a mood to be really fancy, substitute cooked tongue for the ham in this recipe.

1 tablespoon vegetable oil
1 pound ham, run through the hand grinder twice or finely ground in the food processor
6 eggs, separated
½ cup melted butter
½ cup flour
Salt and freshly cracked black pepper to taste

2 tablespoons chopped fresh parsley
1 tablespoon Dijon mustard
¼ cup sherry or Madeira wine
10–12 paper-thin slices Swiss cheese

1. Use the vegetable oil to grease a 10-by-15-by-1-inch jelly-roll pan, line it with wax paper or aluminum foil, then oil again. Let the paper extend over the short ends by 2 or 3 inches, so you can handle the gateau easily after it's baked.

2. Put the ham into a large mixing bowl. Then blend in the egg yolks, melted butter, flour, salt, pepper, parsley, mustard, and wine. Mix well.

3. Using clean beaters and a clean bowl, beat the egg whites until stiff. Fold into the ham mixture. Spread in prepared pan.

4. Bake in a preheated 375° oven for 20 minutes, or until ham mixture pulls away from the sides of the pan.

5. Remove from oven and, using a serrated knife, gently cut the gateau into three equal sections, each 5 inches wide.

6. Remove one of the sections, using two spatulas if necessary, and invert onto a serving platter. Gently pull off wax paper. Top with 2 or 3 slices of the Swiss cheese. Repeat this process with the other two sections, to make three layers in all, with a layer of Swiss cheese on top.

7. Lower oven to 350°, and return the gateau to it for 5 minutes, or long enough to melt the cheese. Serve with the following mustard sauce. Serves 6.

Mustard Sauce✧

✧ This also goes well with sautéed chicken, veal, or pork.

⅔ cup chopped onion
1 large clove garlic, chopped
2 tablespoons butter
½ cup dry white wine

1 teaspoon potato flour
1¼ cups light cream
2 teaspoons Dijon mustard
Salt and freshly cracked white pepper to taste

1. In a saucepan, cook onion and garlic in butter until tender. Add wine; simmer to reduce by half.

2. Blend in the flour and cook, stirring, for 1 minute.

3. Remove from heat. Add 1 cup of the cream, mustard, salt, and pepper.

4. Return to heat; cook and stir until thickened. Add remaining cream, if necessary, to thin sauce. Makes about 1 cup.

French Fried Yams

3 cups vegetable or peanut oil

4–5 medium yams
Salt

1. Preheat oil to 375° in a deep-fat fryer.

2. Meantime, peel yams and slice them about ⅛ inch thick.

3. Deep-fry slices, a few at a time, making sure you do not overload the cooker. Stir occasionally to separate.

4. When done, drain on absorbent paper. Sprinkle with salt. Serves 4–6.

Glazed Baked Apples

6 large, beautiful baking apples
1 cup sugar
1 cup water

2 tablespoons Calvados or apple brandy
6 teaspoons brown sugar

1. Core the apples and neatly peel them a third of the way down, leaving the remaining skin intact. Place in a baking dish so that apples are spaced well apart.

2. Boil together the sugar and water for 5 minutes. Remove from heat, and add the Calvados or apple brandy. Pour this syrup over the apples.

3. Bake at 350° for 30 minutes, spooning syrup over apples from time to time. Remove from oven and sprinkle 1 teaspoon brown sugar on top of each apple. Continue baking for 15 minutes or until apples are soft.

4. Remove apples from oven and run them under a hot broiler to glaze them. Do this carefully, lest they burn. Serve warm. Serves 6.

Family Dinner for 4 or 6 When It's Cold Outside!

MENU   Sausage Bake
Puréed Carrots with Wine
Rum Molasses Cake with Tart, Thin Lemon Sauce

WINE SUGGESTION: Jug of Red or White

WORK ORDER: *Cake, Sausage, Carrots, Lemon Sauce*

Sausage Bake   This is also an excellent brunch dish.

½ pound bulk pork sausage
⅓ cup chopped onions
⅓ cup chopped green pepper
1 teaspoon chopped fresh thyme
About 2 tablespoons freshly grated Parmesan cheese

2 eggs, slightly beaten
1 cup light cream
Salt and freshly cracked black pepper to taste

1. Preheat oven to 450°. In a sauté pan, cook sausage with the onions, green pepper, and thyme until the meat loses its pink color. Stir to separate sausage; drain on absorbent towels.
2. Place the mixture in a 9-inch shallow bake-and-serve dish.
3. Combine grated cheese, eggs, light cream, salt, and pepper and blend well. Pour over sausage mixture and bake 20–25 minutes, or until set. Serves 4–6.

Puréed Carrots with Wine

5 cups peeled and sliced carrots
2 tablespoons butter
⅓ cup light cream
2–3 tablespoons white wine

¼ teaspoon freshly grated nutmeg
Salt and freshly cracked black pepper to taste
1 tablespoon chopped fresh parsley

1. In a pan with a small amount of boiling water, cook the carrots, covered, until tender (about 15 minutes). Drain.

2. Mash carrots, or use food processor to purée them. Combine with all remaining ingredients except parsley. Make sure the mixture is quite smooth. Garnish with chopped parsley. Serves 4–6.

Rum Molasses Cake with Tart, Thin Lemon Sauce

3 tablespoons butter, softened
2 cups all-purpose flour
1 cup granulated sugar
1 teaspoon ground cinnamon
½ teaspoon ground cloves

1 teaspoon baking soda
Pinch of salt
1 egg
¾ cup water
¼ cup dark rum
½ cup dark molasses
Confectioners' sugar (optional)

1. Preheat oven to 375°. Generously grease a 9-inch square cake pan with 1 tablespoon butter.
2. In large mixer bowl, mix together flour, sugar, cinnamon, cloves, baking soda, and salt. Add remaining 2 tablespoons butter, egg, water, rum, and molasses, and mix well at medium speed on mixer. Pour into prepared pan. Bake 30 minutes.
3. Serve with the following lemon sauce, or sprinkle with confectioners' sugar. Makes 9 servings.

Tart, Thin Lemon Sauce

This sauce is good over angel cake, pound cake, or fresh poached fruits. It's very tart and thin—my preference—so I've added notes in case you want to adjust ingredients to suit your own sweet touch.

½ cup sugar
1 teaspoon cornstarch△
Pinch of salt
1 cup boiling water

¼ cup lemon juice☆
1 tablespoon grated lemon rind☆
1 tablespoon butter

△ If you like a thicker sauce, add another teaspoon of cornstarch.

☆ For a sweeter sauce, use 3 tablespoons lemon juice and 1 teaspoon grated lemon rind.

1. In a small saucepan, combine sugar, cornstarch, and salt. Gradually blend in water and lemon juice. Cook, stirring constantly, until slightly thickened.
2. Remove from heat; stir in lemon rind and butter. Makes 1½ cups.

Dinner Before the Movies for 4

MENU   Quick Brandied Chicken Livers
Rutabaga Purée
Fruit Upside-Down Cake

WINE SUGGESTION: Beaujolais Villages or Tavel Rosé

WORK ORDER: *Cake, Purée, Chicken Livers*

Quick Brandied Chicken Livers

5 tablespoons butter
¼ cup chopped shallots
½ pound mushrooms, sliced
1 pound chicken livers, cut into bite-size pieces
¼ cup flour, or less
½ teaspoon salt

Freshly cracked black pepper—a generous twist
¼ cup brandy
1½ cups light cream
4 English muffins, split and toasted

1. Melt 2 tablespoons of butter in a skillet. Add shallots and cook for 2 minutes, or until tender. Add the mushrooms and continue to cook 3 minutes more. Remove from pan.

2. Pat livers dry, coat with flour, and pat again to remove excess flour.

▢ See page 252.

3. Add remaining 3 tablespoons butter to pan, melt, add livers, sprinkle with salt and pepper, and cook over high heat until the pink color disappears. Flame▢ with the brandy. Add mushroom mixture and combine.

4. Remove skillet from heat; blend in the cream. Over low flame, cook, stirring with a wooden spatula, until mixture thickens slightly. Serve over English muffins which have been split and toasted. Serves 4.

Rutabaga Purée

1 pound rutabagas
½ pound carrots
¼ cup light cream
2 tablespoons butter

Salt and freshly cracked black pepper to taste
1 tablespoon chopped fresh parsley

1. Pare rutabagas and cut into cubes. Place in pan of boiling salted water and cook, uncovered, for 5 minutes.

2. Meanwhile, pare carrots and cut into ½-inch pieces. Add

to rutabagas. Cook 15 minutes longer, or until vegetables are tender. Drain well.

3. Place in blender or food processor and add all remaining ingredients except parsley. Purée until smooth. ✧

4. Garnish with parsley and serve. Makes 2 cups.

✧ If mixture is too moist, cook, stirring constantly, over medium flame to evaporate excess liquid.

Fruit Upside-Down Cake

3 tablespoons butter
½ cup firmly packed dark-brown sugar
3 pears, peaches, or plums, cored and cut into eighths
3 tablespoons rum, cognac, or *poire*
¼ cup soft butter

⅔ cup granulated sugar
1 egg
1 teaspoon vanilla extract
1¼ cups all-purpose flour
2 teaspoons double-acting baking powder
½ teaspoon salt
⅔ cup milk

1. Preheat oven to 350°. Melt the 3 tablespoons butter in an 8-inch square baking pan. Stir in brown sugar. Arrange fruit wedges, round side on bottom, in an attractive pattern over the brown sugar. Sprinkle with rum, cognac, or *poire*.

2. Make the cake: cream ¼ cup butter and granulated sugar in a small bowl. Add egg and vanilla, and beat until light and fluffy (about 5 minutes). Combine dry ingredients and add alternately with milk. Blend until smooth.

3. Pour batter over fruit. Bake 40 minutes, or until cake springs back when touched lightly in center with finger.

4. Cool 10 minutes; invert on a serving plate. Serves 4–6.

Festive Fish Dinner for 4

MENU	**Kathy's Baked Stuffed Bluefish** **Glazed Onions** **Asparagus Parmesan** **Pears with Raspberry Sauce**

WINE SUGGESTION: California Pinot Chardonnay or a Gewurtztraminer

WORK ORDER: *Pears, Fish, Onions, Asparagus, Raspberry Sauce*

Kathy's Baked Stuffed Bluefish

Kathy Larson, a dear friend who has assisted me with many writing projects, once taught this recipe to my beginners' cooking class. The recipe works well with any fresh- or salt-water fish, and it can be served without the sauce if you prefer.

3–4-pound bluefish
1 tablespoon lemon juice
 A few sprigs of parsley
 Fresh dill
2–3 slices of lemon
5 tablespoons butter
 Salt and freshly cracked black pepper to taste

Oil for greasing baking dish
3 shallots, chopped
4 scallions, chopped
1 cup white wine
½ cup heavy cream
2 egg yolks

1. Clean fish, remove fins, and wash in acidulated water (a quart of water to which 1 tablespoon lemon juice has been added).
2. Stuff fish with parsley sprigs, dill, and lemon slices. Dot interior with 3 tablespoons of butter and sprinkle with salt and pepper.
3. Oil a baking dish large enough to hold the fish. Put chopped shallots and scallions in dish. Lay fish on top, dot with 2 more tablespoons butter, and sprinkle with salt and pepper. Add the wine. Bake in a 425° oven 20–25 minutes, basting often.
4. Remove the fish to a hot platter. Take out vegetables and add them to the juices in the pan. Put this mixture through a sieve or food mill, then return it to the stove. Add cream and egg yolks. Stir until thickened, but do not boil. Serves 4.

Glazed Onions

✧ Onions will peel more easily if you parboil them for 2 minutes, drain, and cool slightly in cold water.

¼ cup butter
24 small white onions, peeled✧

Salt and freshly cracked white pepper to taste
1 teaspoon sugar

Melt the butter in a skillet. When hot, add the onions, salt, and pepper. Roll onions around in the butter. Put a lid on the pan and cook over medium-high heat, shaking pan frequently.

Cook about 10 minutes, or until tender crisp. Sprinkle the sugar on top and shake pan again. Serves 4.

Asparagus Parmesan

I prepare pokeweed this way, too. Pokeweed looks like baby rhubarb. It is grown in the tobacco barns in Lancaster County, Pennsylvania, and it also grows wild. I buy it in the spring at a local farmers' market. Only the young shoots should be used.

4–5 medium asparagus per person	4 tablespoons melted butter
1 tablespoon salt	¼ cup Parmesan cheese

1. Peel asparagus with a rotary peeler; trim off the rough ends.
2. In a skillet, boil about 1 inch water. Add the salt. Add asparagus and cook at a medium boil for 7–10 minutes, until tender crisp.
3. Remove from pan, drain, and refresh in cold water. (This sets the lovely green color.)
4. Place cooked asparagus in a baking dish, sprinkle with the butter and Parmesan cheese, and bake at 350° for 5 minutes.

Pears with Raspberry Sauce

2 cups dry white or red wine	4 pears, peeled, with stems
1 cup sugar	2 cups fresh raspberries

1. In a small skillet, bring to a boil the wine and sugar.
2. Slice off a small sliver from the bottom of each pear. Simmer the syrup for five minutes to dissolve the sugar and stand the pears upright in the pan. Cover with a lid or an aluminum foil tent and simmer till tender crisp, about 10 to 15 minutes, depending on the ripeness of the pears. Baste frequently with the syrup. Test for doneness with the tip of a little knife.
3. Remove pears to a serving dish. Add the raspberries to the syrup and simmer 10 to 15 minutes longer to reduce and thicken. Mixture should coat a spoon. Strain to remove the seeds of the raspberries and pour around fruit. Serves 4.

Good Old Meatloaf Dinner for 6

MENU   Meatloaf
Perfect Mashed Potatoes Every Time
Snow Peas
Baked Peaches

WINE SUGGESTION: Hearty Burgundy

WORK ORDER: *Meatloaf, Peaches, Potatoes, Snow Peas*

Meatloaf

¼ cup chopped onion
1 clove garlic, chopped
¼ cup chopped green pepper
2 tablespoons butter
1½ pounds ground beef (I use chuck)

1 egg
¼ cup bread crumbs
¼ cup sour cream
Salt and freshly cracked black pepper to taste
1 teaspoon chopped fresh oregano

1. Sauté onion, garlic, and green pepper in butter about 3 minutes, or until partially cooked.

2. In a bowl, combine all other ingredients. Add sautéed vegetables. Pack into an 8-by-4-by-2-inch loaf pan and bake at 375° for 45–60 minutes. Serves 6–8.

Perfect Mashed Potatoes Every Time

Sometimes I cook a peeled garlic clove or peeled cut-up celery root or turnips along with the potatoes and mash them, too. A bit of sour cream added as you mash makes these potatoes sublime. I like to serve them mounded high on a dish, with a chunk of butter on top and melting down the sides.

✧ Amount of cream depends on the starchiness of potatoes.

8 medium potatoes (about 2¾ pounds)
8 tablespoons butter

Salt and freshly cracked white pepper to taste
About 1 cup cream,✧ light or heavy, heated

1. Peel potatoes and cut into chunks. Put in a pan and boil in enough salted water to cover. Cook until tender but not mushy, about 20–25 minutes. Drain. Return potatoes to the pan and shake over flame to remove any water or moisture.

2. Place potatoes in mixer bowl and start beating. Add butter and continue to beat. Add salt and pepper; beat again. Gradually add the cream to the potatoes until they are very smooth. To keep warm, stand the bowl in a shallow pan of hot water or over a double boiler. Or just before serving whisk or beat thoroughly over medium heat. Serves 6.

Snow Peas

4 tablespoons butter
1 pound snow peas, strings removed

Salt and freshly cracked black pepper to taste

Melt butter in a skillet. Add snow peas. Toss or stir-fry for 5–6 minutes, until tender crisp. Add salt and pepper.

Baked Peaches

6 large peaches, peeled, halved, pits removed
2 tablespoons butter
1 cup cake or cookie crumbs
¼ cup melted butter

2 tablespoons brown sugar
1 egg yolk
2 tablespoons rum
¼ cup Madeira wine

1. With a large melon baller or a spoon, scoop out the holes in the peaches to enlarge them. Grease a bake-and-serve dish with 2 tablespoons butter. Lay peaches, cut side up, in dish.

2. Mix together in a bowl the crumbs, scooped-out fruit, melted butter, brown sugar, egg yolk, and rum. Mixture should resemble wet sand. Add more melted butter and rum, if necessary, to achieve proper consistency.

○ You can bake peaches in the same oven as meatloaf, in which case do both at 375°

3. Fill the cavity of each peach with rum mixture and sprinkle the Madeira on top. Bake at 350° for 30 minutes, basting frequently with dish juices.○ Serves 6.

Sliced Steak Dinner for 2

MENU   Sliced Strip Steak
        Sautéed Mushrooms
        Spinach Salad with Blue Cheese–Sour Cream
          Dressing
        Fresh Pears

WINE SUGGESTION: A Beaujolais such as Juliénas

WORK ORDER: *Salad, Dressing, Steak, Mushrooms*

Sliced Strip Steak

△ See page 240

1-inch-thick sirloin steak (should weigh 1 pound after bone has been removed, all fat trimmed)
Salt and freshly cracked black pepper to taste

3–4 tablespoons butter
½ cup chopped shallots or scallions
¼ cup red wine
¼ cup chicken or beef△ stock

1. Cut the steak into strips the size of your index finger. Add salt and pepper.

2. Melt 3 tablespoons of the butter in a heavy skillet. When the foam subsides, put in the steak and cook 2 minutes. Raise the heat and turn pieces over quickly. Cook another minute. (Cooking the meat should be in-and-out, a very quick process.) Remove meat to a warm platter.

3. To the skillet juices, add the shallots or scallions and cook 1 minute, while stirring with a wooden spatula. Next add the wine and stock and cook over high heat to reduce, about 2 minutes.

4. If desired, add another tablespoon of butter to the pan juices before pouring them over the meat. Serves 2.

Sautéed Mushrooms

4 tablespoons butter
¾ pound mushrooms, cleaned and sliced
Salt and freshly cracked black pepper to taste

1–2 tablespoons lemon juice
1 tablespoon freshly snipped chives or parsley

Melt butter in a skillet. Add mushrooms, salt, pepper, and lemon juice. Toss over high flame for 3 minutes; do not overcook. Sprinkle the chives or parsley on top and serve. Serves 2.

Spinach Salad with Blue Cheese–Sour Cream Dressing

☆ This will be more than you need, but clean it all anyway and use it tomorrow.

1 pound☆ fresh spinach, washed, stemmed, and drained
1 cup sour cream
2 tablespoons crumbled blue cheese

1 tablespoon wine vinegar
Salt and freshly cracked black pepper to taste
1 teaspoon Dijon mustard
¼ cup light cream

Place cleaned, drained spinach in a salad bowl and refrigerate until ready to use. Meanwhile, combine remaining ingredients. Pour dressing over spinach just before serving. Toss well to coat leaves. This makes 1¼ cups dressing, which keeps well in refrigerator. If necessary, add a little more cream to thin.

Trendy Hamburger Dinner for 4

MENU   **Hamburgers with Roquefort Cream**
Parsnip Purée
Crisp and Damp Watercress
Grapefruit and Strawberries

WINE SUGGESTION: A Beaujolais such as Brouilly

WORK ORDER: *Parsnips, Grapefruit, Cress, Cream, Hamburgers*

Hamburgers with Roquefort Cream

□ I like to use chuck: it makes a juicier burger.

4 tablespoons butter
1½ pounds ground beef □

Salt and freshly cracked black pepper to taste

Heat butter in a skillet until the foam subsides. Meanwhile, shape beef into four patties. Add to skillet without letting them touch. Cook over high heat 3 minutes on each side, or to desired doneness. Add salt and pepper. Serve plain or with the following Roquefort cream. Serves 4.

Roquefort Cream

¾ cup light cream
½ pound Roquefort cheese
(or blue, Stilton, or
Gorgonzola)

½ teaspoon potato flour
1 tablespoon port wine
Freshly cracked black
pepper—no salt

Heat cream, add cheese, and let it melt. Dissolve potato starch in wine. Use this to thicken the cheese mixture. Add pepper to taste and whisk until mixture coats a spoon. Pour over hamburgers.

Parsnip Purée

1 pound parsnips
6–8 tablespoons light cream,
depending on dryness of
parsnips
⅓ cup butter

Freshly grated nutmeg to
taste
Salt to taste
Generous dash of freshly
cracked white pepper

Peel and slice the parsnips. Cook in boiling salted water until tender. Drain. Place in food processor with remaining ingredients and blend until smooth. If this mixture is too thin, cook in a saucepan over medium flame and stir with a wooden spatula to evaporate liquid. Serves 4.

Crisp and Damp Watercress

2 bunches watercress, washed and trimmed

Soak watercress for 10 minutes in ice water. Shake, but do not dry. Place on a platter and eat with the fingers. You need no pepper because watercress has a natural peppery taste; no salt because the cheese in the Roquefort cream accompanying the hamburgers is probably all you'll need.

Grapefruit and Strawberries

3 grapefruits, peeled and
sectioned
1 pint strawberries

A little liqueur (kirsch,
framboise, Cointreau, etc.)
if desired

Place grapefruit and strawberries in a serving bowl and gently mix together. Add liqueur if desired. Serves 4–6.

Deviled Clam Dinner for 6

MENU **My Deviled Clams**
Carrot Timbales
Bread Pudding

WINE SUGGESTION: Chablis

WORK ORDER: *Pudding, Timbales, Clams*

My Deviled Clams

Deviled clams are among my favorite foods, but I find that too often they taste of mashed potato and are too stiff. Here is my version of this great dish.

6 tablespoons butter
½ cup finely chopped onion
½ cup finely chopped green pepper
¼ cup finely chopped celery
¼ cup flour
2 cups fresh clam juice
1 cup heavy cream
2 cups minced clams
1 tablespoon Worcestershire sauce

¼ teaspoon Tabasco
1 teaspoon thyme
6 tablespoons coarse fresh bread crumbs
1 tablespoon chopped fresh parsley
Salt and freshly cracked white pepper
6 tablespoons fine bread crumbs
6 teaspoons melted butter

1. Melt 6 tablespoons butter in a skillet and sauté the onion, green pepper, and celery.

2. Sprinkle in the flour, clam juice, and cream. Cook until mixture thickens.

3. Add the minced clams, Worcestershire sauce, Tabasco, thyme, coarse bread crumbs, and parsley. Add salt and pepper to taste. Cook until mixture thickens.

4. Put mixture into 6 clam shells or ramekins. Sprinkle each with a tablespoon of fine bread crumbs and a teaspoon of melted butter. Bake 10 minutes at 400°. Serves 6 generously.

Carrot Timbales

If you like small portions of carrots, you may want to cut this recipe in half. I suggest making the whole batch—the leftovers will be delicious reheated, or cold.

Butter for greasing molds
1 pound carrots, peeled and cut into chunks, or 1½ cups cooked mashed carrots
½ cup chopped onion
1 tablespoon finely chopped fresh dill

2 tablespoons butter
Salt and freshly cracked white pepper to taste
4 eggs
1½ cups light cream, scalded
Watercress for garnish (optional)

1. Preheat oven to 350°. Generously butter 12 timbale molds (⅓–½ cup).
2. Cook carrot chunks in boiling salted water until tender, about 25 minutes. Drain well. Purée in blender or food processor until smooth.
3. Meanwhile, cook the onions with dill in 2 tablespoons butter until tender.
4. Add this mixture, along with salt, pepper, eggs, and scalded cream, to the blender or food processor. Blend until smooth.

△ See p. 251.

5. Spoon into prepared molds, filling to the top. Set molds in a bain-marie△ and bake for 25 minutes or until knife inserted near the center comes out clean. Let stand 5 minutes before unmolding. If desired, put a sprig of watercress in the center of each timbale. Makes 4½ cups of mixture, or about 12 individual molds. Serves 6–12, depending on portion sizes.

Bread Pudding

Butter for greasing casserole
7 slices firm white bread, well buttered
⅓ cup white raisins
2½ cups light cream
2 eggs

1 egg yolk
3 tablespoons sugar
1 tablespoon grated lemon rind
1 tablespoon lemon juice
1 teaspoon vanilla extract
Pinch of salt

1. Preheat oven to 350°. Generously butter a 1½-quart shallow casserole.

2. Cut each slice of bread into 4 pieces.

3. Place a layer of bread, buttered side up, in casserole. Top with some of the raisins.

4. Repeat layers, ending with a layer of bread arranged artfully.

5. Beat together the eggs, egg yolk, 2 tablespoons of the sugar, lemon rind and juice, vanilla, and salt. Gradually add the cream and mix well.

6. Carefully pour the cream mixture over the bread in the casserole. Sprinkle top with the remaining tablespoon of sugar. Place casserole in a bain-marie with 1 inch of hot water. Bake 30 minutes, or until set and top is nicely browned. Serves 6–8.

Alone-at-Last Dinner for 2

This is a generous meal, but leftovers will save you time later. The squash and the pudding can be baked in the same oven.

MENU   **Scallops on Skewers**
Spaghetti Squash
Peas with Brown Butter
Orange Cloud Pudding

WINE SUGGESTION: Muscadet

WORK ORDER: *Pudding, Squash, Peas, Scallops*

Scallops on Skewers

1 pound sea scallops
8 large mushrooms, stemmed and cleaned
¼ cup oil
3 tablespoons lemon juice
Salt and freshly cracked white pepper to taste

☆ Or broil in the kitchen. Place skewers 3–4 inches from heat; broil about 10 minutes.

1. Alternate scallops and mushrooms on two 6-inch skewers. Brush with a mixture of the oil, lemon juice, salt, and pepper.

2. Place on grill 3–4 inches from coals☆ and broil about 10 minutes, turning and basting often. Serves 2.

Spaghetti Squash

□ You will need only half of the squash for this meal. Later, for a delicious salad, serve it cold with vinaigrette.

1 spaghetti squash, about 3 pounds□
Salt and freshly grated white pepper to taste

4 tablespoons melted butter
2 sage leaves, if desired
¼ cup freshly grated Parmesan cheese

1. Bake squash whole and unpeeled on a baking sheet in a 350° oven 45–60 minutes, or until it gives a little when you squeeze it.
2. Split open lengthwise and scoop out seeds. With two forks, scrape out interior; it will look like spaghetti and come out in strands.
3. Remember that you will need only half of the squash, as the note mentions. Place this in a serving bowl and toss with salt, pepper, melted butter or sage butter (made by melting the butter with the whole sage leaves, then removing and discarding the sage just before serving), and Parmesan cheese.✧ Serves 2.

✧ Sage leaves are delicious dipped in batter, deep-fried, and served with confectioners' sugar.

Peas with Brown Butter

1½ pounds peas in shell
2 tablespoons butter

Salt and freshly cracked black pepper to taste

Shell peas and place them in a saucepan. Add ¼ cup water. Cook until tender, about 7 minutes. Drain off water. Melt the butter in a pan and allow to brown. Add peas, salt, and pepper, and toss over heat until peas are tender crisp. Serves 2.

Orange Cloud Pudding

Almost like a soufflé, this delicate, refreshing pudding puffs above the top of the dish, cracks, and then settles as it cools.

Butter for greasing baking dish
2 eggs, separated
½ cup granulated sugar
2 cups sour cream

2 tablespoons flour
2 tablespoons Cointreau
1 tablespoon grated orange rind
½ cup confectioners' sugar

1. Preheat oven to 350°. Butter a 1-quart baking dish.
2. In a bowl, combine egg yolks and granulated sugar. Beat on high speed of mixer until thick and lemon-colored, about 5 minutes.

3. Add sour cream, flour, Cointreau, and orange rind. Blend well.

4. In a separate bowl, with clean beaters, beat egg whites until foamy. Gradually add confectioners' sugar, and beat to very stiff thick shining peaks.

5. Fold whites into the yolk mixture. Spoon into prepared casserole. Bake 35–40 minutes, or until just set in center. Makes 4–6 servings.

Guess Who Made the Honor Roll: Family Dinner for 6

MENU   **Roast Filet of Beef with Horseradish Butter**
Two Purées: Mushroom and Carrot
Cherry Tomatoes and Scallions
Fresh Peaches and Grapes

WINE SUGGESTION: Chambertin

WORK ORDER: *Filet, Mushrooms, Carrots, Horseradish Butter, Peaches and Grapes, Tomatoes and Scallions*

Roast Filet of Beef with Horseradish Butter

○ See page 243.

△ I trim off the tips and save them for beef Stroganoff.

This amount of meat should produce enough leftovers to provide makings for open-faced filet sandwiches on black bread with Aïoli○ or salad.

1 whole beef filet, trimmed (about 5 pounds)△
1 tablespoon butter

Salt and freshly cracked black pepper to taste

1. Rub the filet all over with the butter. Season with salt and pepper. Lay in a shallow roasting pan and bake at 475° for about 40 minutes, or until an internal thermometer reads 110°. Unless you have strong preference to the contrary, the meat should be very rare.

2. Let meat rest for about 10 minutes after you remove it from the oven: it continues to cook for a while after it leaves the heat. Carve into thin slices. Serves 6 generously.

Horseradish Butter

△ Try to buy a piece of fresh horseradish, grate it in the food processor—and get ready to cry.

⅔ cup softened butter
2 tablespoons freshly grated horseradish△

1. Place the butter and horseradish in a bowl and beat together with a wooden spatula.
2. On a sheet of wax paper, roll butter mixture into a long roll. Set in freezer until ready to use. Then cut across into disk-shaped pieces. It will melt on contact with the hot meat. Serves 6.

Mushroom Purée

¼ cup butter
¼ cup finely chopped shallots
2 pounds mushrooms, cleaned and finely sliced
3 tablespoons lemon juice

1 cup heavy cream
1 tablespoon flour
Pinch of salt
Few grinds of freshly cracked black pepper
Chopped parsley

1. In a sauté pan, melt 3 tablespoons of the butter. Add the shallots and cook 3 minutes. Add mushrooms and lemon juice and cook, stirring with a wooden spatula, until most of the moisture is evaporated.
2. Place the mushrooms and ¼ cup of the cream in a blender or food processor and purée until smooth.
3. Melt the remaining butter in a saucepan and stir in the flour. Using a wooden spatula, stir and cook for 2–3 minutes. Add the remaining cream; whisk to blend. Add puréed mushroom mixture and whisk until mixture thickens. (At this point, if the mixture seems too thin, cook longer to evaporate the moisture.) Season with salt and pepper and sprinkle with parsley. Serves 6.

Carrot Purée

1½ pounds carrots, peeled
Salt and freshly cracked black pepper to taste

2 tablespoons butter, browned but not burned
Chopped parsley

Cut carrots into chunks and cook in boiling salted water until barely tender, 10 to 15 minutes, depending on age and size of the carrots. Drain. Purée in food processor. Season with salt and pepper, and add butter. Sprinkle with parsley. Serves 6.

Fresh Peaches and Grapes

6 ripe peaches, peeled and sliced
1 pound green grapes, seedless if possible

¾ cup barely whipped cream
2 tablespoons brown sugar

Mix fruits together in a bowl. Fold in the barely whipped cream. Sprinkle top with brown sugar. Serves 6.

Mama Got a Raise: Dinner for 4

MENU   **Veal Chops**
Cucumber Batons
Fresh Artichoke Bottoms with Fluted Mushrooms
Melon with Sherry

WINE SUGGESTION: Swiss Neuchâtel or a white Nuits-Saint-Georges or a California Sauvignon Blanc

WORK ORDER: *Melon, Chops, Artichokes, Cucumber, Mushrooms*

Veal Chops

4 tablespoons butter
4 large veal chops, 1 inch thick
4 tablespoons brandy
2 tablespoons chopped shallots

2 tablespoons port wine
1½ cups heavy cream
Salt and freshly cracked black pepper to taste

△ See page 252.

1. Melt 2 tablespoons of the butter in a skillet. Add the chops and sauté 3 minutes on each side. Pour off butter, and flame△ the chops in the brandy.

2. Remove chops. Add the remaining 2 tablespoons butter and the shallots to the skillet. Stir around for 3 minutes.

3. Add the port wine, cream, salt, and pepper.

4. Return the chops to the skillet and cook until tender—about 20 minutes, depending on the age of the veal. The sauce should coat a spoon when ready. If it doesn't, remove chops, raise the heat under the skillet, and reduce the sauce further. Return chops to pan. Serve with the following cucumber batons, on the side or over the veal. Serves 4.

Cucumber Batons☆

☆ This recipe makes about 4 cups of batons. Leftovers are a bonus: use them as a salad or vegetable next day.

These are also good with fish.

2 large cucumbers
2–3 tablespoons hot butter
Salt and freshly cracked black pepper to taste

1 tablespoon chopped fresh parsley, dill, or mint

1. Peel cucumbers and slice lengthwise. Remove the seeds with the tip of a spoon. Cut across into 1-inch pieces, then cut into matchstick slices.
2. Bring a pan of salted water to a boil. Throw in the cucumbers. Bring back to a boil; cook 1 minute. Refresh in ice water. Dry thoroughly on a towel.
3. Heat the butter in a skillet, add cucumbers, and toss well. Add salt and pepper and fresh herb. Serves 4.

Fresh Artichoke Bottoms with Fluted Mushrooms

□ Instructions for preparing mushrooms are given on page 252.

4 artichokes
About 4 teaspoons lemon juice
2 tablespoons wine vinegar

1 teaspoon salt
4 tablespoons flour
1 tablespoon melted butter
4 mushrooms, fluted□

1. Cut off tops, stems, and leaves of artichokes and trim them neatly around the bottom, leaving about 2 inches of artichoke. Rub with lemon juice.
2. In a pan of cold water, place the vinegar, salt, and artichokes.
3. Put the flour in a small strainer and lower it into the water. Stir inside the strainer to make paste, then remove strainer and cook artichokes about 25 minutes, or until tender. Brush each choke with melted butter, and garnish with a fluted mushroom on top. Serves 4.

Melon with Sherry

2 medium melons (honeydew, Persian, or cantaloupe)

¼ cup honey
½ cup dry sherry

1. Cut each melon in half. Remove fiber and seeds. Trim a tiny piece from the bottom of each melon half so it will stand up without teetering.
2. Spoon into each portion a tablespoon of honey and 2 tablespoons dry sherry. Serves 4.

Favorite Relatives Come to Visit: Dinner for 6

MENU   **Oven-Baked Chicken**
Squash Pancakes
Julienne of Fresh Vegetables
Raspberries

BEVERAGE: A light Médoc, such as Château Beycheville or Beaujolais

WORK ORDER: *Chicken, Pancakes, Vegetables, Berries*

Oven-Baked Chicken

This travels well on a picnic, or in a brown sack.

1 cup dry bread crumbs
1 cup freshly grated
  Parmesan cheese
2 tablespoons chopped fresh
  parsley
2 cloves garlic, chopped

Salt and freshly cracked
  black pepper to taste
¾ cup melted butter
2 small frying chickens, 2–3
  pounds each, cut up

1. In a small bowl, combine bread crumbs, cheese, parsley, garlic, salt, and pepper. Place this in a shallow dish.
2. Place ½ cup of melted butter in a shallow bowl, dip the chicken pieces in it, then coat with the crumb mixture.
3. Arrange chicken pieces in a shallow roasting pan and drizzle remaining melted butter over each piece. Bake at 350° for 45 minutes, turning once. Chicken will be crusty and golden brown. Serves 6.

Squash Pancakes

✧ Summer squash, such as crooked-neck and zucchini, may be used in this recipe but they must be squeezed after cooking to remove liquid.

1 cup flour
1 tablespoon baking powder
2 tablespoons sugar
½ teaspoon salt
¼ teaspoon ground cinnamon

¼ teaspoon grated nutmeg
¾ cup cooked acorn or butternut squash✧
½ cup milk
1 egg, beaten
2 tablespoons oil

1. Preheat griddle according to manufacturer's directions.
2. In a bowl, combine the flour, baking powder, sugar, salt, cinnamon, and nutmeg.
3. In a separate bowl, combine squash, milk, egg, and oil. Add this to the dry ingredients and mix until just barely smooth.
4. For each pancake, pour ¼ cup batter onto hot griddle. Cook until puffed and dry around the edges; turn and brown on second side. Makes a dozen 4-inch pancakes.

Julienne of Fresh Vegetables

1 large turnip (purple and white), peeled
1 rutabaga, peeled
2 carrots, peeled, tapered ends removed

2 leeks, cleaned, white part with 1 inch green
4 tablespoons butter
Salt and freshly cracked black pepper to taste

1. On a mandoline, or by hand, slice the turnip, rutabaga, and carrots and cut into fine julienne pieces, thinner than a matchstick.
2. Do the leeks by hand, cutting the same size as the other vegetables.
3. Plunge all vegetables into boiling, salted water for 2 minutes. Then drain and refresh in cold water and dry on towels.
4. In a skillet, melt the butter. When it is hot, add vegetables and cook for 1–2 minutes, or just until tender crisp. Add salt and pepper. Serves 6.

Raspberries

4½ cups fresh raspberries   2 cups heavy cream

1. Arrange the raspberries in a bowl.
2. *Barely* whip the cream: it should still be almost fluid. Pass cream in a pitcher with the bowl of raspberries. Serves 6.

Delicate Chicken Dinner for 6

○See page 234.

MENU   **Chicken Imbued with Cream**
Rice Pilaf○
Carrot Dumplings
Sandy's Lemon Squares

WINE SUGGESTION: A California Gray Riesling or Puligny Montrachet

WORK ORDER: *Lemon Squares, Chicken, Pilaf, Dumplings*

Try to find really good chicken for this rich, delicate dish; use a cut-up whole chicken if you like. I scout around for real cream with 40 percent butterfat and use the ultra-pasteurized kind only when I have no other choice.

Chicken Imbued with Cream

4 tablespoons butter
3 whole chicken breasts, boned and split, wings attached
2 tablespoons cognac
Salt and freshly cracked white pepper to taste

Freshly grated nutmeg to taste
Ground red pepper to taste
3¼ cups heavy cream
2 egg yolks
2 tablespoons lemon juice
2 tablespoons dry sherry

1. Melt the butter in a skillet. Add the chicken and sauté over *very* low heat. Chicken must not take on any color. Cover with a lid and cook slowly for 10 minutes on each side.

2. Pour off fat and set it aside to supplement the butter in the Rice Pilaf recipe.

△ See page 252.

3. Remove lid and flame△ the chicken with the cognac.

4. Add salt, pepper, nutmeg, and red pepper to chicken; remove it to a casserole.

5. Reduce 3 cups of the cream to 2 cups. Pour it over the chicken.

6. Cover the chicken, and set it on a flame tamer so that the cream barely moves. Cook very, very slowly, basting occasionally with the cream in the casserole, about 40 minutes or until chicken is just done. Do not raise the heat at any time or the cream will separate.

(continued)

7. In a small bowl, beat the egg yolks, lemon juice, sherry, and remaining ¼ cup cream. Warm this mixture with a bit of the cream from the casserole.

8. Remove the chicken from the casserole. Whisk the yolk mixture into the cream in the casserole; return to it the chicken. Serve at once with rice. Serves 6.

Carrot Dumplings

1½ cups sliced carrots
2 tablespoons milk
1 egg
1 cup flour
1 teaspoon baking powder
½ teaspoon salt

Dash of freshly cracked black pepper
1 teaspoon chopped fresh parsley
4 cups chicken broth

1. Cook carrots, covered, in small amount of boiling water until tender (10–15 minutes). Drain. Purée in blender or food processor with milk and egg. Transfer to a bowl and mix in remaining ingredients, except chicken broth.

2. Bring broth to a boil; reduce heat.

3. Drop the carrot batter by tablespoonfuls into broth. When dumplings rise to the surface, cover. Reduce heat and simmer 5–10 minutes, or just until done (they will be soggy if you overcook them). Makes 16 dumplings.

Sandy's Lemon Squares

CRUST

1 cup flour
¼ cup confectioners' sugar
½ cup butter

TOPPING

2 eggs
1 cup granulated sugar

½ teaspoon baking powder
Pinch of salt
2 tablespoons lemon juice
1 tablespoon grated lemon rind
2 tablespoons confectioners' sugar

1. *Make the crust:* Place flour and confectioners' sugar in bowl. Cut the butter into small pieces and add to flour and sugar. Mix together with pastry blender or two table knives, or rub fat and flour together with fingertips, until mixture resembles coarse cornmeal. Press mixture into an 8-by-8-by-2-inch

baking dish or pan, spreading dough evenly. Bake in a pre-heated 350° oven for 20 minutes.

2. *Meanwhile, make the topping:* Beat eggs and add remaining ingredients, except confectioners' sugar. Mix well and pour over the crust. Bake 20–25 minutes. Cut into squares.

3. Sprinkle the confectioners' sugar over the top. Makes about 30 squares.

May Day Dinner for 3

MENU **Rack of Lamb with Orange Rosemary Butter**
Broccoli Pudding
New Potatoes and Peas
Gingersnaps

WINE SUGGESTION: Château Ducru-Beaucaillou (Saint-Julien)

WORK ORDER: *Gingersnaps, Broccoli, Lamb, Potatoes and Peas, Butter*

Rack of Lamb with Orange Rosemary Butter☆

☆ Or serve this with Green Pepper Hollandaise, made by adding 1 tablespoon or more of green peppercorns to hollandaise sauce, page 244.

□ You can also chill this and serve it hardened with pan-sautéed lamb chops.

3 pound rack of lamb, chine bone removed
2 tablespoons olive oil
Salt and freshly cracked black pepper to taste
8 tablespoons butter

1 tablespoon chopped fresh rosemary
1 tablespoon fresh orange rind
2 tablespoons orange juice

1. Preheat oven to 425°.
2. French the lamb chops (scrape the bones bare to about 1½ inches from the tips). Rub the lamb with the olive oil, salt, and pepper. Roast in a shallow pan 30–35 minutes for pink lamb, or until it reads 130 degrees on an internal thermometer.
3. Meanwhile, make the butter sauce. Melt the butter in a pan and add the rosemary and orange rind and juice. Heat over low flame for 5 minutes. Serve as a sauce□ with lamb. Serves 3.

Broccoli Pudding

◇ For a lighter pudding, use 1½ cups cream.

Butter for greasing baking dish
2 pounds fresh broccoli, washed, trimmed, and peeled
3 eggs

½ cup cream◇
1 teaspoon salt
¼ teaspoon ground nutmeg
¼ teaspoon freshly cracked black pepper

1. Preheat oven to 375°. Generously butter a 1-quart shallow casserole.
2. Separate the broccoli florets and cut the peeled stems into pieces. Drop florets and stems into a pan of boiling, salted water. Reduce heat to simmer and cook until tender, 5–7 minutes or longer if necessary to purée easily. Drain well.
3. Place broccoli in blender, add remaining ingredients, and purée until smooth. Pour into prepared casserole.
4. Place in a bain-marie filled with water to half the depth of the casserole. Bake 30–35 minutes, or until a knife inserted near the center comes out clean. Serves 3–4.

New Potatoes and Peas

When I was growing up, we picked the peas and dug up the potatoes from our own garden. This dish was one I could depend on.

12 tiny new potatoes, scrubbed
1½ cups fresh peas
2 tablespoons butter

¼ cup heavy cream
Salt and freshly cracked black pepper

1. Put potatoes in a pan with just enough water to cover them. Cook only until done, about 10–15 minutes, depending on size of potatoes.
2. Five minutes before cooking time is up, add the peas. Cook 5 minutes.

○ You can reduce this to 1 tablespoon and pour back over the vegetables.

3. Drain off water,○ and add butter, cream, and salt and pepper to taste. Shake until butter melts and cream is hot. Serves 3–4.

Gingersnaps☆

☆ To shorten cooking time and reduce quantity, you can cut this recipe by half.

Butter for greasing baking sheets
¾ cup granulated sugar
½ cup brown sugar
⅓ cup softened butter
1 egg
¼ cup dark molasses

1¾ cups flour
1 teaspoon baking soda
¼ teaspoon salt
1½ teaspoons ground ginger
1 teaspoon ground cinnamon
¼ teaspoon ground cloves

1. Preheat oven to 350°. Generously grease 2 baking sheets.
2. In a bowl, cream together ½ cup of the granulated sugar, the brown sugar, and butter. Beat in egg and molasses.
3. Combine flour, baking soda, salt, ginger, cinnamon, and cloves. Add to batter. Beat until blended.
4. Drop batter by level tablespoons into the remaining ¼ cup sugar, coating dough well.
5. Place 1½ inches apart on prepared baking sheets. Bake 10–12 minutes. Makes 3 dozen gingersnaps.

Double-Oven Dinner for 6–8

MENU   **Roast Pork with Thyme and Cheese**
Onion Herb Custard
Wild Rice and Celery
Brandy Lace Cups

WINE SUGGESTION: California Chablis or Graves

WORK ORDER: *Pork, Rice, Cups, Custard*

Roast Pork with Thyme and Cheese

When you're serving roast meat and time is at a premium, compensate by cooking two separate small roasts instead of a single big one. For this recipe, select two center cuts of four chops each. Ask the butcher to crack the chine bones to make carving easier.

○ See page 240.

△ See page 240.

2 center cuts of pork, 4 chops each

2–4 tablespoons vegetable oil

Salt and freshly cracked black pepper to taste

2 tablespoons finely chopped fresh thyme

1¼ cups dry white wine

Ten ¼-inch-thick slices Fontina cheese

½ cup Dijon mustard

¼ cup chicken stock○

2 tablespoons brown stock△

1–2 tablespoons soft butter

1. Brush each roast with 1 or 2 tablespoons oil, and season with salt and pepper. Lay them in a baking pan; make sure they do not touch. Sprinkle over each 1 tablespoon or more fresh thyme.

2. Place in a preheated 375° oven and roast about 1 hour, basting every 15 minutes with 2–3 tablespoons wine.

3. Meat is done when it reaches 165–170° on an internal thermometer. About 5 minutes before it reaches this stage, remove meat from oven to insert cheese and mustard, as follows.

4. In between the bones of each roast make slits—that is, between the bones of the chops, above the chine (or back) bone. Spread the cheese slices on both sides with mustard, and insert in the slits in the meat.

5. Return meat to oven and resume roasting for 5–10 minutes, or until cheese melts. Remove meat from pan.

6. Pour off fat from pan juices. Now add to the pan the remaining ½ cup white wine and the chicken stock. Bring to a boil, scrape, and add the brown stock. Cook until syrupy, then swirl in the soft butter. Rectify seasonings. Serves 8.

Onion Herb Custard

1 pound white onions, peeled and sliced paper thin

4 tablespoons butter

5 eggs

½ cup heavy cream

Salt and freshly cracked black pepper to taste

1 tablespoon chopped fresh parsley

1 tablespoon chopped fresh chives

Freshly grated nutmeg to taste

Butter for greasing baking dish

1. Sauté the sliced onions in 4 tablespoons butter until soft but not browned, about 15 minutes. Cool.

2. Beat the eggs. Beat in the cream, salt, pepper, parsley, chives, and nutmeg. Blend in the onions. Butter a greased shallow bake-and-serve dish, about 1½ quarts, and put mixture in it.

3. Bake uncovered in a 350° preheated oven until set and lightly browned, about 20–25 minutes. Serves 6–8.

Wild Rice and Celery

☆ See page 240.

1 cup wild rice
3 cups chicken stock☆
½ teaspoon salt
1 cup sliced celery

¼ cup chopped onion
¼ cup butter
Salt and freshly cracked black pepper to taste

1. Place rice in a strainer and wash under running water until water runs clear.

2. In a heavy saucepan, combine rice, chicken stock, and salt. Bring to a boil. Reduce heat, cover, and cook over medium heat until rice is tender and fluffy, about 45 minutes. Drain.

3. Meanwhile, in a large skillet, sauté celery and onion in the butter. Add the drained rice and season with salt and pepper. Serves 6–8.

Brandy Lace Cups

The oven temperature is important here: these cups are fragile and will burn or become brittle if the oven is too hot.

1 tablespoon butter for greasing baking sheet
¼ cup butter
¼ cup brown sugar, firmly packed
2 tablespoons light corn syrup

2 tablespoons molasses
1 tablespoon brandy
½ cup flour
¼ teaspoon ground cinnamon
¼ teaspoon ground ginger
1 cup heavy cream, whipped

1. Preheat oven to 350°. Grease baking sheet with butter.

2. In a saucepan, combine ¼ cup butter, brown sugar, corn syrup, and molasses. With heat turned low, bring this mixture to a boil; stir constantly. Remove from heat. Add brandy, flour, cinnamon, and ginger and stir until smooth.

(continued)

3. Drop half-tablespoons of batter 3 to 4 inches apart on greased baking sheet—just four cookies per sheet.

4. Bake (one batch at a time) 5 minutes on middle rack of oven. Remove from oven and let stand just 1 minute.

5. While cookies are still pliable, remove them with a spatula and shape into cups. This can be done inside a greased custard cup or on the end of a greased rolling pin. If cookies become too brittle to handle, return them to the oven for 30 seconds to soften them.

6. Fill cups with whipped cream. Makes 16–18 cups. Unfilled cups keep well in a covered tin.

3 TWELVE LESS POUNDS OF ME: LOW-CALORIE MEALS

There used to be twelve pounds more of me. I am slim now, weight the same as thirty years ago, but it's only because I have embraced dieting with the same fervor I lavish on cooking creatively. This is a balancing act for me. On the one side is the lure, the passion, of food. I love food. I work with it constantly, conceiving and refining new recipes, teaching classes, writing about it. I get up in the middle of the night to record thoughts that rise into my consciousness from deep instinctive obsessions with food. On the other side, equally powerful for me, is the pull of fitness, of vanity, of the ease and grace of slimness.

When the dozen extra pounds congealed, I was horrified. I tried every crash diet known to woman, and what crashed was my disposition. Then I approached classic dieting, no more than 1,200 calories a day, with a new attitude: calories are *food,* and food should always be enjoyable! Like a dedicated poet changing from epics to sonnets, I began to create low-calorie menus, and discovered that people were asking me for recipes.

Gorgeous fresh vegetables, fish, poultry and veal, and herbs and ripe sweet fruits are scrumptious! Luscious soups with piddling calorie counts zinged into my mind. I discovered that a hint of wine can waft plain fare up to sheer tantalization.

I'm sure you've heard of *cuisine minceur*—"lean cooking"—which Michel Guérard introduced by name in 1976. Essentially it relies on skillfully blending light ingredients into exciting dishes. Over the years, my own adventures in creating low-calorie menus have been enriched by the keen powers of observation I have developed. People who eat rich appetizers in quantity, I notice, usually need their appetites roped in, not unleashed. I see as downright wasteful folly the penchant of Americans for serving, and consuming, as much food as they do. I am now an expert on snacking, which I once regarded as part of normal eating. I can now prove it is merely a perverse habit. Once in Italy I lost six pounds while eating pasta, luscious Italian ice cream, and drinking wine with meals. I thought I was sick, or that the scales were off. Then my family joined me in Venice, where I had been directing the Gritti Palace Hotel Cooking School, and we moved to more spacious quarters, with a refrigerator. The six pounds returned along with six more, and I realized that with the fridge I regressed to snacking without even being aware of it.

I've observed that the students in my cooking classes, which certainly do not focus on calorie-watching, are almost all lean beans, though they obviously love good food. I see, at parties, that many people bypass hard liquor in favor of wine. Although I do not claim to be a nutrition expert, I know liquor is loaded with empty calories and I think it bloats people.

Now that my weight is at the right notch, I enjoy an outrageously caloric meal and eat every divine morsel without a single gnawing of guilt. Guilt is an unworthy way to address a superlative meal created for the pure voluptuous joy of eating! For two or three days after a spree, however, I do as other slim people (such as my students) who adore food probably do: I switch back to my 1,200 really good calories and maintain the glorious balance between my love of food and my love of leanness.

Dinner for 4 Flab Fighters

This menu contains no added flour, sugar, fat, or salt.

☆ Follow recipe for Julienne of Fresh Vegetables on page 74, omitting salt and butter.

MENU　**Sherry Steamed Chicken**
　　　　　with Julienne of Fresh Vegetables☆
　　　　Onions and Raisins with Saffron
　　　　Sliced Exotic Fruits

BEVERAGE: Perrier, or 1 glass dry white wine per person

WORK ORDER: *Chicken, Onions and Raisins, Vegetables, Fruit*

Sherry Steamed Chicken

□ See page 240.

2 cups or more chicken stock□
1 piece of ginger the size of a quarter
¼ cup chopped scallions
2 tablespoons soy sauce
Freshly cracked black pepper
3-pound chicken
1 cup sherry

1. Place chicken stock in a pan and put over it a steamer rack or colander. Two cups of stock will probably be enough, but use more if you need it.

2. Put the ginger, scallions, soy sauce, and pepper inside the cavity of the chicken. Pour in the sherry. Holding chicken so that sherry will not pour out, close the cavity by tying the legs, tail, and end of the breast bone together. Place on the steamer over the boiling stock.

3. Steam chicken until tender, about 1 hour. Remove the chicken, tipping so that the juices will run into the stock in the bottom of the pan. Taste stock and rectify seasoning. Reduce to intensify flavor, if necessary. Pour over chicken. Strew julienne vegetables over chicken and carve. Serves 4.

Onions and Raisins with Saffron

24 little white onions, peeled
½ cup white raisins
About ¼ cup white wine
½ teaspoon saffron

Freshly cracked white pepper to taste
1 tablespoon finely chopped fresh parsley

1. Parboil onions for 3–5 minutes, depending on size. Drain.
2. Meanwhile, cover the raisins with white wine. Add saffron and soak mixture for 15 minutes.
3. In a Teflon skillet, put onions, raisins, and 2 tablespoons of the liquid in which the raisins were soaked. Cover pan and shake over the heat until onions are tender crisp. If onions and raisins begin to stick, add more wine. Keep tossing; it will take about 15 minutes. If there is too much liquid in pan, raise heat to reduce it. Season with pepper and parsley. Serves 4.

Sliced Exotic Fruits

Keeping colors and texture in mind, select any combination of fruit available in the market.

1 mango
1 papaya

2 kiwi fruit
Sprig of mint
4 lemon wedges

Peel and slice fruits. Arrange on a serving dish so that slices fan out like a flower. Garnish with mint and lemon wedges. Serves 4.

Lo-Cal Italian Dinner for 4

MENU   Sautéed Mushrooms
Broiled Eggplant with Lo-Cal Tomato Sauce
Broccoli with Lemon
Bread Sticks
Fresh Fruit and Ice Water

WINE SUGGESTION: Soave Bolla or Bertani, or Chianti

WORK ORDER: *Tomato Sauce, Eggplant, Broccoli, Fruit, Mushrooms*

Sautéed Mushrooms

□ See page 252.

4 tablespoons butter
1½ pounds mushrooms, cleaned□ and trimmed
Salt and freshly cracked black pepper to taste

2 tablespoons lemon juice
2 tablespoons finely chopped Italian parsley

1. Melt the butter in a skillet. After it foams and the foam subsides a bit, add mushrooms, salt, pepper, and lemon juice. Toss over heat 3 to 4 minutes, or just until mushrooms are cooked through.
2. Sprinkle parsley over mushrooms. Serves 4.

Broiled Eggplant

❖ Do this by placing a heavy platter or cutting board on top of the slices to squeeze them a bit but not smash them.

1 large eggplant or 2 medium ones
1 tablespoon salt

1 teaspoon vegetable oil for each slice of eggplant

1. Wash the eggplant but do not peel it. Slice lengthwise ¼ inch thick, preferably on a mandoline, or with a knife. You should have about 12 slices, or 3 for each serving.
2. Sprinkle slices with salt and weight down❖ for 10–15 minutes to release excess moisture and bitterness.
3. Wipe each slice dry with a cloth. With a sharp knife, draw a crisscross design on one side of each slice.
4. Brush each slice with a teaspoon of oil. Place slices on a baking sheet and broil 5 minutes (tend them closely so they do not burn). Turn over and broil 1 minute on the second side. Serve crisscrossed side up, with tomato sauce (recipe follows). Serves 4.

Lo-Cal Tomato Sauce

If you can afford some extra calories, sauté the onions and garlic in this recipe in a mixture of 2 tablespoons butter and 2 tablespoons oil.

LO-CAL TOMATO SAUCE

4 pounds plum tomatoes
1 onion, finely chopped
2 large cloves garlic—or more, or less, according to your taste
Tiny pinch of sugar○

Salt and freshly cracked black pepper to taste
4–6 fresh basil leaves, finely chopped
¼ cup chicken stock

○ Not much, but do use more sugar than salt here.

1. Slice off the tips of the tomatoes. Drop them into boiling water for 10 seconds, then plunge into cold water with ice cubes. Squeeze each tomato in your hand and skin will slip off in one piece. Finely chop the tomatoes.

2. In a pan (any kind but aluminum) combine all ingredients and simmer until the sauce gives up its liquid and thickens, about 25 minutes. Serves 4.

Broccoli with Lemon

△ If you can handle the guilt, add ¼ cup melted butter to the juice.

1 head broccoli, dark green with no yellow on the head

3 tablespoons lemon juice△
Salt and freshly cracked black pepper to taste

1. Trim away leaves from the broccoli, and if the stems are tough, split them. Arrange broccoli in a pan with 2 inches of boiling water. Partially cover and cook for 10–15 minutes, depending on size of broccoli and desired doneness.

2. Drain broccoli. Sprinkle with lemon juice, salt, and pepper. Serves 4.

Fresh Fruit and Ice Water

Fresh peaches, cherries with stems, apricots— whatever is in season

A bowl of water with lots of ice

Wash the fruit and arrange it decoratively in a bowl. Place bowl in the center of the table, and set the bowl of ice water alongside it. Invite each guest to refresh the fruit (in the ice water) before eating it. Provide dessert plates, fruit knives, and forks.

A Rich But Guilt-Free Dinner for 3

MENU   Vegetable Soup
Scallops Minceur
Salad with Julie's Lo-Cal Dressing
Fruit with Sauternes

WINE SUGGESTION: Pouilly-Fumé

WORK ORDER: *Soup, Shallot reduction, Sauternes reduction, cut up Fruit, Dressing, Scallops*

Vegetable Soup

□ See page 254.

2 large onions, peeled and cut into eighths
2 cups mushrooms, wiped clean and cut into quarters
3 large tomatoes, quartered
½ head cabbage, shredded
5 unpeeled carrots, cut into bite-size pieces

4 cloves fresh garlic, smashed, then peeled □
Chicken stock
2 pounds fresh spinach, washed, stems stripped off
Salt and freshly cracked black pepper to taste
Yogurt, if desired
Chopped fresh parsley, if desired

1. Put onions, mushrooms, tomatoes, cabbage, carrots, and garlic into an 8-quart kettle or stock pot. Add chicken stock to cover vegetables.

2. Bring to a boil. Cover and lower heat to a simmer. Cook until vegetables are tender but not mushy. Stir in the spinach and cook, uncovered, for another 5 minutes.

3. Put the mixture through the food mill, using the finest disk.

4. Rectify seasoning. Serve hot, or cold with a tablespoon of yogurt on top. Sprinkle with chopped parsley, if desired. Makes 12–14 cups. Freezes well.

Scallops Minceur

I created this on a cold winter's night when my husband and I were home alone. When he wanted seconds but not calories—"It's so rich!" he said—I told him it's a skinny dish and served him another portion.

1 pound sea or bay scallops
¼ cup finely chopped shallots
¾ cup dry white wine
1 ripe tomato, peeled, seeded, and finely diced

2 tablespoons finely chopped fresh dill (or ½ teaspoon saffron threads crushed in a mortar and moistened with wine)
3 egg yolks
Salt and freshly cracked white pepper to taste

1. If you use sea scallops, cut them into 4 disks each. Leave bay scallops whole.
2. Toss scallops over high heat in a sauté pan, preferably Teflon, until they yield their juices, 3–5 minutes but no longer.
3. Reserve juices. Set scallops aside.
4. Place shallots in a small heavy saucepan and add the wine. Place over medium heat and reduce the mixture to 2–3 tablespoons of liquid.✧

✧ Don't rush this process. It will take about 15 minutes or more to achieve reduction.

5. To the shallot-wine reduction, add the tomato and fresh dill. Set aside.
6. Make a *sabayon:* Whisk the egg yolks with 3 tablespoons scallop juice.○ Put into a heavy pan and whisk over medium flame until mixture mounts and is lemony and thick. Raise and lower pan off heat; be careful not to curdle the yolks. When *sabayon* is thick, combine with the scallops, dill, tomato, and reduction of shallots.

○ If you do not have enough juice, add water. Sometimes scallops will not give up their juice!

7. Reheat slowly and cook a bit, only until mixture is slightly thick and creamy-looking. Season with salt and white pepper. Serve at once! It will not hold! Serves 3.

Julie's Lo-Cal Salad Dressing

△ Crisp Belgian endive leaves are my special favorite.

Rather than putting the dressing directly onto the greens, I make an assorted platter of greens△ in season and use the dressing as a dip. I find I use less dressing and don't have to worry about its coating the greens.

½ teaspoon salt
½ teaspoon freshly cracked black pepper
2 teaspoons strong prepared mustard
1 clove fresh garlic, peeled

¼ cup roughly chopped onion
1 egg yolk
¼ cup tarragon vinegar
¾ cup chicken stock
1 tablespoon parsley sprigs

1. Place all ingredients in blender and blend until creamy, about 2 minutes.
2. Refrigerate until ready to use. Makes a little more than 1 cup.

Fruit with Sauternes

☆ Reducing the wine will intensify its sweetness and eliminate the need for sugar.

1 bottle inexpensive Sauternes
Any combination of fresh fruit in season, such as orange slices, strawberries, pears, etc.

1. Pour Sauternes into a pan and cook on a medium flame until it reduces to about 1 cup. ☆
2. Stir the warm Sauternes over ice, and continue stirring until it is cold. Pour over the fruit just before serving.

An Interesting Dinner for 4 Dieters

MENU   **Roast Chicken with Herbs**
Celery and Cucumbers
Shaved Carrots with Yogurt Dressing
Grapefruit Sections with Candied Peel

WINE: 1 glass dry red or dry white wine per person

WORK ORDER: *Chicken, Grapefruit, Celery and Cucumbers, Carrots, Dressing*

Roast Chicken with Herbs

3–4-pound chicken
1 cup finely chopped fresh parsley
2 chopped garlic cloves
¼ cup finely chopped shallots
2 tablespoons any chopped fresh herb (rosemary, thyme, etc.)

Salt and freshly cracked black pepper to taste
1 tablespoon prepared mustard
1–2 tablespoons freshly grated Parmesan cheese
Chicken stock for basting

1. Remove all the fat in the cavity of the chicken. Loosen skin over the breast.

2. Mix parsley, garlic, shallots, and herb of your choice in a small bowl. Add salt and pepper, mustard to moisten the mixture, and grated cheese. Mix well.

3. Stuff parsley mixture under the skin of the chicken. Place it on a rack in a roasting pan, sprinkle with salt and pepper, and place in a 375° oven.

4. Baste with chicken stock about every 15 minutes, and turn chicken from side to side during roasting. Roast 1 hour. Serves 4.

Celery and Cucumbers

The celery and cucumbers look alike when cooked, and in this dish they taste so good they don't seem lo-cal.

8 ribs celery, cut into 1-inch diagonal pieces
4 cups chicken stock
4 cucumbers, peeled, seeded, and cut into 1-inch diagonal pieces

Juice of 1 medium lemon
Salt and freshly cracked black pepper to taste
1 tablespoon finely chopped fresh parsley

1. Place celery in a pan with 3 cups of the chicken stock. Bring to a boil, cover, and simmer until barely tender, about 10–15 minutes. Drain. Save stock to freeze or reuse.

2. Place cucumbers in a pan and cover with 1 cup chicken stock. Bring to a boil, cover, and simmer until barely tender, 7–10 minutes. Drain. Save stock.

3. Combine the two vegetables. Sprinkle them with lemon juice, salt, pepper, and chopped parsley. Serves 4.

Shaved Carrots with Yogurt Dressing

Usually I loathe yogurt, have difficulty downing it, but this dressing is one I like.

4 large carrots, peeled
1 cup yogurt
   Juice of 1 medium lemon
1 teaspoon Dijon mustard
   Salt and freshly cracked
   black pepper to taste

½ cup chicken stock (you can use the reserve from the celery and cucumbers dish above)

1. Peel the carrots and shave them lengthwise with a rotary peeler or mandoline. Soak in ice water in refrigerator for 15 minutes, drain, and dry on a towel. Place in serving bowl.

2. For the dressing, combine remaining ingredients and mix well. Use as a dip for the carrots.

Grapefruit Sections with Candied Peel

4 grapefruits

1 cup curaçao

1. Peel the skins of 2 of the grapefruits carefully, so that no pulp is on the skin. Julienne with a knife, cutting into very fine slivers. Put into a pan and cover with curaçao. Bring to a boil, then turn to a simmer and cook 18–20 minutes. If you have time, cool to room temperature. Otherwise, set pan over ice and stir until cool.

2. Section the grapefruits and place in a crystal bowl. Pour the peel-curaçao mixture on top. Serves 4.

4 FROM CHINA TO ITALY

❖ *The Pantropheon, or A History of Food and Its Preparation in Ancient Times*, distributed by Grosset & Dunlap, 1977 (originally published in 1853), p. 51.

More than a century ago Alexis Soyer, gastronome, legendary chef, and author of a number of classic books on cooking, wrote: "So true it is that the genius of man develops itself more particularly under difficult circumstances, and that the art of cookery owes, perhaps, the perfection and glory which it has attained to the impediments which its formidable enemy, frugality, seems always ready to surround it."❖

Until quite recently, isolation no less than frugality influenced and perhaps forced the creation of great national cuisines. Chinese cooking, as we all know, *had* to be completed quickly because of the scarcity of wood, which could not be imported because inexpensive transportation had not yet been invented. Thus the great chefs and creative cooks of China were challenged not only to plumb the deepest nuances of available fresh foods and glean inspiration for great harmonies of ingredients, but also to cook them fast over the precious fire.

Nowadays, of course, the Chinese use gas and electric stoves, but they, and the rest of us, are glad that their ancestors did not have long-burning appliances and devised instead the tender-crisp cooking technique that is one of the highest tributes one can pay to a beautiful fresh vegetable.

Most of us think that the Chinese gave Italy pasta, thanks to Marco Polo, but I've discovered that we are probably wrong. According to the *Horizon Cookbook*, "an ancient tool identified as a macaroni-maker can be seen in the frescoes of an Etruscan tomb." It

○ Time-Life Books.

seems, moreover, that well before Polo ever set sail, in 1290, an Italian cookbook detailed the methods for making various pastas.○ As far as I'm concerned, this mistaken myth is just one more proof that Italian *cucina* has not been paid its due homage for vast originality and excellence. I will stand up and be counted as one who defends Italian cooking and would remind the French that they are indebted to the Italians for teaching them how to cook. Their first lessons date back to 1533, the year Catherine de'Medici left Italy to marry King Henry II of France and took her chefs with her.

Exquisite vegetables, meats, fish, and fresh foods of all kinds reaped from the plenitude of spendthrift Nature—these are the foundations of great cooking, and the cuisines of all countries rest securely upon them. Even now, have you noticed that many of the truly knowledgeable authorities on cooking spent their formative years on isolated farms?

Of course, not many of us live on farms anymore. Most of us are within easy distance of a good supermarket where an abundance of fresh food, in season, awaits preparation according to the marvelous methods developed by "the genius of man."

Italian Menu for a Quartet After the Concert

> **MENU**   Musician's Pasta
> Carpaccio with Watercress Sauce
> Italian Bread Sticks
> Sliced Blood Oranges with Maraschino Liqueur
>
> WINE SUGGESTION: Valpolicella
>
> WORK ORDER: *Watercress Sauce, Beef, Oranges, Pasta*

Musician's Pasta

Chef Mosca, one of Italy's most venerable pastry chefs, taught me this creation in Venice. He told me the sauce is quite popular among musicians, particularly late in the evening after a performance. Perhaps the reason is that the ingredients are usually on the shelf at home. Arthur Rubinstein is known to be partial to this dish. While sometimes a boxed pasta is used,

I like it best over pasta from scratch. When I prepared pasta for a group of Italian food writers and food experts from Venice, they gave me and my method rave reviews. (Much has been written about the virtues of hand-rolled pasta, but I don't blush when I get out my electric pasta machine.)

3 cups flour
4 whole eggs
Salt
1–2 tablespoons olive oil
12 tablespoons soft butter
½ cup strong meat juices left over from a roast△

½ cup freshly grated Parmesan cheese
3 eggs, beaten
Freshly cracked black pepper, if desired

△ Or use 1 cup chicken or beef stock boiled until reduced to ½ cup.

1. A food processor is necessary for this method. Using the steel blade, put the flour, 4 whole eggs, and a pinch (about ½ teaspoon or according to your taste) of salt into the processor and spin for 3 or 4 seconds.

2. Add olive oil through the feed tube; continue to spin.

☆ All flours are different. See page 249.

3. Mixture should begin forming a large lump around the blade. If this does not happen☆ add a few drops of warm water through the tube. The machine will clog and the pasta will be ready.

4. Remove the pasta and place on a floured pastry board or counter top. Knead for a minute or two; the dough will become as smooth as satin.

5. Roll pasta dough into a sausage shape and cut into 6 equal pieces.

6. Flatten each piece. Using widest opening of electric pasta machine, feed each piece of pasta through the wringer. Fold pasta into three and continue kneading through machine till very smooth. Set the wringer of the pasta machine down a notch and pass pasta through. Do not fold. Continue passing pasta through wringer, setting lower each time, till pasta is very thin. Then put through noodle or fettucine cutting blades of machine.

7. Get out the largest kettle you possess, fill with water, and boil. Add 2 tablespoons salt and drop pasta into the boiling water.

(continued)

8. Fresh pasta cooks fast! Cook only 2–3 minutes, and, using a wooden fork or pasta comb, keep it moving.

9. Drain pasta through a sieve. Place on a warm serving dish and add the soft butter.

10. Add the meat juices and toss pasta, coating each strand.

11. Add grated Parmesan cheese, continuing to toss.

12. Add the 3 beaten eggs *gradually* while tossing so that the egg will cook, but not curdle, on the hot pasta.

13. Add freshly cracked pepper, if desired. Usually no salt is necessary; the cheese will probably be salty enough. Serves 4.

Carpaccio with Watercress Sauce

This is my version of Carpaccio, invented in Venice at Harry's Bar (the most famous of all Harry's bars, no relation to its dozens of namesakes) in honor of the great sixteenth-century Venetian artist Vittore Carpaccio. Carpaccio has made its way to France (where all great Italian recipes seem to travel) and, with the *nouvelle cuisine* wave, I have seen it on menus in New York and Philadelphia. It is an Italian answer to steak tartare. Carpaccio, incidentally, was influenced in his work by Giovanni Bellini, an earlier Italian painter who lived to be ninety and inspired several generations of artists. Harry's Bar has also honored Bellini (see the chapter "Cheers: Drinks Homemade and Otherwise").

□ Have butcher slice meat ¼ inch thin, or do it yourself.

2 pieces of beef filet per person□

1. If you're to be the butcher, don't neglect to put the beef into the freezer for 15 minutes to make the slicing job much easier.

2. Lay beef slices on a sheet of wax paper, leaving a good space between each slice. Put another piece of wax paper on top.

3. Pound with the flat side of a meat cleaver very gently, so as not to break the membranes or cause holes. Meat should be ⅛ inch thick after pounding. Do not brutalize it; merely subdue it.

4. Remove meat to a platter and cover with the following watercress sauce.

Watercress Sauce

1 egg yolk
1 teaspoon salt
½ teaspoon freshly cracked black pepper
1 teaspoon good mustard (Dijon, maybe)
½ cup good olive oil
Juice of 1 lemon

½ cup corn or vegetable oil
1 large bunch really fresh watercress, finely chopped
2 tablespoons finely chopped shallots, if desired
2 tablespoons finely chopped fresh parsley

1. In a small bowl, whisk the egg yolk, salt, and pepper until combined.
2. Add mustard; continue whisking.
3. Whisking constantly, add the olive oil in a thin stream. Do not rush this. Add lemon juice, continue whisking, and slowly add the corn or vegetable oil.
4. Rectify seasoning—add a little salt, or more lemon juice, or, if too tangy, just a bit more oil.
5. Fold in watercress. Add shallots, if desired.
6. Spread over beef and sprinkle with the chopped parsley.

Sliced Blood Oranges with Maraschino Liqueur

❖ Or slice the oranges into a crystal bowl, pour over about ½ cup liqueur, and refrigerate until serving time.

While I dislike maraschino cherries, I do enjoy the flavor of maraschino liqueur over oranges or, occasionally, peaches. Blood oranges are scarce as hen's dentures, so substitute any orange of your choice: large navels are quite good. If you are feeling dramatic, serve the oranges as an Italian waiter does. Inspired showmen, these waiters magically peel an orange on a fork while guests sit, enchanted. The slices are arranged like a beautiful flower on the serving plate. I like to serve these on crystal, or green majolica.❖

1 orange, peeled, per person
1–2 tablespoons maraschino liqueur per serving

Sugar, if desired

1. Slice oranges ¼ inch thick and lay them overlapping on a dessert plate.
2. Pour liqueur over the oranges.
3. If oranges are not sweet enough, sprinkle with a little sugar.

Delicately Delicious Chinese Dinner for 2

It's beginning to look as though we are heading back to where those brilliant Chinese were when they created fast-cooking techniques thousands of years ago. We are becoming as hard up for gas and electricity as they were for firewood, but they've given us magnificent cookery to make fuel shortages almost pleasant.

A little bit of fish or meat goes a long way in Chinese cuisine. The tender crisp vegetables are heavenly. The total wallop is so delicately delicious it is difficult to understand how this food can taste so good and be healthful, too!

○ The Chinese usually skip dessert, but fruit is good for you.

MENU   **Chicken Broth with Carrots, Cucumbers, and Soy**
Steamed Scallops with Ham, Ginger, and Scallions
Really Good Rice
Bowl of Fresh Apricots or Other Fruit in Season○

BEVERAGE SUGGESTION: Hot Tea (see page 230).

WORK ORDER: *Scallops, Chicken Broth, Rice*

Chicken Broth with Carrots, Cucumbers, and Soy

△ See page 240.

4 cups well-flavored chicken stock△
1 small cucumber, about 4 inches long, peeled and sliced into thin rounds

1 small carrot, peeled and sliced very thinly on the diagonal
1 tablespoon soy sauce
A few drops of sesame oil

1. Bring chicken stock to a boil in saucepan. Lower heat and add cucumber and carrot. Turn to simmer and cook until vegetables are tender crisp, about 3 minutes.

2. Add the soy sauce and sesame oil and simmer 1 minute.

3. Serve in warm bowls. Enough for seconds for 2.

Steamed Scallops with Ham, Ginger, and Scallions

¼ pound sea scallops, cut into 4 disks each
3 tablespoons dry sherry
½ teaspoon sugar
1 tablespoon soy sauce
1 teaspoon fresh ginger root, shredded fine

2 tablespoons finely chopped ham, preferably smoked
3 scallions, chopped with tops

1. Put the scallop disks in a bowl and add sherry, sugar, soy sauce, and ginger root. If time is limited, let stand about 10 minutes; if you can, marinate 30 minutes. Turn frequently.

2. Put scallops, ham, and scallions on a heatproof dish and place on a rack in steamer. Cover and steam for about 10–15 minutes.

3. Serve with rice. Serves 2.

Really Good Rice

1 cup long-grain rice

1. Wash the rice in cold water until it is no longer milky—about three or four times. Drain.

2. Place rice in pan with a heavy bottom and cover with fresh cold water until water is 1 inch above rice.

3. Cover and bring to a boil. Reduce heat to a simmer and cook for 25 minutes without peeking. When you lift the lid, water should be absorbed and little holes should be visible on the surface of the rice. Fluff up the rice with chopsticks or two forks.

4. Rice can be kept warm over an asbestos mat, on low flame. Serves 2–4.

A Dramatic Northern Italian Dinner for 8

MENU   Mushrooms with Parmesan Cheese
Broccoli Mousse Encased in Prosciutto Ham
Romaine Salad
Melon Balls with Melon Purée

WINE SUGGESTION: Chianti Riserva or Bardolino

WORK ORDER: *Broccoli Mousse, Melon Balls and Purée, Salad, Mushrooms*

Mushrooms with Parmesan Cheese

□ See page 252 for directions on cleaning mushrooms, which require gentle treatment.

○ Instead of tossing, you can use a wooden spatula if you choose.

The wild porcini mushrooms of Italy, although very large, are perfect for this dish, but use the best of what is available.

8 tablespoons butter
48 medium mushrooms, carefully cleaned□
Juice of ½ lemon
Salt and freshly cracked black pepper to taste

½ cup Parmesan cheese
2 tablespoons finely chopped fresh parsley

1. Melt the butter in a large skillet. When the foam subsides, add the mushrooms.
2. Toss mushrooms until they are well coated with butter, only about 1 minute. Squeeze on the lemon juice. Add salt and pepper and continue to toss for 4–5 minutes.○
3. Just before serving, add the Parmesan cheese and toss 1 minute longer, or until the cheese melts.
4. Arrange on a platter, sprinkle with chopped parsley, and serve. Makes 8 servings.

Broccoli Mousse Encased in Prosciutto Ham

This idea came to me in the middle of the night. It is a gorgeous presentation. A ring mold is lined with overlapping paper-thin slices of ham and filled with a creamy broccoli mixture. The ends of the ham are folded over to cover the top, and the mousse is baked in a water bath (bain-marie) and inverted onto a platter. The recipe will also work with cauliflower, carrots, spinach, asparagus (use your own ideas!): use 3 cups of the cooked fresh vegetable instead of the broccoli. This mousse is splendid hot or cold.

1 tablespoon vegetable oil	1 teaspoon salt
½ pound prosciutto ham, sliced paper-thin△	½ teaspoon freshly cracked black pepper
About 1¾ pounds fresh broccoli	¼ teaspoon nutmeg
2 tablespoons butter	6 eggs
1 small onion, finely chopped	1½ cups light cream or milk
1 clove garlic, peeled and chopped	Cherry tomatoes, if desired
	Mushrooms, if desired

△ This works well with country ham, too.

1. Brush a 6–8-cup ring mold with vegetable oil. Line with overlapping slices of ham. Let it lounge over the sides; later you will arrange it over the filling.

2. Steam the broccoli, or plunge it into a large kettle of salted water and boil uncovered until barely tender (10 minutes or so), remove, and drain.

3. Put first the broccoli florets, then the stems, through the food processor. Remove to a bowl.

4. Heat the butter in a sauté pan until the foam subsides. Add onion and garlic and cook 1–2 minutes.☆

☆ This removes the raw onion taste. Otherwise the onion will steam in the mousse and impart a bitter flavor

5. Add onion-garlic mixture to the broccoli, then the salt, pepper, and nutmeg. Mix well.

6. In a separate bowl, beat eggs and add light cream or milk. Add this to the broccoli mixture and blend well.

7. Pour mixture carefully into the ham-lined mold.□

□ To avoid spilling, I usually use a metal measuring cup.

8. Drape the ends of the ham over the mold.

9. Place a round of buttered wax paper over the mold to keep it from drying out while cooking.

10. Place mold in a bain-marie, or water bath, set into a preheated 350° oven, and bake until set, about 25–30 minutes.

11. To unmold, remove wax paper and, using an up-and-down sawing motion, run a thin knife around the edge of the mold. Lay a round serving platter over the mold and carefully invert. Shake gently to release mousse.

12. The center can be filled with sautéed cherry tomatoes or fluted mushrooms.✧ But do not use mushrooms if you are serving them in another course! Serve in wedges, warm or at room temperature. Generous portions for 8.

✧ See page 252.

Romaine Salad I cut greens with a knife, for I am a firm believer that cutting does less damage than tearing. If you are emotional about this, go ahead and tear your greens. One of my students once claimed that her palate could distinguish between cut and torn greens. "With a delicate palate such as yours," I said, "you are wasting time in my classes. You should be a tea or spice taster, or perhaps a lettuce taster." I never saw her again.

I am also opposed to wooden salad bowls. They are rarely "mellow." They are more often rancid. I prefer clear bowls for salads, but if you insist on a wooden one, wash it with warm sudsy water, rinse in warm water, and dry thoroughly before using—for my peace of mind. Whatever your method of preparing greens and selecting bowls, you will enjoy this Italian salad dressing, which is relaxed and good-tempered.

3 large bunches of romaine lettuce
Salt and freshly cracked black pepper to taste
1 tablespoon any fresh chopped herb

4 tablespoons red wine vinegar
¾ cup good Italian olive oil

1. Wash lettuce thoroughly and remove outer leaves if they are wilted or brownish. Cut off root end. Lay romaine on cutting board and cut across into inch-wide pieces. Dry in a salad spinner or roll in a paper towel, then in a dish cloth, and refrigerate.

2. Place the greens in a bowl of china, porcelain, plastic, glass, earthenware, etc.

3. Add to the greens the salt, pepper, and herb. Sprinkle the vinegar and olive oil over and toss well. Taste to adjust seasoning.

4. Serve on chilled salad plates. Serves 8.

Melon Balls with Melon Purée Whenever I made melon balls, I became vexed because so much fruit was wasted, but the balls are so scrumptious! Finally I devised this no-waste method.

△ See page 226.

1 medium watermelon
A little simple syrup△

A few tablespoons of light or dark rum

1. Cut watermelon in half lengthwise. Use a melon baller and remove as much of the interior as possible, discarding the seeds.

2. With a large metal spoon, scrape out the rest of the melon. Usually it comes to 2 cups or more.

3. Put melon scrapings into blender or food processor, purée, and sweeten with simple syrup and rum. I would use 1 tablespoon of rum to a cup of purée, but check to suit your own taste.

4. Pour purée over melon balls and chill.

5. If desired, serve in one half of the melon shell. Serves 8.

Dinner with an Italian Dash for 6

MENU   **Semolina Gnocchi**
Veal with Lemon
Medallions of Broccoli Stems and Carrots
   Vinaigrette
Marinated Fresh Fruit

WINE: Pinot Grigio or Orvieto

WORK ORDER: *Gnocchi, Fruit, Vegetables, Veal*

Semolina Gnocchi

These gnocchi, a specialty of Rome, can be prepared with either water or milk, but somehow milk makes them so much richer.

1 quart milk or water
1 teaspoon salt
1 cup semolina
8 tablespoons butter

2 beaten eggs
1 cup freshly grated imported Parmesan cheese
½ teaspoon freshly cracked white pepper

1. Put milk or water into a saucepan. Bring to a boil and add the salt.

✧ Use a funnel made of wax paper to make semolina flow in a very fine stream, or shake through a fine sieve into the liquid.

○ At this point, you can also add some bits of prosciutto ham, truffles, or even chopped hard-cooked egg.

△ At this point you can store this dish in the refrigerator. It will keep 1 or 2 days. Cover with plastic wrap, and make sure you let it come to room temperature before baking.

2. Carefully add the semolina✧ to the boiling liquid, stirring the mixture all the while to avoid lumps.

3. When the mixture pulls away from the sides of the pan—about 5 minutes—add 4 tablespoons of the butter and beat it in.

4. Add the beaten eggs and continue to stir.

5. Add ½ cup of the cheese○ and the pepper. Beat to make sure there are no lumps.

6. Spread mixture out, ½ inch thick, onto a wet baking sheet or counter top. Let cool to room temperature or put into the refrigerator to chill.

7. Cut the dough with a round cutter, 1½ inches wide, or cut into diamond shapes.

8. Butter a baking dish with 1 tablespoon of the butter and place gnocchi dough therein, using the leftover dough first, then covering with overlapping rounds or diamond shapes.

9. Melt remaining butter and sprinkle over gnocchi.

10. Add remaining ½ cup Parmesan cheese.△

11. Place in a 375° oven until hot and bubbly, 15–20 minutes. Run under broiler for a minute or two to develop a rich brown crust. Serves 6.

Medallions of Broccoli Stems and Carrots Vinaigrette

If you'd like to use this as a hot dish, omit the vinaigrette dressing and simply serve the cooked broccoli-carrot mixture with butter. Save the stems from another broccoli dish for this salad, or save and peel the stems from artichokes and use them as you would the broccoli. Nobody can guess the artichokes!

2 pounds broccoli
4 carrots
1 teaspoon salt
  Freshly cracked black pepper

2 tablespoons red wine vinegar
4 tablespoons olive oil
1 tablespoon finely chopped fresh parsley

1. Remove stems from the broccoli, peel, and slice ⅛ inch thick on a mandoline or vegetable cutter. Reserve the florets for another use.

2. Peel the carrots and slice the same way.

3. Add broccoli slices to rapidly boiling water seasoned with 1 teaspoon salt and cook until barely tender, about 3 minutes.

4. Cook carrots the same way, in a separate pan.

5. Drain vegetables. Combine in a salad bowl. Season with salt and pepper to taste.

6. While the broccoli and carrots are still warm, add the vinegar, oil, and parsley. Toss and serve. This tastes good warm or at room temperature. Serves 6.

Veal with Lemon

If you want this dish to be a bit more festive, make caramelized lemon rind (following recipe) and sprinkle it over the veal along with the parsley.

☆ Or substitute chicken or turkey breast scallops.

1½–2 pounds veal☆ loin, cut into thin scallops
¼ cup flour
Oil to film bottom of sauté pan
2 tablespoons butter

Salt and freshly cracked black pepper to taste
Juice of 1 medium lemon
1 tablespoon finely chopped fresh parsley

1. Place veal scallops on chopping board and with a metal pounder dipped in ice water, give each 3 or 4 light swipes or poundings. Dip each in flour and pat to remove excess.

2. Add oil gently to pan, being careful not to overdo it, then add the butter.

3. Heat, being careful not to burn butter.

4. Add the veal scallops a few at a time. Do not let them touch each other in the pan. Cook 2–3 minutes on each side. Salt and pepper them and add the lemon juice.

5. Remove to a serving platter and sprinkle parsley over the top. Serves 6.

Caramelized Lemon Rind

Rinds of 3 medium lemons
2 tablespoons melted butter
1 teaspoon sugar

1. Peel the lemon rinds with a swivel-bladed knife and julienne them as finely as possible.

2. Melt butter in a sauté pan. Add lemon rinds and sugar.

3. Cook very slowly while stirring with a wooden spatula until the rinds are tender and caramelized.

Marinated Fresh Fruit

Fresh fruit (whatever is in season)
1 tablespoon sugar

2-3 tablespoons cognac

The possible fruit combinations are endless. Peaches, bananas, pears, berries, melon, oranges, and grapefruit are just a few suggestions. Do go easy on apples, however. Nothing bugs me more than fresh fruit "combinations" that are mostly apples. Gauge the amount of fruit you need by its size: whether or not each person can eat two peaches depends on the size of one peach. Select enough for 6 people.

1. Cut up the fruit into a special serving bowl.
2. Arrange attractively and sprinkle with the sugar.
3. If you're feeling dramatic, put your thumb over the cognac bottle and shake it over the fruit.
4. Let chill in the refrigerator before serving.

Greek Feast for 6 or 8

> **MENU**   Feta Cheese with Black Bread, Butter, and Assorted Olives
> Avgolemono (Greek Egg-Lemon Soup)
> Keftedes (Greek Meat Rolls)
> Sliced Oranges with Ouzo
>
> **WINE SUGGESTION:** California Cabernet Sauvignon
>
> **WORK ORDER:** *Cheese, etc., Keftedes, Oranges, Soup*

Avgolemono (Greek Egg-Lemon Soup)

□ See recipe for chicken stock on page 240. To make it stronger, reduce it: start with about 11 cups.

8 cups strong chicken stock□
½ cup rice

2 eggs
Juice of 1 medium lemon

1. Bring the stock to a boil. Add rice and cook until it is tender, about 15 minutes.
2. Just before serving, use a rotary beater to beat the eggs until they are light and frothy.

3. Beat in the hot stock, *a little at a time.* Unless the temperature of the eggs is raised slowly with the addition of the hot liquid, the eggs will curdle.

4. Beat in the lemon juice; adjust seasonings. Reheat gently, but do not boil. Serves 6–8.

Feta Cheese with Black Bread, Butter, and Assorted Olives

1 pound Feta cheese
A loaf of good black bread
Butter in a crock

1 or 2 bowls of assorted olives

1. Rinse the cheese under water, drain, and place on a serving board.

2. Place the bread on another board. Serve with a knife, the butter, and the olives.

Keftedes (Greek Meat Rolls)

These are splendid as canapés; just form the meat mixture into 40–50 tiny rolls.

1 tablespoon olive oil
1 small yellow onion, finely chopped
2 slices firm white bread
2½ pounds ground beef sirloin
1 egg
1 tablespoon lemon juice
1 tablespoon chopped fresh mint

2 tablespoons chopped fresh parsley
¼ teaspoon ground cinnamon
Salt and freshly cracked black pepper to taste
¼ cup butter

1. In the olive oil, sauté the onion until soft but not brown, about 10 minutes.

2. Meanwhile, toast the bread and put into a large mixing bowl with ½ cup water. Let soak for 5 minutes, then squeeze out any excess water.

3. Add to the soaked toast the meat, egg, lemon juice, mint, parsley, cinnamon, salt, and pepper. Using your hands, work the mixture until it is well blended. Form into 12 large sausage-shaped rolls.

4. In a skillet, heat the butter. When it is hot, add the meat rolls and sauté until well browned all over. Serves 6–8.

Sliced Oranges with Ouzo

Use a light touch with the ouzo. Otherwise it will overwhelm the oranges.

8–10 oranges, depending on size

1 tablespoon honey, or more

1–2 tablespoons ouzo

1. Peel the oranges and cut into thick slices. Do this over the serving bowl so as not to squander any juices.
2. Add the honey, then gently drizzle over the ouzo. Serves 6–8.

A West Virginia Breakfast for 8

MENU　Caramelized Bacon
Rosemary's Grits Crêpes
Applesauce

BEVERAGE: Café au Lait

WORK ORDER: *Applesauce, Crêpes, Bacon*

Caramelized Bacon

24 slices good grade of bacon　½ cup honey

1. Place the bacon on a rack on a baking sheet. Bake 5 minutes in a 400° oven. Remove from oven, pour off fat, and save it for another day.
2. Drizzle the honey over the bacon; allow about a teaspoon per slice.
3. Lower oven to 350°. Return bacon to oven and bake about 15 minutes, making sure it does not burn. Baking time will depend on thickness of slices. Serves 8.

Rosemary's Grits Crêpes

Rosemary Lanahan, a super lady, extraordinary cook, and wife of the former president of the Greenbrier Hotel in West Virginia, shared this recipe with me. When I am at the hotel to direct its cooking school, we dine together frequently and swap ideas.

4 medium ears fresh white corn
⅓ cup light cream
1⅓ cups water
1¼ teaspoons salt
⅓ cup white hominy grits— the quick-cooking kind
4 eggs, lightly beaten

½ cup sifted flour
2 cups scalded milk
½ cup melted butter
A generous dash of nutmeg
Freshly grated Parmesan cheese

1. Scrape the corn to make 1 cup. Combine with the cream in a blender. Purée and set aside.

2. In a large saucepan, bring water and salt to a boil. Slowly stir in the grits. Reduce heat and cook uncovered, stirring occasionally, 3–5 minutes.

3. To the slightly beaten eggs, add a small amount of the grits. Mix. Return this mixture to the pan with the rest of the grits.

4. Remove pan from heat. Blend in flour, scalded milk, melted butter, and nutmeg.

5. To make each crêpe: Pour ⅓ cup of the batter into a slightly buttered crêpe pan. Be sure to dip to the bottom of the bowl each time, since the grits and corn tend to settle there.

6. Cook over medium-high heat 2–3 minutes, *on one side only.*

7. Carefully *slide*✧ crêpe out of the pan and onto a dish. Continue making and stacking crêpes until all the batter is used.

✧ Do not try to lift these from a pan with a spatula; crêpes are very fragile and will break if you do.

8. To assemble, start with the top crêpe, and roll○ up each crêpe. Roll each crêpe from the stack; do not lift unrolled. Place 2 crêpes each into 8 individual casseroles.

○ If desired, fill with slivered ham or a creamed mixture such as mushrooms before rolling.

9. Sprinkle the rolled-up crêpes with the grated cheese. Place under broiler until brown. Makes 8 servings.

Applesauce

4 pounds apples
(Baldwins, McIntosh,
Granny Smith, Red
Delicious, etc.)
1 cup water
½–1 cup sugar, depending on
sweetness of apples

A little grated nutmeg
1 cup heavy cream, barely
whipped, if desired

1. Quarter and core the apples, but do not peel them. The skins will add flavor to the sauce.

2. Put into a large saucepan and add the water. Bring to a boil, cover, and simmer until soft and mushy, about 30 minutes.

3. Add ½ cup sugar, stir until it dissolves, then taste for sweetness. Add more sugar if you like. Sprinkle with nutmeg.

4. Remove from the heat. Put through a food mill (fine disk) to remove the skins. Serve warm or cold with barely whipped cream, if desired. Serves 6–8.

Deep South Menu for 6

If only one oven is available, you can bake the spoon bread and the Bourbon sponge in the same oven at 350°.

MENU   **Batter-Fried Chicken**
Spoon Bread
Warm Okra Vinaigrette
Bourbon Sponge

LIBATION: Mint Juleps before dinner

WORK ORDER: *Sponge, Spoon Bread, Chicken, Okra*

Batter-Fried Chicken

1½ cups chicken stock
2 eggs
  Salt and freshly cracked
  black pepper to taste

2 teaspoons baking powder
1½ cups flour
2 chickens, cut up

1. Mix all ingredients except the chicken together. Beat with a whisk until smooth, but do not overbeat. Cook as for Aunt Sophie's Fried Chicken (page 204). Serves 6, with leftovers.

Spoon Bread

2 cups milk
1 teaspoon salt
½ cup white or yellow stone-
  ground corn meal

3 egg yolks, beaten
2 tablespoons butter
½ teaspoon baking powder
3 egg whites

1. Bring milk to a boil. Add salt to the corn meal, then add this mixture to the milk. With a wooden spatula, stir until thick, about 5 minutes.

2. Beat in the egg yolks, butter, and baking powder. Let rest a few minutes.

3. Meanwhile, beat the egg whites until stiff. Fold into the corn meal mixture. Put into a buttered 1-quart bake-and-serve dish. Bake at 350° for 40 minutes, until puffed. Serves 6.

Warm Okra Vinaigrette

Okra was a vegetable my brothers and I detested when we were kids. I remember trying to hide it under the skins of baked potatoes, or holding it in my mouth to flush away in the powder room. Now I love okra—especially this way, or fried in batter.

△ See page 245.

1½ pounds smallest okra,
  sliced crosswise or left
  whole, ends trimmed

1 cup vinaigrette△

1. In a pan of briskly boiling salted water, cook okra 5 minutes, or until tender crisp. Do not cover. Drain and refresh in cold water for a minute or so. Dry.

2. While okra is still a bit warm, place in a bowl and cover with vinaigrette. Serves 6.

Bourbon Sponge

1 tablespoon butter
3 eggs, separated
1 tablespoon grated orange
    rind

¼ cup Bourbon
1 cup sugar
2 tablespoons flour
1 cup cream

1. Preheat oven to 350°. Grease a baking dish with butter.

2. Beat egg yolks until thick. Stir in the orange rind and Bourbon. Beat in the sugar and flour and continue to beat until smooth.

3. Gradually add the cream.

4. Beat the egg whites until stiff, then fold into the Bourbon mixture.

5. Put mixture into prepared dish. Place in a bain-marie with boiling water coming halfway up the dish. Bake until lightly browned, about 35 minutes. Serves 6.

Hungarian Rhapsody Dinner for 6 or 8

MENU   **Maria's Stuffed Peppers
Pumpernickel Bread
Hungarian Sausage Bake
Cherry Compote**

WINE SUGGESTION: Egri Bikover

WORK ORDER: *Peppers, Sausage, Compote*

Maria's Stuffed Peppers

My good friend Maria Donovan, the Hungarian food writer, gave me this recipe for peppers. They are purely fabulous with cocktails. You can also chill these peppers overnight in the refrigerator. The cheese will set. To serve, slice peppers horizontally, with a sharp knife, into rings about ¼ inch thick.

2 large green or red
  peppers
1¼ cups drained ricotta
  cheese
¼ pound unsalted butter
½ cup blue cheese
2 tablespoons Dijon
  mustard

Salt to taste
1 tablespoon caraway seeds
¼ cup finely chopped chives
¼ cup chopped anchovies
1 tablespoon sweet
  Hungarian paprika
A little beer, if needed

1. Remove tops from peppers about 1 inch down. Discard seeds and fibers.

2. Place all remaining ingredients in large bowl of mixer. Beat until creamy. If needed, add a little beer to smooth the mixture.

3. Pack cheese mixture into the empty pepper shells and replace the tops. Set in refrigerator.

4. Remove the tops and use the cheese to spread on black bread. Serves 6–8.

Hungarian Sausage Bake

1½ pounds potatoes
½ pound Polish sausage,
  thinly sliced
4 hard-cooked eggs, sliced
  Salt to taste
1 tablespoon medium-
  sweet Hungarian paprika

2 tablespoons butter
2 cups sour cream
1 teaspoon potato flour
¼ cup light cream
2 tablespoons buttered
  bread crumbs

1. Preheat oven to 350°.

2. Boil potatoes, covered and in their skins, in salted water for 10–15 minutes. When cool enough to handle, peel and thinly slice.

3. Butter a 2-quart shallow baking dish, 12 by 8 by 2 inches. Arrange half of the potatoes, sausage, sliced eggs, salt, paprika, and butter in a single layer.

4. Combine sour cream, potato flour, and light cream. Spread half over mixture in baking dish.

5. Make a second layer using the remaining half of ingredients. Top with buttered bread crumbs.

6. Bake 25 minutes. Let stand 5 minutes before serving. Serves 6–8.

Cherry Compote

1 quart Bing cherries, washed, stemmed, and pitted

3 cups simple syrup☆
2–3 tablespoons kirsch

☆ See page 226.

1. Put the cherries in a pan and cover with simple syrup. Bring to a boil and cook for 7 minutes.

2. Remove cherries with a slotted spoon and place in a crystal bowl. Add kirsch and toss.

3. Reduce syrup to half, being careful not to let it caramelize. Remove from fire and pour over cherries. Serve at room temperature. Serves 6–8.

Cheers to the English Dinner for 4

If you think there is too much cream in this menu, you can make the Brussels bisque with only chicken stock, adding enough to replace the cream. Or you can serve the strawberries with only confectioners' sugar, for dipping.

MENU   **Brussels Bisque**
Sirloin of Beef
New Potatoes in Mint Cream
Herbed Popovers
Strawberries with Crème Anglaise

WINE: Chambertin or California Pinot Noir

WORK ORDER: *Beef, Crème Anglais, Bisque, Popovers, Potatoes*

Brussels Bisque

1 quart Brussels sprouts, washed and trimmed
2 cups chicken stock
2 tablespoons minced shallots
1 large clove garlic, minced
2 tablespoons butter

2 tablespoons flour
2 cups light cream
Salt and freshly cracked white pepper to taste
Sour cream, if desired
1 tablespoon chopped fresh dill

1. Cook Brussels sprouts in boiling salted water until tender, 10–15 minutes. Drain.

2. Place Brussels sprouts and chicken stock in blender; purée until smooth.

3. Cook shallots and garlic in butter until tender. Blend in flour. Stir with a wooden spatula and cook 3 minutes.

□ Or 2 cups chicken broth.

4. Add puréed vegetables, cream,□ and remaining ingredients. Change to a whisk and cook until the mixture is slightly thickened and smooth. If necessary, thin with a little more cream or chicken stock.

5. If desired, serve with a dollop of sour cream.

6. Sprinkle dill on each serving. Serves 4 generously.

Sirloin of Beef

✧ If you have the time and the need for leftovers, use a larger sirloin.

4 pounds sirloin of beef✧ at room temperature
1 tablespoon coarse salt

Freshly cracked black pepper
Watercress

Rub the sirloin of beef with the coarse salt and pepper. Place on a rack in roasting pan. Roast at 375° for 15 minutes per pound, or until thermometer reaches 110° (for rare). Carve into very thin slices. Garnish with watercress. Serves 4 or more.

New Potatoes in Mint Cream

1½ cups heavy cream
2 tablespoons chopped fresh mint leaves
16 small new potatoes, scraped and washed

Salt and freshly cracked white pepper

1. Put the cream and mint into a small heavy pan and simmer until cream is reduced to half.

2. Place the potatoes in enough water to cover them, add salt, and boil 15 minutes or until barely tender. Drain; pierce each potato in 2 places so that cream will be absorbed. Sprinkle with salt and pepper.

3. Pour the minted cream over them. Serves 4.

Herbed Popovers

2 eggs
1 cup milk
1 cup flour

1 tablespoon mixed fresh herbs
Oil for greasing molds

1. Break the eggs into a bowl and beat for 1 minute. Add the milk and beat until blended.
2. Mix together flour and herbs and combine with the milk mixture. Blend thoroughly, but do not overbeat.
3. Brush 8 custard cups with the oil. Fill half full with batter.
4. Bake in a 425° oven 30 minutes, then turn oven down to 350° and bake 15–20 minutes longer to dry out popovers. Makes 8.

Strawberries with Crème Anglaise

Place a quart of strawberries, gently washed and drained, into a large crystal bowl. Pour over them the following crème Anglaise—which sounds so much better than "vanilla sauce"! If you like you can substitute a liqueur for the vanilla.

4 egg yolks
2 cups milk or cream

¼ cup sugar
1 teaspoon vanilla extract

1. Beat egg yolks in a bowl.
2. Heat milk or cream and sugar in pan until bubbles form around the edge. Add vanilla.
3. Carefully, very carefully, combine the yolks and milk or cream mixture and cook it until it coats the back of a spoon. Strain and cool. This is a thin sauce. Makes 2 cups.

Provencal Dinner for 2

MENU   **Tender Radishes with Butter**
Baby Frog Legs
French Fried Zucchini
Fresh Purple and Green Figs

WINE SUGGESTION: White Côtes du-Rhône

WORK ORDER: *Radishes, Zucchini, Figs, Frog Legs*

Tender Radishes with Butter

1 or 2 bunches radishes, depending on size

¼ pound unsalted butter
1 small loaf French bread

1. Wash radishes and trim bottoms, leaving stems on. Arrange neatly on a platter.
2. Put butter in a small crock.
3. Serve radishes, butter, and French bread together.

Baby Frog Legs

Provide big, thick napkins: you eat these with your fingers.

24 frog legs, no bigger than your little finger
¼ cup flour
8 tablespoons butter
2–3 cloves garlic, chopped (use more if you like)

Salt and freshly cracked black pepper to taste
Juice of 1 medium lemon
1 tablespoon finely chopped fresh parsley

1. Roll frog legs, a few at a time, in flour and pat off excess.
2. Heat 6 tablespoons butter in a skillet until sizzling. Add frog legs and sauté rapidly—this should require no more than 5 minutes. Remove to a platter with a slotted spoon.
3. Add 2 tablespoons butter to the pan, along with garlic, lemon juice, salt and pepper, and parsley. Heat a minute or two and pour over the frog legs. Allow 12 per person. Serves 2.

French Fried Zucchini

4–6 small zucchini
2 cups shortening

½ cup flour
Salt to taste

1. Wash the zucchini, leaving skin on. Slice paper-thin on a mandoline or in a food processor.
2. Meanwhile, heat shortening to the point of smoking.
3. Put flour in a bowl and roll zucchini in it. To shake off excess, place zucchini in a strainer and tap it over the flour.
4. Drop zucchini, a few at a time, into the hot fat. Pay attention here: it will brown in mere seconds. Remove with a slotted spoon; drain on a brown paper bag. Salt just before serving. Serves 2.

Fresh Purple and Green Figs

Wash and dry figs, place in a bowl, and eat them out of hand.

Fire 'n' Ice for 6

MENU   No-Bean Chili
Corn Bread
Grapefruit Snow

BEVERAGE: Beer

WORK ORDER: *Chili, Corn Bread, Grapefruit*

No-Bean Chili   According to some friends of mine in Arizona, the best way to put out the fire of hot chili in the mouth is to douse it with a teaspoon of honey.

2 tablespoons vegetable oil
3 cloves garlic, chopped
2 onions, chopped
1 green pepper, chopped
3 pounds beef, finely chopped (not ground)
Salt and freshly cracked pepper to taste

1 teaspoon ground cumin
1 teaspoon ground oregano
2–3 tablespoons chili powder
12 medium tomatoes, peeled, seeded, and chopped
12-ounce can of beer

1. Heat oil in a large skillet or saucepan. Add garlic, onions, and green pepper. Sauté about 5 minutes, or until soft.
2. Add the beef and stir until it loses its pinkness.
3. Add remaining ingredients, cover partially, and simmer for about an hour. Skim fat from top as the chili cooks, and stir occasionally to keep it from sticking. Serves 6.

Corn Bread   1 cup yellow corn meal, preferably stone-ground
1 cup flour
1 tablespoon baking powder
1 teaspoon salt
2 tablespoons sugar

2 eggs, beaten
1 cup milk
¼ cup melted butter
1 tablespoon butter for greasing baking dish

1. Combine in a bowl the corn meal, flour, baking powder, salt, and sugar.

2. Beat together the eggs, milk, and melted butter. Add to dry mixture carefully. Do not overbeat.

3. Butter an 8-by-8-by-2-inch baking dish and pour in the corn meal mixture. Bake in a preheated 425° oven 20–25 minutes. Cut into squares. Serves 6.

Grapefruit Snow

This is a cool and sassy dessert that must be served at once, since it melts quickly. The following amounts make one serving: I prepare two for each whirl-round with the blender.

½ cup unsweetened grapefruit juice

5 cracked ice cubes

○ Before you sit down to dinner, put the goblets into the freezer to chill until dessert time.

1. Blend the juice and ice cubes until slushy.
2. Remove to a goblet. ○ Serve immediately.

Puerto Rican Repast for 4 to 6

MENU   **Arroz con Pollo (Chicken with Rice)**
Salad Platter with Garlic Vinaigrette
Rum-Filled Pinwheels

WINE SUGGESTION: Red Spanish Rioja

WORK ORDER: *Arroz, Pinwheels, Salad*

Salad Platter with Garlic Vinaigrette

2 carrots
2 turnips
2 beets

1 large tomato
2 bunches watercress
1 cup garlic vinaigrette △

△ See page 245.

1. Shred the peeled carrots, turnips, and beets in a food processor.

2. Peel the tomato and cut into ⅛-inch wedges.

3. Arrange vegetables on a round serving platter. Put the tomato wedges in the center, then arrange the carrots, turnips, and beets in six alternating sections, with a strip of watercress bordering each section.

4. Serve with a bowl of vinaigrette. Serves 4–6.

Arroz con Pollo (Chicken with Rice)

☆ See page 240.

1 chicken, 3½–4 pounds
3 tablespoons butter or
olive oil
Salt and freshly cracked
black pepper to taste
2½ cups chicken stock ☆
½ teaspoon saffron

1 small yellow onion,
chopped
1 cup long-grain rice
1 bay leaf
1 pound fresh peas, shelled
A few strips of pimiento, if
desired

1. You will need 8 pieces of chicken: 2 drumsticks, 2 thighs, 2 wings, and the breast cut in half.
2. Heat the butter or olive oil in a large skillet. Salt and pepper the chicken and cook over moderate heat until well browned on all sides.
3. Meanwhile, add the neck, giblets, and any trimmings to the stock and boil in a separate pan.
4. Place the saffron in a small bowl and add 1 tablespoon of the chicken stock to extract the flavor. (Be miserly with the saffron; too much will make everything taste like medicine.)
5. When the chicken is beautifully browned, remove it from the pan. To the same skillet, add the chopped onion and cook for 3–4 minutes.
6. Next, add the rice. Cook and stir for 2–3 minutes.
7. Pour on the chicken stock, and strain the saffron liquid into the mixture as well. Bring all to a boil. Add the bay leaf.
8. Place in a casserole, and artfully arrange the pieces of chicken on top.
9. In a preheated 350° oven, cook, covered, for 35–45 minutes, or until the rice has absorbed the liquid and both it and the chicken are tender. Just before this point is reached, cook the peas in a small pan of water for about 5 minutes.
10. Drain peas and use them to garnish the casserole. If desired, add pimiento. Serves 4–6.

Rum-Filled Pinwheels

If you want to bake these in the same oven with arroz con pollo (preceding recipe), keep the temperature at 350° and bake pinwheels a bit longer. They should be served warm: if necessary, wrap them in foil and reheat.

BISCUITS

2 cups flour
2 tablespoons granulated sugar
1 tablespoon baking powder
¾ teaspoon salt
¼ cup shortening
¼ – ⅓ cup milk
¼ cup white rum
¼ cup melted butter

TOPPING

½ cup firmly packed brown sugar
4 tablespoons butter
2 tablespoons white rum

FILLING

⅓ cup firmly packed brown sugar
1 teaspoon cinnamon
1 tablespoon white rum

1. Preheat oven to 400° (or bake at 350° in same oven with arroz con pollo; see note above). Grease 12 muffin cups.

2. *Make the topping*: In a saucepan, combine the brown sugar, butter, and white rum. Bring to a boil, reduce heat, and simmer for a few minutes. Spoon a teaspoon or so of this mixture into each of the muffin cups. Save the remaining topping, for you will need it later.

3. *Make the filling*: Combine the ⅓ cup brown sugar, cinnamon, and white rum in a bowl. Set aside.

4. *Make the biscuits*: In a bowl, combine the flour, sugar, baking powder, and salt. Cut in shortening until the mixture looks like corn meal. In another bowl, combine ¼ cup milk with the white rum (start with this much milk; add more if you need it). Add milk-and-rum to the flour mixture, mixing only enough to moisten dry ingredients. Dough is right when it leaves the sides of the bowl. Turn dough onto a lightly floured board and knead it gently, 6–7 turns, about 30 seconds.

5. *Assemble the pinwheels*: On lightly floured wax paper, roll the dough into a 12-by-18-inch rectangle. Brush with the melted butter, then spread with the filling mixture. Using wax paper as a guide, roll loosely from the long side, as you would a jelly roll. Cut into 1-inch slices; place in prepared muffin cups. Bake 15 minutes. Let stand 1 minute. Loosen edges and turn out of pan. Spoon any remaining topping over the pinwheels. Makes 12.

Far West Dinner for 4 or 6

MENU   **Salmon Steaks with Shallot Butter Sauce**
Cucumbers in Cream
Sliced Kiwi Fruits

WINE SUGGESTION: Montrachet or Meursault

WORK ORDER: *Salmon, Cucumbers, Fruit, Shallot Sauce*

Salmon Steaks with Shallot Butter Sauce

This recipe works well with any fish except oily ones, and can also be used with fish fillets.

½ cup chopped shallots
4 salmon steaks, ¾ to 1 inch thick, about 3 pounds in all
¾ cup white□ wine

½ pound unsalted butter
Salt and freshly cracked black pepper to taste
1 tablespoon finely chopped fresh parsley

□ Or use a red wine, and serve red wine with the meal. This recipe definitely refutes the old white-wine-white-fish bromide.

1. Spread the shallots in a Pyrex baking dish. Lay the salmon steaks over them. Pour in the wine.
2. Cover casserole with a sheet of aluminum foil or wax paper (this will keep steaks from becoming dry on top). Bake in a preheated 350° oven until the fish flakes. Twenty minutes should be about right—I find that salmon requires more cooking time than other fish steaks; it is still too raw at the bone after the standard 10 minutes. Be careful not to overcook, however.
3. When fish is *almost* done, remove it to a serving platter and cover loosely with the aluminum foil or wax paper you used earlier. Turn off the oven, then return fish to it to keep warm while you make the sauce.
4. *The sauce*: Place the shallot and wine mixture, which will have absorbed a goodly taste of fish, into a heavy saucepan (I use copper). Reduce over a medium flame until the shallots are just wet and most of the liquid has evaporated. Remove pan from the burner and begin whisking in the butter, a tablespoon at a time.

5. When half the butter has been whisked in, return pan to a low flame and whisk in the remaining butter. Do not let the butter become completely melted; this mixture should look like thin mayonnaise.

6. Season with salt and pepper, and add the parsley. Pour over the salmon, or serve in a warm sauceboat. Serves 4–6.

Cucumbers in Cream

2 large cucumbers, peeled and seeded
1 teaspoon salt
Freshly cracked white pepper to taste
3–4 tablespoons sherry wine vinegar
1 tablespoon finely chopped fresh parsley or chives
½ cup barely whipped cream

1. Slice the cucumbers very thin, either by hand or on a mandoline.

2. Place them in a bowl and sprinkle the salt over them. Refrigerate about 15 minutes, then squeeze the cucumbers to drain off the liquid.

3. Add remaining ingredients, fold together gently, and serve. Serves 4–6.

Sliced Kiwi Fruit

Kiwi fruit has been overworked by *nouvelle cuisine*, which hasn't really surpassed what Australians and New Zealanders have been doing with this fruit for years! Nonetheless, it's nice to have one kiwi fruit recipe around the house. This one—not with meat or fish, nor in a tart—is sheer simplicity, and properly so.

4 or 5 kiwis
A thin slice of lemon for each portion
Sprigs of mint, if available

1. Peel and slice the fruit as thin as possible. Arrange the slices on individual dessert plates. Fan them out so that they resemble a flower.

○ Notch with a lemon stripper, removing small slivers from top to bottom of lemon. Then cut across into thin slices.

2. Notch the lemon○ before cutting thin slices from it. Place one lemon slice in the center of each plate of fruit. Garnish each with a mint sprig. Serves 4–6.

5 BREAKFASTS AND BRUNCHES: FACING THE DAY

Some of my most festive parties have been breakfast for a crowd. Redolent with smells and tastes that transform grouches into sweethearts and make early birds chirpier, breakfast is the day's best deal, in my opinion. It's the least complicated, most informal meal of all— and you have to work hard to make it expensive. Even an inexperienced cook can pull off, with a flourish, breakfast for company.

It's a mistake to be a curmudgeon about choices: there's more to the morning than bacon and eggs. In my travels to other countries, I've learned that vegetables and other combinations of foods I once thought reserved for other times can be delicious fast-breakers.

If your kitchen is large enough, it's the place to serve breakfast. The family-size kitchen is becoming an important architectural feature in new homes and apartments, and high time. I've always had giant kitchens, and now, in our Philadelphia house, everyone loves to congregate in the big country-French-style kitchen. (One of my fond memories is of the time when James Beard came to visit and insisted on having all meals there, rather than in the formal dining room.)

For busy people, brunch often works out as an even more convenient way to entertain. I don't know who coined the word, but it's a nifty improvement on "late breakfast," which is what I used to call it. And brunch is interchangeable, in terms of the dishes you can serve, with lunch or light supper (see Chapters 6 and 9).

Picture a Hunt Breakfast by a roaring fireplace, or an Easter Brunch or Joggers' Breakfast—you can see the charming possibilities. I predict front-of-the-day meals are going to become among the most popular of parties.

The menus and dishes I've devised for this chapter take minimal time. Because of my promise that recipes in this book can be produced quickly, I've had to forgo yeast breads. One can do magical things with biscuits, popovers, crêpes, and other quick breads. They are adaptable, instantly, for sack lunches and snacks, and many can be toasted for tomorrow's breakfast.

North Country Breakfast or Brunch for 3 or 4

MENU   **Baked Canadian Bacon**
Ginger Pancakes with Ginger Syrup or Sauce
Frosted Green and Black Grapes

BEVERAGE: Bloody Marys

WORK ORDER: *Grapes, Bacon, Syrup or Sauce, Pancakes*

Baked Canadian Bacon

If you use as much as 3 pounds of Canadian bacon (and 3 tablespoons of melted butter) to allow for abundant leftovers, you won't be sorry. It is delicious served cold with red-skin potato salad, or in sandwiches made with lettuce, tomato slices, and mayonnaise.

1 pound Canadian bacon   1 tablespoon melted butter

1. Place bacon on a rack in a small roasting pan with ¼ inch hot water in the bottom. Brush with melted butter and bake 30 minutes in a preheated 325° oven.
2. Slice very thin and serve. Serves 3–4.

Ginger Pancakes

1¼ cups flour
1 tablespoon sugar
1 tablespoon baking powder
¼ teaspoon salt
2 teaspoons ground ginger

¼ teaspoon ground allspice
1¼ cups milk
1 egg, beaten
2 tablespoons melted butter

1. Heat griddle according to manufacturer's directions, greasing if necessary.
2. In a bowl, mix together the dry ingredients.
3. Add remaining ingredients, and stir just until flour is moistened. Mixture will be lumpy.
4. For one pancake, pour ¼ cup batter onto preheated griddle.
5. Turn each pancake when its rim is full of broken bubbles and the underside is browned. Remove to a heated platter. Makes 10 pancakes about 4 inches in diameter. Serves 3–4.

Ginger Syrup or Sauce

¾ cup light corn syrup
½ cup firmly packed brown sugar
2 teaspoons ground ginger

¼ teaspoon ground allspice
3 tablespoons butter
3 tablespoons water

1. Combine all ingredients in a saucepan. Stir slightly to blend the mixture as it comes to a boil.
2. Reduce heat and simmer 5 minutes. Cool slightly to serve. Makes 1 cup.

Frosted Grapes

1½ pounds green or black grapes, or a combination of both, washed and dried

3 egg whites
¾ cup sugar

1. In a shallow bowl, beat the egg whites until frothy.
2. Place sugar on a sheet of wax paper.

3. Cut grapes into serving-size clusters. Dip into egg white, then roll in sugar. Place clusters on a rack over a baking sheet and let dry. Serves 4.

A Hunt Breakfast for 6

MENU   **Sautéed Crabmeat with Newburg Sauce**
       Green Bean Salad
       Strawberries with Strawberry Purée

LIBATION: Highballs

WORK ORDER: *Salad, Purée, Berries, Crab and Sauce*

Sautéed Crabmeat with Newburg Sauce

2½ pounds lump crabmeat
9 tablespoons butter
2 tablespoons cognac
Salt and freshly cracked white pepper to taste
Juice of 1 medium lemon
3 tablespoons flour
2 cups heavy cream
4 egg yolks
½ cup sherry
1 tablespoon chopped fresh parsley

△ See page 252.

1. Remove any cartilage from the crabmeat, but be careful not to mangle it.
2. Melt 6 tablespoons of the butter in a skillet, but do not brown it. Add crabmeat and toss 3–4 minutes until hot, then flame△ with cognac. Season the mixture with salt and pepper, and sprinkle the lemon juice over it.
3. Remove crabmeat from skillet with slotted spoon.
4. To the skillet juices add remaining 3 tablespoons butter. Rub in the flour with a wooden spatula and cook 3–4 minutes. Add cream.
5. In a separate bowl, beat the egg yolks and sherry together. Whisk this into the skillet mixture, and season with salt and pepper. Continue to whisk; cook for 3 minutes.
6. Add crabmeat and reheat. Keep warm in a chafing dish. Garnish with parsley. Serves 6.

Green Bean Salad

Since it does not wilt, this salad is a bright idea for a buffet. If you like, you can let it marinate for several hours.

2 pounds green beans, young as possible
¾ cup sliced walnuts
½ cup thinly slivered mushrooms
½ cup walnut oil

¼ cup vinegar
1 tablespoon Dijon mustard
Salt and freshly cracked black pepper to taste
1 tablespoon chopped fresh parsley

1. Bring 3 quarts salted water to a rolling boil.
2. Remove tops and tails of green beans. Add to the water a few at a time so that the water holds its boil. Cook 7–10 minutes, until tender crisp.
3. Drain in a strainer and refresh in a bowl of ice water. Dry on a cloth or paper towels and place in a salad bowl.
4. Add walnuts and mushrooms.
5. Combine remaining ingredients and pour over the salad. Toss. Serves 6.

Strawberries with Strawberry Purée

1 quart strawberries, gently washed and hulled
1 pint strawberries, also washed and hulled

1 cup Beaujolais wine
2 tablespoons sugar

1. Place the quart of strawberries in a crystal bowl.
2. Purée the pint of strawberries in the blender or food processor and add the wine and sugar. Pour over the whole strawberries. Serves 6.

An Early Summer Brunch for 4

MENU   Stewed Rhubarb
Spicy Baked Eggs
Walnut Raisin Bread

BEVERAGE: Coffee or Tea

WORK ORDER: *Bread, Rhubarb, Eggs*

**Stewed
Rhubarb**

I remember when I was a kid sent to pull up stalks of rhubarb from our garden early in the summer. I'd brush off the dirt, bite into a piece—and make a horrible face to protest the sour taste. I still dislike rhubarb, but it's one of those things *other* people always seem to enjoy. So I keep on serving and eating it.

1½ pounds rhubarb (ends and leaves trimmed), cut into 1-inch pieces

¾ cup sugar, maybe more

1. Wash the rhubarb and place in a saucepan with the water that clings to it. You need no extra water because rhubarb gives off liquid as it cooks. Add the sugar.
2. Simmer very slowly, about 15–20 minutes, until it reaches the doneness desired. Some people like rhubarb a bit firm; others like it very mushy.
3. Serve warm, or place in refrigerator and chill to serve cold. Serves 4.

**Spicy Baked
Eggs**

5 tablespoons butter
2 large onions, peeled and sliced
6 tomatoes, peeled and sliced
1 tablespoon finely chopped fresh basil

½ teaspoon hot pepper sauce
Salt and freshly cracked black pepper to taste
4 eggs

1. Preheat oven to 350°. Grease four individual ramekins with a tablespoon of the butter.
2. Melt the remaining butter in a saucepan; add onions and cook until tender. Add tomatoes, basil, hot pepper sauce, and salt and pepper. Simmer, stirring ocasionally, for 10 minutes.
3. Divide mixture among the baking dishes, and top each with a raw egg.
4. Bake 5–10 minutes, or until eggs are done to your taste. Serves 4.

Walnut Raisin Bread   This is especially good when served warm with cream cheese or butter.

1 tablespoon butter	1 cup milk
1½ cups flour	⅓ cup dark molasses
½ cup sugar	1 egg, beaten
1½ teaspoons baking powder	¾ cup uncooked oatmeal
1 teaspoon baking soda	¾ cup seedless raisins
¾ teaspoon salt	¼ cup chopped walnuts

1. Preheat oven to 375°. Lightly grease a loaf pan (8½ by 4½ by 2½ inches) with butter.
2. In a large mixer bowl, mix together dry ingredients.
3. Add milk, molasses, and egg. Mix well. Stir in oatmeal, raisins, and walnuts.
4. Pour into prepared pan and bake 45 minutes. Let stand 5 minutes before removing from pan. Makes 1 loaf.

An Easter Brunch for 6

This could also be used as a luncheon, dinner, or supper menu. The corn can be baked in the same oven as the ham, but make sure the temperature is 350° if you do it this way.

MENU   **Ham Loaf**
Corn in Saffron Cream
Bibb Lettuce Salad, Mimosa
Honeydew Melon with Green Chartreuse

WINE SUGGESTION: Champagne or California Pinot Chardonnay

WORK ORDER: *Melon, Ham, Corn, Eggs for Mimosa, Salad*

Ham Loaf

□ If sausage is not highly seasoned, you may want to add sage, thyme, or fennel.

About 1 pound ham
¼ cup chopped scallions, including green part
1 tablespoon butter
½ pound pork sausage□
¾ cup rye bread cubes
2 tablespoons brown sugar
1 tablespoon Dijon mustard
2 eggs, slightly beaten
2 tablespoons milk
1–2 tablespoons dry sherry

1. Preheat oven to 375° (or 350° if you plan on baking the corn in saffron cream at the same time).
2. Grind the ham. If you are using a hand grinder, make sure all sinew is trimmed off; otherwise meat will catch in the holes. If you are using a food processor, there's no problem. You should have about 2 cups ground ham.
3. Sauté scallions in butter.
4. Combine all ingredients in a bowl and mix well. Shape into a firm loaf and place in a shallow 1-quart baking pan. Bake 45 minutes. Serves 6–8.

Corn in Saffron Cream

5 tablespoons butter
6 medium ears yellow corn
⅓ cup chopped onion
⅓ cup chopped green pepper
1 cup light cream
½ teaspoon saffron threads
4 eggs, slightly beaten
Salt to taste
Dash of ground red pepper

1. Preheat oven to 350°. Grease a 1-quart baking dish with a tablespoon of the butter.
2. Scrape corn to measure 3 cups.
3. In a skillet, melt the remaining butter, but do not brown it. Sauté onion and green pepper until tender. Add corn and cook 1 minute.
4. In a separate pan, heat cream and saffron to the boiling point.
5. Combine eggs with the corn and saffron cream, being careful not to let the eggs curdle. (To prevent curdling, first add some of the hot mixture to eggs, and whisk while adding.) Season with salt and pepper.
6. Run the mixture through the blender or food processor. It will become very, very creamy.
7. Pour into baking dish, and set this in a bain-marie (or a deep baking pan) filled with 1 inch of water. Bake 30–35 minutes or until set. Serves 6.

Bibb Lettuce Salad, Mimosa

✧ See page 245.

3 or 4 heads Bibb lettuce, washed and cut into bite-size pieces

¾ cup vinaigrette✧
2 hard-cooked egg yolks

1. Place lettuce in a salad bowl. Dress with vinaigrette and toss. Arrange on serving plates.
2. Press the hard-cooked egg yolks through a sieve, using the back of a spoon. Sprinkle a teaspoon of this mixture over each salad. Serves 6.

Honeydew Melon with Green Chartreuse

Chartreuse is a very exotic, very potent liqueur made by French monks who use a secret blend of herbs.

1 very large ripe honeydew melon

Green chartreuse, as much as the melon will take

1. Stand melon on end. Cut a little piece off bottom to allow melon to stand up. Cut off top about 2 inches down. Remove seeds and fiber with a long spoon.
2. Fill the melon with as much green chartreuse as it will take. Replace lid, and set in refrigerator until serving time. Give melon a shake once in a while to distribute the liqueur.
3. At dessert time, scoop out fruit and juices, and place in goblets. Serves 6.

Back-Home Breakfast for 6

MENU   **Pitcher of Freshly Squeezed Orange Juice**
Eggs in Black Butter
Herbed Muffins with Some of Mom's Good Jam

BEVERAGES: Coffee, Tea, Milk

WORK ORDER: *Muffins, Juice, Eggs*

Freshly Squeezed Orange Juice

The number of oranges you'll need will depend on how juicy they are, but usually 2 per person is about right. Fresh mint leaves make a perky garnish.

Eggs in Black Butter

8 tablespoons butter, and more if needed
12 eggs
4 tablespoons red wine vinegar
4 tablespoons drained capers

Salt and freshly cracked black pepper to taste
1 tablespoon finely chopped fresh parsley

1. Melt 4 tablespoons butter in a heavy skillet over medium heat. Fry 4 eggs at a time, adding more butter for second and third batches if necessary.
2. As eggs are fried, remove with a spatula to an ovenproof platter and set in a 250° oven to keep warm.
3. Add more butter to the skillet, if needed, along with vinegar and capers. Some of the vinegar will evaporate quickly in the heat of the pan. Pour this mixture over the eggs, sprinkle with salt and pepper, and garnish with parsley. Serves 6.

Herbed Muffins

○ Or substitute an equal amount of chopped fresh basil, dill, or chives.

1 tablespoon butter
2 cups all-purpose flour
2 tablespoons sugar
2 teaspoons baking powder
½ teaspoon salt

3 tablespoons chopped fresh parsley○
1 cup milk
1 egg, slightly beaten
3 tablespoons melted butter

1. Preheat oven to 450°. Generously grease muffin pans with 1 tablespoon butter.
2. Mix together in a bowl the flour, sugar, baking powder, and salt. Add parsley or other fresh herb.
3. Combine remaining ingredients and add all at once to dry mixture. Stir just enough to moisten; batter will be lumpy.
4. Fill each muffin cup two-thirds full, or with about ¼ cup batter.
5. Bake 20–25 minutes until golden brown. Makes 12 muffins.

6 LUNCHES: SAVVY FARE AND SACK STUFF

To paraphrase Will Rogers' comment about the weather, almost everybody eats lunch but nobody does much about it. Most of the time, that's probably the way it should be. Yet when a special occasion arises and provides an excuse for getting people together in a better-than-routine way, luncheons can be a luscious solution. Simple to prepare, easy to make elegant-looking, luncheon at home extends a warmth and hospitality that dates out just cannot match. Ordinarily, I do not look upon this as a time for cocktails; usually wine or something like dry sherry will suffice.

Because this meal lends itself to frivolous or light-hearted entertaining, one can celebrate an event (such as Social Security Check Day) just for an excuse to lift the midday. Other times, when lunch is going to be the habitual quickie, there's no excuse to make a rut out of it. Sometimes I have nightmares that future generations of Americans will go through life thinking that "luncheon" means "peanut butter." Even if you're home alone watching a soap opera you don't tell your friends about, you can feel like royalty at a command performance if you prepare yourself a tray with a special touch or two.

Sack lunches—brown bags—now are found everywhere! They can make noontime interesting and are a great way to educate a child's palate and tickle his appetite: vegetables on a skewer are a breeze to prepare, and dramatic to find in a sack. The office set has taken to bring-along luncheons for economy of time as well as money. Then, too, with so many people taking bus tours and adventuring about, sack stuff can add to the outing when the quality of restaurant food along the way is chancy.

In this chapter, I've devised menus for several occasions, from kids' lunches to rather luxurious viands. Change and mix menus as you please, invent some yourself—and put the peanut butter back on the shelf!

Fridge Raid for a Kid's School Lunch

There's rarely any need to buy cold cuts and junk goodies for school lunches. They cost more than homemade, usually, and aren't as good. Look in the fridge, get out the leftovers—and start packing. The one rigid rule I observe for sack lunches is not to use mayonnaise: it can become rancid very quickly. Be sure to include a piece of fruit and a leftover cupcake or slice of last night's dessert. A sample sack lunch could be:

MENU	**Cheese and Bacon Finger Sandwiches**
	Fresh Veggies on a Skewer
	Cupcakes
	Fresh Fruit

Cheese and Bacon Finger Sandwiches

A piece of Cheddar cheese   Sour cream
Leftover cooked bacon

In a blender or food processor, grind cheese with the bacon. Add a little sour cream to smooth and bind the mixture. Spread on a roll or bread and cut into finger-size pieces.

Variation

△ See page 194.

Instead of cheese, use a hard-boiled egg,△ finely chopped. Mix it with bacon, and add salt, pepper, and sour cream.

Fresh Veggies on a Skewer

This is a kind of clean trick to get your children to eat raw vegetables. Put an assortment of fresh vegetables (carrots, celery, green pepper, raw mushrooms, whatever is in the bin) on a *wooden* skewer stick and wrap it and stash it in the sack.

Lunch for 4 Before the Horse Show

MENU   **Steaming Oyster Bisque**
Black Radish Vinaigrette
Fresh Fruit and Cheese

WINE: Muscadet

WORK ORDER: *Bisque, Radishes, Fruit*

Steaming Oyster Bisque

☆ If you want to serve this bisque cold, use *heavy* cream instead.

1½ pints oysters
4 tablespoons butter
1 quart light cream ☆
Salt and freshly cracked white pepper to taste

1 tablespoon finely chopped fresh parsley
Paprika

1. Heat oysters in a pan with their juice just until the edges curl. Add the butter.
2. In a small pan, heat the cream until bubbles form around the edges.
3. Add scalded cream, salt, and pepper to oysters.
4. If you like, purée bisque in blender or food processor. Garnish with parsley and paprika and serve hot. Serves 6.

Black Radish Vinaigrette

□ See page 245.

4 medium black radishes
2 tablespoons finely chopped fresh parsley

¾ cup vinaigrette□
Salt and freshly cracked black pepper to taste

1. Wash and trim radishes, but do not peel them. Slice each one very thin, either by hand or on a mandoline, then cut into julienne strips as fine as a match. Place in ice water in refrigerator for 15 minutes.
2. Drain radishes on a towel, put into salad bowl, and toss with parsley, vinaigrette, salt, and pepper. Serves 4.

Fresh Fruit and Cheese Select fresh fruit in season and present with a platter of three kinds of cheese—hard, medium, and soft. Serve with crackers or French bread with unsalted butter.

Lunch or Light Dinner for 4 or 6 Football Widows

> **MENU** **Cheese Strata**
> **Romaine and Mushroom Salad**
> **Sliced Peaches and Blueberries**
>
> **WINE SUGGESTION:** Red Saint-Julien
>
> **WORK ORDER:** *Peaches, Cheese Strata, Salad*

Cheese Strata This cheese dish is rich, filling, and flexible. Its texture combines qualities of a soufflé and a custard. It can be set up an hour ahead of baking, if you have time. To pad out a menu, serve it with sautéed Canadian bacon slices or a few strips of crisp, well-drained bacon for each serving. For a less rich dish, use milk instead of cream.

Butter
4 slices stale bread
2 cups grated sharp Cheddar cheese
1 cup light cream

½ cup white wine
3 eggs
1 tablespoon potato flour
Salt to taste
Dash of ground red pepper

1. Preheat oven to 350°.
2. Butter bread and place, buttered side down, on bottom and sides of a 1-quart casserole (I use a casserole 6½ inches square and 1¾ inches deep).
3. Combine remaining ingredients and pour into prepared casserole. Bake 40–45 minutes, until set. Makes 4–6 servings.

Romaine and Mushroom Salad

Romaine is a sturdy lettuce, one of those substantial lettuces that work so well for buffets. Unlike Bibb, Boston, or loose-leaf varieties, it does not wilt rapidly in the bowl.

✦ This will serve 4 generously; if you are preparing for 6, add another small head.

○ See page 245.

1 large head of romaine, washed, trimmed, and cut into bite-size pieces✦
1 pound very fresh white mushrooms, wiped clean, stems removed, and sliced

¾ cup vinaigrette○

1. Place romaine and mushrooms in a salad bowl.
2. Pour over the vinaigrette, toss, and serve. Serves 4–6.

Sliced Peaches and Blueberries

8–10 fresh medium peaches, skinned, stoned, and sliced
2 tablespoons lemon juice

2 cups (1 pint) blueberries
2 tablespoons sugar, more or less, depending on tartness of fruit

Put peaches in a bowl and sprinkle with lemon juice. Add blueberries. Mix together, and sprinkle sugar over the fruit. Toss fruit and chill until serving time. Serves 4–6.

Luncheon for 6 or 8 Before the Preview at the Art Gallery

MENU **Green Spring Soup with Asparagus and Spinach**
Herbed Sponge Roll Filled with Shrimp Salad
Endive Sticks
Spicy Nut Meringues

WINE SUGGESTION: California Chablis or Macon Pinot Chardonnay

WORK ORDER: *Meringues, Roll, Soup, Endive*

Green Spring Soup with Asparagus and Spinach

1 cup chopped scallions
¼ cup butter
6 cups chicken stock, or more to cover vegetables
2 cups peeled and thinly sliced potatoes
2 large carrots, peeled and thinly sliced

4 tablespoons raw rice
Salt and freshly cracked black pepper to taste
1 pound asparagus, cut up
1 pound spinach, torn in pieces

1. In a large kettle, cook scallions in butter until tender. Add stock, potatoes, carrots, rice, salt, and pepper. Bring to a boil. Reduce heat, cover, and simmer 15 minutes.
2. Add asparagus and cook 15 minutes more.
3. Add spinach and cook about 10 minutes, or until tender. Serves 6–8.

Herbed Sponge Roll Filled with Shrimp Salad

1 tablespoon oil
6 eggs, separated
½ cup hot chicken stock
1¼ cups flour
1½ teaspoons baking powder
Salt and freshly cracked black pepper

⅓ cup chopped fresh parsley
2 tablespoons chopped fresh dill
2 tablespoons grated imported Parmesan cheese

1. Preheat oven to 375°. Oil a jelly-roll pan (10 by 15 by 1 inch), line with wax paper, and oil wax paper, too. Set aside.
2. In mixer bowl, beat egg yolks until thick and lemon-colored, about 5 minutes.
3. Put mixer on low setting, and add the chicken stock.
4. Combine flour, baking powder, salt, pepper, parsley, and dill and add to egg yolk mixture. Mix *just until smooth*.
5. Using clean bowl and beaters, beat egg whites until they form stiff peaks. Gently fold them into yolk mixture.
6. Pour mixture into prepared pan; spread evenly. Bake 12–15 minutes.
7. Sprinkle a sheet of wax paper with the grated cheese. Loosen the sides of the baked sponge roll along the long edges of the pan and invert onto wax paper. Carefully peel off wax paper from bottom of roll.
8. Spread filling (recipe follows) evenly over the roll. Starting with the narrow end, roll it up like a jelly roll. Slice to serve. Serves 6–8.

Shrimp Salad Filling

△ See page 242.

4 cups chopped, cooked shrimp (1½ pounds of cleaned medium shrimp)
¼ cup finely chopped celery
¼ cup finely chopped onion
1 tablespoon lemon juice

Salt and freshly cracked black pepper to taste
8–10 tablespoons homemade mayonnaise△
2 tablespoons finely chopped fresh dill
2 tablespoons finely chopped fresh parsley

Combine all ingredients. Use as a filling for preceding sponge roll. Serves 6–8.

Endive Sticks

☆ See page 245.

6–8 Belgian endives, trimmed and washed
1 tablespoon finely chopped fresh parsley

¾ cup vinaigrette dressing☆

▢ I've never seen any reason to core endives. They taste bitter anyway, and the core is not particularly tough.

1. Cut endives in half, lengthwise. Remove core, if desired.▢ Lay each piece flat on the cutting board and slice into long, thin sticks. Chill in ice water for 15 minutes.
2. Drain and dry on towels or in a salad spinner.
3. Remove to a bowl. Sprinkle parsley over and dress with vinaigrette. Serves 6–8.

1 tablespoon butter
1 egg white
    Pinch of cream of tartar
¼ cup sugar

1 teaspoon ground cinnamon
¾ cup ground almonds

Spicy Nut Meringues

1. Preheat oven to 350°. Grease a baking sheet—even if it's the no-stick kind—with butter.
2. In a bowl, combine the egg white and cream of tartar and beat until foamy.
3. Combine sugar and cinnamon. Gradually add to egg white, beating until stiff peaks form. Fold in ground almonds.
4. Drop by level tablespoons about 2 inches apart on prepared baking sheet; cookies spread and flatten during baking, so make sure they are spaced well apart.
5. Bake 10 minutes, or until they are a pale beige color. Makes 18 cookies.

Lunch for 4 After Browsing Through the Flea Market

MENU Roquefort Cheese Soufflé
Carrot and Watercress Salad
Scalloped Apples with Whipped Cream Sauce

WINE SUGGESTION: A Beaujolais such as Morgon

WORK ORDER: *Apples, Salad, Soufflé, Sauce*

Roquefort Cheese Soufflé

3 tablespoons butter
3 tablespoons flour
¾ cup milk
1 cup Roquefort cheese
5 egg yolks

Salt and ground red pepper to taste
7 egg whites
Pinch of cream of tartar (optional)

✧ Unlike most cooks, I do not grease my soufflé dishes, nor do I dust them with bread crumbs or Parmesan cheese. I think soufflés rise higher my way.

1. Get out a 1-quart soufflé dish, but do not grease or otherwise coat it.✧ Preheat oven to 375°
2. Melt butter in a small heavy pan. Be careful not to brown it.
3. Add the flour and stir with a wooden spatula for 3–4 minutes.
4. Switch to a whisk and add the milk. Whisk until thick and smooth.
5. Add the cheese and allow to melt.
6. Whisk in the egg yolks and cook about 3 minutes longer.
7. Add salt and red pepper.
8. Let this mixture cool at room temperature 5–10 minutes. Transfer to a large bowl.
9. In a separate bowl, beat egg whites with the mixer or by hand until they form firm peaks. Add cream of tartar, if you like.

○ For a spongier soufflé, place dish in a bain-marie and bake 45 minutes.

10. Fold into cheese base and pour into soufflé dish.○
11. Place on bottom shelf of preheated 375° oven and bake 25–30 minutes. Serves 4.

Carrot and Watercress Salad

△ See page 245.

2 bunches watercress, tough
　stems removed
2 carrots, peeled

½ cup vinaigrette△ or more

1. Wash watercress and place in a salad bowl.
2. With a rotary peeler or mandoline, cut long, thin strips from carrots. Cut 4 slits lengthwise on each carrot slice, leaving a ¼-inch margin on each end. Fasten the ¼-inch ends of each carrot slice together with a toothpick, thus forming a circle, and soak in ice water, in refrigerator, 15 minutes.
3. Remove toothpicks, drain carrot curls on a towel, and add to watercress. Toss with vinaigrette. Serves 4.

Scalloped Apples with Whipped Cream Sauce

☆ I like Granny Smith or Golden Delicious apples in this dish.

□ Or place in a prebaked pie shell and bake at 400° for 30 minutes.

These scalloped apples can be baked in a prebaked pie shell for an apple tart if you have time and need a splurgy dessert.

6 tablespoons butter
2½ pounds (6 medium)
　apples,☆ peeled, cored,
　and thinly sliced
¾ cup brown sugar
　Juice of 1 medium lemon

2 tablespoons Calvados or
　applejack
2 teaspoons ground
　cinnamon
¼ teaspoon freshly grated
　nutmeg

1. Melt butter in large saucepan. Add remaining ingredients.
2. Cook over medium heat□ for approximately 25–30 minutes, turning frequently. Apples should be caramelized and tender. Serve warm with following sauce.

Whipped Cream Sauce

1 cup heavy cream
2 tablespoons confectioners'
　sugar

¼ teaspoon freshly grated
　nutmeg

1. Whip the cream, but only barely. It should form soft peaks.
2. Fold in confectioners' sugar and nutmeg. Serves 4.

Lunch for 4 Before the Tennis Doubles

Despite its lightness, this high-protein menu is an energy-generator.

MENU   Cheddar Cheese Soup
Mushrooms and Smoked Salmon Vinaigrette
Coffee Ice Cream with Fernet

BEVERAGE: Perrier Water

WORK ORDER: *Ice Cream, Soup, Salmon*

Cheddar Cheese Soup

3 large onions, peeled and chopped
1 green pepper, seeded and chopped
2 celery ribs, chopped
8 tablespoons butter
4 tablespoons flour
6 cups chicken stock
Juice of 1 medium lemon
1½ pounds Cheddar cheese, grated
2 cups milk
Salt and freshly cracked white pepper to taste
2 tablespoons chopped fresh parsley

1. Sauté onions, pepper, and celery in the butter until soft (about 5 minutes).
2. Using wooden spatula, rub in the flour and cook 3 minutes.
3. Add the chicken stock, lemon juice, and cheese. Cook until everything is tender (about 15 minutes).
4. Put through blender, food processor, or fine disk on food mill. Add milk.
5. Reheat. Season with salt and pepper. Garnish each serving with parsley. Serves 8–10, but you'll probably need seconds.

Mushrooms and Smoked Salmon Vinaigrette

½ pound firm white mushrooms
¼ pound smoked salmon
Juice of 1 medium lemon
½ cup olive oil
Salt and freshly cracked white pepper to taste

1 teaspoon ground oregano
1 tablespoon chopped fresh parsley
2 bunches watercress, tough stems removed

✧ See page 252.

○ See page 252.

1. Clean mushrooms.✧ Reserve four of the most beautiful ones and flute them○ for the garnish.

2. Thinly slice rest of mushrooms and place in a bowl. Chop the salmon, add to mushrooms, and mix. Sprinkle over the lemon juice, oil, salt, pepper, oregano, and parsley.

3. Arrange mixture in the center of a flat platter and surround with watercress. Set fluted mushrooms on top. Serves 4–6.

Coffee Ice Cream with Fernet

This is an unusual and exotic dessert, but remember that Fernet is very bitter and you must be stingy with it! In Italy and other European countries, it is used to settle the stomach. It's also good on chocolate ice cream. Don't tell anyone what it is and create a little mystery.

△ See recipe on page 196.

Vanilla ice cream△
3 tablespoons very strong coffee (espresso if possible)

3 drops—hold it!—Fernet for each serving

1. Follow the directions for vanilla ice cream but add the coffee to the basic mixture.

2. To serve, carefully, carefully drop the Fernet over each portion.

New Orleans Luncheon for 4

MENU   **Cold Tomato Cream with Basil**
Shrimp with Mustard Mayonnaise
Parsley Toast Strips
Banana Soufflé

WINE SUGGESTION: Muscadet

WORK ORDER: *Shrimp, Toast, Soup, Soufflé*

Cold Tomato Cream with Basil

☆ See page 240

□ You can use 1 tablespoon fresh chives or dill instead. Adjust garnish accordingly.

This super-simple soup has a delightfully fresh taste.

1½ pounds ripe tomatoes
1 cup chicken stock☆
Salt and freshly cracked black pepper to taste

6 fresh basil leaves□
¾ cup sour cream
Basil sprigs for garnish

1. Remove stem ends of tomatoes, but do not skin them.
2. Put tomatoes into blender with chicken stock, salt, pepper, and 6 basil leaves. Blend a few seconds, until smooth. Remove to a bowl.
3. Whisk in sour cream.
4. Ladle soup into attractive serving bowls or cups and garnish each with basil sprig. Makes 5 cups, or about 4 servings.

Shrimp with Mustard Mayonnaise

◇ See page 238.

○ See page 242.

5 cups court bouillon◇
2 pounds medium shrimp in shell
Ground red pepper, if desired
1 cup homemade mayonnaise○

½ cup Creole mustard (hot)
2 tablespoons lemon juice
2 tablespoons chopped fresh dill
2 garlic cloves, chopped
Salt to taste
½ cup sour cream

1. Bring court bouillon to a boil and drop in the shrimp. Add a little ground red pepper if you like. Cover and simmer 5 minutes. Turn off heat and let shrimp cool.

2. Remove shrimp. At this point, you can serve them as is for an informal get-together; they are called shrimp *à la nage.* I like them best served peeled with the following mustard mayonnaise.

3. Put mayonnaise in a bowl, add mustard, lemon juice, dill, garlic, salt, and sour cream. Blend well. Makes 2 cups.

Parsley Toast Strips

△ Save crusts for bread crumbs.

1 loaf very thinly sliced bread, crusts removed△ (called Melba thin by some companies)
½ pound butter
1 teaspoon minced garlic

2 tablespoons chopped fresh parsley
1 tablespoon chopped fresh oregano leaves
1 teaspoon salt
1 tablespoon chopped fresh thyme

1. Preheat oven to 325°. Cut slices of bread diagonally into quarters. Arrange on a baking sheet and dry in oven 10 minutes.

2. Meanwhile, combine remaining ingredients in a small saucepan. Heat to melt the butter. Lower heat and simmer a few minutes to blend the flavors.

3. Brush butter mixture over partially dried bread. Bake about 7 minutes, or until edges begin to brown and bread becomes crisp. Makes 120 pieces. (Leftovers keep well in a covered container.)

Banana Soufflé

4 medium bananas, ripe but firm
4 tablespoons lemon juice
Confectioners' sugar

1 tablespoon cornstarch
½ cup light cream
2 eggs, separated
2 tablespoons rum

1. Preheat oven to 350°. Remove one section of skin from each banana, or cut a thin slice off the top. Carefully remove fruit: you want to keep enough skin intact to make shells.

2. Place 1 banana shell in each of 4 individual baking dishes. Sprinkle with lemon juice.

3. In a saucepan, combine 1 tablespoon confectioners' sugar with cornstarch and light cream. Cook, whisking constantly, until mixture becomes very thick.

☆ Save remaining purée to
use in a fruit cup later.

4. In a blender or food processor, purée 2 bananas,☆ or enough to make 1 cup purée.

5. In a saucepan, combine cream mixture, banana purée, egg yolks, and rum, and mix well. Cook, whisking until mixture thickens. Remove from heat, transfer to a bowl, and chill slightly.

6. Using a clean bowl and beaters, beat egg whites until stiff peaks form. Add a small amount of the whites to the banana mixture; mix well. Gently fold remaining whites into the mixture.

7. Spoon into banana shells, piling slightly. Sprinkle with confectioners' sugar.

8. Bake 15 minutes or until top is slightly browned. Sprinkle with confectioners' sugar and serve at once. Serves 4.

Day-after-a-Holiday Meal for 6

MENU   **Horseradish Ham Mold**
Mashed Sweet Potatoes
Relishes from Refrigerator
Fruit Cake Gems

BEVERAGE: Coffee or Tea

WORK ORDER: *Fruit Cake Gems, Ham, Potatoes, Relishes*

Horseradish Ham Mold

1–2 tablespoons butter
1 pound ham or tongue, chopped (2 cups)
1 cup heavy cream
3 eggs, separated
1 tablespoon Dijon mustard

1 tablespoon grated horseradish
Salt and freshly cracked black pepper to taste
1 tablespoon chopped fresh tarragon

1. Preheat oven to 350°. Generously butter a 5-cup ring mold or charlotte mold.

2. In blender or food processor, combine 1 cup of the ham and ½ cup of cream. Blend until smooth. Place mixture in

(continued)

bowl. Blend the remaining ham and cream the same way, and place in the same bowl.

3. Add to ham mixture the egg yolks, horseradish, mustard, salt, pepper, and tarragon. Mix well.

4. Beat egg whites until stiff peaks form. Fold into ham mixture. Spoon into prepared mold.

5. Set mold in a bain-marie. Bake 40–45 minutes, or until knife inserted near center comes out clean. Let stand 5 minutes before unmolding. Makes 6 servings.

Mashed Sweet Potatoes

1½ pounds sweet potatoes
2 tablespoons butter
2 tablespoons brandy
Salt and freshly cracked black pepper to taste
Cream, if necessary

□ To paint this lily, place potatoes in a casserole, top with chopped pecans, and drizzle with 2 tablespoons butter. Bake at 350° for 15 minutes.

1. Peel potatoes and cut into small pieces. Cook in boiling salted water until tender, about 15–20 minutes. Drain.

2. Add butter and brandy; mash with mixer until smooth. Add salt and pepper. If necessary, add a little cream to achieve desired consistency: this will depend upon the texture of the potatoes.□ Serves 6.

Relishes

Raid the fridge for raw, crunchy veggies. Just after a holiday you should have a good supply.

Fruit Cake Gems

This is a delicious, light variation on the fruit cake theme—and it's quick.

CAKES

Butter for greasing muffin cups
⅓ cup softened butter
⅓ cup light-brown sugar
½ teaspoon vanilla extract
2 eggs
1 cup flour
1 teaspoon baking powder
½ teaspoon salt

¼ cup orange juice
2 tablespoons brandy
1 cup (½ pound) mixed candied fruit
⅔ cup chopped dates

GLAZE

⅓ cup sugar
⅓ cup orange juice
2 tablespoons brandy

1. Preheat oven to 350°. Generously butter 12 individual muffin cups.

2. In mixer bowl, cream together the softened butter, brown sugar, and vanilla. Add eggs, one at a time, beating well after each addition.

3. Mix together flour, baking powder, and salt. Add alternately with the orange juice and brandy to the creamed mixture. Stir in fruits.

4. Fill each muffin cup almost to the top (about ¼ cup batter). Place a pan of hot water on bottom rack of oven. Bake gems on middle rack for 25 minutes.

5. Meanwhile, make the glaze: Combine sugar, orange juice, and brandy in a saucepan. Heat.

6. When cakes are done, remove from oven and cool for about 10 minutes. Prick tops with a two-tined fork. Spoon the glaze over. Makes 12 little fruit cakes.

A Light Oriental Lunch for 4 to 6

MENU **Shrimp Tempura with Soy Dipping Sauce**
Bean Sprout Salad
Grapefruit with Ginger

BEVERAGE: California Pinot Chardonnay or Hot Tea

WORK ORDER: *Sauce, Grapefruit, Salad, Shrimp*

Shrimp Tempura with Soy Dipping Sauce

2 eggs
1½ cups cold water
1 teaspoon salt
1¼–1½ cups flour
Solid shortening or peanut oil for deep frying

2 pounds shrimp, shells removed, tails left on, cleaned

1. Beat eggs and add to water in a bowl. Add salt and enough flour to make a batter that is not too thick but will stick to the shrimp.

2. Meanwhile, heat the fat to 375°. Dip shrimp in batter and fry a few at a time until brown. Drain on brown paper. Serve with the following sauce for dipping. Serves 6.

Soy Dipping Sauce
¾ cup soy sauce
¾ cup red wine vinegar
2 tablespoons vegetable oil

2 cloves garlic, chopped
2 tablespoons grated
  horseradish, if desired

Combine all ingredients and serve with shrimp.

Bean Sprout Salad
4 cups fresh bean sprouts,
  cleaned
6 scallions, finely chopped,
  including most of green
  tops
½ cucumber, peeled, seeded,
  and very thinly sliced

¼ cup finely chopped green
  pepper
Rice wine vinegar to taste
¼ cup sesame seed oil
Salt and freshly cracked
  black pepper to taste

Place vegetables in a bowl and sprinkle over the rice wine vinegar, sesame seed oil, salt and pepper. Toss and serve. Serves 6.

Grapefruit with Ginger
½ grapefruit, sectioned, per
  person

½–1 teaspoon chopped
  crystallized ginger per
  person

Sprinkle grapefruit with ginger, or serve ginger separately.

Scandinavian Lunch for 6 to 8

MENU   **Sweet-and-Sour Red and White Radishes**
Thin Rye Bread Sandwiches
Scandinavian Fish Pudding
New Potatoes with Dill
Rich Butter Balls

BEVERAGE: Aquavit

WORK ORDER: *Cookies, Fish Pudding, Potatoes, Radishes, Sandwiches*

Sweet-and-Sour Red and White Radishes

2 bunches red radishes
1 bunch white radishes
Salt to taste, and maybe a little pepper
½ cup vinegar
2 tablespoons sugar
¼ cup water

1. Thinly slice the radishes and put into a serving bowl. Salt to taste, but go easy on the pepper—radishes can be bitey.

2. Heat together the vinegar, sugar, and water. Cook only until sugar dissolves. Pour over the radishes. Serve at room temperature, or chilled, with the following sandwiches.

Thin Rye Bread Sandwiches

1 small loaf rye bread, thinly sliced
8 tablespoons or more softened butter

Make sandwiches and cut into small sizes, or finger shapes.

Scandinavian Fish Pudding

Butter for greasing ring mold
¼ cup chopped onion
¼ cup grated carrot
2 tablespoons butter
1 tablespoon flour
1¼ cups light cream
1 pound flounder fillets, or fillets of any white fish
2 eggs, separated
Salt and freshly cracked white pepper to taste
1 tablespoon chopped fresh parsley
Pinch of ground cardamom

1. Preheat oven to 350°. Generously butter a 5-cup ring or charlotte mold.

2. Cook onion and carrot in 2 tablespoons butter until tender. Add flour and cook 3 minutes. Blend in ¼ cup of the cream; cook and stir until thickened.

3. In blender, combine fish and remaining cream; blend until smooth. Add egg yolks, salt, pepper, parsley, cardamom, and vegetable mixture to blender✧ and blend until smooth.

✧ Do not try to use the food processor here, else the dish will come out grainy.

4. In a clean bowl with clean beaters, beat egg whites until they form stiff peaks. Fold into fish mixture. Spoon into prepared mold. Set mold in a pan of hot water.

5. Bake 35–40 minutes, or until a knife inserted near the center comes out clean. Let stand 5 minutes before unmolding. Serves 6–8.

New Potatoes with Dill

4 tiny potatoes per person
8 tablespoons butter
¼ cup finely chopped fresh dill

Salt and freshly cracked black pepper

1. Thoroughly scrub the potatoes. Cook in boiling salted water until just barely tender, about 10–15 minutes. Drain.
2. Melt butter in pan, and add the dill to it.
3. Salt and pepper the potatoes to taste. Pour the dill butter over them.

Rich Butter Balls

½ pound unsalted butter, at room temperature
½ cup granulated sugar
1 teaspoon vanilla extract
Pinch of salt

⅓ cup ground almonds
⅓ cup ground walnuts
⅓ cup ground hazelnuts
1¾ cups flour
1 cup confectioners' sugar

1. With electric mixer, beat the butter in a bowl. Gradually beat in the granulated sugar. Add vanilla and salt. Add nuts and flour. Roll dough into a ball and chill 15 minutes.
2. Break off pieces of cookie dough, roll between palms of your hands, and form balls the size of a small walnut. Bake on an ungreased baking sheet at 300° for 18–20 minutes. Remove and roll while still warm in confectioners' sugar. These cookies store well in a covered tin. Makes about 5 dozen.

A Philadelphia Luncheon for 6

Food lovers know that Philadelphia has in recent years burst forth as a truly great restaurant town. They also know that this city has long been famous for a number of really excellent dishes—pepper pot soup, sticky buns, scrapple, and ice cream. On election night here, even the losers take comfort from the traditional dinner of terrapin, planked shad, and fried oysters. Another Philadelphia classic is shrimp Lamaze, created by George Lamaze, a versatile fellow who was a New Jersey speakeasy operator before he became the chef at the Warwick Hotel. I don't know how he did at the speakeasy, but his shrimp Lamaze is a classic which remained on the Warwick's menu for years. Here is the authentic recipe.

MENU **Consommé Bellevue**
Shrimp Lamaze
Philadelphia Ice Cream with Chocolate Nut Sauce

BEVERAGE: Fish House Punch (page 224) before Lunch

WORK ORDER: *Ice Cream, Shrimp, Lamaze Sauce, Consommé, Chocolate Nut Sauce*

Consommé Bellevue

○ See page 240.

△ I alert my fish man in advance, and he saves this for me.

The Bellevue was for years Philadelphia's best-known hotel.

4 cups chicken stock ○
4 cups clam broth △
Salt and freshly cracked black pepper to taste

½ cup heavy cream, whipped

1. In a large pan, mix together the stock, broth, salt, and pepper. Heat and pour into serving cups.
2. Top each with a tablespoon of whipped cream and serve. Serves 6–8.

Shrimp Lamaze

☆ See page 242.

1½ cups homemade mayonnaise ☆
1 cup chili sauce
¼ cup India relish
1 chopped hard-cooked egg
1 tablespoon chopped chives
½ chopped pimiento
1 tablespoon freshly chopped parsley

1 tablespoon sharp Dijon mustard
Salt and freshly cracked black pepper to taste
1 tablespoon A-1 sauce
Dash of paprika
1 head red lettuce
1 head green lettuce
2 pounds shrimp, cooked, cleaned, and deveined

1. In a large bowl, mix together all ingredients except the lettuce and the shrimp. This is the Lamaze sauce, which should be chilled a while before serving. (It keeps well in the refrigerator if you want to make it ahead of time.)
2. On a large platter, arrange the red and green lettuce, washed and spun dry. Next arrange the shrimp. Cover with the Lamaze sauce. Serves 6.

Philadelphia Ice Cream with Chocolate Nut Sauce

This sauce is a favorite in a number of Philadelphia's busy restaurants.

1 recipe ice cream□

□ See page 195.

Chocolate Nut Sauce

❖ I'm partial to walnuts or almonds.

1 6-ounce package semisweet   ½ pound butter
   chocolate morsels   ½ cup finely chopped nuts❖

1. Melt the chocolate morsels over simmering water in a double boiler.
2. In a separate pan, melt the butter. Add it to the chocolate and stir well.
3. Add the chopped nuts.
4. Pour this warm over the ice cream. It will harden almost at once. (If necessary, it will hold over hot water, or it can be reheated.) Makes 2 cups.

Luncheon for 6 Artichoke Addicts

This meal also makes a lovely light supper.

○ Artichokes tend to kill the flavor of wine, so a lesser wine such as this will suffice. Some people don't bother to serve wine with artichokes at all.

MENU   **Baked Artichokes with Meat Filling**
French Bread and Butter
Fruit (and Cookies from Yesterday)

BEVERAGE: Tavel Rosé ○

WORK ORDER: *Artichokes, Fruit*

Baked Artichokes with Meat Filling

These can be served hot, or at room temperature.

6 rather large artichokes
½ cup olive oil, or more
1½ cups chopped onion
1 cup chopped celery
3–5 cloves garlic, peeled and chopped
1 pound ground lean veal△
1 pound ground lean pork△
1 tablespoon salt
Freshly ground white pepper to taste

1 tablespoon finely chopped fresh basil
Zest, grated, of 2 medium lemons
Juice of 1 medium lemon
1½ cups fresh soft bread crumbs
1 cup chopped fresh parsley

△ Or substitute 2 pounds chicken or 2 pounds ham for the veal and pork.

1. Prepare the artichokes according to instructions on page 190, but boil them only 20–25 minutes, until tender-firm when pierced with a knife. Drain, and remove "chokes" as directed.

2. While artichokes are boiling, make the meat filling. In a large skillet heat about ¼ cup of the oil until it begins to ripple gently. Add the onion and sauté over medium heat until it begins to soften, about 5 minutes.

3. Add the celery and half the garlic and cook, stirring, about 5 minutes. Add the veal and pork, salt, pepper, and basil. Cook and stir to break up the clumps. When the meat loses its raw look, remove from heat.

4. Add lemon zest and juice. Toss in the bread crumbs, most of the parsley (save some for garnish), and the remaining garlic. Toss together, and correct seasonings.

5. Spoon the filling mixture into the centers and between the outermost rows of each artichoke. Arrange upright and close together in a baking dish. Sprinkle over the remaining chopped parsley, and drizzle over all the remaining ¼ cup oil.

6. Set the baking dish in a pan filled with boiling water to a depth of about ½ inch. Cover all with a sheet of aluminum foil and bake 35–40 minutes in a preheated 375° oven. Artichokes are done when the base of one can easily be pierced with a knife. Serves 6.

A Light, Unusual Luncheon for 2

MENU   Belgian Endive Salad
Dutch Babies

BEVERAGE: A Glass of Dry Red Wine

WORK ORDER: *Salad, Dutch Babies*

Belgian Endive Salad

☆ See page 245.

3 Belgian endives, trimmed, washed, and dried
1 tablespoon chopped fresh chives

½ cup vinaigrette☆

Cut endives lengthwise, remove cores if desired, and julienne or cut on the diagonal into small pieces. Put into a salad bowl with chives. Toss with vinaigrette. Serves 2.

Dutch Babies

This is nothing more than a popover batter with a little sugar added, but it makes a fabulous puffy pancake. It's fun to serve when you need to improvise for an unexpected guest.

2 tablespoons butter
4 eggs
1 tablespoon granulated sugar
½ cup flour
½ cup milk

Dash of grated fresh nutmeg
Juice of 1 medium lemon
2 tablespoons sifted confectioners' sugar

1. Put the butter into a 10-inch skillet and place in a preheated oven set at 400°.

2. Mix and whisk together eggs, granulated sugar, flour, milk, and nutmeg. Pour into the hot skillet, return to oven, and bake 12–15 minutes.

3. Remove from oven and sprinkle with lemon juice and confectioners' sugar. Serves 2–3.

7

BARBECUES AND PICNICS: ENERGY SOLUTIONS

In summer most people take to the backyard or the woods rather than turn on the air conditioning. In winter the widespread use of wood-burning stoves makes the rooms where they're located natural settings for warm eating. In other words, the energy crisis is creating new possibilities for unusual and delightful picnics and barbecues, outdoors and indoors.

I love picnics and will connive to give them. My preference is to prepare everything in advance and avoid makeshift cooking. But with the new gas grills (if you can afford the gas!) and other cooking devices, I will concede that barbecuing has moved out of the dark ages of smoke, sputter, and scorch. (To make a charcoal fire do extra duty, throw on some herbs to complement what's cooking—rosemary for chicken, fennel for fish, etc.)

I've suggested several menus here, but don't confine your choices to this chapter. Browse through the rest of this book and fly with your fancy. With all the clever and inexpensive picnic gadgets now on the market, you can easily take just about any kind of dish, hot or cold, almost anywhere. The one rule is: Be downright lavish with food! Fresh air, or the homey feeling of a warm wood fire, charges up appetites!

Hot Picnic in the Woods for 8 at Tree-Cutting Time

MENU **Zucchini, Carrot, and Leek Soup in a Thermos**
Sausages Poached in White Wine
Buttered Hard French Rolls
Apple Cake with Cinnamon Sauce

BEVERAGE: Hot Apple Cider

WORK ORDER: *Apple Cake, Soup, Sausages, Cinnamon Sauce*

Zucchini, Carrot, and Leek Soup

□ See page 240.

6 leeks
8 tablespoons butter
4 zucchini, diced but not peeled
6 carrots, washed but not peeled
3 large potatoes, peeled and diced

8 cups chicken stock,□ or more
1 bay leaf
½ teaspoon saffron threads
Salt and freshly cracked black pepper to taste
1 cup chopped fresh parsley
1 cup heavy cream

1. Clean the leeks. Chop the white part, plus 1 inch of the green.
2. Melt the butter in a large pan. Add the vegetables. Add chicken stock; if it does not cover the vegetables, use more. Add bay leaf, saffron, salt, pepper, and parsley.
3. Bring to a boil, then turn to simmer. Cover and cook 25–30 minutes, or until vegetables are tender crisp. Put through the blender, food processor, or food mill, using medium disk.
4. Add cream, reheat, and rectify seasonings. Place in a thermos to take on a picnic. This soup freezes well. Serves 12.

Sausages Poached in White Wine

✧ I buy mine at a local farmers' market.

8–16 sausages, depending on size✧
1 cup chopped shallots

1 tablespoon butter
2 cups white wine

1. Prick the sausages with a skewer or put a toothpick through each one to keep them from bursting.

2. Sauté the shallots in the butter for 3 minutes. Add sausages and roll them around in the butter-shallot mixture.

3. Pour in the wine, and turn burner to simmer. Poach 15–20 minutes.

4. Remove sausages.

5. Raise flame and reduce the wine left in skillet by half. Pour this mixture over the sausages. Serves 8.

Apple Cake with Cinnamon Sauce

1 tablespoon butter
2 eggs
2 cups sugar
½ cup vegetable oil
1 teaspoon vanilla extract
2 cups all-purpose flour
1 teaspoon baking powder
1 teaspoon baking soda
½ teaspoon salt

1 teaspoon ground cinnamon
½ teaspoon freshly grated nutmeg
⅛ teaspoon ground cloves
4 cups diced, peeled apples (about 2 pounds)
½ cup chopped walnuts

1. Preheat oven to 350°. Grease a 10-by-15-by-1-inch baking sheet with butter.

2. In large mixer bowl, beat eggs until light and fluffy. Gradually add sugar, oil, and vanilla.

3. Mix together flour, baking powder, baking soda, salt, and spices. Add to egg mixture and blend well.

4. Mix in apples and nuts. Spoon into prepared pan. Bake 30 minutes.

5. Slice 8 servings for the picnic, and freeze the rest. (Recipe makes 24 small but very rich and moist servings.) Take along a container of the following sauce to go with the cake.

Cinnamon Sauce

This is also complementary to ice cream or fruit.

1 cup dark-brown sugar
2 teaspoons cornstarch
1 teaspoon ground cinnamon

2 cups boiling water
2 tablespoons butter
2 teaspoons vanilla extract

In a saucepan combine the brown sugar, cornstarch, and cinnamon. Gradually blend in the water. Cook, stirring constantly, until slightly thickened. Remove from heat; blend in butter and vanilla. Makes 2½ cups.

Barbecued Ribs for 6

MENU   **Barbecued Spareribs**
Fresh Vegetable Kebabs
Green Salad, Sour-Cream Dressing
Watermelon

BEVERAGE: Beer or Ale

WORK ORDER: *Ribs, Kebabs, Dressing, Salad, Melon*

Barbecued Spareribs

○ I count at least 1 pound per person; ribs disappear rapidly.

If time allows, these ribs will benefit from marinating.

6–7 pounds pork spareribs○
2 onions, sliced
1 teaspoon ground red pepper
Salt
3 cloves garlic, peeled and mashed

2 cups brown sugar
½ cup soy sauce
2 cloves garlic, chopped
A little cider vinegar

1. Cut the ribs into serving-size pieces. Place them in a shallow roasting pan and barely cover with water. Add onions, red pepper, salt, and mashed garlic. Bring to a boil, then simmer for 45 minutes. This will eliminate much of the fat and partially cook the ribs.
2. Remove ribs from water and lay them on a large dish or several small ones.
3. In a bowl, place brown sugar, soy sauce, and chopped garlic. Add just enough cider vinegar to dilute the brown sugar: mixture should look like a paste. Use it to brush the ribs.
4. Lay the ribs on a hot grill 4 inches from coals and baste with a long-handled brush, turning and basting on both sides. Since ribs are already partially cooked, this process will take only about 15 minutes.

Fresh Vegetable Kebabs

12 large mushrooms, cleaned, stems removed
2 green peppers, cut into chunks, seeds removed
1 red pepper, cut into chunks, seeds removed
1 medium eggplant, cut into chunks

2 red onions, peeled and cut into chunks
1 pint cherry tomatoes, stems removed
½ cup olive oil
Salt and freshly cracked black pepper
½ cup lemon juice

1. Using 6 metal skewers, about 6–8 inches long, thread the vegetables, thinking of colors and alternating for beautiful effect: pale colors (mushrooms, eggplant, onions) should go between the bright ones (green and red peppers, cherry tomatoes).

2. Brush with a marinade of olive oil, salt, pepper, and lemon juice. Grill 4 inches from hot coals, turning and basting frequently, for 10–15 minutes. These can also be grilled in the broiler. Serves 6.

Green Salad, Sour-Cream Dressing

2 heads romaine lettuce
2 heads Boston lettuce
1 bunch watercress

2 tablespoons freshly chopped chives

Wash lettuces and watercress, cut into bite-size pieces, and dry in a salad spinner. Place in a large salad bowl, add the chives, and toss with the following dressing.

Sour-Cream Dressing

If you omit the light cream, this recipe makes a nice dip for crudités.

1 cup sour cream
2 tablespoons wine vinegar
1 tablespoon chopped shallots

Salt and freshly cracked white pepper to taste
3 tablespoons light cream

In a bowl, combine all ingredients and mix well. If necessary, add more cream to achieve desired consistency. Makes 1¼ cups.

Watermelon Cut a watermelon into wedges and serve ice cold. Pass a plate of cookies, if you have some.

Middle Eastern Barbecue for 6

Lamb and rice combine like ham and eggs.

MENU **Lamb Shish Kebabs**
Baked Rice with Bay Leaves
Sliced Tomatoes, Creamy Onion Dressing
Melon Fingers with Lime

WINE SUGGESTION: Pitcher of Rosé

WORK ORDER: *Rice, Lamb, Dressing, Tomatoes, Melon*

Lamb Shish Kebabs

△ Beef can be substituted.

4 pounds cubed lamb,△ cut in 1½ inch cubes, from leg or shoulder
2 tablespoons freshly chopped oregano or rosemary

3 cloves garlic, peeled and chopped
½ cup olive oil
½ cup lemon juice
Salt and freshly cracked black pepper to taste

1. You should have 36 cubes of meat. Thread meat onto six metal skewers, 6 inches long. Place in a shallow dish.

2. Mix remaining ingredients and pour over the skewers of lamb. Let marinate at least 30 minutes, longer if you have time.

3. Place skewers 4 inches above the hot coals. Turn and baste often with the marinade. Cook until nicely browned and crisp, about 20 minutes. Serves 6.

Baked Rice with Bay Leaves

☆ See page 240.

4 tablespoons butter
1 medium onion, chopped
1½ cups long-grain rice
3 cups chicken stock☆

8 bay leaves·
Salt and freshly cracked black pepper to taste

1. In a small, heavy casserole, melt the butter. When butter is hot, add the onion and stir around for 3 minutes, being careful not to brown it.

2. Add rice, stock, bay leaves, salt, and pepper. Bring to a boil, lower heat to simmer. cover, and simmer for 23 minutes. Remove the lid, fluff up rice with two forks, remove bay leaves, and serve. Serves 6.

Sliced Tomatoes, Creamy Onion Dressing

□ See page 242.

4 pounds tomatoes, thinly sliced (skinned if desired)
½ cup homemade mayonnaise□
¼ cup chopped scallions, white part only
2 tablespoons light cream

1 tablespoon tarragon vinegar
Salt and freshly cracked white pepper to taste
1 tablespoon chopped fresh parsley

1. Arrange sliced tomatoes on a serving platter.

2. Make dressing: Combine all remaining ingredients except the parsley and mix well. Refrigerate until serving time.

3. Cover tomatoes with dressing. Sprinkle parsley on top. Serves 6.

Melon Fingers with Lime

This is a refreshing dessert after a rich meal.

1 *large* honeydew melon
½ cup fresh lime juice

Grated rind of 2 limes (no pith or white part)

Peel honeydew. Remove seeds and fibers. Cut into finger-size pieces. Place in a serving bowl and sprinkle the lime juice and grated rind on top. Serves 6.

Inside-Outside Dinner for 4

MENU   **Grilled Baby Chickens**
            Tomatoes in Cream
            Onion Salad
            Bananas and Cream in Nut Crust

WINE SUGGESTION: A Beaujolais such as Fleurie

WORK ORDER: *Bananas and Cream, Chickens, Salad, Tomatoes*

Grilled Baby Chickens

You can use Cornish hens or squabs here. If you're cooking outside, toss a bunch of rosemary over the coals just before you start the chickens. The rosemary will permeate the fowl with a delicious, exotic flavor. While you're at it, grill an extra chicken for a sack lunch.

4 small chickens, 1 pound
  each, split
8 tablespoons butter
  Salt and freshly cracked
  black pepper to taste
  Juice of 2 medium lemons
  or limes

1 tablespoon or more
  chopped rosemary
  Watercress
1 lemon or lime, cut into
  wedges

1. Lay chickens flat and pound with flat side of a meat cleaver to level them out.
2. Mix together butter, salt, pepper, lemon or lime juice, and rosemary, and rub into both sides of the chicken.
3. Place on a rack 3–4 inches under broiler or over hot coals. Broil 10 minutes on each side. Garnish with watercress and citrus wedges. Serves 4.

Tomatoes in Cream

¼ cup chopped onion
2 tablespoons butter
8 thick tomato slices

Salt and freshly cracked
  black pepper to taste
½ cup heavy cream

1. Sauté onion in butter until soft, about 3 minutes.
2. Place the tomato slices on broiler pan. Sprinkle the onion, salt, and pepper over them. Broil 3–4 inches from flame for 6

minutes. Pour the cream on top and broil 2–3 minutes longer, or until bubbly. Serves 4.

Onion Salad

3 large white onions
Salt
½ cup vegetable or olive oil
¼ cup vinegar

Freshly cracked black pepper to taste
1 tablespoon chopped fresh parsley

Peel the onions and slice paper-thin. Put in a bowl, sprinkle with salt, and cover with ice water. Set in fridge for about 15 minutes. Drain and pat dry. Place in a salad bowl and add the oil, vinegar, pepper, and parsley. Toss and serve to 4.

Bananas and Cream in Nut Crust

CRUST

1 cup ground nuts, the oilier the better (macadamia or Brazil nuts work fine)

3 tablespoons sugar
2 tablespoons melted butter

Mix together and pat into an 8-inch pie plate. Bake in a 375° oven until set, about 10–15 minutes. Remove from oven and let cool.

FILLING

1 cup heavy cream
2 tablespoons confectioners' sugar
2 tablespoons dark or light rum

2 bananas
1–2 tablespoons lemon juice
1–2 tablespoons shaved chocolate

1. Whip the cream and add the sugar. Blend in rum and whip a minute longer. Place in cooled nut crust.
2. Peel bananas, slice on bias, and sprinkle with lemon juice. Lay these artfully on top of the whipped cream mixture. Set in refrigerator.
3. Just before serving, use a rotary peeler to shave chocolate over top. Do this from the side of the chocolate so that curls will form. Serves 4–6.

Dress-Up Barbecue for 4

MENU   **Flank Steak on the Grill**
Asparagus Gratin
Mushrooms with Madeira
Nectarines with Champagne

WINE SUGGESTION: A Beaujolais such as Moulin-à-Vent

WORK ORDER: *Marinate Meat, Asparagus, Mushrooms, Nectarines*

Flank Steak on the Grill

1 flank steak, 2½–3 pounds (must be prime)
½ cup soy sauce
¼ cup sherry
2 tablespoons honey
1 clove garlic, finely chopped
Freshly cracked black pepper to taste
2 tablespoons vegetable oil
1 teaspoon freshly grated ginger

1. Place steak in a Pyrex dish. Blend all remaining ingredients together. Brush this mixture on both sides of the steak. Set aside to marinate while you prepare the remainder of dinner.

2. At cooking time, broil 4–5 minutes on each side, 3–4 inches from coals. Or you can place steak in the broiler inside, 3–4 inches from flame. Meat must be rare.

3. Carve horizontally across the grain into paper-thin slices. Serves 4 with leftovers, maybe.

Asparagus Gratin

In this recipe, you can use leeks instead of asparagus. Finely chop 6 leeks, white part only, sauté in butter, and finish as for the asparagus.

2 tablespoons butter
1 pound asparagus, peeled and cut into ½-inch pieces
1½ cups heavy cream
Salt and freshly cracked black pepper to taste
¾ cup freshly grated imported Parmesan cheese

1. Melt the butter in a skillet and quickly sauté the asparagus. Toss over the flame for 2–3 minutes.

2. Transfer to a bake-and-serve dish. (I use a small copper gratin dish.) Pour the cream on top and add salt and pepper. Sprinkle the cheese over the top. Place in a pan of hot water and bake at 350° until fairly set, about 30–35 minutes. Serves 4–6.

Mushrooms with Madeira

4 tablespoons butter
¼ cup chopped shallots
1½ pounds mushrooms, quartered
¼ cup Madeira wine

¾ cup heavy cream
Salt and freshly cracked white pepper to taste
1 tablespoon chopped fresh parsley

1. Heat the butter in a skillet. Add shallots and cook while stirring with a wooden spatula for 3 minutes. Add mushrooms and toss or stir for 3 minutes longer. Add Madeira and cook until all the juices in the pan are evaporated. (This intensifies the flavor.)

2. Add the cream and continue to cook until it coats a spoon. Season with salt and pepper, and garnish with parsley. Serves 4–6.

Nectarines with Champagne

4–6 nectarines, peeled and sliced
4 teaspoons liqueur (Cointreau, framboise, kirsch, etc.)

Split of champagne, chilled

Divide nectarines evenly among 4 goblets. Add 1 teaspoon liqueur per serving, then fill each goblet with champagne. If you have some champagne left over, drink it. Serves 4.

Celebration Barbecue Dinner for 4 or 6

MENU　Curried Duck with Crisp Watercress
Potatoes Gratin
Fresh Peach Cobbler

BEVERAGE: Pale India Ale or Iced Tea

WORK ORDER: *Potatoes, Cobbler, Duck*

Curried Duck with Crisp Watercress

These instructions are for outdoor barbecuing, but you can achieve the same results, in the same time, in your kitchen broiler. Or roast the duck in the oven at 350° for about 1 hour, brushing on the honey glaze after the first 30 minutes of roasting.

2 ducks, 4 pounds each, cut
　into 4 pieces each
1 cup honey
2 tablespoons curry powder

1 tablespoon Dijon mustard
¼ cup soy sauce
¼ cup brandy
Crisp watercress

1. Remove all visible fat from ducks. Set them aside.
2. In a small bowl or saucepan, mix together honey, curry powder, mustard, soy sauce, and brandy.
3. Lay duck pieces on grill, 3–4 inches from the hot coals, for 10 minutes on each side.
4. Now begin to brush the ducks with the honey mixture. Keep turning and basting; grill 30–40 minutes, depending upon how well done you want the duck. The skin will be very crisp when duck is ready.
5. Present on a platter surrounded by bunches of crisp watercress. Serves 4–6.

Potatoes Gratin

1 whole clove garlic, peeled
4 baking potatoes
2 cups heavy cream
　Salt and freshly cracked
　black pepper to taste

A little freshly grated
　nutmeg
¾ cup freshly grated
　Parmesan cheese

1. Rub the garlic clove over a 2-quart bake-and-serve dish. Finely chop what remains and scatter over the bottom of the dish.

2. Wash and peel the potatoes, but do not wash after peeling,✧ and slice them ⅛ inch thick on a mandoline. Place slices directly in baking dish.

✧ This will preserve the potatoes' natural starch, which will serve to bind the dish and eliminate the need for flour.

3. Pour over the cream, salt, pepper, and nutmeg. Use your hands to mix these ingredients. Make sure the potatoes are well coated with the cream.

4. Sprinkle the Parmesan cheese over the top and bake in a bain-marie at 400° for 30 minutes. Then reduce heat to 350° and bake 20–30 minutes longer, or until creamy. Serves 4–6.

Fresh Peach Cobbler

Let the time of the year decide which fruit to use in this cobbler. The recipe works with almost anything—blueberries, sliced apples, pitted cherries, blackberries, or sliced plums, to name a few.

3 cups peeled and sliced fresh peaches	2 teaspoons baking powder
½ cup sugar	1 tablespoon sugar
8 tablespoons butter	1 teaspoon salt
1 cup flour	½ cup heavy cream, or less

1. Lay fruit in a 1½-quart baking dish. Sprinkle over ½ cup sugar; dot with 4 tablespoons of the butter.

2. Make a crust of the remaining ingredients: Mix together flour, baking powder, 1 tablespoon sugar, and salt. Cut in the 4 remaining tablespoons butter; then add enough heavy cream to make a manageable dough. Mix with a *light* touch.

3. Roll out dough on a lightly floured board and place over the fruit. Bake at 375° for 35–40 minutes. Serves 6.

Swaparounds and Leftovers

Using mostly leftovers, which you wisely planned for as you prepared other meals, you can do wonders with quick picnics and sack lunches.

CHICKEN PICNIC IN THE PARK

Cold Fried Chicken
Red-Skin Potato Salad
Crudités and Salt
Apple Cake or Molasses Cake

SACK LUNCH FOR A DESK CONFERENCE

Black Bread with Horseradish Butter
Leftover Filet of Beef
Marinated Olives
Gingersnaps

STRETCH-IT-OUT PICNIC

Leftover Roast Sirloin or Leftover Filet with Vinaigrette
Bread Sticks
Cold Cucumber Batons
Sandy's Brownies

Leftover Roast Sirloin or Filet with Vinaigrette

○ See page 245.

Leftover meat, cut into strips
Vinaigrette○
½ cup chopped onion
½ cup chopped celery

Dress beef strips with vinaigrette, and stretch with onion and celery. Serves 2 or more.

Sandy's Brownies

2 squares unsweetened chocolate
½ cup butter
1 cup sugar
2 eggs, beaten
½ cup flour
Pinch of salt
1 teaspoon vanilla extract
½ cup chopped walnuts

Over low heat or over water, carefully melt chocolate and butter. Remove from heat. Blend in sugar and eggs. Add flour and salt; stir well to mix. Add vanilla and walnuts. Pour batter into an 8-by-8-by-2-inch greased pan. Bake at 400° for 15–20 minutes (do not overbake). Makes 16 squares.

Car or Bus Picnic for 2 or More

MENU	**Raw Mushroom Sandwiches, Alfalfa Sprouts** **Cheese Salad** **Cherry Tomatoes** **Bing Cherries**
BEVERAGE:	Thermos of Coffee or Lemonade
WORK ORDER:	*Cheese Salad, Sandwiches, Cherries, Tomatoes*

Raw Mushroom Sandwiches, Alfalfa Sprouts

△ See page 70.

Brown bread, 2 slices per person
Horseradish butter△
Sliced fresh mushrooms, 2–3 per person

½ cup alfalfa sprouts, or more

For each sandwich, spread 2 slices of brown bread with horseradish butter. Layer on the sliced mushrooms, top with alfalfa sprouts, and cover with the second slice of bread. Cut into pieces and wrap well.

Cheese Salad

☆ See page 145.

2 cups diced Gruyère cheese
1 tablespoon caraway seeds
Salt and freshly cracked white pepper to taste

½ cup mustard mayonnaise,☆ or more
1 tablespoon finely chopped fresh parsley

Mix all ingredients in a bowl, adding enough mustard mayonnaise to bind the salad. Serves 2.

Cherry Tomatoes   Wash a generous supply of these, and don't forget the salt.

Bing Cherries   Wash and pack an abundance of these. They are ideal for picnics because they will not crush—but people tend to dip into them before the picnic begins, so you'll need a lot.

Chicken Chest Picnic for 2

> **MENU**   **Chicken Chest**
> **Fresh Fruit**
> **Brandy Lace Cups**□
>
> **BEVERAGE:** Chianti

Chicken Chest

□ See page 81.

◇ See page 204.

1 loaf unsliced home style bread, day old, if possible
4–6 tablespoons melted butter

Fried chicken◇
Pickles, olives, and radishes

1. Remove top of bread, lengthwise, to form a lid. Hollow out the interior, leaving a 1-inch margin all around. (Save the center for making crumbs.) Brush the box, inside and out, and the underside of the lid with the melted butter.
2. Place container and lid on a baking sheet and put into a 350° oven for 20 minutes to toast. Remove from oven.
3. Fill with fried chicken. Replace lid. Decorate the top with toothpicks holding pickles, olives, and radishes, arranged so that the colors form an attractive pattern. Serves 2.

Eastern Shore Crab Party in Kitchen or Yard for 12

This is a fun and wonderfully messy way to entertain. Spread newspapers on the table, the way they do it in Maryland. Provide lots of *large* napkins, small hammers (real crab eaters will bring their own), seafood fork or lobster crackers and picks. The menu can be expanded to a veritable feast. Homemade ice cream is a must, however.

○ See index.

△ See page 50.

☆ See page 195.

MENU   **Cold Soup**○
Sliced Beefsteak Tomatoes with Oil and Vinegar
Hard-Shell Crabs from Maryland
Matchstick Potatoes△
Corn on the Cob
Homemade Ice Cream☆

BEVERAGE: Cold beer or champagne

Hard-Shell Crabs From Maryland

Measurements depend on the size of the kettle. The larger it is, the more you'll need of condiments. These quantities are for a giant kettle.

1 handful salt
1 cup or so of vinegar
  Crab boil (I sometimes use a whole package of Zatarain, a super mixture from New Orleans)

As much ground red pepper as you and your guests can bear
1 bushel hard-shell Maryland crabs

1. Into kettle put salt, vinegar, crab boil, and red pepper. Add crabs, a few at a time, and cook until they turn reddish, about 20 minutes (depending on size of kettle and crabs).

2. Serve at room temperature. To eat, start hammering and cracking. Lift up the apron (the piece of the shell that comes to a point) and pull out the spongy material. Eat the remainder, and don't forget the claw meat. I can eat about 8 of these, but I've had guests who could pack away 18!

8 COCKTAIL PARTIES: A COMEBACK

Cocktail parties are coming back in style, though for me they never went out. A merry do with drinks and finger foods for a milling crowd is one of my favorite celebrations! With time and money overtaxed for most of us, this beloved classic is being rediscovered as a spiffy way to entertain without having to take a week off from work to prepare for it, or sell the silver to pay for it.

Flexibility and a sense of humor are apt guidelines for this kind of party. It's a good idea to provide a variety of foods in appealing shapes and colors, but a mistake to aim for a gallimaufry that exhausts you and bewilders your guests. Let the occasion generate offerings that add to the fun. A cocktail party for the author of a new book, for example, could feature Scarlett O'Hara Vegetables (served with red caviar) and Good-as-Gold Cheese Fondue.

I plan on four drinks and six hors d'oeuvre per person, as a basic rule. White wine is a must, and so is a nonalcoholic beverage (see chapter on "Cheers: Drinks Homemade and Otherwise"). Using 10- or 12-ounce wineglasses for everything is a neat trick: they look ultrasmart, and are so much easier to cope with than separate-size glasses for different drinks. Don't be "the kind of people who run out of ice." Figure out what you think you'll need, then add some for your own peace of mind.

The rigid 5–7 P.M. time slot for cocktail parties can become a bit too finicky for busy people: if you want to make it 4–6 P.M. or even 6–8 P.M., you can. A relatively recent version is called a "heavy cocktail buffet," which means that abundant food will be served, so that guests won't need dinner afterward. More interpretations of this versatile social will appear, since it adapts so well to new needs for simple but civilized forms of quick-do entertaining.

A Medley of Makings for a 60-Minute Cocktail Party

Here is a list of suggestions, many of them new recipes, others from elsewhere in this book, for you to pick and choose from when you're long on time and lavish with good intentions. Included are a mixaround menu for a Suit-the-Season Cocktail Buffet (you'll use this one over and over) and nine menus for simple but stunning cocktail party fare. Keep in mind that *presentation* is a magic key. The Sausages in White Wine, for example, are terrific as a main course. If you but slice the sausages into bite-size pieces, they turn into delicious hors d'oeuvre. After the party's over, I encourage you to use this list to conjure up menus for other occasions, at other times of day or evening.

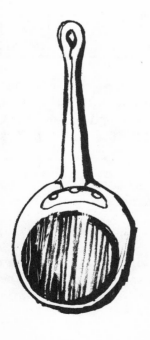

Rat Cheese in Phyllo Dough
Walnuts Wrapped in Prosciutto
Red-Skin Potatoes, Aïoli
Fried Cheese
Crudités with Almond Mayonnaise or Seasoned Salt
Puffed Potato Wedges
French Fried Zucchini
Greenbrier Radja
Oysters in Beer Batter
Lady Apples with Blue Cheese
Roquefort Cream with Chopped Celery
Continuous Cheese Crock
Broccoli Florets in Cherry Tomatoes
Sliced Sausages in White Wine
Salted Nuts
Roasted Chestnuts
Mexican Stuffed Avocados, Pappadums
California Appetizers
Stemmed Radishes with Butter
Crabmeat Canapés
Cucumber Slices with Egg Salad
Scallions and Cherry Tomatoes
Shellfish on Ice

Suit-the-Season Cocktail Buffet

When you decide on recipes for this menu, take advantage of fresh foods that are in season. Your party will taste better—and cost less.

□ Consult the list of ideas in this section, or look through recipes for appetizers in the rest of this book.

❖ See index.

MENU   Cocktails
Canapés or Hors d'Oeuvres□
Any Soup from This Book❖
Filet, Sirloin Strips, or Flank Steak❖ Served at
   Room Temperature
Breads and Mustards
Any Salad from This Book❖

One-Hour Party #1

○ See page 117.

MENU   Rat Cheese in Phyllo
Walnuts Wrapped in Prosciutto
French Fried Zucchini○

Rat Cheese in Phyllo

This cheese is plain old store cheese, or sharp cheese, but it was called rat cheese when I was growing up and I still think of it this way. It was so sharp it felt as though it would cut your lips when you tasted it—but I loved it! If the name makes you tetchy, call it something else.

4 phyllo leaves
4 tablespoons melted butter
½ pound rat cheese, in one
   piece, rind removed

2 tablespoons Creole
mustard

1. Spread the phyllo leaves on a work surface or clean counter top, and brush each one with melted butter, piling them in a neat stack as you go.

2. Place the cheese in the middle of the phyllo stack, and brush over sides and top with mustard. Fold edges of phyllo leaves over to enclose the cheese envelope-fashion. Brush all over with melted butter.

3. Lay "package" on a baking sheet and bake in a preheated 350° oven for 25 minutes, or until brown. Let stand 5 minutes before cutting into wedges. Serves 4–6.

Walnuts Wrapped in Prosciutto

1 pound fresh walnut halves
¼ pound thinly sliced prosciutto ham

Cut pieces of ham into shapes larger than the walnuts, and wrap nuts in ham. Yields approximately 4 cups.

One-Hour Party #2

> **MENU**   Red-Skin Potatoes, Aïoli
> Oysters in Beer Batter with Horseradish Sauce
> Roasted Chestnuts

Oysters in Beer Batter with Horseradish Sauce

△ Or shrimp, if you wish. Remove the shells, but leave the tiny tails intact.

☆ See page 237.

30 oysters△
1 cup flour
   Beer batter☆

2–3 cups solid shortening or peanut oil

1. Dry oysters on a paper towel. Dip in flour, then in beer batter.

2. Meanwhile, melt the shortening in a heavy saucepan.

3. Drop oysters, a few at a time, into hot (375°) fat. They will puff and cook in 2 minutes.

4. Drain on brown paper, and serve with the following sauce. Serves 6–10.

Horseradish Sauce

□ See page 240.

1 cup chicken stock□
2 tablespoons sugar
6 tablespoons soy sauce

2 tablespoons freshly grated
    horseradish
1 clove garlic, chopped

Combine all ingredients, blending well.

One-Hour Party #3

✧ See page 202.

> **MENU**   **Fried Cheese**
> **Salted Nuts**✧
> **Broccoli Florets in Cherry Tomatoes**

Fried Cheese

I'd never dream of doing this to a fresh cheese; I use an old Brie or Camembert. It's impossible to give precise measurements, but you won't need them, anyway. If someone gives me a Brie which refuses to ripen, I make this dish. Everybody thinks it's super.

Cheese, cut into triangles
Flour
1 egg, beaten
Bread crumbs or ground
    almonds

2–3 cups solid shortening or
    peanut oil

Roll the cheese in the flour. Dip in beaten egg. Roll in bread crumbs or ground almonds. Fry in hot fat 1–2 minutes. Drain on a clean paper bag or paper towels, and serve.

Broccoli Florets

○ See page 245.

1 quart cherry tomatoes
1 cup broccoli florets

Vinaigrette○

1. Remove the stem from each cherry tomato and dig out a small piece from the center.

2. Separate broccoli florets into tiny pieces. Insert them in the holes in the little tomatoes. Brush with vinaigrette.

One-Hour Party #4

△ See page 186.

☆ See page 27.

> **MENU**   **Crudités with Almond Garlic Mayonnaise**△
> **Puffed Potato Wedges**☆
> **Lady Apples with Blue Cheese**

Lady Apples with Blue Cheese

As many lady apples as you wish
As much blue cheese as you need

Remove a core from the *bottom only* of each tiny apple. Insert a small piece of blue cheese into the empty cavity. Arrange on a platter, stems up.

One-Hour Party #5

□ See page 158.

✧ See page 237.

> **MENU**   **Roquefort Cream with Celery**
> **Sliced Sausages in White Wine**□
> **Marinated Olives**✧

Roquefort Cream with Celery

1 pound Roquefort cheese
½ pound butter, softened
½ cup heavy cream, whipped
1 cup finely chopped celery hearts

Ground red pepper to taste
Salt if necessary
Crackers

1. With mixer, beat the Roquefort cheese until smooth. Beat in the butter and continue beating until creamy.
2. Gently fold in the whipped cream.
3. Lastly, fold in the celery, red pepper, and salt, depending on saltiness of the cheese.
4. Serve with crackers. Makes 5–6 cups cream.

One-Hour Party #6

○ See page 203.

△ See page 166.

☆ See page 243.

MENU	Continuous Cheese Crock,○ crackers
	Flank Steak△
	Aïoli☆
	Greenbrier Radja

Greenbrier Radja

This is a favorite with cocktails at the famous Greenbrier Hotel in White Sulphur Springs, West Virginia. Since it's usually made with country ham, leave out the salt; because of the curry, skip the pepper.

□ See page 241.

1 cup chopped cooked ham
   or turkey
2 tablespoons butter
1 tablespoon curry powder
2 tablespoons chutney, finely
   chopped

1 cup heavy béchamel
   sauce□
36 toast fingers
¼ cup freshly grated
   Parmesan cheese
¼ cup melted butter

1. Sauté the ham or turkey in the 2 tablespoons butter. Add curry and cook, stirring with a wooden spatula, for 2 minutes.

2. Add the chutney and béchamel and mix well. Spread this mixture over the toast fingers.

3. Sprinkle with Parmesan cheese and drizzle the melted butter on top.

4. Lay on a baking sheet and bake in a preheated 375° oven 5–7 minutes. Makes 36 pieces.

One-Hour Party #7

MENU	Mexican Stuffed Avocados with Poppadums
	California Appetizers
	Stemmed Radishes with a Crock of Butter

Mexican Stuffed Avocados

3 ripe avocados
1 tomato, chopped
1 medium onion, chopped
1 teaspoon ground red
   pepper

Salt to taste
1 tablespoon olive oil
1 teaspoon chopped coriander
   leaves
Lemon or lime wedges

1. Being careful not to mar the shells, which you will need later, cut the avocados in half. Remove pits.

2. In a bowl, mash the pulp with a fork. Add the tomato, onion, ground red pepper, salt, olive oil, and coriander.

3. Fill the avocado shells with this mixture and serve with lemon or lime wedges and the following poppadums.

Poppadums

These are thin Indian wafers, sometimes made with pea flour, often served with curry dishes. Available in specialty food shops, they are deliciously crisp when fried in a shallow layer (about 1 inch) of bacon fat or vegetable shortening. Just heat the fat to the smoking point, drop in a poppadum, and keep alert—in just a few seconds, it will ruffle and brown.

California Appetizers

Butter for greasing pan
8 eggs
1 teaspoon Tabasco sauce
½ cup flour
1 teaspoon baking powder
½ teaspoon salt

3 cups shredded Monterey
   Jack cheese
1½ cups shredded sharp
   Cheddar cheese
⅓ cup minced green pepper

1. Preheat oven to 375°. Lightly butter a 9-inch square baking pan.

2. In mixer bowl, combine eggs and Tabasco. Using high-speed setting, beat until light and fluffy, about 5 minutes.

3. Add the flour, baking powder, and salt. Mix well. Stir in cheeses and green pepper.

4. Spoon into prepared pan. Bake 20–25 minutes. Let stand 5 minutes before cutting. Makes 36 appetizers or 9 luncheon servings.

One-Hour Party #8

MENU	**Crabmeat Canapés** **Cucumber Slices and Onion Egg Salad** **Cherry Tomatoes with Coarse Salt**

Crabmeat Canapés

2 tablespoons minced shallots
2 tablespoons minced green pepper
3 tablespoons butter
3 tablespoons flour
½ teaspoon salt
1 cup light cream
¼ teaspoon Tabasco sauce

1 teaspoon lemon juice
2 egg yolks, slightly beaten
1 pound crabmeat
36–40 two-inch toast rounds
½ cup grated Swiss cheese
7 slices bacon, cooked and crumbled

1. In a saucepan, cook shallots and green pepper in butter until tender. Blend in flour and salt. Cook and stir 1 minute, making sure vegetables do not brown.

2. Blend in cream, Tabasco sauce, and lemon juice. Cook, stirring, until mixture thickens.

3. Add a small amount of the hot mixture to the beaten egg yolks so as to raise temperature of yolks gradually (this will keep them from curdling in the next step).

4. Add yolk mixture to pan and cook a few minutes. Stir in the crabmeat.

5. Place about 1 tablespoon of mixture onto each toast round; put on a baking sheet. Top each with a small amount of the cheese and crumbled bacon.

6. Bake in a preheated 350° oven for 15 minutes. Makes 36–40 canapés, or 4 luncheon servings.

Cucumber Slices and Onion Egg Salad○

○ You can also use this salad to make 4 sandwiches, or to fill 4 hollowed-out tomatoes.

△ See page 194.

2 large cucumbers
2 medium onions, finely chopped
6 hard-cooked eggs,△ chopped

¼ cup mayonnaise
Salt and freshly cracked white pepper to taste
Parsley sprigs

1. Slice cucumbers into ¼-inch slices.
2. Mix onions, eggs, mayonnaise, and salt and pepper. Pile this mixture onto the cucumber slices, and dot each with a sprig of parsley. Makes 30–40 pieces.

One-Hour Party #9

```
MENU    Shower of Shellfish on Ice
        Assorted Accompaniments
        Brown Bread and Butter Sandwiches
```

Shower of Shellfish on Ice

☆ Have the fishmonger open these.

□ See page 153.

✧ See page 145.

We usually serve this in winter, when the ice will not melt too quickly. I let a waiter drain off the excess water and replenish the ice, or sometimes a friend pitches in.

Oysters☆
Clams☆
Fresh crabmeat

Shelled cooked shrimp
Lobster meat

1. Let the kinds of shellfish you select be determined by your taste and budget, and the quantity by the number of guests. About 4–6 ounces of shellfish per person is a generous, but reasonable, amount.
2. Embed shellfish on a bed of cracked ice. (I use a huge serving bowl which covers my hall table.) Place small plates and oyster forks around the edge.
3. Serve with Lamaze Sauce,□ Mustard Mayonnaise,✧ pepper in a mill, and lemon wedges.

9 SUPPERS AND BUFFETS: VICTUALS WITH FLAIR

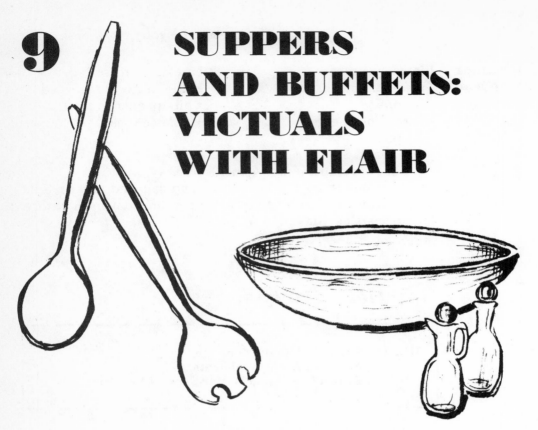

I've read that King Louis XV enjoyed cooking *petits soupers*, little suppers, which helps to prove my theory that cooks have a royal time of it. Suppers, which I think of as rather late meals, somewhere around eleven or eleven-thirty at night, and buffets, do bring out the inner queen or king in every cook! There is an aura of grace and grandeur to this kind of deliberately elegant entertaining.

Part of the fun is the appointments—tablecloth, dishes, and other props that set the scene. The menus should include colors that blend, smells that entice, arrangements that attract, but the food need not be heavy. With so many fresh foods to choose from at any time of the year, your approach to this kind of entertaining probably requires much less fuss than you might think.

Buffets are parties that I think of as including too many people for sit-down serving. They're comfortable, and many guests prefer them because the informal, help-yourself style means the host or hostess without servants (and that means most people) can join the party, too. For buffets, I refuse to ask my guests to juggle food on their knees. If you try, you can figure out a way to provide everyone with a place to sit down and eat.

The recipes in this chapter are titled for occasions that suit certain times of the year, so as to take advantage of fresh foods available at the time. You can also use ideas from the other chapters in this book: some brunches adapt delightfully to suppers; you can find some buffet ideas in the chapter on picnics and barbecues. The main thing is to tailor your menu to the mood of the evening, keep it uncomplicated—then join your own party, and sup!

A Tree-Trimming or Make-a-Wreath Party for 8

> **MENU** **Crudités with Almond Garlic Mayonnaise**
> **Baked Potatoes with Caviar and Sour Cream**
> **Lemon Ice**
>
> **LIBATION:** Chilled Vodka
>
> **WORK ORDER:** *Lemon Ice, Potatoes, Mayonnaise, Crudités*

Crudités
○ See page 252.

1 pint cherry tomatoes, stems on

2 cucumbers, peeled, seeded, cut into strips

1 cauliflower, cut into small florets

2 bunches radishes with stems

1 bunch carrots, peeled and shaved thin on mandoline and soaked in ice water to curl

1 pound raw mushrooms, cleaned○

1 stalk celery, trimmed and cut into sticks

1 green and 1 red pepper, seeded and cut into strips

½ pound snow peas, cleaned of strings

You can add or substitute vegetables according to your taste and what is in season. Arrange on a platter around a bowl of the following mayonnaise. Serves 8.

Almond Garlic Mayonnaise

△ See page 242.

2 cups homemade mayonnaise△
2 large cloves garlic, chopped very fine

½ cup finely chopped toasted almonds
Salt and freshly cracked white pepper to taste
1 tablespoon chopped parsley

1. Put mayonnaise in a bowl. Whisk in garlic, almonds, salt, pepper, and parsley.
2. Transfer to a serving bowl that looks beautiful in the center of the vegetable platter.

Baked Potatoes with Caviar and Sour Cream

This is one of my favorite elegant-but-simple dishes. On the rare occasions when I am dining alone, I like to bake one potato and lavish it with these trimmings.

8 large baking potatoes
A bowl (about 2 cups) of thick sour cream
Red or black caviar, as much as the budget allows

A crock of butter for those who prefer it

1. Preheat oven to 425°. Wash the potatoes well and place directly on oven rack. Bake 40–60 minutes.
2. Split open by making a cross on top of each potato and plump it up. Serve with the sour cream, caviar, and butter. Serves 8.

Lemon Ice

Simple syrup: 2 cups water and 1 cup sugar
2 cups fresh lemon juice

Grated rind of 1 lemon
2 egg whites, beaten into soft peaks

1. Make the simple syrup by combining the water and sugar in a pan. Bring to a boil and hold it there for 5 minutes or until sugar is dissolved. Cool the mixture.
2. Put lemon juice, lemon rind, and syrup into electric ice cream maker and, following manufacturer's directions, churn for 15 minutes. Stop machine and check mixture: it should look like slush.

3. Add the egg whites and churn for another 15 minutes. When ready, it should be on the soft side. Makes about 1 quart, or 8 servings.

Sunday Supper for 8 After a Day at the Fair

This meal also makes a good breakfast or brunch.

MENU   **Celery Soup**
            Deviled Ham and Eggs
            Cup Custard

WINE SUGGESTION: Mountain Red in a Carafe

WORK ORDER: *Custard, Soup, Ham and Eggs*

Celery Soup

☆ Or use 2 medium bunches of celery plus 6 bulbs of fennel.

□ See page 240.

12 tablespoons butter
3 pounds celery,☆ chopped, with tops
3 cups chopped onion
2 ripe tomatoes, peeled and chopped
3 quarts chicken stock□ (more or less, depending on size of pan)

1 bay leaf
1 teaspoon crushed thyme
Salt and freshly cracked black pepper to taste
1 tablespoon chopped fresh parsley
1 tablespoon Pernod

1. Melt 6 tablespoons of the butter in a large pan and sauté the celery and onion.
2. Add the chopped tomatoes. Cover with chicken stock. Add bay leaf, thyme, salt, and pepper. Bring to a boil and simmer until vegetables are tender crisp—don't let them get mushy.
3. Purée in blender or food processor or put through the fine disk of a food mill. Rectify seasoning.
4. Whisk in the remaining 6 tablespoons of butter and add the parsley and Pernod.
5. This serves 20–24. Freeze what you don't use today; you'll want more soon.

Deviled Ham and Eggs

Ask your butcher to do this, or grind the ham yourself in a food processor. Do not use a meat grinder: it won't work right because of the gristle in the ham.

3 cups ground✧ ham
¼ cup butter
½ cup chopped onion
2 tablespoons flour
¼ cup chicken stock
1 cup light cream
3–4 tablespoons Dijon mustard
1 tablespoon grated horseradish
¾ cup sliced stuffed olives
Salt and freshly cracked black pepper to taste
16 slices buttered toast
8 hard-cooked eggs, sliced

1. Preheat oven to 350°. In a saucepan, brown the ham in the butter. Add onion and cook until tender. Add flour and cook and stir 3 minutes. Remove from heat.

2. Blend in the stock, cream, mustard, and horseradish. Cook, stirring, until thickened. Add olives, salt and pepper.

3. For each serving, place 1 slice of toast in the bottom of an individual ramekin. (You will need 8 in all.) Top toast with ½ cup of the sauce and 1 sliced egg. Cut another slice of toast into triangles and place around edges of the ramekin.

4. Return to oven and bake 5–10 minutes, until bubbly. Serves 8.

Cup Custard

Maybe custard is always such a popular dessert because it's so downright homey. This one is especially rich and creamy.

Butter
3 cups light cream
3 eggs
3 egg yolks
5 tablespoons sugar
2 teaspoons vanilla extract
Freshly grated nutmeg

1. Preheat oven to 325°. Lightly butter 8 custard cups, 6 ounces each.

2. In a saucepan, scald the cream.

3. In a bowl, mix together eggs, egg yolks, sugar, and vanilla. Gradually add the scalded cream. Strain through a sieve.

4. Pour ½ cup mixture into each custard cup, and sprinkle generously with nutmeg. Place cups in a pan of boiling water 1 inch deep. Bake 30 minutes, or until set. Makes 8 servings.

A Cook-In Buffet: Spaghetatta for 12

○ See page 95 for pasta recipe. You will need 4 batches.

I'm not going to mislead you: one person cannot execute this entire menu in 60 minutes, but it's easy to do if your guests join in—and it's fun. Get two helpers to make the pasta,○ another to do the sauces, and a fourth to prepare the artichokes and vinaigrette. The host or hostess can prepare the zabaglione at the end of the meal. If everybody's too shiftless to make pasta, buy it in a box, if you have the heart. Or, if you insist on doing everything yourself, you can make the pasta ahead of time and freeze it.

MENU   **Pasta with Four Kinds of Sauce:**
           Braci di Fero   Fresh Tomato
           Butter and Cheese White Clam
           Artichokes Vinaigrette
           Bread Sticks
           Espresso Zabaglione

WINE SUGGESTION: Red and white jug wine

WORK ORDER: *Pasta, Sauces, Artichokes, Zabaglione*

I call this Popeye Sauce because it's made with spinach.

Braci di Fero Sauce△

△ This means "Arm of Iron."

1 cup heavy cream
¼ cup chicken stock
½ cup Swiss cheese cut into small cubes
2 cups fresh *raw* spinach, cleaned, stems removed
Freshly grated nutmeg

8 tablespoons butter
¼ cup freshly grated Parmesan cheese
Salt and freshly cracked black pepper to taste
1 pound fresh thin pasta, cooked and drained

1. Heat the cream, stock, and Swiss cheese together until cheese is melted.

2. Add remaining ingredients, except the pasta. (The raw spinach leaves will cook a bit on the hot pasta.)

3. Pour the sauce over 1 pound of fresh pasta and toss. Serves 4.

White Clam Sauce

☆ See page 241.

Do it the Italian way: forgo cheese with seafood.

6 tablespoons olive oil
3 cloves garlic, peeled
½ cup chopped fresh Italian parsley
36 tiny clams in shell (washed)
¼ cup dry white wine

Salt and freshly cracked white pepper to taste
¼ cup medium béchamel sauce☆
1 pound fresh thin pasta, cooked and drained

1. Heat oil in a large pan. Add garlic cloves and cook until the oil is perfumed. Remove the garlic.
2. Add parsley, clams and wine. Cover the pan with a lid until the clams open. This takes very little time, so pay attention.
3. Add salt, pepper, and béchamel sauce to clam mixture in pan. Stir 1 minute. Serve, shells and all, over pasta. Serves 4.

Butter and Cheese Sauce

8 tablespoons soft butter
½ cup freshly grated Parmesan cheese
¾ cup heavy cream
Salt and freshly cracked black pepper to taste

1 pound fresh thin pasta, cooked and drained
2 tablespoons chopped fresh Italian parsley

Mix all ingredients, except the pasta and parsley, together and beat until creamy. Toss sauce with pasta. Garnish with parsley. Serves 4.

Fresh Tomato Sauce

Make sauce according to instructions on page 87. Toss with 1 pound fresh thin pasta, cooked and drained.

Artichokes Vinaigrette

□ See page 245.

12 artichokes
6 quarts water, more as needed

3 tablespoons salt
1 cup vinaigrette□

✧ Some people insist on rubbing artichokes with lemon juice to keep them from discoloring during preparation, but I've found this really doesn't help much.

1. Wash the artichokes well in cold water. Cut the stems even with the base so they can sit without wobbling.✧

2. Lay each artichoke on its side on a cutting board. Cut about 1 inch from the top. Use scissors to trim away the prickly points of the top two or three rows of leaves, and any dried or bruised leaves. In the center, within the leaves, you will find a fuzzy tuft—the "choke"—which is inedible. It's a job to remove the chokes before cooking, but you can do it by pulling the leaves apart, reaching into the center, and pulling away the prickly leaves around the hairy choke. Then use a spoon or small paring knife to scrape away the fuzz. The advantage to completing this chore first is that the artichokes will cook in about half the time. (I still prefer to wait until after cooking the artichokes, when the "chokes" pull right out.)

3. Meanwhile, bring the water to a boil in a large kettle or fish poacher. Do not use aluminum, else the artichokes will turn dark gray! Add the salt after water begins to boil.

○ I prefer to overcook these a bit so I can get at the last morsel of the luscious pulp. I think they are ready when a leaf can be pulled away from the base with ease.

4. Now add the artichokes and try, if you can, to keep the bases down. Return the water to a boil and cook the artichokes rapidly for 30–45 minutes.○ Add more water if too much boils away, and rotate artichokes in the pot if they are crowded.

5. Using a slotted spoon, remove from the water. Turn upside down on a dish or paper towels to drain. At this point, the fuzzy "chokes" will be easy to remove.

6. Turn the artichokes right side up on a platter, or special artichoke plates if you have them, and serve with vinaigrette in little individual dishes for dipping. Serves 12.

Espresso Zabaglione

This should be served warm the instant it is made. Make two batches, in front of guests.

3 eggs
6 egg yolks
⅔ cup sugar

½ cup very strong espresso coffee

1. Put all ingredients into a bowl and beat with a whisk.

2. Set over a pan of simmering water and beat until mixture thickens and is doubled in volume. Serve in small stemmed glasses. Serves 6-8.

10 CHILDREN'S PARTIES

Life styles flourish, fade, and change, but something there is in the instinct of a parent that vibrates to the call of a child's celebration— a birthday party, an occasion that commands attention. Today that parent may be Mom, the vice-president, or Dad, a single. While some roles may have changed, organizing a memorable party for one's child is something parents, even the busiest ones, do because they want to.

From bringing up three children, after many years of gaggles of kids gathered to celebrate every significant event from a second birthday to a high school graduation, I know that young people are bored by sit-down, stuffy parties. Action is what they crave. Once I rented a carousel to put in the backyard for a birthday party. At other times I've hired entertainers (there's always an older kid around who can do some confoundingly good magic tricks) or recruited an innocent bystander to dress up in a clown suit. Games are always good, provided they're carefully selected for the specific age group and attention span of the guests.

The menus in this chapter can easily be put together in an hour. I'm particularly proud of the Shell Game Party, which features hard-boiled eggs with shells that absolutely refuse to ravage the eggs when they are peeled, even by children. The eggs are cooked in very heavily salted water. It's a wonderful method I learned from one of my cooking school students, who heard about it from a poultry farmer.

If you haven't time for an afternoon or evening party, let your imagination control your schedule. How about breakfast? I once gave a graduation breakfast at 7:30 A.M. Some of the guests are now giving parties for their own small children, but they still tell me that morning party was one of their all-time favorites.

Letting the kids do a lot of the food work, with careful supervision when needed, subtly teaches them about cooking, handling utensils, and entertaining others, and it keeps them so happily occupied they don't even know they are being educated. In a real way, parties are a portion of their heritage from you. Have a good time!

"Shell Game" Party for 12 Children

Children love things in shells, husks, etc., and they love to have things to do. This party will keep them occupied! It sounds like a glorious mess, but really isn't. You can let the kids eat everything with their fingers and serve the ice cream in cones. That way, the only supplies you'll need are tons of paper napkins, some cups—and at least one large trash can.

MENU **Hard-Cooked Eggs in the Shell**
Peanuts in the Shell
Chicken Wings Lavished with Paprika
Corn on the Cob with Herb Butter
Half-Hour Homemade Philadelphia Ice Cream

BEVERAGE SUGGESTION: Lemonade

WORK ORDER: *Chicken Wings, Ice Cream, Hard-Cooked Eggs, Corn, Lemonade, and Peanuts*

Chicken Wings Lavished with Paprika

4 dozen chicken wings
½ cup vegetable oil
1 tablespoon finely chopped fresh garlic
1 tablespoon salt
1 tablespoon freshly cracked black pepper
¼ cup paprika

1. Lay chicken wings in a baking dish. You may need two dishes—make sure you have enough room to accommodate the wings comfortably. Brush them with oil, sprinkle the garlic over, then sprinkle on the salt, pepper, and paprika.

2. Place in a 350° oven. Bake 45 minutes and turn every 15 minutes to brown wings evenly.△

△ For further browning, you can run these under the broiler.

3. Serve warm or cold. Serves 4 wings each to 12 people.

Hard-Cooked Eggs

If you are an advanced cook, you will certainly share my excitement over this method of preparing hard-cooked eggs! For years the food establishment has been in a hullabaloo over how to boil eggs so that they can be peeled without being annihilated. It has been fashionable to blame the poulterers, the freshness of the eggs, the wax they are sealed in, and the background of the chicken that laid them. Everyone, and that includes me, griped. This fabulous method came from a student in my Crash Course. It works every time, with cold or room-temperature eggs, just-laid or a week old, in cold or boiling water. This is a wonderful trick and proves again the old adage that the best way to learn is to teach.

☆ If eggs are left over, they'll be good for salad or sandwiches later. Or prepare more for parents who call to claim their offspring.

□ 12 minutes for regular large eggs, 14 minutes for jumbos. If you keep them on much longer, they will develop a green ring around the yolk. It won't hurt anyone, but it looks awful.

◇ You can cook the eggs the night before and store them in the refrigerator.

24 eggs☆
2 tablespoons, no less, of
    salt

1. Drop eggs gently into boiling water to which you've added the salt. Reduce heat to a generous simmer and cook 12 minutes.□
2. Remove eggs from boiling water and plunge at once into a large bowl of ice water with a few ice cubes therein. Let cool 2-3 minutes.◇
3. Allow the children to peel their own eggs. Serves 12.

Peanuts in the Shell

Nut shops are appearing everywhere. If one is near you, get your peanuts there and know they'll be very fresh. Since peanuts keep well, it won't hurt to have some left.

3–5 pounds very fresh
    peanuts

1. Place peanuts on a baking sheet and warm them in a preheated 350° oven for about 10 minutes.
2. Place in a large bowl or serving basket and let the children shell as they go.

Corn on the Cob with Herb Butter

○ I like to use these in a combination of three. Use only one or two, if you prefer.

24 ears very fresh corn in the husk
¾ pound melted butter
Juice of ½ lemon, if desired
1 tablespoon finely chopped fresh herbs, such as parsley, tarragon, and chives○

Salt and pepper for the table

1. Let the children shuck the corn.
2. Place ears in a large kettle of boiling, unsalted water. Let water return to boil. Cook 3–6 minutes, depending on whether the ears are large or small.
3. Season the melted butter with lemon juice, if you like, and the chopped herbs. Provide paintbrushes so the children can dip into the butter bowl and "paint" their corn. Serves 12.

Half-Hour Homemade Philadelphia Ice Cream

One of my fondest childhood memories is our Sunday ritual of making ice cream. Mother prepared a very rich mixture, usually vanilla, and placed it in a can with a dasher, then into a wooden bucket filled with ice and rock salt. My three brothers and I sat on the outer cellar steps and took turns cranking the dasher until we could no longer budge it. Then Father appeared to give it a few more turns, and how we marveled at his strength! Arguments over who'd lick the dasher were settled by a toss of a coin. The bucket was emptied and repacked with more ice and rock salt and the ice cream was set to mellow in a dark corner of our cool cellar. Layers of newspapers and an old, tattered piece of Oriental carpet were put over the bucket to hold in the cold. I still make ice cream, and homemade always tastes best to me.

This version, Philadelphia ice cream, contains no eggs. I prefer to use unscalded whipping cream, about 35 percent butterfat content, to give the final creation a stick-to-the-roof-of-your-mouth texture. *For this party, you'll need to make two separate batches. Borrow an ice cream maker from a friend to help do the job.*

(continued)

1 quart whipping cream
¾ cup sugar
Pinch of salt

1 tablespoon pure vanilla flavoring, or the seeds scraped from one whole vanilla bean

1. Mix all ingredients together; stir till sugar dissolves.
2. Place in metal container of ice cream maker and arrange in the bucket of the machine. Pack with ice and rock salt, according to factory directions,△ and plug in.
3. Ice cream should require 20–30 minutes to freeze.
4. Repack with ice and salt until ready to use. Makes a little more than 1 quart. Serves 6.

△ The usual salt and ice ratio is 1 part salt to 8 parts ice. More salt will freeze ice cream faster, but makes it grainy.

Lemonade

☆ See p. 226.

1½ cups fresh lemon juice
Simple syrup to taste☆

Thin lemon slices

1. Fill a very large pitcher with ice cubes. Add lemon juice.
2. Sweeten to taste with simple syrup. Place in refrigerator.
3. Just before serving fill pitcher with water and stir well.
4. Serve from pitcher or pour into a large punch bowl and float lemon slices on top. This recipe makes a gallon, or a bit more than 1 cup each for 12 children. Since kids are always thirsty you'll probably need a second batch. Serves 12 children who are not very thirsty.

A Spud Party for 12 Kids

This is a nifty way to entertain when the budget is bent. The menu works fine for adults, too, but tell them it's a Baked Potato Party.

MENU   **Baked Potatoes with Trimmings**
Wilted Spinach Salad with Bacon Dressing
Caramelized Bananas

BEVERAGE: Lemonade for Kids, Beer for Adults

WORK ORDER: *Potatoes, Bananas, Trimmings, Salad*

Baked Potatoes with Trimmings

Thoroughly scrub 12 Idaho potatoes, more if you think you'll need them. Place on a rack in a 425° oven and bake 40–60 minutes. Remove, cut a cross on top, and fluff up each potato. Let each guest help himself or herself to trimmings from an assortment such as this:

1 pound butter
  Salt and pepper in mills
  Bowl of chopped chives or scallion tops
1 pound bacon, cooked and chopped (save grease for later use)
1 pint sour cream
  8-ounce jar Creole mustard

8-ounce jar sharp horseradish, or some freshly grated horseradish, if available
1 pint cottage cheese
  Bowl of freshly grated Parmesan cheese

This array will serve 12.

Wilted Spinach Salad with Bacon Dressing

3 pounds spinach, washed
2 cloves fresh garlic, chopped
1 tablespoon dry mustard
1 tablespoon sugar

½ cup red wine vinegar
  Bacon fat, saved from preceding recipe
  Salt and freshly cracked black pepper to taste

1. Wash the spinach by soaking it in tepid water to loosen dirt. Then rinse in cold water. Pat or spin dry. Remove stems by pulling them back. Place spinach in salad bowl.

2. Prepare salad dressing by placing the garlic, mustard, sugar, and vinegar into the skillet with the bacon fat. Bring to a boil and pour over salad. Toss and taste before adding salt and pepper—the bacon fat may be salty enough and the mustard may be hot enough. Add bacon bits, if you have them. Serves 8-12.

Caramelized Bananas

8 tablespoons butter
13 bananas, peeled
   Juice of 1 medium lemon
1 cup honey

2–3 tablespoons dark rum

1. Butter a baking dish with 2 tablespoons of the butter. Put bananas, whole or cut into 2-inch pieces, if you prefer, in a single layer, and sprinkle with lemon juice. Pour the honey on top and dot with the remaining 6 tablespoons of butter.

2. Bake at 350° for about 20 minutes; turn bananas over in the honey as they bake.

3. Just before serving, heat the rum and ignite. Pour over bananas. Serves 12.

11

IMPROVISING FOR DROP-INS

Sometimes I decide I love to cook because my life is interesting, and sometimes I think my life is interesting because I love to cook. Either way, spontaneity—no time to panic—brings out the best in me. When unexpected company comes, I gun into high gear and ask myself, "What's around here that I can throw together so it will land right?" Often I invent a new dish: once you've learned something about combinations of foods and techniques, this is the easiest kind of cooking.

My husband always calls before bringing anyone home to dinner, though he knows I'm not tetchy about cooking for drop-ins. On one occasion, he called to say an important client from Europe had dropped by the office. The man had been eating the *oeuvres* of great chefs in famous restaurants. In other words, he'd be a joy to cook for!

Now do you suppose that I thought of all the lavish meals he'd been eating and tried to dream up a yard-long menu? I'm at ease with *haute cuisine*, of course, and love to teach it to the most exacting students I can find, but in this case I would have been off the wall to aim for something ultrafancy. Besides, I knew my audience. A person who has been eating in restaurants for some time hankers for a good, simple, home-cooked meal. That evening we dined on baby lobster tails and soft-shell crabs from the freezer, rice, salad greens, and homemade ice cream served in meringues (made from leftover egg whites) with fresh raspberry syrup. Our guest said it was his favorite meal of the trip.

Spur-of-the-moment entertaining for a group, a party that just happens because we're having so much fun with friends that nobody wants to break up the evening, is another favorite of mine. After a concert, for example, serving Musician's Pasta and Carpaccio with Watercress Sauce is a charming way to keep the melody going. Or when everyone's smugly bushed and starving after a tennis workout, crêpes or omelets filled with something fresh, such as a green vegetable in a light sauce, can score aces at the table.

Whether you have an hour or a month, there are some fundamentals for planning a meal, and once you have them engraved on your mind, the rest flows naturally. Colors, textures, and balance of dishes are important, and so is presentation. If you haven't time to make a dish look really good, think of another one. No one wants a dish that does not excite the eye. Don't worry about sauces; one sauce per menu is quite enough. Oversaucing is a clue that you are a beginner, or are emotionally insecure and lack self-confidence. It's also a mistake to repeat any particular food in a later course, even if someone just gave you a whole crate of beautiful oranges, or your tomatoes are ripe and overabundant. The one exception to this rule is truffles, but most of us do not have truffle surpluses.

While the menus in this chapter require straightforward ingredients, I strongly urge you to read Chapter 14, "Weekends and Cooking Days." They are designed to help you deposit time when you have it, and cash in when you don't.

Truly great chefs improvise all the time. It's a mistake to forget that, after all, the art of cooking evolved from using foods that were available. *You* have more choices and better storage methods than any cook at any other time in the history of civilization!

The important thing is sincerely to want to serve your guests good food, to keep your menu simple and interesting—and then to enjoy yourself.

A Treat After the Little League Game

MENU   **Banana Doughnuts**
Fresh Cider from the Farmers' Market

Banana Doughnuts   These are quick and easy to make, and the delicate banana taste is fresh and unusual.

DOUGHNUTS

3 cups solid shortening or peanut oil
4 cups flour
¾ cup sugar
4 teaspoons baking powder
1 teaspoon salt
½ teaspoon ground cinnamon
½ teaspoon grated nutmeg
¼ cup butter
1 cup ripe mashed bananas
2 eggs, well beaten

TOPPING

¾ cup sugar
2 teaspoons ground cinnamon

1. In deep-fat fryer, heat oil to 375°.

2. In a large bowl, mix flour, sugar, baking powder, salt, cinnamon, and nutmeg. Cut in the butter.

3. Make a well in the center of the flour mixture; add bananas and eggs. Mix well; you may need to do this by hand with a wooden spoon, or even without one, since the dough will become rather heavy.

4. Turn out onto a lightly floured board and roll to ½-inch thickness. Cut with a floured 2½-inch doughnut cutter.

5. Deep-fry, a few at a time, until golden brown. Fry the "holes," too. Drain on absorbent paper.

6. Combine the ingredients for the topping. Roll warm doughnuts and holes in this mixture. Makes 22 doughnuts and 22 centers.

Junking Out: Any Number Can Play

MENU   **Popcorn**
       Salted Nuts
       My Mother's Fudge

BEVERAGE: Fruit Punch

WORK ORDER: *Fudge, Nuts, Popcorn*

Popcorn   2 tablespoons vegetable oil   Salt, if desired
¼ cup popcorn

Put the oil in a 2½-quart pot with a lid. Add the corn. Cover and turn flame to high. Shake the pan with authority. In a few minutes the corn will explode; keep shaking until most of the racket dies down. Remove lid and put into a bowl. Sprinkle with salt, if desired. Serves 4 (6 cups).

Salted Nuts   This is another of my favorite goodies. Prepared at home, they taste better because they're warm from the oven.

2 pounds pecans, almonds, cashews, walnuts, macadamias, or any combination you like	¾ cup French peanut oil Sea salt to taste

1. Put the nuts on a large baking sheet so they are in a single layer. Drizzle the oil over them with a large spoon; move the nuts around to coat them really well.
2. Put baking sheet on middle rack of a 375° oven. After 15 minutes, turn nuts over. Bake another 15 minutes, and remove from oven just before they burn. Be careful here—I think the nuts taste best when they have a deep, dark, roasted flavor, but not charred!
3. Remove nuts and place in a strainer for 10 minutes, to allow excess oil to run off. Shake strainer occasionally. Lay the nuts on a clean baking sheet and sprinkle with ground sea salt.
4. You can freeze these for later use by storing them in a tight can. Reheat for 5 minutes in a 350° oven.

My Mother's Fudge   How many times I've eaten this fudge from a spoon because I couldn't wait for it to set!

2 cups sugar	4 tablespoons butter
½ cup cocoa	1 teaspoon vanilla extract
1 cup milk	

1. Combine the sugar, cocoa, and milk in a saucepan. Stir to blend. Bring to a boil, stirring constantly. Then turn to simmer, and stir no more.
2. Cook until it reaches 238° on a candy thermometer, or until a drop of the mixture in a cup of cold water goes together and forms a soft ball in the fingers.
3. Remove from fire and add butter and vanilla.
4. Beat with a wooden spatula until the mixture loses its sheen. Pour into a buttered 8-by-8-inch pan and cool. Cut into squares. Makes about 5 dozen small pieces.

Come Over After Dinner for Backgammon—4 Players

> **MENU**   **Continuous Cheese Crock with Crackers, French Bread, or Thinly Sliced Black Bread**
> **Roasted Chestnuts**
> **Bowl of Fresh Ripe Apples**
>
> **WINE SUGGESTION:** A Jug of White or Red
>
> **WORK ORDER:** *Cheese Crock, Chestnuts*

Continuous Cheese Crock

I call this "continuous" because I store what is left over in the fridge. As I accumulate tidbits of cheese, I grind them and beat them in the mixer with the cheese from the crock. It goes on forever.

1 pound Cheddar cheese, ground or grated
½ pound soft butter
¼ cup brandy, sherry, or beer
1 teaspoon hot pepper sauce
2 tablespoons Worcestershire sauce
Salt, if needed

1. Beat the cheese in the mixer bowl about 5 minutes, or until very light and fluffy. Add the butter and continue to beat until quite creamy. Slowly beat in the remaining ingredients and taste for seasoning; you may need salt if the cheese is bland.

2. Pack into a crock or bowl and serve. Makes 12–16 servings.

Roasted Chestnuts

When I was a kid we roasted chestnuts in our big open fireplace. My father would sit in his huge leather chair and use his penknife to slit the chestnuts and cut up apples for us. The apples, picked from our own orchard and stored in our cold cellar, were so succulent the juices would run down our chins.

(continued)

1 pound chestnuts, or more if   Coarse salt, if desired
  desired

1. Cut a cross on the convex (round) side of each chestnut. Lay them on a baking sheet and place in a 400° oven for about 20 minutes, or until the cross opens up a bit.

2. Serve hot and let guests remove the shells. Eat plain, or dip into coarse salt. Serves 4.

Feeding 6 Football Fans

MENU   **My Aunt Sophie's Fried Chicken**
Red-Skin Potato Salad with Lettuce Leaves
Dione Lucas's Chocolate Roll

BEVERAGE: Beer

WORK ORDER: *Chocolate Roll, Salad, Chicken, Fill Roll*

My Aunt Sophie's Fried Chicken

My Aunt Sophie, my mother's sister, was almost as great a cook as my mother. The rivalry intensified because Aunt Sophie led a glamorous life: she was married to the first cornet player in John Philip Sousa's band and traveled with her husband. My mother had a lovely singing voice and had always wanted to be in musical comedy—but she was stuck at home with four kids. Sometimes one of Aunt Sophie's triumphs, such as this fried chicken, was enough to keep mother from speaking to her.

2–3 pounds frying chicken,   ½ teaspoon ground red
  cut up   pepper
1 cup flour   2 cups solid shortening
1 tablespoon salt   (Aunt Sophie used half
1 tablespoon paprika   lard and half rendered
                                           chicken fat)

1. Wash chicken and dry it well on a towel.

2. In a brown paper bag, mix the flour, salt, paprika, and pepper together. Shake the chicken, a few pieces at a time, in the bag.

3. Heat the shortening to the point of smoking in two 10-inch black iron skillets, if you have them, or any heavy pan or pans. The objective is to have enough pan space to keep the pieces of chicken from touching. Put 6 pieces of chicken, skin side down, in each pan. Leave flame on high for 5 minutes. Reduce heat to medium, cover pan, and cook 15 minutes. Lift lid, turn chicken over (do not pierce skin: the juices will run out), and fry covered for another 10–15 minutes. Chicken should be crisp on the outside and moist inside.

4. Lay on a brown paper bag to drain, then place on a baking sheet on a rack and keep warm in a 300° oven. Serves 6.

Red-Skin Potato Salad with Lettuce Leaves

24 red-skin potatoes (about 3 pounds)
1 tablespoon salt
½ cup vegetable oil
¼ cup red wine vinegar
¼ cup finely chopped white of scallions
Salt and freshly cracked black pepper to taste
2 tablespoons finely chopped fresh parsley
A few large lettuce leaves

1. Wash potatoes. If they are large, cut them in half but leave the peel on. Put them in a pan and cover with water. Add the salt; bring to a boil. Lower heat to medium, cover, and cook 15–20 minutes, or until potatoes can be pierced easily with the tip of a sharp knife. Drain.

2. Pierce each potato with the tip of a knife or skewer in a couple of places. Put them in a bowl and, while still warm, pour over them the oil, vinegar, scallions, salt, pepper, and parsley. Toss well and let stand at room temperature to marinate.

3. To serve, place in a bowl and surround with tender lettuce leaves standing up around the edge of the bowl. I like to use oak-leaf or red-leaf lettuce if possible. Serves 6.

Dione Lucas's Chocolate Roll

There is no chocolate dessert in the world like this one from my beloved teacher. In this recipe, try to use *couverture,* or coating, chocolate.

2 tablespoons vegetable oil
½ pound dark sweet chocolate
5 tablespoons liquid coffee
7 eggs, separated
1 cup sugar

½ cup sifted cocoa
1 cup heavy cream
2 tablespoons confectioners' sugar
1 teaspoon vanilla extract

1. Oil a 10-by-15-inch jelly-roll pan with 1 tablespoon of the oil. Cover with aluminum foil, and coat with the other tablespoon of oil.

2. Melt the chocolate in a pan with the coffee and cool.

3. Beat the egg yolks and mix in the sugar. Beat until thick and pale yellow. Carefully add the coffee-chocolate mixture.

4. Beat the egg whites until fairly stiff. Fold into the egg yolk–chocolate mixture.

5. Spread evenly on the baking sheet and bake on the middle shelf of a 350° oven for 15 minutes.

6. Remove and cover with two layers of paper towels which have been wrung out in cold water, then cover with a dish towel and allow to cool to room temperature. Remove towel; dust roll with cocoa.

7. Whip the cream with confectioners' sugar and vanilla. Spread over the cake and roll it up as you would a jelly roll.

8. Present, uncut, on a wooden board. Serves 6.

Come Over for Dessert and Coffee for 8

MENU　Two-Kinds-Chocolate Cake Roll with White Chocolate Sauce

BEVERAGE: Coffee or Ice Water

WORK ORDER: *Roll, Sauce*

Two-Kinds-Chocolate Cake Roll

White chocolate—the good kind, not the imitation variety—is made of cocoa butter, vanilla bean, sugar, and milk. This recipe originally appeared in my book *Menus for All Occasions* in 1974—well before white chocolate was "discovered" by *nouvelle cuisine*.

CAKE

½ pound white chocolate
5 tablespoons strong coffee
2 tablespoons vegetable oil
7 eggs, separated
1 cup granulated sugar
2 tablespoons dark crème de cacao or Kahlúa

FILLING

1½ cups heavy cream
½ cup unsweetened cocoa, less if desired
¼ cup confectioners' sugar, more if desired
2 tablespoons dark crème de cacao or Kahlúa

1. *Make the cake:* Melt the white chocolate in the coffee over low heat. Set aside to cool.

2. Oil an 11-by-17-inch jelly-roll pan, line with wax paper, and oil the wax paper. Set aside.

3. With electric mixer, beat egg yolks in a bowl. Gradually add granulated sugar and beat until mixture is very light and creamy. Add the chocolate-coffee mixture and blend well. Add 2 tablespoons crème de cacao or Kahlúa.

4. In another bowl, with clean beaters, beat egg whites until stiff. Fold them into the chocolate mixture and spread in jelly-roll pan.

5. Bake 15 minutes in a 350° oven. Turn oven off, but leave pan in oven 5 more minutes.

6. Remove cake from oven and turn out onto two overlapping strips of wax paper. Carefully remove the wax paper with which you have lined the cake pan, then cover cake with a double thickness of paper towels wrung out in cold water. Cool.

7. *Make the filling:* Whip the cream, and add ¼ cup of the cocoa, confectioners' sugar, and crème de cacao or Kahlúa. Spread on cake and roll up as you would a jelly roll.

8. Just before serving, dust the cake with the remaining ¼ cup cocoa or with an equivalent amount of confectioners' sugar. Serve with the following sauce. Serves 8–10.

White Chocolate Sauce

This very rich and creamy sauce has a delicate chocolate flavor and looks beautiful on the pale yellow and chocolate-brown cake.

3 ounces white chocolate
1 egg, well beaten
¾ cup light cream, or 1 cup if you like a thin sauce

⅓ cup sugar
1 teaspoon vanilla extract

1. Melt chocolate in a pan over hot water.
2. Combine egg, cream, and sugar. Blend well. Add this mixture to melted chocolate, whisking until mixture is smooth.
3. Cook over hot water, stirring occasionally, for 15 minutes.
4. Remove from heat. Add vanilla and beat until smooth. Makes about 1⅓ cups sauce. Serve hot or cold.

Anywhere, Anytime Meal for 10 to 12

MENU   **Delancey Place Fish Soup**
Toasted French Bread
Fruit and Cheese

WINE SUGGESTION: Pouilly Fuissé or Pinot Chardonnay

Delancey Place Fish Soup□
□ My guests have dubbed this dish Delancey Place after the street where I live.

✧ See page 238.

¼ cup or more olive oil
2 large onions, chopped
4 garlic cloves, chopped
1 cup chopped celery
4–5 pounds very ripe tomatoes, peeled, seeded, and chopped
1 bottle dry white wine
Salt and freshly cracked black pepper to taste
A few fresh basil leaves
½ teaspoon saffron threads

½ teaspoon thyme
4 pounds thick fish fillets, cut into chunks (I use haddock, grouper, or halibut)
2 cups fish stock✧ or enough to cover fish
24 cleaned mussels, or more
24 cleaned clams
⅓ cup finely chopped fresh parsley

1. Heat olive oil in a large kettle. Add onions, garlic, and celery. Cook, stirring with a wooden spatula, about 15 minutes.

2. Add tomatoes, wine, salt and pepper, basil leaves, saffron threads, and thyme. Cook 10 minutes more.

3. Add fish. Pour on the fish stock and bring to a boil. Lower heat. Add mussels and clams, throw the chopped parsley on top, cover, and simmer 15–20 minutes. Serves 10–12.

Homemade Pizza for 4 After a Movie

Homemade Pizza

CRUST

1 package dry yeast, or 1 cake

¼ cup water, about 110° for dry yeast, 95° for cake Olive oil

1 teaspoon salt

⅔ cup lukewarm water About 3 cups flour

FILLING

4–5 pounds tomatoes, peeled

6 tablespoons olive oil

6 sliced onions

1 tablespoon chopped fresh oregano

Salt and freshly cracked black pepper to taste

½ pound mozzarella cheese, coarsely grated

½ cup grated Parmesan cheese

1. *Make the crust:* Soak yeast in ¼ cup water, at temperature directed, for at least 5 minutes.

2. Meanwhile, put 2 tablespoons olive oil, salt, and ⅔ cup lukewarm water in a large bowl. Add the yeast.

3. Add the flour, a cup at a time, beating after each addition. After the second cup the mixture will be stiff. Add the third cup, turn out on a lightly floured board, and knead for about 5 minutes. Brush lightly with olive oil, cover with a cloth, and let stand 30 minutes—no longer.

4. Brush a 12-inch pizza pan lightly with olive oil. Roll dough into a large circle and place in the pan. Form a slight rim around the edge. Prick all over with a fork and let stand about 15 minutes.

(continued)

5. Bake in a preheated 400° oven 10–12 minutes, until very lightly browned. Remove to a cake rack and cool. This shell can be filled, cooled, and baked again. It can also be refrigerated or frozen.

6. *Meanwhile, make the filling:* Cook the tomatoes in 2 tablespoons of the oil for about 10 minutes.

7. Cook the sliced onions in the remaining 4 tablespoons of oil until they are soft, about 20 minutes.

8. Mix onions and tomatoes together and arrange over pizza shell. Sprinkle on the oregano, salt, and pepper; then layer on the mozzarella and add grated Parmesan. Heat in a 400° oven for 5 minutes. Serves 6.

Anytime Snack for 6

French Toast Rounds with Maple Syrup

These toast rounds are a variation on the usual French toast theme, and they have a beautiful golden color. You can use them for a kids' snack, breakfast, brunch, dessert, whatever.

TOAST

2–3 cups oil or solid shortening
1 loaf Italian or French bread, 2 inches in diameter
1½ cups milk
2 egg yolks
2 tablespoons Madeira or sherry
1½ tablespoons confectioners' sugar

TOPPING

½ cup confectioners' sugar
½–¾ teaspoon ground cinnamon
1½ cups pure maple syrup

1. In the deep fryer, heat the oil to 375°.

2. Cut bread into 1-inch slices; remove crusts.

3. In a bowl, combine the milk, yolks, wine, and 1½ tablespoons confectioners' sugar. Soak bread in this mixture.

4. Deep-fry rounds, a few at a time, in the hot fat, about 1½–2 minutes on each side. Drain on absorbent paper.

5. Combine the ½ cup confectioners' sugar and the cinnamon. Roll toast rounds in this mixture, and place in a pyramid on a platter.

6. In a small saucepan, heat the maple syrup until it nearly boils. Serve in an earthenware pitcher with the toast rounds. Serves 6.

Main-Course Soufflés: Improvisations

How well I remember Dione Lucas beating egg whites in her copper bowl when she taught her famous TV cooking classes in the late 1940s! She'd throw the bowl over her head, the egg whites never dropped out, and everyone oohed and aahed. I could not wait to buy a bowl and beat egg whites in it—and I did, for years. When I became a cooking teacher and opened my own school, I continued to teach that method for years—until I became bored with what I thought was nonsense. To all the conversation and written pieces on chemical reactions between egg whites and copper, electrolytic reactions, etc., I say—Balderdash!

By now I have made thousands of soufflés, and given a choice, I'll beat, with my Hobart mixer, egg whites—and nothing else. Knowing when to stop beating is the secret: the whites must be stiff but not dry. In my classes, using the same recipe and same ingredients, we've experimented three ways: mixer, rotary beater, and whisk with copper bowl. The ones made with the mixer are the highest. No acid, such as cream of tartar, is necessary, though this is great if you want a soufflé to hold up a bit longer, as restaurants do. Let's remember that copper was the most readily available metal in France when these techniques were first written down. All my French chef friends use the mixer, too!

I'm still devoted to the old rule about soufflés that everybody knows: people wait for soufflés—they don't wait for people.

Main-Course Soufflé

3 tablespoons butter
3 tablespoons flour
1 cup milk

5 egg yolks
6–7 egg whites, at room
    temperature

1 cup whatever is handy, such as:

Crumbled cooked bacon
Cheese, shredded or
    grated
Spinach or sorrel,
    cooked and squeezed
    dry
Broccoli and sautéed
    onion, chopped fine

Crabmeat flavored with
    2 tablespoons Madeira
    and sautéed shallots
Cooked chicken, turkey,
    or ham, chopped
Sautéed sliced onion

1. In a nonaluminum saucepan, melt the butter over high heat. Stir in the flour with a wooden spatula. Cook, stirring constantly, for a few minutes. Do not let the flour brown.

2. Remove saucepan from heat and add the milk, whisking vigorously, then return to the heat and cook. Stir constantly until the mixture comes to a boil and is thick and smooth. Add the cup of "whatever is handy." Set aside to cool○ slightly before adding the egg yolks.

○ This step is important: if mixture is too hot, the yolks will curdle when you add them in the next step.

3. Beat yolks together in a small bowl, then beat them into the basic mixture.

4. With a clean bowl and clean beaters, use electric mixer to beat egg whites until stiff, but not dry.

5. Take about a third of the beaten whites and stir them into the basic mixture. This will make it lighter, so that the rest of the beaten whites will blend in more easily. Then fold in the remaining whites with a rubber spatula. Work quickly and gently: it's better to leave a few little white bubbles showing than to overmix and deflate the whites.

6. Using an ungreased, 1½-quart soufflé dish, bake in a preheated 375° oven for 30 minutes, or until nicely browned on top. If you want the outside to be crusty, bake on the bottom shelf of the oven; for a creamier version, place the soufflé in a pan of hot water and bake 45 minutes. Serve immediately. Serves 6–8.

Basic French Omelets: Improvisations

Perfect for any impromptu occasion at any time that calls for quick thinking and good cooking, the omelet is the stock-in-trade of a cook. Once you get the knack of it—and this requires practice—it's easy to make beautiful omelets every time. As for fillings, improvise! Spinach, cheese, tomato, bits of ham, meat, fish, or bacon, vegetables, avocado, sausage, jam, smoked salmon—almost anything can be used to make a crowd-pleasing omelet.

If you haven't mastered omelets yet, use these instructions—and I repeat, *practice.* Your finished product should be a perfect oval shape, pointed at both ends, plump in the center. The outside should always be pale yellow in color; the inside, mellow or creamy. Try to use a rather heavy pan that is not too large: one that measures about 8 inches across the bottom is perfect. For a large group, it's much easier to make a lot of small omelets than a few large ones: a small one cooks in only 30 seconds anyway. This basic recipe is for one omelet.

Basic Omelet

THE OMELET

3 large fresh eggs
Salt and freshly cracked white pepper to taste

1 generous tablespoon butter

THE FILLING (use one of the following)

½ cup fresh spinach leaves, sorrel, or watercress (not cooked—they cook in the egg)

2–3 tablespoons grated or shredded Cheddar, Parmesan, Roquefort, or blue cheese

½ cup fresh tomato, peeled, seeded, and chopped

¼ cup diced cooked ham, chicken, or fish

¼ cup cooked sausage, drained

2–3 tablespoons jam or jelly

¼ cup diced smoked salmon

1. Heat the pan as slowly as you can. Test it with a little piece of butter to see if it sizzles. The butter must not brown. If it does, wave pan in the air a couple of times to cool it. Add rest of butter.

(continued)

2. Meanwhile, put the eggs in a bowl with salt and pepper. With a fork or whisk, beat 30–40 times.

3. Pour eggs into the pan. The second they hit, take a fork in your right hand and hold the handle of the pan in your left hand. Stir mixture with the flat of the fork, tines flat on the bottom, while you shake the pan to and fro. Stir first clockwise, then counterclockwise, shaking pan all the while. Do this with spirit and zeal; in about 30 seconds, remember, you will have made a beautiful omelet!

4. As soon as the omelet looks as though it is *starting* to set, pat it out evenly to the sides of the pan. If you are using a filling, this is the time to add it.

5. Slide the fork around the edge of the pan, fold the omelet over, and turn out onto a dish. Serves 1.

Flat Omelets: Improvisations

Flat Omelet

△ See preceding recipe.

☆ Serve with sour cream and a lime wedge on the side.

□ Serve with freshly grated Parmesan cheese on top.

Proceed as with French omelets,△ but do not stir with the fork; simply cook the eggs flat. Toss one of the following directly on top of the eggs (or add to beaten egg):

½ cup shredded raw carrot☆

½ cup shredded zucchini☆

¼ cup raw minced onion□

½ cup peeled, seeded, and chopped tomato□

¼ cup crumbled bacon□

Cook omelet flat and turn out on platter. Cut in wedges and sprinkle with parsley. Serves 1.

Basic Crêpes: Improvisations

Basic Crêpes

½ cup flour
¼ teaspoon salt
2 eggs
2 egg yolks

¼ cup vegetable oil
½ cup milk
Oil for pan

1. Put flour, salt, eggs, egg yolks, the ¼ cup vegetable oil, and milk into a blender and blend at top speed, or whisk until smooth. If batter is lumpy, strain it. Refrigerate for 45–60 minutes.

2. Before frying, check consistency of batter. It should be that of heavy cream. If it is too thick, thin with a little milk or water.

3. Film a seasoned crêpe pan with oil, heat it over high flame to the point of almost smoking, then fry the crêpes.✧ You will need 2–3 tablespoons of batter for a dessert crêpe, a scant ¼ cup batter for an entrée crêpe.

4. Fry each crêpe 1 minute, or until the edges are brown, as you tilt the pan in all directions to spread batter evenly. Crêpe should be very thin. Turn crêpe and fry on other side for about 30 seconds.○ Film pan lightly with oil before making each crêpe. Makes twelve 5-inch crêpes or eight 7-inch crêpes.

✧ Use a 5-inch pan for dessert crêpes; a 7-inch pan for entrée crêpes.

○ Put the 30-second side *inside* when you fold or roll each crêpe.

Fillings for Crêpes

☆ See page 241.

| 1 recipe Basic Crêpes | Grated Parmesan cheese |
| 1 teaspoon melted butter for each crêpe | 2½ cups Béchamel Sauce☆ |

1 cup of something, such as:

Crumbled cooked bacon
Grated Cheddar, Parmesan, Roquefort or blue cheese
Cooked spinach or sorrel, drained and squeezed dry
Chopped cooked broccoli

Crabmeat sprinkled with 2 tablespoons Madeira
Cooked chopped chicken or turkey or ham
Sautéed sliced onions

1. Into 1½ cups of the béchamel, fold 1 cup of "something."

2. Fill crêpes with the mixture, roll, and place in gratin dish. Pour over the remaining béchamel and melted butter, and dust with grated cheese. Bake at 350° for about 15 minutes, or until bubbly. Makes eight 7-inch crêpes.

Basic Quiche: Improvisations

Basic Quiche

☆ See page 246.

1 partially baked 9-inch Pâte Brisée Shell☆
2 eggs
2 egg yolks

2 cups light cream
Salt and freshly cracked white pepper

1½ cups of something, such as:

Crumbled cooked bacon
Grated or shredded Cheddar, Parmesan, blue, or Roquefort cheese
Cooked spinach or sorrel, squeezed dry

Cooked broccoli, chopped
Crabmeat sprinkled with 2 tablespoons Madeira
Cooked ham, chicken, or turkey, chopped
Sautéed sliced onions

1. Prepare and partially bake the pâte brisée shell.
2. Beat together in a bowl the eggs, yolks, cream, salt, and pepper. Add "something" and mix. Fill shell and bake at 350° for 30 minutes, or until set.

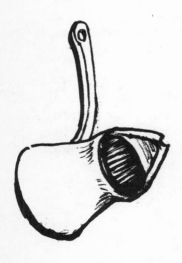

12 COME FOR CASSE-CROÛTE!

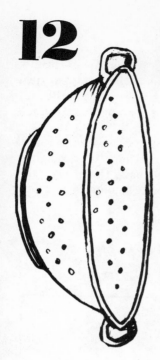

I have borrowed from the French a charming phrase to describe a casual little party. It is *casse-croûte* and means, literally, "to break a crust"—from *casser le croûte*. What I am offering, really, is a suggestion for a name for a form of entertaining that provides more food (and less booze) than a cocktail party, but requires less time (and money) than a cocktail buffet or traditional dinner. When you invite your guests to *casse-croûte,* they'll soon learn what they can expect is a hearty main dish and good, crusty bread (so you will have a crust to break).

A quick meal, an ample repast—a *casse-croûte*—fits comfortably into today's design: there is space for a name for a simple party that is big-hearted with food. *Casse-croûte,* while nothing pretentious, isn't makeshift, either. The term suits the occasion: a tad low-key, but with a certain elegant friendliness.

I realize that I might be accused of taking license with the French language. So? Isn't it true that the French snitch words from us all the time?—witness *le cowboy, le diet, le cocktail.*

I would not, however, want to do harm to a beautiful language, so I consulted with professors of French at two major universities, Temple and Pennsylvania, along with a French-born and -educated expert on current idiomatic usage of her native tongue. All were marvelously enthusiastic about the idea of an American version of *casse-croûte.* The Temple University professor, who is himself the author of several books, said, "It's a great name for a party, and I'd like to come."

Then he added, "Besides, if the French can market a little thing called Le Car in the United States when the word *car* in French means 'a big vehicle'—a *bus,* for God's sake—they haven't much room to talk about linguistic purity. Just be sure you serve some good bread."

The University of Pennsylvania professor agreed, but to cover all bases, she referred me to the expert on idiomatic usage. This lady told me that *casse-croûte* in French is a delightfully flexible term, extremely informal, with usage varying according to the region in which you travel. In her liltingly accented English, she said, "Be surrre to serrrve a good crrrusty bread!"

How about a late-evening Casse-Croûte After the Championship

Basketball Game? Or a Come Straight from Work Casse-Croûte, which will enable you to entertain your friends without a great deal of time and trouble, and let everyone make a merry but early evening of it? I hope *casse-croûte* can do for the evening what brunch has done for the middle of the day.

Following are some menus to lead you onto the *casse-croûte* route. The form of the function is flexible, its applications wide-ranging. Along with letting people know you'd like to have them over, the only other sure bet about *casse-croûte* is nobody's going to go home hungry.

Casse-Croûte for 6 to 8 After the Championship Basketball Game

□ See page 106. This soup is ideal for people on diets

MENU   Four Kinds of Soup
           Double Mushroom Bisque
           Squash Soup
           New England Clam Chowder
           Avgolemono□
         Loaf of French Bread
         Loaf of Unsliced Rye-and-Pumpernickel Bread
         Crock of Sweet Butter
         Cookies

BEVERAGE: Little Glasses of Sherry

WORK ORDER: *Bisque, Squash Soup, Chowder, Avgolemono*

Double Mushroom Bisque

✧ See page 240.

2 tablespoons dried mushrooms	1 tablespoon flour
½ cup Madeira or sherry	2 cups chicken stock✧
6–8 tablespoons butter	2 cups milk
½ cup chopped onions	Salt and freshly cracked white pepper to taste
1½ pounds fresh mushrooms, chopped	½ cup heavy cream
2 tablespoons lemon juice	2 tablespoons chopped fresh parsley

1. Soak the dried mushrooms in the Madeira or sherry for 15 minutes.

2. Meanwhile, place 6 tablespoons of the butter in a pan. Sauté in it the onions and mushrooms. Add lemon juice and stir with a wooden spatula for 5 minutes.

3. Chop the soaked mushrooms. Add them, along with the soaking liquid, to the onion-mushroom mixture. Sprinkle in flour, stir in with a wooden spatula, and cook 5 minutes longer.

4. Add the chicken stock, milk, salt, and pepper. Bring to a boil, cover, and simmer 20 minutes. Add heavy cream. Swirl in 2 tablespoons of butter to enrich, if desired. Sprinkle parsley on top before serving. Serves 8.

Squash Soup

○ You can substitute other varieties of squash, such as zucchini, crookneck, or patty pan.

△ See page 240.

2 tablespoons butter
¾ cup chopped green onions
2 pounds butternut squash, sliced○
6 cups or more of chicken stock△

Salt and freshly cracked black pepper to taste
Freshly grated nutmeg
1 cup thick sour cream

1. In a pan, melt butter and sauté the onion in it. Add the squash, cook, and stir for 5 minutes. Add chicken stock—enough to just cover the squash—and cook until tender, about 20 minutes. Add salt, pepper, and nutmeg.

2. Purée in the blender or on fine disk of food mill. Blend in the sour cream. Serves 8.

New England Clam Chowder

☆ Add these to the clam liquor.

6 slices bacon, diced
2 medium onions, chopped
¼ cup chopped celery
4 cups peeled, cubed potatoes
2 cups boiling water
3 cups cream
2 tablespoons butter

1½ cups clam liquor (if necessary, use water)
Salt and freshly cracked white pepper to taste
2 dozen large clams, opened, cut into bite-size pieces, all juices saved☆

1. In a large kettle, cook bacon, onions, and celery until bacon is cooked and vegetables are tender, about 10–12 minutes. Add potatoes and boiling water and cook 5 minutes longer.

2. Add cream, butter, clam liquor, salt and pepper. Cook 10–15 minutes. Adjust seasoning. Add clams and cook 5 minutes. Serves 8.

Winter Night Casse-Croûte for 8

MENU   **Sausages (from a Farmers' Market):**
Unsliced Whole Rolls of German Bologna
Braunschweiger
Hard Salami
Small Whole Roll of Provolone
Creole and Düsseldorf Mustards
Shredded Carrots Vinaigrette□
Rye and French Loaves
Baked Apples with Barely Whipped Cream✧

□ See page 245 for vinaigrette sauce.

✧ See page 242.

BEVERAGE: Dark Beer

WORK ORDER: *Apples, Carrots, Arrange Wursts on Cutting Board*

Casse-Croûte à l'Italienne for 8

MENU   **Pasta with 2 Sauces: White Clam○**
Braci di Fero△
Sliced Tomatoes, Cucumbers,
and Onions Vinaigrette
Italian Bread
Fresh Orange Slices with Curaçao

○ See page 190.

△ See page 189.

WINE SUGGESTION: White Corvo

WORK ORDER: *Pasta, Sauces, Oranges, Tomatoes, Cucumbers, and Onions*

Casse-Croûte After Leaf-Raking for 6

MENU   **Keftedes (Greek Meat Rolls)☆**
Feta Cheese with Black Bread, Butter,
and Assorted Olives□
Cherry Tomatoes with Scallions
Pears Poached in Wine✧

☆ See page 107.

□ See page 107.

✧ See page 36.

WINE SUGGESTION: Zinfandel

WORK ORDER: *Pears, Keftedes, Feta Cheese, Tomatoes*

13 CHEERS: DRINKS HOMEMADE AND OTHERWISE

Every household has a list of drinks, alcoholic and nonalcoholic, that are house specials. Sometimes a drink rates because it's a holiday tradition (the only reason I can think of for the popularity of eggnog, which I consider dreadful); sometimes a particular drink conjures up memories of a person, or occasion, that we remember fondly. The recipes I've included for drinks in this chapter are ones that are my favorites, for various reasons.

I'm pleased to see that drinks made with fruit juices are back in vogue. Some restaurants make a point of using only freshly squeezed juices, which I think is a wonderful idea. The fresh tastes and lovely colors of fruit drinks enhance a festive gathering. By considering the fruits that are in season before you decide on what to serve, you'll give yourself and your guests a bonus in pleasure and interest.

Salute!

Bloody Mary

This is probably the most common morning drink in the United States today. (When I order a Bloody Mary in a restaurant, I always ask for vodka on the side, just to be certain I'm not being shortchanged.)

☆When fresh tomatoes are in season, squeeze them for this drink, and revel in the difference!

2 ounces vodka
3 ounces tomato juice☆
2 tablespoons lemon, lime, or sauerkraut juice

Worcestershire sauce and Tabasco to taste
Salt and freshly cracked black pepper to taste
Slice of lemon or lime

Shake all ingredients (except lemon or lime slice) with ice. Serve, with or without ice, in a glass garnished with lemon or lime slice. Serves 1.

Charles Baker's Sunday Morning Cocktail

1½ ounces cognac
1 ounce port wine
    Demitasse of espresso or strong coffee

1 egg
Sugar to taste

Shake with ice and pour into a stemmed cocktail glass. Serves 1.

Milk Punch: My Answer to Eggnog

This is good both for the holiday season and for hangovers.

2 ounces brandy
1 ounce rum

1 lump of sugar
3 ounces milk

Shake with ice. Serves 1.

Cuba Libre

Today this is just plain Rum and Coke, but in the Havana of thirty years ago the Cuba Libre was quite romantic.

2 ounces rum
Coca-Cola

Juice of ½ lime

Over ice in a glass, pour the rum and fill with Coca-Cola. Squeeze in lime juice, stir, and serve to 1.

Screwdriver   2 ounces vodka   Fresh orange juice

Into a 6-ounce glass, place ice cubes, vodka, and enough fresh orange juice to fill the glass. Stir and serve to 1.

Kir   3–4 ounces white wine   ¼ ounce cassis

Pour ingredients into a white wine glass. Stir lightly. Serve with or without ice, as preferred. Serves 1.

Sangría   ½ cup sugar   1 pint brandy
1 cup water   1 pint club soda
1 thinly sliced lime   Lime and orange slices for
1 thinly sliced orange   garnish
1 bottle dry red wine

1. Combine sugar and water in a small saucepan and heat, stirring, until sugar is dissolved. When syrup reaches the boiling point, remove from heat and add lime and orange slices. Let cool before using.

2. At serving time, fill a pitcher one-fourth full with ice cubes. Add fruit syrup, wine, brandy, and club soda and stir with a wooden spoon. Garnish each glass with citrus slices. Serves 6.

Bellini   This drink originated at Harry's Bar in Venice; the recipe I like is from the Gritti Palace Hotel in that city. It is especially delightful and refreshing in the summer, at the height of the peach season. (If peaches are not really sweet, a tiny bit of sugar and lemon juice can be added.)

2 very ripe fresh cold peaches   Italian champagne

Remove skins and pits of peaches. Purée peaches in blender or food processor. Add enough Italian champagne to equal the amount of peach purée and mix well. Serve in chilled wine goblets. Serves 2.

Mint Julep   Since I was recently named a Kentucky Colonel by the governor of that state, I have taken to mint juleps all over again. This drink also brings me fond memories of my late brother-in-law, who used to claim that for a decent mint julep, the mint had to come from "the shady side of the barn." Well, even though we have no barn, our friends supply us with fresh mint and we serve a pretty mean julep at our house.

4 large sprigs mint   2½ ounces bourbon
1 small lump sugar

     1. Chill a large highball glass or julep cup in the freezer for 15 minutes.
     2. In a separate glass, muddle 3 sprigs of mint with a teaspoon of water and a small sugar cube.
     3. Remove glass from freezer and add muddled mixture.
     4. Fill glass with crushed ice.
     5. Add bourbon, but do not stir. (Some of my friends insist on stirring juleps with a silver spoon until the outside frosts. Take your pick of methods.) Decorate with a mint sprig. Serves 1.

Fish House Punch   This famous punch is supposed to be from a secret recipe of a men's dining club in Philadelphia. Most Philadelphians, however, have their own versions. Fish House Punch is especially popular after football games. This recipe comes from *The Philadelphia Cookbook* by Anna Wetherill Reed, published in 1940 by Barrows.

¾ pound loaf of sugar   1 quart cognac
2 quarts water○   1 wineglass peach brandy
1 quart lemon juice

○ In winter, when the ice in the punch bowl melts slowly, you may want to use more water; in summer, you may need less.

     1. Dissolve sugar loaf in water in the punch bowl. When all the sugar is dissolved, add lemon juice, cognac, and brandy.
     2. Put a large lump of solid ice into punch bowl and allow mixture to mellow until serving time, or at least 30 minutes, stirring occasionally. This recipe will make 1½ gallons. Serves 10–12.

1-2-3-4 Planter's Punch

△ See page 226.

This recipe was given to me by my husband, who is an excellent maker of drinks and has his own formula for this one.

1 ounce sour,
2 of sweet,
3 of power, and
4 of weak

1 part lemon or lime juice
2 parts simple syrup△
3 parts rum
4 parts crushed ice

Mix juice, syrup, and rum. Pour over crushed ice. Serves 1.

Negroni

The first time I had a Negroni (a popular drink in Italy) was in Rome, in the 1950s. Actually, I had two or three—and that night I slept for fourteen hours.

1½ ounces gin
1½ ounces sweet vermouth

1½ ounces Campari
Lemon twist

Stir together all ingredients except lemon twist. Pour into a glass filled with cracked ice. Decorate with twist. Serves 1.

Old White Club White Spider

This is one of the most popular—and most lethal—drinks from the Greenbrier Hotel in West Virginia.

2 ounces vodka

1 ounce white crème de menthe

Shake over ice and serve in a glass filled with chipped ice. Serves 1.

Irish Coffee

I'm not a connoisseur of alcohol-and-coffee drinks; usually I prefer my coffee strong and black. Nonetheless, I'd rather have this than dessert.

1 teaspoon brown sugar
1 cup hot, strong coffee

2 ounces Irish whiskey
2 tablespoons whipped cream

Put the brown sugar into a large, *thick* highball glass. Add coffee to two-thirds of the way up; stir to dissolve sugar. Add Irish whiskey, leaving room in the glass to add the whipped cream on top. Serves 1.

Homemade Fruit Cordials

Homemade fruit cordials, with vibrantly natural flavors and bouquets, add a dramatic finale to your home-cooked meals and are superb gifts for friends. I discovered these gorgeous concoctions in Italy, where almost every little restaurant has its own special creation, and wrote about them in the May 1979 issue of *House and Garden*.

The Italians use the fermented pressings of grapes, *grappa,* as a base. Since we in the United States do not ordinarily have access to *grappa,* I experimented and found that a number of white liquors, among them vodka, gin, tequila, and white rum, work fine.

In Venice, I consulted with several chefs and found that the basic ingredients they use in fruit cordials are white spirits, simple syrup, and fresh, peak-ripe fruit. This mixture is stored in a covered crock or wide-mouth jar in the refrigerator for three months. After the first three weeks, taste the mixture and adjust; if it's too sweet, add more white liquor; if it's too spirited, more sugar syrup.

When the three months are up, serve your cordials in tiny vodka glasses, if you have them, or use the colorful drink, fruit and all, as a sauce for ice cream. Each season you can have your own house-brand cordials that evoke the bounties of the months just past. Keep the seasons rotating!

I realize these cordials cannot be made and served on the spot, but they require so little preparation time and are such glowing treats I wanted you to know about them.

Basic Simple Syrup

☆ Sometimes I cut this to 1 cup, which makes for a lighter, less sweet syrup.

2 cups water   2 cups sugar☆

Mix together in a pan, bring to a boil, and allow to boil for 5 minutes. Let cool.

Raspberry Cordial☐

☐ Or use other berries, such as strawberries or blackberries.

2 cups simple syrup (above)   1 bottle vodka
1 pound raspberries

1. In a crock with a cover or a wide-mouth jar, place the simple syrup and raspberries. Add vodka. Cover and place in refrigerator.

2. Wait at least two weeks to let fruit mellow. Taste for sweetness and adjust by adding more simple syrup or more vodka. Tighten lid and let mellow for about eleven weeks longer. At first the berries will float on the top, then gradually they will sink to the bottom.

Orange and Coffee Bean◇ Cordial

◇ Or leave out the coffee beans and use prickly pears, mangoes, or persimmons instead of oranges.

3 oranges
27 coffee beans, plus ¼ cup coffee beans

2 cups simple syrup
1 bottle tequila

1. Cut three slits down the side of each orange. Insert 3 coffee beans in each slit. Put into a jar and add the ¼ cup coffee beans.
2. Add simple syrup and tequila, seal, and store in refrigerator for three months. The liquid will probably turn dark from the coffee beans, but the orange flavor will still be there and the cordial will look deliciously unusual. Serve in frosted, tiny glasses.

Ginger Cordial

1 cup crystallized ginger
1 cup sugar

1 bottle vodka

Note that plain sugar, not simple syrup, is used here. Place all ingredients in a jar, cover, and let mellow in refrigerator for three months.

Fresh Pineapple Cordial

☆ See page 226.

1 fresh pineapple, peeled, cored, and cut into rings

2 cups simple syrup☆
1 bottle white rum

Place all ingredients in a container with a cover. Seal and let stand in a refrigerator for three months.

Fresh Fig Cordial

◇ See page 226.

12 fresh figs, green or purple
1 cup simple syrup◇

1 bottle vodka or gin

Place all ingredients in a container. Cover and allow to mellow in refrigerator for three months.

Seckel Pear Cordial

12 little seckel pears
½ cup sugar

1 bottle vodka

Mix ingredients in a container, cover, and refrigerate for three months.

Prune and Raisin Cordial

□ Or use a pound of dried apricots and omit the raisins.

○ See page 226.

1-pound box dried prunes□
Handful of white raisins

1 cup simple syrup○
1 bottle vodka or white rum

Mix ingredients in a container, cover, and refrigerate for three months.

Mint Cordial

☆ See page 226.

Large bunch of mint, crushed

2 cups simple syrup☆
1 bottle white rum

Mix ingredients, put in a covered container, and allow to mellow for three months. This is good for adding to a fruit compote.

Lady Apple Cordial

□ See page 226.

About 12 little lady apples, whole and pricked
2 cups simple syrup□

½ cup sugar
1 bottle rum or gin

Mix ingredients in a container, cover, and allow to mellow in a refrigerator for three months.

Fresh Peach Cordial

○ See page 226.

About 6 fresh peaches
Handful of almonds in the skin

2 cups simple syrup○
1 bottle vodka or gin

Mix all ingredients in a container and cover. Let mellow in refrigerator for three months.

Cherry or Kumquat Cordial

☆ See page 226.

1½ pounds Bing cherries or 12 fresh kumquats

1 cup simple syrup☆
1 bottle sake or vodka

Mix ingredients in a container, cover, and let stand in refrigerator for three months. Try this as a substitute for dessert after a Chinese dinner.

Zesty Winter Cordial

✧ See page 226.

About 2 cups zest (no pith) from oranges, lemons, grapefruits, or limes

2 cups simple syrup✧
1 bottle vodka or gin

Mix ingredients in a container, cover, and let stand in refrigerator for three months.

Nonalcoholic Fruit Punch

△ See page 226.

4 cups fresh orange juice
2 cups fresh grapefruit juice
1 cup fresh lemon juice
¼ cup grenadine syrup (optional)

Simple syrup△ to taste
1 quart club soda
Orange slices

Pour all juices into a large pitcher of cracked ice. Mix together. Add grenadine, if you wish, and simple syrup. Fill pitcher with club soda, taste again for sweetness, adjust accordingly, and stir to chill. Float orange slices on the top. Serves 8.

My Favorite Strong Coffee

Most often I buy a blend of mocha and Java coffee beans and have them finely ground at the shop, or grind them myself as I use them. While I have a number of coffee makers, my standby is a Chemex, which uses a paper filter and keeps the coffee clear. Whatever your choice of pots, remember that the finest coffee in the world can be ruined by a pot that is not thoroughly clean. You also diminish the flavor of the coffee by using the wrong size of pot: it should be brewed full (but if you use a percolator, make sure the water in the pot does not touch the bottom of the coffee basket). Almost everyone needs at least two pots, a smaller one for just the family and a larger one for entertaining.

(continued)

Terrible tap water makes terrible coffee. At home in Philadelphia (where no honest person would claim our city water tastes good; we just brag that it's plentiful), I use water from a filter in my kitchen.

If you like your coffee feckless and submissive, I can't help you: I make mine strong! I use 2 tablespoons of finely ground coffee for each cup of water, plus an extra tablespoon for the pot.

Since it has become a pricy item on the marketing list, nobody wants to waste coffee. If you've made too much, don't let it stand in the pot overlong; it will take on an acrid taste. Keep it in a tightly covered jar in the refrigerator.

Iced Coffee

I make double-strength coffee for this.

☆ See page 226.

| 1 cup double-strength brewed coffee | Simple syrup☆ Cream |

Pour coffee over ice cubes in a tall glass. Sweeten with simple syrup to taste and add cream if desired. Serves 1.

Barbara's Iced Capuccino

For a hangover pick-me-up, add a bit of brandy.

| 1 heaping teaspoon instant coffee | 1 teaspoon sugar 2 ice cubes |
| 1 cup cold milk | Dash of nutmeg |

In a blender, mix all ingredients except nutmeg until smooth. Sprinkle with nutmeg. Serves 1.

Hot Tea

Like most Americans, I am not much of a tea drinker. I like it only when I'm sick, and usually I am quite healthy. Someone once said that Americans don't incline toward tea because they still haven't gotten over the Boston Tea Party, and he was probably right. Yet—after water—tea is the most popular beverage in the world. Its endless varieties and legends are as romantic as those of wine.

This method for making hot tea is the one recommended by most tea experts:

1 teaspoon loose tea or	Water in full boil
1 teabag for each cup	

Before brewing the tea, rinse the pot with hot water to warm it. Pour out this water. Put tea or teabag in pot. Meanwhile, bring *cold* water to a full, rolling boil and at the moment this occurs, pour it over the tea in the pot. Let stand and steep at least 3 minutes, no longer than 5, lest it begin to release tannin, which changes the flavor to great disadvantage. Serve with lemon or cream and sugar—or straight, depending on the kind of tea you are using.

Iced Tea

While hot tea leaves me cold, I adore iced tea and could drink it all year round. The one gripe I have is that cold tea sometimes clouds up, which looks awful. Years ago a friend taught me a method I have used ever since: it's delicious, and the tea does not diminish in clarity. Put 12 tea bags into a half-gallon jar. Fill with cold water and tightly cover the jar. Place in refrigerator for 12 hours before using.

Cocoa for (Big or Little) Kids

½ cup cocoa	more, to taste
3 tablespoons sugar, or	4 cups milk or half-and-half

Mix cocoa and sugar together. Heat the milk to the boiling point. Add a bit of the hot milk to the cocoa-sugar mixture and stir to blend. Add remaining milk. Serves 4.

Espresso

A friend in Italy gave me a little octagonally shaped coffee pot called a Moka Express which I cherish. It makes three cups of espresso for me. These pots are now common in this country, and I urge you to buy one if you haven't done so already. The pot comes in three parts. You fill the bottom part with water up to the little steam valve. Insert the middle part, the coffee basket, and fill it with 2½ tablespoons of finely ground strong coffee, then screw on the top part. Put over a direct flame. Soon you'll hear a noise like a gurgling baby volcano: the coffee will shoot up through a spout in the center of the top of the pot, and that's all there is to making delicious espresso.

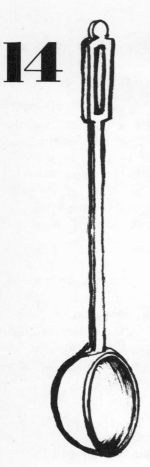

14 WEEKENDS AND COOKING DAYS: SAUCES, STOCKS, AND OTHER INDISPENSABLES

Even though neither you nor I have time to make every day a cooking day, there are certain fundamentals—homemade stocks, bread from scratch, your own mayonnaise—that separate the women from the girls and the men from the boys in the kitchen. Homemade touches just won't keep their secret!

The recipes in this chapter are referred to repeatedly in the marginal notes throughout this book. If you can't merge your time with an all-out cooking spree, you can let your time do double duty. A recipe that calls for three hours in the oven is often no more trouble than one which screams for thirty minutes of constant tending. A stock simmering contentedly needs only an occasional skimming.

When a food you like is fresh and in season, it's a shame not to take advantage of its abundance. If mushrooms are a good buy, make and freeze *duxelles*. Exquisite ripe berries can be transformed into sauces and syrups and great drinks. Make a double recipe of the dish you'll serve tonight and freeze the other half for a frantic day two weeks from now. While you have the rolling pin out, make several pie crusts and freeze them. Yeast breads keep beautifully when frozen and will emerge to comfort you on a day when everyone's crabby and the washing machine breaks down.

Along with the practical benefits, there are other rewards from a cooking day. There are times when one *wants* to cook, when out must come the pots and pans, the bones saved in the freezer, the fresh vegetables and fruits demanding attention. The sheer, lusty urge to work with food, pat and touch it, feel its textures, bite into its lusciousness, and behold its natural gorgeousness overwhelms the creative cook, generates an energy demanding expression. Yield to the impulse!

A Well-Stocked Freezer

☆ Cook when in season, freeze in small containers for soups and sauces. Just stew in butter 2–3 minutes, put in plastic bags, and seal.

□ I wash, dry, and cut these to freeze in the early fall, when they are abundant. I store them in a plastic bag, with air pushed out, top tied, and set in a coffee can with a plastic lid. Sometimes I put a basil leaf on top before sealing.

Tart shells, baked or
    unbaked
Stocks, in 1-cup containers
    Chicken
    Fish
    Beef or Veal
Fresh tomato sauce
Cookie doughs
Breads
Nuts
Leek and sorrel bases☆
Duxelles
Tiny bread cups
Croutons
Filo leaves

Bread crumbs
Meat juices
Ice cream
Fresh homemade pasta
Melba toast
Boned chicken breasts
Crêpes
Shrimp
Bacon
Frozen fresh herbs
Soups
Applesauce
Cupcakes
Fresh tomatoes□

A Well-Stocked Refrigerator

△ See page 203.

Vinaigrette
Homemade mayonnaise
Chocolate sauce
Raspberry and
    strawberry sauce
Simple syrup
Selection of cheeses:
    Block of Parmesan
    Gruyère
Garlic
Shallots
Fresh ginger
Sour cream
Continuous Cheese Crock△

Salad greens
Selection of fresh fruits
Milk
Cream
Eggs
Butter
Jelly glazes:
    Apricot
    Currant
Marinated olives
Meat juices from roasting
    pans and skillets
Vegetable water

Raspberry Vinegar

In the nineteenth century, most cookbooks featured recipes for raspberry vinegar. This is one of them. Raspberry vinegar at that time was made with sugar and used as a base for summer drinks. It is used now in mayonnaise, vinaigrette, and some chicken dishes.

3 quarts raspberries (1 quart a day for 3 days)
1 quart vinegar

2 cups sugar for each pint of mixture

1. Wash 1 quart raspberries; drain. Place in a crock or jar, pour in the vinegar, and let stand one day.
2. The second day, strain off the vinegar onto a second quart of fresh raspberries. Let stand overnight.
3. On the third day, strain off the vinegar again and pour it over the third quart of raspberries.
4. On the fourth day, strain off the vinegar a third time. Add 2 cups of sugar to each pint of vinegar mixture, place in a pan, and bring to a slow simmer. When it is scalded through, place in jars and seal while still hot.

Basic Rice Pilaf

✧ See page 240.

○ See page 240.

½ cup butter or other fat
1 medium onion, chopped fine
1 cup long-grain rice
2 cups chicken stock,✧ brown stock,○ or water

Salt and freshly cracked black pepper to taste
2 tablespoons chopped fresh parsley

1. Melt ¼ cup of the fat in a heavy casserole (one with a tight-fitting lid) and sauté the onion over high heat. When onion is translucent but not brown (about 2 minutes), add the rice. Stir it around to coat the grains with butter.
2. Add stock or water, salt, and pepper. Bring mixture to a full boil over high heat, then cover it tightly and reduce heat to simmer.
3. Cook exactly 23 minutes (use a timer, if possible), and do not lift the lid during this time. Then lift the lid, fluff up the

rice with two forks, sprinkle with the remaining ¼ cup butter, which you have melted, and border with chopped parsley. Serves 6–8.

Rice Timbales

△ See page 234.

1 recipe Rice Pilaf△
2 tablespoons finely
   chopped celery
1 clove chopped garlic

Freshly grated nutmeg to
   taste
Oil to grease molds

1. Follow recipe for Rice Pilaf, but add celery, garlic, and nutmeg to the cooking liquid. Bring liquid to a boil and continue with recipe as directed.
2. When rice is cooked, pack it while hot into 8 small oval molds greased with oil. Pack firmly. Let molds set for 1 minute before turning them out. Serves 8.

Saffron Rice Pilaf

☆ See page 240.

This is a spicier version of the basic pilaf.

2 tablespoons butter
2 tablespoons olive oil
1 medium onion, finely
   chopped
½ teaspoon chopped garlic
1½ cups long-grain rice

1 teaspoon saffron threads
3 cups chicken stock ☆ or
   water
Salt and freshly cracked
   white pepper to taste

1. Using a heavy casserole that has a tight-fitting lid, heat the butter and oil. Sauté, but do not brown, in it the onion and garlic (this will take about 3 minutes).
2. Add the rice, stirring it around to coat the grains with butter and oil.
3. Dissolve saffron in 1 tablespoon of the stock. Pour remaining stock into the casserole and add the dissolved saffron, salt, and pepper. Bring to a full boil over high heat; immediately cover tightly and reduce heat to simmer.
4. Without lifting the lid, cook for 23 minutes. Then remove lid and fluff the rice with two forks. Makes 6–8 servings.

Rice Salad

1 cup long-grain rice
Salt and freshly cracked
  black pepper
¼ cup olive oil
2 tablespoons wine vinegar
2 teaspoons Dijon mustard

2 cups mixed cooked
  vegetables: carrots, green
  beans, peas, corn, etc.
½ green pepper, finely diced
½ cucumber, peeled and
  diced

1. Put rice, salt, and pepper and 2 cups water in a small heavy pan or casserole with a tight-fitting lid. Bring to a boil, cover, then reduce heat and simmer for 20 minutes. Do not remove the lid during this time.

2. Put cooked rice in a bowl, add oil, vinegar, and mustard, and toss with a fork to mix.

3. Gently mix in the cooked vegetables (leftovers will work well), green pepper, and cucumber.

4. Taste to adjust seasoning. Place in refrigerator 30 minutes or more before serving. (If you wish to serve this in a special shape, oil a mold and pack rice into it before refrigerating. Unmold at serving time.) Serves 8.

Bread Crumbs

Save all old or leftover bread. Dry out in a 350° oven for 10 minutes. Grind in food processor or blender. One slice bread makes ½ cup crumbs.

Duxelles

This mixture of very finely chopped mushrooms and shallots cooked in butter is one of the most versatile basics in cooking. It can be frozen almost indefinitely and will keep in the refrigerator for as long as ten days. Use *duxelles* to stuff a fish; combine with bread crumbs to stuff chicken; fill whole tomatoes; stuff chicken breasts; stuff eggplant; stuff under skin of chicken; stuff deviled eggs; or spread on Melba toast that you sprinkle with grated Parmesan cheese and melted butter, and heat under a broiler.

½ pound mushrooms, very
    finely chopped
¼ cup butter

¼ cup finely chopped
    shallots
Salt and freshly cracked
    black pepper

1. Put chopped mushrooms in the corner of a tea towel and wring them out to remove excess liquid.
2. Melt butter in a skillet. When it is foaming, add chopped shallots. Cook over high heat for a few minutes, stirring with a wooden spatula until shallots are transparent. Do not let them brown.
3. Add mushrooms and cook 15–20 minutes. Stir constantly with wooden spatula until mushrooms look dry. Season with salt and pepper. Cool. Makes about 1 cup.

Marinated Olives

Your own home-marinated olives are elegant to serve when unexpected guests arrive. I buy them in large jars, or loose at the deli. Just pour the brine off the olives, place them in a jar, and add 4 cloves mashed garlic. Fill the jar to the top with olive oil, cover, and refrigerate. They will keep indefinitely.

Beer Batter

Make this at least an hour before you use it, and let it stand at room temperature. It will keep in the refrigerator for up to three or four days. Use beer batter for frying almost anything—shrimp, oysters, onion rings, mushrooms, eggplant, zucchini, finger-size pieces of fish, apple rings, and fresh pineapple chunks, to name a few ideas.

12-ounce can beer
1–1¼ cups flour, lightly
    spooned
1 tablespoon salt

1 teaspoon paprika
½ teaspoon baking powder

Pour the beer into a bowl. Add the flour (the mixture will foam). Stir in the salt, paprika, and baking powder. The mixture will thicken as it stands. Makes about 2½ cups.

Court Bouillon   Use court bouillon for poaching any fish or shellfish, but put them into simmering, not boiling, court bouillon, so as not to toughen the fish.

2 cups dry vermouth or other dry white wine, or 2 cups cider vinegar	2 teaspoons salt
	8 peppercorns
	3 sprigs parsley
½ cup chopped onion	1 bay leaf
½ cup chopped carrot	1 clove
½ cup chopped celery	½ teaspoon dried thyme

Put all ingredients and 2 quarts cold water into a large saucepan or kettle. Bring to a boil, and boil rapidly for 30 minutes. Strain and cool. Makes 9–10 cups.

Meat Glaze   When a recipe calls for beef concentrate, it is only beef stock, strained and reduced to a syrup, or meat glaze. Simply boil 3 quarts of beef stock in a large kettle for 30 minutes, or until it is reduced to 1 quart. Strain this into a small saucepan and boil 30 minutes longer, or until it is reduced to 1½ cups. Pay attention as the mixture intensifies, and do not let it scorch. Cool about 1 hour; store in a covered jar in refrigerator, where it will keep for about two months. Makes 1½ cups.

Fish Stock

□ Recipe follows.

1 cup sliced onion	1 cup dry white wine
½ cup sliced celery	Bouquet garni□
½ cup sliced carrot	Salt and freshly cracked white pepper to taste
2 pounds fish bones and trimmings, all from lean fish	

Put all ingredients and 1 quart of cold water into a kettle or stock pot and bring to a boil. Skim. Reduce heat, half-cover the pot, and simmer another 30 minutes. Strain through a fine sieve. Makes 3–4 cups.

Bouquet Garni

1 rib celery
1 bay leaf
3–4 sprigs parsley

¼ teaspoon dried thyme (or fresh if available)

Make a sandwich of the celery: lay herbs on half the rib, fold the other half over, and tie with a string. Leave one end of the string long enough to tie to the handle of the pot or casserole so it will be easy to remove.

Velouté Sauce

○ See page 240.

✧ See page 238.

☆ See page 241.

¼ cup butter
¼ cup flour

2½ cups chicken○ or fish✧ or veal☆ stock

1. Melt butter in a saucepan. Stir in flour with a wooden spatula and cook over high heat, stirring constantly, for 2 minutes.
2. Remove from heat, switch to a whisk, and add the stock. Whisk vigorously for 3 minutes.
3. Return pan to heat and cook, stirring, until sauce thickens and comes to a boil. Makes 2 cups.

Basic Brown Sauce

□ See following recipe.

✧ See recipe above.

○ See page 238.

3 tablespoons butter
¾ cup finely chopped onion
½ cup diced carrot
4½ teaspoons flour
2 cups brown stock□
1 tablespoon chopped shallot

2 cloves garlic, chopped
Bouquet garni✧
2 teaspoons tomato paste
Freshly cracked black pepper
½ teaspoon meat glaze○

1. Melt butter in a small pan. Add onion and carrot and cook over high heat for 5 minutes, stirring with a wooden spatula. Blend in flour and cook, stirring constantly, about 10 minutes, or until nicely browned.
2. Remove pan from heat and change to a whisk. Add the brown stock, beating vigorously. Add shallot, garlic, bouquet garni, tomato paste, pepper, and meat glaze.
3. Return pan to heat and bring mixture to a boil. Reduce the heat, cover pan, and cook over *very* low heat for 30–60 minutes to intensify flavor.
4. Strain through a fine sieve; adjust seasonings. Store in a covered jar in refrigerator for up to 1 week, or in freezer for 2 months. Makes 1 cup.

Brown Stock

2 pounds cubed lean veal
brisket or shin
2 pounds split veal bones
1 veal knuckle
1 cup sliced carrots
1 cup sliced celery, with
leaves
2 medium onions, peeled
4 whole cloves △

1 cup dry white wine
1 clove garlic, mashed
½ teaspoon dried thyme
1 bay leaf
3 sprigs parsley
2 tablespoons tomato paste
Salt and freshly cracked
black pepper to taste

△ Stick cloves into onions before cooking.

1. In a roasting pan, put the veal, veal bones, knuckle, carrots, celery, and onions with cloves. Place in a preheated 450° oven for about 30 minutes, or until veal is thoroughly browned. Stir vegetables occasionally to prevent scorching.

2. Remove vegetables when browned; place them, and the meat and bones, in a deep kettle or stock pot.

3. Pour 1 cup of water into the roasting pan; scrape up the brown bits. Pour this mixture into the kettle.

4. To the mixture in the kettle, add enough water to make 4 quarts in all. Add the wine, garlic, thyme, bay leaf, parsley, tomato paste, salt, and pepper and slowly bring to a boil. Skim. Reduce heat, half-cover the kettle, and simmer gently for 4 hours.

5. Strain through a sieve which has been lined with a double thickness of cheesecloth, wrung out in cold water. This will keep in refrigerator for up to 1 week, if boiled every day, or frozen for up to 2 months. Makes 2–3 quarts.

Extra-Strong Brown Stock

If a recipe requires this, simply boil brown stock without a cover over moderately high heat until it is reduced by one-third.

Chicken Stock

4 pounds chicken backs,
wings, necks, and giblets, or
a 4-pound whole chicken
1 cup sliced carrots
1 cup sliced celery, with
leaves
4 medium onions, peeled
4 whole cloves □

1 cup dry white wine
1 clove garlic, mashed
1½ teaspoons thyme
1 bay leaf
3 sprigs parsley
2 tablespoons tomato paste
1 tablespoon salt
Freshly cracked black
pepper

□ Stick the cloves into the onions before cooking.

1. Place all ingredients and 4 quarts of cold water in a deep kettle or stock pot. Slowly bring to a boil. Skim; reduce heat and half-cover the kettle. Simmer gently for 1½ hours.

2. Remove the chicken, strip the meat✧ from the bones, return bones to the kettle, and simmer for another 2½ hours.

✧ Use the meat in any recipe that calls for cooked chicken, or freeze.

3. Wring out in cold water a cheesecloth, double thickness, and use it as a lining for the sieve. Strain the stock through this.

4. Stock can be stored in refrigerator for up to a week, if boiled every day, or in the freezer for up to 2 months. If a recipe calls for extra-strong stock, boil, uncovered, over moderately high heat, to reduce by one-third. Makes 2–3 quarts.

Veal Stock

Follow the preceding recipe for chicken stock, substituting veal and veal bones for the chicken.

Béchamel Sauce

This basic white sauce has a number of uses which call for differences only in consistency.

	BUTTER	FLOUR	MILK
Thin—			
for cream soups	1 tablespoon	1 tablespoon	1 cup
Medium—			
for sauces	2 tablespoons	2 tablespoons	1 cup
Thick—			
for soufflé bases	3 tablespoons	3 tablespoons	1 cup

1. Melt the butter in a saucepan, being careful not to let it brown. Add the flour and stir with a wooden spatula, moving the mixture all around the bottom of the pan. Do not allow this roux to take on any color. Let it bubble and foam on the bottom of the pan for 3 to 5 minutes.

2. Add the milk (hot or cold) and switch to a whisk immediately. Whisk mixture until it thickens. Cook over low heat for 20–30 minutes. Season with salt, freshly cracked black or white pepper, and freshly grated nutmeg to taste. Makes 1 cup.

Whipped Cream   I still prefer to whip heavy cream with a piano-wire balloon whisk, using a metal bowl set in another bowl of ice. Whipped by this method, and sweetened with confectioners' sugar (about 1 tablespoon for each cup of heavy cream), whipped cream is less likely to turn into butter and will not separate on standing. Confectioners' sugar should be added when the cream is mounding softly.

Barely Whipped Cream   This is somewhere between heavy cream that you can pour and whipped cream that stands tall: with a piano-wire balloon whisk, in a metal bowl over ice water (unless the cream is thoroughly chilled), whip the cream until it *just barely* begins to mound.

Basic Mayonnaise   Learn to make mayonnaise with a whisk—the classic method—before you use any machines. It's so simple, and satisfying, you may never want to give up your whisk.

Before you begin, bear in mind that if you add the oil too quickly, the mixture will separate. (Please do not listen to anyone who tells you mayonnaise *curdles*: it *separates*. Curds must form if a mixture curdles; this is what happens to hollandaise when the egg yolks are overheated.)

Should you goof, the easiest method for rectifying mayonnaise is to put 1 egg yolk into a small bowl. Whisk and gradually add the separated mixture teaspoon by teaspoon while whisking. Eventually the mixture will recombine.

1 teaspoon salt	1½ cups oil (any kind you select)
3 egg yolks	
½ teaspoon freshly cracked black or white pepper	1–2 tablespoons vinegar or lemon juice
1 teaspoon mustard, Dijon style or dry	

1. In a bowl, mix the salt, egg yolks, pepper, and mustard. Whisk well. Begin adding the oil a teaspoonful at a time. Continue to whisk until the mixture emulsifies (thickens).

2. Add the oil a little more rapidly, in a thin stream, as you whisk.

3. Finish with 1–2 tablespoons vinegar or lemon juice, depending on consistency desired. Makes 1½ cups.

Variations

Add to Basic Mayonnaise any of the following puréed vegetables:

The white part of cooked leeks
A carrot, peeled and cooked
A little cooked fresh spinach or sorrel. (This is quite good with fish.)

Blender Mayonnaise

Use the same ingredients, in same amounts, as for basic mayonnaise, but note that the sequence for mixing is a bit different.

1. Blend salt, pepper, egg yolks, mustard, and vinegar or lemon juice with *2 tablespoons* of the oil for a few seconds to mix.
2. With blender on high speed, add the remaining oil in a thin stream. Stop blender as soon as mayonnaise thickens.

Quick Aïoli

○ See page 242

1 cup basic mayonnaise○
2–3 teaspoons chopped garlic
  (to taste)

2 tablespoons dry bread
  crumbs
A touch of ground red pepper

Mix all ingredients in a bowl.

Hollandaise Sauce

Remember that the butter must be very hot for hollandaise. Use a heavy pan that is not aluminum (which will make the eggs turn greenish). I like to use a small, heavy copper pan. Hollandaise should not be served hot: the food on which it is served should be hot. You can make this sauce in advance and reheat it by placing it in a pan over a pan of simmering water; whisk and serve.

(continued)

½ cup butter

3 egg yolks

2 tablespoons lemon juice

¼ teaspoon salt

¼ teaspoon freshly cracked white pepper

1. Melt the butter, but be careful not to brown it.

2. In a small heavy pan that is not aluminum, place the egg yolks and 3 tablespoons of cold water. Over high heat, raising and lowering the pan constantly so as not to let it overheat, whisk together the yolks and water.△ If the outside of the pan gets too hot, the sauce will curdle. If necessary, remove the pan from the heat entirely—but don't stop whisking. Do this for about 10 minutes, or until the mixture begins to mound. It should have the consistency of heavy cream.

△ This egg yolk and water mixture is called a *sabayon*.

3. Remove the pan from the heat, and whisk in ¼ cup of the hot melted butter, *a tablespoon at a time* (4 tablespoons in all).

4. Return the pan to high heat, keep whisking, and add the remaining hot melted butter in a thin stream. Whisk until the mixture is thick and creamy—this should take about 5 minutes—and continue to move the pan on and off the heat.

5. Add lemon juice, salt, and pepper. If necessary to wait a while before serving, place the pan over a pan of warm water and whisk now and then. If the sauce seems too thin, return it to the stove—still moving pan to keep it from overheating—and whisk until it thickens.

6. If the sauce should curdle, you can rectify it by whisking in 1 tablespoon of cold water or 1 tablespoon of boiling water. Another method is to whisk an egg yolk in a bowl, then whisk the sauce into it, very slowly.

Blender Hollandaise

Using the same ingredients, same measures, as preceding hollandaise sauce, blend the egg yolks, lemon juice, salt, and pepper for 1 minute. Turn blender to high speed and pour in the very hot melted butter in a thin stream. The sauce will thicken, and it will hold over warm water until serving time—but whisk it now and then.

Béarnaise Sauce

Béarnaise is a relative of hollandaise and thus requires the same care in handling over the heat. Also, it should be served warm (not hot) over food that is hot.

1 tablespoon chopped
  shallots
½ cup tarragon vinegar
3 tablespoons finely
  chopped fresh tarragon
3 egg yolks
½ cup melted butter, very
  hot but not browned

¼ teaspoon salt
¼ teaspoon freshly cracked
  white pepper
2 tablespoons chopped fresh
  parsley, if desired

1. In a small heavy pan, over moderately high heat, put shallots, vinegar, and tarragon. Cook, stirring with a wooden spatula, for about 5 minutes or until all the liquid evaporates. (Be careful not to let it burn.)

2. Remove pan from heat. Add the egg yolks and 2 tablespoons of cold water; whisk together until well blended.

3. Return pan to heat, and raising and lowering the pan to keep mixture from becoming hot, whisk until mixture is the consistency of heavy cream.

4. Remove pan from heat and whisk in 4 tablespoons of the hot melted butter, *1 tablespoon at a time.*

5. Again returning the pan to the heat, keep whisking as you add the remaining hot melted butter in a thin stream. Whisk until the mixture is thick. Season with salt and pepper.

6. If you want to stir in the parsley, you might want to strain the béarnaise sauce first. Makes ¾–1 cup.

Basic Vinaigrette

A true vinaigrette is simply salt, freshly cracked pepper, oil, and vinegar. The oil can be olive, vegetable, French peanut, or any oil you choose, straight or in combination. I cut olive oil with vegetable oil, or use French peanut oil.

Yes, I put olive oil in the refrigerator, even though it does become cloudy when it's chilled. This does not impair the flavor, and at the price of olive oil today, I prefer cloudiness over rancidity. While I like a reasonable supply of vinegars, I do not care for the fancy ones that have been introduced by the *nouvelle cuisine* rage. I usually stock tarragon, cider, red wine, sherry wine, and raspberry vinegar. (Raspberry vinegar, incidentally, has been around for a long time and was turned into cooling summer drinks a century ago. See page 234 for the recipe.) Sherry wine vinegar is one I really like: I buy it in

Spanish neighborhoods, where it is less expensive. Sometimes, for the acid, I prefer to use lemon juice in vinaigrette, and sometimes I add a few chopped shallots, a touch of chopped garlic, a little Dijon mustard, or a fresh herb.

☆ Or lemon juice.

1 teaspoon salt
½ teaspoon freshly cracked
  black pepper

2 tablespoons vinegar ☆
6 tablespoons oil

Whisk all ingredients together in a bowl. Pour over salad just before serving. Makes ½ cup.

Pâte Brisée Shell

This buttery, flaky crust is my preference for quiches. It also makes lovely tarts and turnovers.

□ If you use salted butter, cut salt to ½ teaspoon.

2 cups loosely packed flour,
  plus extra for dusting on
  rolling surface
1 teaspoon salt

½ cup chilled unsalted
  butter□
¼ cup vegetable shortening

1. In a bowl, place the 2 cups flour and stir in the salt. Cut in the butter and shortening with a pastry blender. If you use your fingertips, lift the mixture up and let it fall off your fingers. Work quickly so the mixture will stay cool; when ready, it should look like small peas.

2. Add just enough ice water, a tablespoon at a time, to hold the mixture together. You will need about 3–4 tablespoons of water. Sprinkle the water on the flour mixture and toss with a fork. Mixture is ready when it can be formed into a dough ball: if it is still crumbly, add another tablespoon of water. The more humid the air, the less water you will need. If you use too much water, the crust will be tough.

3. On a lightly floured pastry board or marble surface, flatten the ball of dough and roll it in all directions with a rolling pin that has been lightly floured. Keep turning the dough to roll it into an even circle. Use more flour on the rolling surfaces if needed, to keep dough from sticking.

4. Use a pastry scraper to roll the dough around the rolling pin, then unroll it over a 9-inch pan or flan ring. Take care not to stretch the dough as you ease it into the pan. Trim off excess by gliding and moving the rolling pin over the top of the

pan or flan ring. Press dough over the top edge of the pan or ring to keep it from shrinking away from the pan as it bakes. Prick dough with a fork, all over the bottom.

5. Before baking, line dough with wax paper or aluminum foil and fill it with dried beans or rice to keep crust from puffing up during baking.

For a quiche: Bake at 375° for 20–25 minutes, or until set, then remove beans, wax paper, and flan ring, add the filling, and continue baking as recipe directs.

For tarts: Bake in a 350° oven for 30 minutes, then remove beans, wax paper, and flan ring, reduce heat to 325°, and bake 20–25 minutes longer, or until pastry is a pale gold color. Remove from oven and cool on a rack at room temperature.

Parmesan Bread Crumb Crust
✧ See page 236.

If you are *really* in a hurry, use this crust for quiches.

¾ cup dry bread crumbs✧   3 tablespoons grated
¼ cup melted butter   Parmesan cheese

Mix all ingredients together in a bowl and press into a 9-inch pie dish. Bake at 400° for 5 minutes, or until set.

Praline Powder

This will keep, in a covered container, on the shelf for a month. Use it on ice cream.

Butter   ¼ teaspoon cream of tartar
1 cup blanched or   1½ cups sugar
  unblanched almonds

1. Grease a baking sheet with butter.

2. Put almonds, cream of tartar, and sugar in a heavy saucepan; over medium heat, stir constantly with a wooden spatula until the sugar melts and mixture turns a dark-brown color. After about 15 minutes, the mixture will be ready: it will give off a slight puff of smoke and boil up vigorously. When this happens, remove saucepan from heat at once.

3. Immediately pour the mixture onto the buttered baking sheet. When mixture hardens, break it into pieces. Use blender, food processor, rolling pin, or a mallet to pulverize it.

60-Minute Bread Sticks

2 tablespoons oil
1¾ cups flour
1 tablespoon sugar
1 teaspoon salt
1 package (¼ ounce) active dry yeast
¼ cup softened butter
⅔ cup lukewarm milk
1 egg white, beaten
1 tablespoon water
Sesame seeds

1. Preheat oven to 375°. Generously grease 2 baking sheets.

2. In a bowl, combine ½ cup of the flour, sugar, salt, and yeast. Add butter. Gradually add milk. Beat at medium speed on mixer for 2 minutes.

3. Add ¼ cup more flour; beat at high speed for 2 minutes. Add enough of the remaining flour to make a soft dough (you will probably use all of the flour).

4. Turn out onto a well-floured board. Roll into 12-by-8-inch rectangle. Cut in half to make two pieces, 6 by 8 inches. Cut each piece into sixteen 6-inch strips. Roll each between floured hands to make a rope.

5. Arrange ropes of dough 1 inch apart on baking sheet; roll to grease all sides. Cover. Let rise in a warm place 15 minutes.

6. Combine beaten egg white with water; brush sticks with mixture. Sprinkle with sesame seeds. Bake 20 minutes. Remove from sheet; cool on a wire rack. Makes 32 bread sticks.

15 FOOD HAS FEELINGS, TOO: METHODS AND TECHNIQUES

Whenever my mother left my brothers and me at home, she always told us not to cook anything. So, of course, we raced to the kitchen the minute the door closed behind her. We always made fudge which never turned out right, and we'd eat the evidence before Mother returned. When I became a mother and warned my children against using the stove while I was away, they, of course, always made fudge and it never turned out right. Failures can be fun, and one certainly can learn from them. Repeating the same mistakes over and over, however, is kids' stuff.

Along with techniques and methods, which are liberally described throughout these pages, one needs to acquire an understanding that foods are living things, each with a nature of its own. Take flours, for example: all are different. If you measure flour improperly, you can ruin the best recipe without ever knowing why. Flour should be stirred up, *aerated*, before it is measured. Never pack or shake it down into the cup: scoop it in lightly. To spare yourself cooking failures and learn more about flour's fascinating traits, read a good book on baking.

Everyone has theories about pastry crusts and what makes them succeed or fail. I learned from Dione Lucas, who insisted on blending the flour and fat *up*. I can still hear that dear genius saying, "Up to the heavens! Up to the heavens!" as I labored. She was right. The initial upward-blending incorporation of fat into flour *is* all-important. You can develop a feel for this, along with the amount of liquid to use. As a rule, pastry crust requires less liquid on humid days and more on dry days. If your pastry shrinks, you are using too much fat. If it is tough, you've been heavy-handed with the liquid.

For baking, all ingredients should be at room temperature unless otherwise specified. The oven should always be preheated. Some energy experts who are dodos at cooking addle me when they advise cooks to save energy by not preheating ovens. You will ruin costly ingredients and waste your own energy if you start with a cold oven.

If you need to bake two different dishes at the same time, and one recipe calls for a 350° oven and the other 375°, do so fearlessly! When you cook a dish ahead and reheat it, undercook it slightly and let it stand at room temperature for about an hour before you pop it into the oven. Otherwise, the dish will emerge lukewarm and unlovable. About 15–20 minutes of reheating time is necessary for most dishes, unless they are straight from the freezer or the refrigerator.

So many people are intimidated by yeast that its reputation as a temperamental mystery needs to be debunked. The only smart way to work with yeast is to get a cooking thermometer and precisely measure the temperature of the liquid you are using. When a recipe says 105° or 115°, respect it. Yeast is a living substance and it will be good to you if you are considerate of it.

Unlike flours, the standard thickeners—arrowroot, cornstarch, and potato starch—are virtually interchangeable. If a recipe calls for one you do not have, use another.

Herbs are a miracle! Fresh ones are always better, and I specify fresh parsley, dill, and garlic in my recipes always. Any time I can get fresh tarragon, thyme, basil, whatever, I grab it. One must, however, be realistic and use dried herbs on occasion. One teaspoon dried equals one tablespoon fresh, as a rule of thumb.

Contemplate the egg. It is one of nature's most glorious creations, with literally thousands of uses. Eggs have a character all their own, and it's not determined by whether the shell is brown or white. Contrary to myth, egg whites blended into a soufflé are not all that delicate. (Just add some of the egg whites to the soufflé sauce to lighten it a bit, then incorporate the rest of the whites. It won't hurt a thing if you leave a few bubble pockets—*over*blending is what kills soufflés.)

I think it takes diabolical skill to wreck an innocent fresh vegetable, but you can do it by overcooking, oversaucing, or otherwise denying its simple needs. Why abuse an innocent mushroom by soaking it in water, which draws away its succulence?

One must make value judgments in cooking. For purées, I sometimes do not peel turnips, carrots, or potatoes. Whether or not I peel broccoli depends on who's coming to dinner. Sometimes, too, food can become a matter of ethics and principles. Once I killed a lobster during a televised cooking class. I did the decent thing by plunging a knife into the cross-pattern in the middle of its head. The television station was later deluged with letters from furious viewers who accused me of being guiltier than Lady Macbeth. But I ask you, how would *you* feel if somebody dropped you alive into boiling water?

Be they lobsters, eggs, yeast breads, or soufflés, good things come out better when the cook practices! If you want to make beautifully shaped, moistly creamy omelets, get three dozen eggs and experiment, each time thinking through what you did wrong the previous time. If no one else will eat your mistakes, perhaps the dog will help you out. Once you've caught the knack of it, you'll love making omelets. Good cooking methods and techniques call for the kind of concentrated practice you use when you learn to play the piano. The resulting harmonies, in each case, are worth the effort.

This does not aspire to be a book with complete information on methods and techniques; I've jotted down a few fundamental suggestions to save you time. For the library of every cook, I recommend two books by my friend Jacques Pepin: *La Technique* (Times Books, 1976) and *La Methode* (Times Books, 1979).

Methods and Terms

Bain-Marie (Mary's Bath) or Water Bath
A pan half-filled with hot water in which another pan or dish containing food is to be placed. Food cooked this way will not brown on edges or around the bottom.

Deep-Frying
Usually I prefer solid shortening for this because it gives off less odor than other kinds of fat—but oil is fine. When deep-frying, never add too much food to the pan at once or the temperature of the fat will plummet; your fried foods will take longer to cook and lose in quality.

Deglazing Pans
After you brown meat, salvage the juices and brown bits in the pan for added flavor in your sauce. Remove the meat from the pan and pour off the excess fat except, in most cases, for about 1 tablespoon. Add about ¼ cup liquid (wine, stock, or water) to the pan, boil it up over heat, and scrape up the brown bits with a wooden spatula. To deglaze the pan with brandy, flame (see *Flaming*), and when the flames have died down, scrape the brown bits they have loosened.

Enriching Sauces with Egg Yolks
Beat the yolks with a fork. Then, to avoid curdling the sauce while adding the yolks, warm them gradually by stirring a little of the hot sauce into them. Stir this warmed yolk mixture

into the sauce. Do not boil a sauce after you have added egg yolks: it may curdle.

Coating a Spoon

When a sauce reaches this consistency, it will just cling to a metal spoon. If you draw a vertical line down the back of the spoon, it will remain.

Flaming

Heat brandy or other liquor in a small, long-handled pan just until finger warm (warm to touch). Keep your head back, ignite the brandy, and pour it, flaming, into the pan or over the dish to be flamed, then shake pan or dish until the flames die.

Folding

This technique is used to combine a fairly delicate substance with a heavier base. Pour the ingredient to be folded in over the original mixture. Using a large rubber spatula, cut down through the center of the mixture to the bottom of the bowl; move across the bottom, up a side, over to the center, then down again. Keep turning the bowl as you fold.

Mushrooms

CLEANING: Never soak mushrooms. Wipe them clean with paper towels dipped in acidulated water (water with a little lemon juice—1 tablespoon to a quart of water—in it) or dip them quickly in acidulated water, then dry them out with paper towels.

SLICING: To keep the distinctive mushroom shape, trim off the stems, then slice mushrooms vertically from top to stem.

FLUTING MUSHROOM CAPS: Cut off the stems of the mushrooms even with the caps—don't twist the stems out. Then, with a small curved knife or a lemon stripper, cut grooves that spiral out from the center of each cap to the edges, all around.

SAUTÉING: Melt butter, 1 tablespoon for each ¼ pound of mushrooms, in a skillet. When it is hot and foaming, add mushrooms, squeeze on a few drops of lemon juice, sprinkle with salt and freshly cracked black pepper, and toss over high heat for about 3 minutes.

Tomatoes

PEELING: Spear a tomato on a fork, twirl it in the flame of a gas range for a few seconds, and the skin will loosen. The skin will also loosen if the tomato is blanched—that is, plunged into boiling water for about 30 seconds. (*Use this method for peaches, too.*)

SEEDING: Cut each tomato in half crosswise, hold a half in the palm of your hand, and squeeze out the seeds.

SLICING: For salads, slice tomatoes from stem to bottom. They'll lose the least juice this way.

Vegetables—Refreshing

As soon as fresh vegetables have boiled to the tender-crisp stage, drain them and plunge immediately into cold water. This stops the cooking and helps set the color—thus "refreshing" the vegetables. They can be cooked in the morning, refreshed, drained, covered and stored in the refrigerator, then reheated at night with butter and seasoning.

Salt

Coarse salt (sea salt or kosher salt) seems saltier than table salt to me. When you rub coarse salt on the exterior of roasts or steaks, an attractive crust will form. Many chefs use coarse salt exclusively. The crystals are slower to dissolve than those of table salt, which makes coarse salt ideal to use in salad dressings—but not a very practical idea for salting greens directly.

Washing Salad Greens

See page 102 for general comments on cutting and serving salad greens. Greens should be washed thoroughly in cold water, shaken to remove excess, and placed on paper towels. Roll up loosely, wrap in a tea towel, and place in a refrigerator for at least 30 minutes to crisp and become dry. (A salad spinner is a real time saver.)

Washing Spinach

Pick over the spinach, discard damaged leaves, and remove stems by tearing them back. Wash thoroughly first in warm water, then in cold. Dry the leaves thoroughly by rolling up in paper towels and putting in a refrigerator to crisp for at least 30 minutes.

Cleaning Leeks
Cut roots and tops off the leeks, leaving about 1 inch of green. Split lengthwise and hold under running water, separating the layers to wash thoroughly.

Preparing Baby White Onions
Unlike a number of cooks, I do not put a cross on the end. I find that if I do not overcook them, the onions remain intact and I've skipped a time-consuming chore.

To Chop Parsley
Remove stems and gather parsley into a ball on cutting board. Chop from the back of a chef's knife, keeping point of knife on board. Can do in blender or processor, but make certain parsley is *dry*.

Mandoline
An instrument that has an adjustable blade. It will enable you to cut vegetables into nice, uniform slices, thick or thin.

To Chop Garlic
Smash garlic clove with side of chef's knife. The peel will slip off. Chop garlic finely from the back of the knife.

Grating Cheese
Use a hand grater, blender, or food processor. For Parmesan in the food processor, start the machine and drop small pieces of cheese down the feed tube. Grate as needed.

To Open a Coconut
Punch eyes with ice pick. (There are usually three eyes.) Let the liquid run out into a bowl. Put coconut in a 350° oven for 30 minutes. Remove from oven and drop on floor to crack open the shell. Skin will peel away readily. Grate coconut in food processor.

Measuring Flour
Unless a recipe specifies sifted flour, all flour in my recipes is measured without this step. Before measuring, I stir or aerate the flour (which is stored in a canister) with a scoop or a spoon, to loosen it. Then I lightly scoop it into the measuring cup. I do not pack or shake flour down in the cup.

Flouring

To coat food to be cooked with flour, roll it in flour, but be certain to pat it lightly to remove excess.

Reheating on a Brown Paper Bag

Set cake racks on a baking sheet. Cover with brown paper bag. Put whatever is to be reheated on the paper, and set in a 350° oven for as long as recipe directs.

Peeling Citrus Fruit for Julienne

Peel off skin gently with a rotary peeler. The white pith will remain behind. Layer pieces one on top of another and cut as finely as possible with a chef's knife.

To Section Citrus

Use a serrated knife and peel away all white. Lift out sections by placing knife next to membrane; cut down and come up the other side. Section will fall out. Do this over a bowl to save the juice.

Squeezing Lemons

Cut lemon in half crosswise and squeeze through fingers. No gadgets are necessary, and the seeds will remain in your hand.

To Grate Citrus Peel

Use a small hand grater.

Roasting on a Rack

I like to roast on a rack because the heat can circulate underneath. This way the meat won't stew in its own juice.

Skimming

Excess fat makes sauces and stocks look and taste greasy. The easiest way to remove it, if you have time, is to chill the sauce or stock; the fat will rise to the top and solidify, and you can lift it off. Or you can tilt the cooking vessel and spoon off the excess fat. If stock or sauce must be absolutely fat-free, finish skimming with a paper towel: lay it on the surface to pick up remaining fat.

How to Bone and Skin a Chicken Breast

1. Work with whole chicken breasts; they are easier to bone than split ones. Place chicken breast on a cutting board with breastbone up and, if you are right-handed, wishbone to the left. Then, with a short, sharp boning knife or a 3-inch utility knife, make a slit the full length of the breastbone.

2. Working first on the side away from you (you can see what you are doing more easily this way) use the knife with a cutting-scraping motion against the breastbone and rib bones, peeling back the flesh with your free hand as you cut.

3. Turn the breast around so that the wishbone is at the right, then free the other side the same way.

4. Pull off the skin.

You can bone chicken breasts a day ahead if you cover them with plastic wrap and refrigerate. Bring to room temperature before using.

Trussing a Chicken

1. Cut about 36 inches of butcher's cord. Lay the bird on its back with the tail away from you. Bring the cord under the tail and legs and loop it, making a half knot. Then draw legs close to tail.

2. The string has two equal ends now. Pass each end of the cord between a leg and the body of the bird.

3. Flip the bird over, breast down, then go under the wings with the cord ends and bring the neck flap down over the bird's back.

4. Loop the cord over the flap, making a half knot to hold the flap in place.

5. Turn the bird onto its back again, then bring the cord ends over the wings and tie a knot on the breast.

Killing a Lobster

Place lobster on a cutting board with claws to your left, shell side up. Insert a knife point into the center of the cross on the lobster's head: it is clearly marked. Split lengthwise. Remove the sac (behind the eyes) and the intestinal membrane (the little membrane running the length of the lobster). Cut off the large claws with a knife or scissors. Remove any tomalley and red coral (the roe).

16 TOOLS OF THE TRADE: UTENSILS AND APPLIANCES

Where would Michelangelo be without his chisels and mallets, or Rembrandt minus brushes and palettes? Creative work requires more than talent and inspiration: one must possess tools. In cooking, the greatest brioche this side of Valhalla would look pitiable if it were baked in a square pan. One's heart goes out to the poached fish that never had a chance to lie on some kind of rack or a hammock. *Coeur à la crème* without heart-shaped molds is not a *coeur*, which means heart.

Today almost everyone has access to excellent cooking supply shops bulging with almost every kind of gadget and gimcrack. The wise cook equips with caution, though, so when you size up your own kitchen and its appointments, think in terms of your own patterns. If five-and-ten pots and utensils are your preference, fine.

Do you like large parties, or small ones? If you love to serve soup, you perhaps need a magnificent soup pot or tureen that can be set on the table. Unless poached fish is your specialty, it's almost silly to invest in a copper poacher. Control yourself when you feel the urge to buy a piece of exotic equipment: it probably will end up in a closet or at a rummage sale.

There are certain basic supplies which everyone needs, and that goes for people in small apartments. If there isn't enough room for pots and pans in your kitchen, put them under the bed. The list of equipment I have compiled here has been carefully thought out and I've tried to keep it—like the recipes—simple.

I rarely specify any particular brand of appliance. Cooking, not pushing merchandise, is my interest. Some brands suit me better than others; some are more economical and durable, in my opinion. In the rare instances where I specify a brand name, I urge you to shop around. American ingenuity and mass production are such that we're blessed with constantly improving products. One example is the food processor. Some purists hate it, but they would have said that Henry Ford's Model T would never sell, or that a woman's place would never be anywhere but at home. Food processors are rapidly becoming a necessity for good cooks with little time. A person who loves homemade bread but can't spare the extra minutes for kneading dough by hand can use a food processor—or a mixer with a dough hook—with the same sense of liberation our forefathers felt when they revved up their Model T's.

You will not find a microwave oven on my list. Perhaps these appliances appeal to you, but I just cannot warm up to them. To me they seem sterile, and I think they steam the food rather than bake it; anyway, the flavor changes. Nor do I recommend pressure cookers. Maybe I'm put off by both the oven and the cooker because they seal up all the cooking smells, and cooking isn't any pleasure without its wonderful aromas.

I cannot understand trying to cook without at least two good whisks, a collection of quality sauté pans (the professional variety, if possible), and a few fantastic knives. Three—a chef's knife, a utility knife, and a paring knife—are the minimum. Carbon steel is my first choice, although stainless steel looks prettier. Carbon steel begins to look old very soon, but that to me is part of its charm.

As you look over my list, make additions and subtractions to suit yourself. And remember not to be squeamish about using the best tools a creative cook has—*hands*. I squeeze lemon juice through my fingers; it flows through perfectly strained, removes garlic odors, and keeps my rings clean. Mostly, though, I use my hands because I love the *feel* of beautiful, natural food.

Necessary Equipment

Electric pasta machine
Cutting board or chopping block, 18 by 20 by 1 inch
3 saucepans with lids
      1 quart
      1½ quarts
      3 quarts
Knives, carbon steel if possible
      9–10-inch blade
      4–5-inch blade
      2–3-inch blade

3 sauté pans with lids; all pans with sloping sides
> 10 inches across bottom
> 8 inches across bottom
> 6 inches across bottom

Mixing bowls: a nest of small, medium, and large
6 custard cups
Measuring cups (4-, 2-, and 1-cup sizes; ½-, ⅓-, and ¼-cup sizes)
2 heavy professional-weight baking sheets 18 by 12 inches
Roasting pan with rack
2 muffin tins
3–4-quart casserole with lid
Wooden spatulas (small, medium, and large)
Meat pounder or cleaver
Metal spatula
Strainers: 1 large and 1 small
Rolling pin
Whisks
> 16-inch (optional) or large
> 10-inch or medium
> 7-inch or small

2 heavy copper saucepans (if possible!)
Crêpe pan, 5 inches across bottom
Set of Pyrex baking dishes for cakes, coffee cakes, etc.
6-cup soufflé dish
Lemon stripper
Trussing needle and string
Stainless serving platters
> Oval
> Round

2 copper au gratin serving dishes
> Large
> Small

Good scissors
Rotary peeler
Mandoline, Feemster Slicer, or any vegetable slicer
6-cup ring mold
Ladle
2 large kitchen spoons, 1 with holes
Long kitchen fork
1½-quart casserole with lid

Food processor
Hobart Kitchen Aid Mixer, 2 bowls, 2 whips, and 2 whisks
Blender
9-inch flan ring or quiche pan
8-inch omelet pan
Foley hand grater
12-quart kettle with lid, for boiling pasta, making stock
Tongs
Jelly-roll pan, 15 by 10 inches
Can opener
Wine bottle opener
Rubber spatulas
    Large
    Small
Pepper mills (dark wood for black pepper; light wood for
    white pepper)
Timer
9-inch pans with removable bottoms
Juicer (Foley)
Scale
Food mill
Pastry blender
Pastry scraper
Rotary beater
2 pastry brushes
Professional meat thermometer
Ice cream machine (I prefer Waring or the Minigel, which
    uses no salt, no ice, and makes ice cream in 15–30
    minutes)

Nice to have:
    Jelly-roll board
    Large pastry bag
    Large star tube
    Large plain tube
    Salad spinner

17 THOUGHTS FROM A COOKING TEACHER

In the seventeen years since I became a professional cooking teacher, I have joyfully participated in a revolution in the American understanding of cooking as an art. Certainly this happy transformation began long before, in the mid-1940s, when World War II ended and our soldiers brought home from their tours of duty a vast new knowledge of, and appreciation for, the cuisines of the countries in which they had served.

Now as Americans are traveling everywhere, to a degree beyond the wildest dreams of their grandparents (except the H. G. Wells types), they are adding to their awareness of good food, and their palates are being educated as never before.

Along with this we have produced cooking experts, cooking school teachers, and a whole new breed of gifted American-born-and-trained chefs, restaurateurs, and thousands of creative cooks who have taken to their kitchens as never before. Cooking has become a major industry, not just through the direct route, but via the production and sale of cooking equipment, appliances, gadgets of all kinds. People are taking food more seriously than at any other time in our history.

This is all to the good. Along with it, however, we seem to have spawned a breed of people who make things uncomfortable for the rest of us: these are the food Snobs and Purists (S&P's).

Some S&P's are people who take a single cooking course, or a short trip abroad, then enter a restaurant looking for trouble. They tell the waiter the butter tastes refrigerated (of course it does—it has been in the refrigerator). They join a mediocre wine and food society that requires only the payment of dues as a qualification for membership, and suddenly they begin to send back every bottle of wine because it tastes "corky."

S&P's cringe at the thought of drinking a white wine with cheese because "it isn't done." (Little do they know that it is done, with great success, in certain areas of the world, and that a certain white wine is the finest kind to drink with an Emmenthal or a Gruyère.)

They also discuss *nouvelle cuisine* and *cuisine minceur* with no understanding of either, and after having bored their companions with an evening of food petticisms, they offend everyone in the room by lighting up a foot-long cigar.

S&P's follow not their palates, but the gossip columns and headlines. Because some trendy member of the food establishment says nasty things about iceberg lettuce, the S&P's hate it, too.

S&P's frequent only the most expensive, "in" places, never giving smaller and perhaps better ones—or themselves—a chance.

On the restaurant side of the S&P line looms the Snooty Sommelier. With a long chain, a cup, a fake French accent, and a scornful mien, he arrives at table to intimidate a nice couple who are trying to find a pleasant wine to enjoy with their dinner. I shall tell you what I tell my students: drink what you like! If Snooty Sommelier raises an eyebrow, ask him what he drinks, and see if he doesn't decide from the right side of the wine list.

Cooking teachers are not exempted from my list of S&P's. I have taught thousands of students from all over the world and am appalled by some of the stories I have heard from them. These students insist there is only *one* way to do this or that—the way some dogmatic (and ill-informed) teacher said to. Here are some of the sillinesses I have heard:

1. *"Pasta is no good unless made by hand."* While I prefer to make pasta by hand, I am not at all shy about using an electric machine. I have done so while preparing a meal for a number of prominent Italian chefs who applauded my efforts. I also teach my students to make pasta by machine. The amusing skirmishes that spring from these precious niggles about handmade versus machine-made seem to be developing into a War of the Pastas. Now some "experts" insist that because plastic rollers on electric machines are "porous," they make a pasta to which *the sauce clings better*. To all this I say—Hogwash! I agree with that astute food writer, Nika Hazelton, who says in her book *Italian Regional Cooking* that "whether made by machine or rolled by hand, being made *well* is what counts."

2. *"It is impossible to make a soufflé without beating the egg whites in a copper bowl."* I have detailed my opinions, and experiments, on this matter on page 211.

3. *"Unless you use this pan, you cannot make an omelet."* When you hear this from a teacher, start wondering if s/he is being paid to push pans.

4. *"Certain dishes will work only if you use clarified butter."* Frankly, I never clarify butter and do not see any reason to. I've never burned a chicken suprême, a fish fillet, etc. I fortify the butter with a spoonful of oil, which allows me to heat the mixture to a higher temperature—and I *watch* while I'm sautéing. Just because the old masters wrote down in their words of wisdom to clarify butter does not mean that I have to, a century or two later. I use the

finest butter available, with government controls on it. It is allowed only a certain content of whey. Years ago it was probably necessary to clarify butter—and back then they probably did not have widely available vegetable oils.

5. *"Only dry ingredients should be measured in metal cups, and only liquids in Pyrex or glass cups."* It's becoming a little irritating to me continually to read or hear about how to measure properly. Some of my students have been citing the "fact" that certain ingredients must be measured in certain kinds of cups. I bought some metal cups and measured back and forth between them and the glass ones and there is not one bit of difference. The only thing to watch is that it is not possible to sweep off dry ingredients level in a glass cup. I teach my students that we are in a kitchen, not a chemistry lab, and a bit less or more of any ingredient is not going to matter. What matters is learning how to avoid, or correct, failures.

As far as I am concerned, those cute little sets of measuring spoons all hooked together are the institution of the devil. Americans are filling up their kitchens with every conceivable professional gadget, to the point of measuring out ⅛ of a teaspoonful with a special spoon. Use ordinary teaspoons and tablespoons from your kitchen drawer—they are accurate enough for my kind of cooking.

7. *"People who smoke and drink hard liquor cannot possibly possess sensitive palates."* Richard Olney smokes Gauloises and drinks, and he can taste and define wine and food better than anybody I've ever known. I know because I've been to blind tastings with him.

Some cooking teachers try to enhance their authority by actually belittling students in front of others. Some never permit, or answer, any questions. I will have to confess that I am capable of being less than understanding when a student interrupts me during a lesson with something I consider overpicky. If a teacher is truly intimidating, or refuses to answer questions, I advise my students to walk up to the teacher in front of the rest of the class, ask for their money back, and say, "Julie Dannenbaum told me to do this."

I urge you to read, take lessons, experiment with foods, and learn all about cooking that you can—it's a wonderful journey, one you will never tire of. If you spend your whole life exploring this world, you can never know all there is to know—nobody can. That's what makes it so fascinating! When good cooking loses its natural purposes—necessity, pleasure, sociability—it becomes an unpleasant subject, and a noble work loses dignity. There is room aboard for just about everybody to join the fun and adventure of good food and good cooking—but no room at all for S&P's who would make this a vehicle for insulting, intimidating—and exploiting—others.

MORE
FAST
&
FRESH
Cooking

CONTENTS

DEDICATED TO MY CHILDREN

Thanks to Betty Barlow and Grace Benson, who tested recipes. Thanks to Rose Guarrera and Will Kratz, who supplied me with recipes and encouragement. Thanks, too, to my husband, who ate all manner of weird combinations while I was working on this book. A special thanks to longtime good friend Jim Quinn, who kept my thoughts together in preparation of this book. More thanks to Jay Acton, the very best agent, and to Larry Ashmead, the very best editor anybody could have.

J.D.

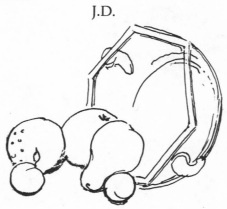

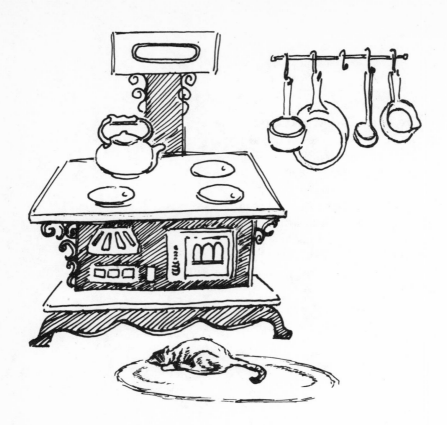

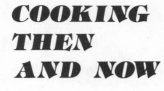

COOKING THEN AND NOW

For years I've kept a notebook of meals I've had in famous restaurants—meals that were especially good or especially disappointing. I frequently look back through it to the trips I took to Europe twenty-five to thirty years ago and I am amazed. Two restaurant meals a day, each loaded with cream sauces, hollandaise, béarnaise, buttery soups, rich desserts. I don't understand how I managed never to gain weight. And I wonder how I managed to survive!

No one eats like that anymore. Part of it is that all of us eat less as we grow older. But a more important part is that our children, people in their twenties and thirties today, have too much sense. I remember when we all used to laugh at the "kid's food"—everything cooked with raisins and honey and nuts. But there really has been a revolution in American cooking, one which trusts the food to taste good.

In a way, this revolution seems like a step backward: back to Grandma's cooking. I remember my grandmother's kitchen and my mother's kitchen. My grandmother's kitchen was the most important room in the house. I remember the big round table, big enough for four or five children, grown-ups, and any guests who might show up. The chairs were high-backed old wooden ones, so that you could see a foot or so of chair over the heads of the other children at the table. My grandmother served all weekday meals in the kitchen, and on Sunday everybody moved to the dining room. We all loved that kitchen. Grandmother didn't have a bare wood table, of course, but one covered with oilcloth. I haven't seen oilcloth for years, but I still remember the smell; no matter how old it got, it still reminded you of new machine crank case oil or kerosene. And, of course, all the children would spend their time picking at the holes in it, peeling it down to the canvas backing underneath. It gave the grown-ups something to complain about—my aunt was forever telling us to sit up straight, eat properly, and quit picking at the oilcloth like monkeys picking fleas in the zoo. Things were meant to last in those days, though, and no matter how we picked at the oilcloth, the same old oilcloth stayed on the table. We grew up with it, we went away to college, we came back to visit Grandma, and there was the same oilcloth with the same holes in it.

I remember when my mother remodeled her kitchen. The table was chrome and plastic; the appliances were stark white; the kitchen cabinets were stark white. If you looked in the ladies' magazines of the time, the women in the kitchens sometimes dressed in stark white dusters, with their hair pulled back in severe little buns, looking something like scientists concocting a new formula. New formulas were all around then. Frozen food had just appeared—and the frozen spinach tasted

pretty good to anyone who had actually managed to eat that canned soggy spinach. There were new mixes. Everything was designed to take place in minutes; just add water and serve. All new, all improved. I could hear my mother talking on the phone to a friend and saying, "Have you tried that new meringue mix?" There actually was a meringue mix, also a cream puff mix, cake mixes, etc. God knows what was in them, or in the rest of that instant stuff. They certainly didn't have to tell us on the label. And if they did nobody would have read it. Our children had to teach us to read labels. The pages of the food sections and the magazines were full of new convenience ideas: how you could combine tuna fish with noodles and make a fabulous casserole topped with French-fried onion rings from a can. Instant cake mixes that were no quicker than making a cake from scratch. Instant mashed potatoes that tasted like papier-mâché run through a paper shredder.

There had to be a reaction to all that scientific convenience, and there was. Suddenly everybody had to learn the most complicated and difficult techniques of French haute cuisine. Every woman had her own batterie de cuisine, and nothing was too difficult or too time-consuming to be made for family dinner. There were recipes for ratatouille that took lots of pots and hours to prepare. Ingredients were boned and fussed over at great length, as if we didn't trust food to be good enough to eat without working our mysterious kitchen magic on it. The convenience kitchens were spare and white, like little laboratories, where you combined the latest in chemical ingredients to produce the most scientifically correct food the world has ever known.

The contrived food kitchens filled up with gadgets. What was a home without a flan ring? Or a nest of soufflé dishes or bowls ranging in size from four-quart to a thimble-sized unusable one in the middle? One set of pots was no longer enough. You had to have

three or four. Aluminum pots and pans were suddenly a no-no, since they discolor sauces. (The visiting chefs who teach at my school pull them off my wall and make perfect sauces in them.) My pots are in constant use, and that seems to make the difference. If you cook every day in your home, you can cook in just about anything. I dislike stainless steel because it develops hot spots. I'll take professional aluminum or tin-lined copper. But when it comes to pots—pots is pots.

Some of the complicated recipes tried to make things seem a little simpler. They'd print a little star at one point in the recipe and say, "Can be prepared ahead to this point, then frozen and reheated." Then all you had left was fifteen minutes of hysteria in the kitchen as you simultaneously reheated the dish, finished the béarnaise, and whipped a little cream for dessert—by hand, of course. There is nothing wrong with mastering traditional kitchen techniques. It will always improve your style of cooking. But for most family dinners and most entertaining it's more important that the cook be relaxed and worry-free, and it's hard to be that when you're worrying your way through a recipe designed around some crucial ambidextrous juggling performed at top speed with three saucepans and a wire whisk. There is a lot of good food without agony.

The young people today taught us that, too. The young people in my family not only eat less than I did at their age, they also eat better. They don't bother with frozen or canned food, they never buy mixes, and they read the labels on everything. They work, as do their friends, and food shopping and food preparation are shared chores. They plan out menus in advance, the only way to do it if you want to shop once a week. They visit the supermarkets when the produce is the freshest. And they usually manage to find time over the weekend to go to a farmer's market for more fresh produce, local chickens, local cheeses, anything that is in season or in good supply. Food is important enough to the children in my family that they are willing to spend the time looking for the best available ingredients.

Kitchens have changed once again. When I first had my kitchen installed eleven years ago, my friends were horrified. Quarry tile floors, tile and natural wood, rough plaster on the walls, a professional stove, and a professional butcher block work table on stainless steel legs. Some people thought it looked too old-fashioned. Some of them thought I'd ruin my feet standing on that tile floor. I told them I'd put a small rug in front of the stove just the way my grandmother used to do. I never figured out what that rug was for; the family pets used to sleep on it. I always suspected that rug was there just to

make sure everybody knew what an important place the front of the stove was. The tile floor is comfortable and easy to clean. In a few years, all my friends had tile floors too. We all wanted a country kitchen look, like Grandma, to go with our new simple and sensible and healthful style of cooking, which was similar to the best of Grandma's.

This book, like the first *Fast and Fresh,* was designed for quick and easy cooking and for the working couple. It is not written only for them, as everyone can use good, fast, easy recipes, but it is designed for people who share the young people's appreciation of good food and their appreciation for the uses that can be made of time not spent in the kitchen.

The approach is simple—fast and fresh. Look at any recipe, and you will see it does not rely on a myriad of spices and herbs. The basic flavors of these recipes come from the food itself. This isn't plain cooking, but the kind of cooking that recognizes the elegance of simplicity. There are a few show-stoppers in the book; who doesn't like coming out of the kitchen with a platter that looks just as spectacular as it is going to taste? But you don't have to combine the skills of Oriental flower arrangement and origami with broccoli florets and flounder filets to have a great-looking and good-tasting food.

Whenever I go to a restaurant and get a plate of food on which every Brussels sprout seems turned with its best side to the light, and the potato slices are laid one on top of the other as

if they were dominoes fallen in a long sinuous line, I think: How pretty. Then I wonder how long the chef had his hands in my food in order to get everything so perfect. A little raggedy humanness in food is an advantage; it's as if you tried to make your own clothes. You'd want to get good enough so that they looked beautiful, but not so good that everybody thought you bought them off a rack ready-made. Don't try to make your food look professionally gussied up by a finicky restaurant chef; first of all, you might not be able to do as well, and even if you could, all that work isn't worth the effort in home cooking.

What is worth the effort is making good food properly. And that is easy. There are no complicated techniques in this book. No chicken or rabbits to bone, no long and involved sauces, no stirring gingerly for an hour while everything else gets cold or burns. You can tell from the list of ingredients in the recipes that it isn't going to take all day to buy them. And you can tell from the short and simple list of directions that it's not going to take all day to cook. Relax. Trust the taste of fresh food. And trust your own pace. Nobody is going to mind if you take an hour and fifteen minutes instead of an hour to prepare a menu. This is fast cooking, but not breakneck cooking.

A few cautions. I urge you to substitute ingredients when necessary and when something in your area is especially fresh and good. But I also urge you to spend a little time looking for hard-to-come-by ingredients. It seems strange to me that sometimes students in my classes are so disheartened when I mention a new product I've found in New York.

"Oh, New York," they sigh, as if New York were halfway across the continent from Philadelphia, instead of ninety miles away—and as if they didn't go to New York once a month or so for the theater and opera and art galleries. New York, a wonderful source of imported foods from almost every corner of the world, may actually be half a continent from your home. But surely you have a major city near you, where you can find ethnic and Oriental ingredients. If not, there are mail order catalogs in which you can find anything short of bear paws. And no matter where you live there is a farmer's market, a street fruit and vegetable stand, or a store that specializes in fresh produce. And someplace where you can find cheeses that do not come presliced,

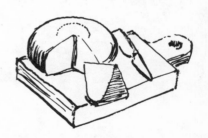

and tasting predigested, in neat little plastic envelopes. American farmer Swiss is not Gruyère, but it works a lot better as a substitute for Gruyère than the processed milkfat solids sold in supermarkets under that name. Not all supermarkets are equally bad—many suburban markets have a fresh vegetable department that a farmer's market could envy. But one of the pleasures of life is discovering a new source of good ingredients. Shopping for food is at least as much fun as shopping for clothes, and a lot cheaper.

I also urge you to find some way to get fresh herbs for your home. If you have any kind of garden, you can easily grow basil, rosemary, thyme, and oregano. I can do it, and I have a black thumb for every kind of houseplant and

garden flower. Remember herbs are only weeds that taste good. Even if you do not have any garden space at all, there are window boxes and tabletop greenhouses where herbs will grow fairly well. If all else fails, try the specialty shops in your area or even the local supermarket. I always find fresh dill year round, and in season basil and chives. Nothing will improve your cooking as

much as using fresh herbs, whatever herbs you can find, and throw away all those little boxes of things that all taste and look like lawnmower sweepings. If you must use dried herbs, at least dry them yourself—that way they retain some of their taste.

Most of us like to think that the family stove is perfect. We tend to think those little oven knobs are as accurate as room thermostats. Sometimes that's true in a very new oven. But gas and electric pressures vary from time to time; and dials, knobs and thermostats get out of whack. Buy yourself an oven thermometer, and you'll go a long way toward making your cooking consistent.

But, of course, no cooking can be perfectly consistent. I can prepare a poached fish dish one week and write down exactly the ingredients and the procedure. I make it again, and when I taste as I go along, I realize it is going to be different. The fish is always a little more or less fresh and firm (it has had different parents), the butter is different, the wine a little sour or sugary, the gas or electric pressure is stronger, the cream is older or younger, or richer or thinner, and sometimes I am different. In my own kitchen, at my own stove, I can easily adjust for all those changes. I can't do the same in your kitchen. Each time you make a dish you essentially conduct an experiment with changing ingredients, and with your own changing taste. Don't say "I can't understand it—I used exactly the same amount of butter and it doesn't taste as rich." Use the right amount of butter to make it taste the way you want. A recipe is not the

Constitution or the Bible; it is meant to be changed at will.

Finally, have fun. There are people for whom cooking is one of life's dreariest chores. They expect everything they make to be a long and complicated failure, and somehow they manage to live down to their expectations. But cooking is a chance to be creative and exciting—every day of our lives. You don't have to spend hours in the kitchen for the pleasure of taking good ingredients and combining them in delicious ways. Among the most sincere and heartfelt compliments most of us will ever receive is one from the guest who says, "This tastes great! May I have the recipe?"

I remember the beautiful country where I grew up in central Pennsylvania: an old red brick house with acres and acres of land, streams, orchards—a wonderful place to raise a family. My grandmother lived nearby and had the same kind of property. In the middle of her backyard stood an old pump, where pure spring water came up icy cold in winter and summer. These were depression days. The roads in the early thirties were filled with tramps, men out of work, wandering across the country. The grown-ups always thought these men had a series of signs to let each other know where to get a good handout. My grandmother's house was famous for miles around, as she always had something on hand to feed these men who were hungry. Men would come through alone and sometimes in twos or threes, asking for food.

"Go get yourself a drink of cold water from the well," my grandmother would tell them, "and I'll fix you something." She'd make up sandwiches, or bowls of soup, slices of pie, or just leftovers; those men would eat anything. I remember as little children my brothers and I would go watch them sitting on my grandmother's back porch, those strange and dusty men, eating steadily and hungrily whatever was brought to them, taking long drinks of that cold water. Maybe that's when I decided that making food was one of the most important things you could do in life. And I still think so. Try it and see.

Recipes in this chapter:

ASPARAGUS TIP CONSOMMÉ
SPINACH CONSOMMÉ
ZUCCHINI AND POTATO
CRAB AND CORN CHOWDER
SUMMER VEGETABLE WITH BASIL
CURRY
JULIENNE OF VEGETABLE
JERUSALEM ARTICHOKE
CREAM OF CAULIFLOWER
EGG DROP
PUMPKIN
SWEET POTATO BISQUE
MULLIGATAWNY
BUTTERMILK, WATERCRESS, AND
   CUCUMBER
GREEN PEA
THICK AND HEARTY POTATO AND
   CARROT
SHREVEPORT CLUB SHRIMP AND
   CRABMEAT
CARROT AND MUSHROOM
BACON, LETTUCE, AND TOMATO
"ONE-OF-EACH"
AVOCADO WITH GOLDEN CAVIAR
WILD RICE
CHICKEN BROTH WITH POACHED
   EGGS
COLD BLUEBERRY
COLD CHERRY

SOUPS

I love soup—from the clearest and most delicate consommé down to thick rich chowders where the spoon stands straight up in the middle of the bowl. And I think everybody who loves to cook loves soup. Because soup is the bonus dish we get out of fresh scraps, trimmings, and bones—all the things we save that people who hate to cook call "that mess in the kitchen." Soup is a wonderful dinner, a hearty lunch, or even a delicious breakfast. On a cold dark day, full of snow or winter rain, a big warming soup for breakfast will take you a lot further than oatmeal or one of those sugary cold cereals. And on fewer calories, too.

Back in Grandmother's day there was always a big kettle of soup on the back of the old wood stove, kept at a constant simmer. All the bones and peels and parings of everything went into that soup pot. Nothing was thrown away in Grandmother's kitchen. You can still make soup that old-fashioned way— I do. Just strain off the stock after simmering, let cool, put in the refrigerator, and remember to reboil it every two to three days. Add some fresh bones and scraps to intensify its flavor, simmer, strain, and put it back into a clean container.

Not everyone has the time to boil and reboil stocks, but with kitchen gadgets we have around now, everyone can make delicious soups in less than an hour. Like all soups, these quick soups keep for weeks in the freezer and make great emergency meals. Every year I teach a course at the Gritti Palace Hotel in Venice, and every year I seem to fly back home on a slower and later flight. All I can think of when I get off that plane at some ungodly U.S. time is that at least there is soup in the freezer at home. "Soup is a great comfort," my mother used to say; and she was right. It even takes the edge off jet lag.

A deceptively simple soup, and refreshing at the same time. These broth-type soups may be garnished with chopped cooked bacon, croutons, grated Parmesan cheese, chopped parsley or chives, then lemon slices, or a dollop of sour cream or whipped cream. A few grinds from the pepper mill enliven all soups. If calories are no problem add a spoonful of one of the butters.

Asparagus Tip Consommé

6–8 cups well-flavored chicken
    stock
2 cups thin asparagus tips

Salt and fresh pepper to taste
2 tablespoons chopped chervil
    (or less)

Bring stock to boil in saucepan. Add asparagus, salt, pepper, and chervil and return to a boil. Turn heat to a simmer. Cook 5 minutes; asparagus should still be crunchy. Serve.

Serves 4–6.

VARIATION:

You can add up to 1 cup grated carrot and/or finely chopped celery instead of the asparagus tips if desired.

Spinach Consommé

6 ounces spinach, with stems	Salt and fresh pepper to taste
6–8 cups strong chicken stock	1 lemon, thinly sliced
Freshly grated nutmeg to taste	

Remove spinach stems by pulling them back from the leaves. Wash spinach leaves in warm water to loosen dirt or sand. Rinse in cold water, and dry well with paper towel or cloth. Gather spinach together and cut into chiffonade or thin strips, using chef's knife with spinach placed on cutting board (should be 2 cups spinach, well packed, after removing stems).

Heat chicken stock. When really hot, add spinach. Cook while stirring 5 minutes. Grate nutmeg on top and season with salt and pepper. Float thin lemon slices on each serving.

Serves 4–6.

VARIATION:

Substitute 1 cup sliced mushrooms for the spinach. In this case, omit the nutmeg.

Zucchini and Potato Soup

4 tablespoons butter	2–3 cups chicken stock
1 medium onion, chopped	2 pounds zucchini, diced
1 garlic clove, chopped	1½–2 cups cream
2 medium potatoes, peeled and diced	Salt and fresh pepper to taste
1 tablespoon chopped fresh marjoram	

Melt butter in saucepan. Add onion and garlic and cook 3–4 minutes. Add potatoes, marjoram, and enough chicken stock to cover potatoes. Cover, bring to a boil, reduce to a simmer, and cook 5–10 minutes, or until potatoes are soft. Add zucchini and cook 10 minutes more. When zucchini is added to soup, add water, if necessary, to cover. Add cream, salt, and pepper.

Purée and serve hot or cold. Thin, if necessary, with cream.

Serves 4–6.

VARIATION:

Yellow squash may be used in place of the zucchini.

For a richer chowder, substitute chicken stock for the water. This chowder can stand on its own as a main course, in which case add more crab.

Crab and Corn Chowder

4 tablespoons butter or bacon fat
2 medium onions, finely chopped
1 small green pepper, finely chopped
2 large potatoes, peeled and diced
3 cups corn, cut off cob

2 cups milk or more
1 cup cream
½ pound crabmeat
  Salt and red pepper to taste
2 tablespoons finely chopped parsley

Melt butter or bacon fat in pan. When hot, add onions and green pepper. Sauté 5 minutes. Add potatoes and cover vegetables with water. Cook 10 minutes. Add corn and continue to cook until potatoes are tender. Add 2 cups milk and the cream. Stir and bring to a boil. Add crabmeat and just heat through. If too thick, thin with milk. Season with salt and pepper. Stir in parsley.   *Serves 6–8.*

The basil sauce here is similar to a pesto but without pine nuts. Try this sauce on potatoes, vegetables, and especially sliced tomatoes.

Summer Vegetable Soup with Basil

¼ cup olive oil
2–3 zucchini, chopped
4 carrots, peeled and chopped
2 medium onions, chopped
3 cups green beans
4 leeks, chopped (white part)
3 celery ribs, chopped
3 potatoes, peeled and diced
3 tomatoes, peeled, seeded, and chopped

2 cups shelled lima beans
4 cups chicken stock
2–4 cups water
  Salt and fresh pepper to taste
½ teaspoon chopped thyme
2 cups julienned spinach
  Basil sauce (see below)

Put oil in soup kettle. When hot, add the vegetables except spinach and stir well. Add the chicken stock and water to cover vegetables. Add salt, pepper, and thyme. Bring to a boil. Half-cover with a lid. Simmer 30–40 minutes or until vegetables are barely tender. Stir in spinach. It will cook in 1–2 minutes. Taste and rectify seasoning. Serve in soup bowls and spoon the basil sauce in each serving to taste.

Serves 6–8.

Basil Sauce

1 cup basil leaves	6–8 cloves garlic, chopped
¾ cup Parmesan cheese, freshly grated	1–1½ cups olive oil

Place the basil, cheese, garlic, and half the oil in blender. Blend 1 minute. Slowly add rest of oil to mixture and blend well.

Makes about 2 cups.

Curry Soup

1 medium onion, finely chopped	2 tomatoes, peeled and chopped
2 tablespoons butter	Juice of 1 lemon
2 tablespoons flour	2 tablespoons freshly grated coconut
1 tablespoon curry powder	1 cup light cream
4 cups chicken stock	Salt and fresh pepper to taste
1 large apple, peeled, cored, and chopped	

In medium saucepan, cook onion in butter until tender. Add flour and curry. Cook 2 minutes. Gradually add chicken stock. Cook, stirring, until slightly thickened. Add remaining ingredients except cream. Bring to a boil, then reduce heat. Cover and cook over medium heat 20 minutes. Purée a small amount at a time in electric blender, food processor, or food mill. Chill in a bowl placed in a bowl of ice cubes, stirring frequently. Just before serving, add cream, salt, and pepper.

Serves 4–6.

This soup can be prepared rapidly if all vegetables are julienned in the food processor or done on a Mouli-julienne. A fresh, elegant flavor.

Julienne of Vegetable Soup

3 carrots, peeled and julienned
2 potatoes, peeled and julienned
1 turnip, peeled and julienned
2 onions, peeled and finely chopped
1 tomato, peeled, seeded, and diced
½ pound green beans, slivered
2 celery ribs, julienned
1 garlic clove, chopped
Chicken stock to cover (about 8 cups)
Salt and fresh pepper to taste
¼ cup chopped parsley

Put everything except parsley into a kettle. Bring to a boil, then reduce to a simmer. Put on lid and cook until vegetables are tender, about 20 minutes. Sprinkle parsley over.

Serves 8.

Mystify your family and guests with this soup. No one will be able to identify the Jerusalem artichoke. If the artichokes are terribly knobby and difficult to peel, simply scrub them to death.

Jerusalem Artichoke Soup

4 tablespoons butter
1 large onion, chopped
4 celery ribs, chopped
2 pounds Jerusalem artichokes, peeled and coarsely chopped
2 tablespoons flour
4 cups chicken stock
2 cups milk
Salt and fresh pepper to taste
Few grains of freshly grated nutmeg
1 cup heavy cream
2 tablespoons chopped parsley

Melt the butter in a saucepan and sauté onion 1 minute. Add celery and artichokes and stir for 1–2 minutes. Rub in flour with a wooden spatula. Pour on chicken stock and milk and bring to a boil. Season with salt, pepper, and nutmeg. Put on lid and simmer, covered, for 20–30 minutes or until vegetables are tender. Purée in food mill or food processor. Return to pan and add cream. If too thick, thin with chicken stock or cream to desired consistency. Reheat. Garnish with parsley.

Serves 6–8.

Cream of Cauliflower Soup

4 cups cauliflower, cut into
   small pieces
5–6 cups chicken stock
4 tablespoons butter
4 tablespoons flour

3 cups milk, light cream, or
   heavy cream
Salt and fresh pepper to taste
Few grinds of fresh nutmeg
2 tablespoons chopped parsley

Put cauliflower in pan. Cover with stock. Bring to a boil. Cover and turn to simmer. Simmer 20 minutes or until cauliflower is tender. Purée in food mill, blender, or food processor. Return to pan.

Melt the butter in a saucepan. When the foam subsides, add flour. Turn heat to medium and stir with wooden spatula, getting into corners of pan. Let mixture bubble up without browning. Cook for 3 minutes or until flour taste is gone. Add milk or cream and switch to a whisk, whisking until sauce comes to a boil. Boil gently 5 minutes. Add salt, pepper, and nutmeg. Combine sauce with puréed cauliflower. Thin to desired consistency with cream or stock. Garnish with parsley.

Serves 6–8.

VARIATION:

Any of these vegetables can be substituted for the cauliflower: spinach, broccoli, carrots, peas, lettuce, onion, mushrooms, leeks, potatoes, turnips.

Egg Drop Soup

6 cups chicken stock
4 scallions, thinly sliced
2 eggs

1 tablespoon water
Salt and fresh pepper to taste

Combine stock and scallions in a saucepan. Bring to a boil. Combine eggs and water; mix well. Gradually pour in a thin steady stream into boiling stock, stirring constantly. Heat a few minutes to cook egg. Season if desired.

Serves 4–6.

VARIATION:

To make Greek lemon soup, omit water and add 1 tablespoon lemon juice after egg has been added.

I usually serve this soup at Thanksgiving dinner and let everybody try to figure out what it is. Garnish with slivers of chestnuts.

Pumpkin Soup

3 pounds pumpkin, cut into cubes and peeled
3 cups chicken stock or more to cover pumpkin
1 medium onion, chopped
2 celery ribs, chopped

Salt and fresh pepper to taste
Few grains of freshly grated nutmeg
2–3 tablespoons butter, softened
1 cup heavy cream
2–3 tablespoons rum, or to taste

Put all ingredients except butter, cream, and rum into saucepan. Bring to a boil and cover. Simmer until pumpkin is tender, about 15 minutes. Purée in food processor, blender, or food mill. Return to saucepan. Beat in the butter with a whisk. Add heavy cream and rum to taste. If too thick, thin with chicken stock or cream. Reheat.   *Serves 4–6.*

Another hard-to-guess soup—people think it may be squash.

Sweet Potato Bisque

1½ pounds sweet potatoes
2 celery ribs, chopped
1 large tart apple
2 tablespoons butter
¼ cup chopped shallots

2½ cups light cream
Salt and fresh pepper to taste
2 tablespoons sherry or Madeira
1 tablespoon finely chopped parsley

Peel and cube the sweet potatoes. Put into a saucepan, add the celery, and cook, covered, in a small amount of water 10–15 minutes. Meanwhile, peel, core, and chop the apple. Melt the butter and, when hot, add the shallots and sauté 1 minute. Add the apple and cook, while stirring, for 5 minutes. Drain potatoes and combine in pan with the apple mixture. Purée through blender, food mill, or food processor until smooth. Return to pan and add cream, salt, and pepper. Add the sherry or Madeira and bring to a boil. Stir the parsley through the bisque for color. Serve hot.   *Serves 4–6.*

Mulligatawny is usually made with chicken or at least garnished with chicken. To shorten the cooking time, I eliminated the chicken.

Mulligatawny

4 tablespoons butter	½ cup freshly grated coconut
2 apples, cored, peeled, and chopped	1–2 teaspoons sugar
1 medium onion, chopped	Salt and fresh pepper to taste
1 garlic clove, chopped	2–3 tablespoons chopped parsley
1 small green pepper, chopped	4 tomatoes, peeled, seeded, and chopped
2 medium carrots, chopped	Cooked rice
2 tablespoons flour	Thin lime slices
1–2 tablespoons curry powder	2 tablespoons finely chopped fresh coriander
8 cups chicken stock	

Melt the butter in a large saucepan. Sauté apples, onion, garlic, green pepper, and carrots for 3–4 minutes. Sprinkle on the flour and curry. Rub them into the vegetables thoroughly with a wooden spatula, and cook for 2–3 minutes. Add the stock and bring to a boil. Turn to a simmer and add the coconut, sugar, salt, pepper, parsley, and tomatoes. Cook 20 minutes or so until vegetables are tender. Rectify seasoning. Place a good spoonful of rice in each soup bowl. Ladle soup over. Garnish each serving with a thin slice of lime and a bit of fresh coriander.

Serves 8–10.

Nothing could be quicker than this delightful soup. If the soup is too thick after puréeing, simply thin with a bit of buttermilk or stock.

Buttermilk, Watercress, and Cucumber Soup

2 cucumbers, peeled, seeded, and cut into chunks	3 cups buttermilk
1 cup watercress leaves	2 tablespoons chopped fresh dill
1 cup chicken stock	Salt and fresh pepper to taste

Place all ingredients in blender jar or food processor in batches. Purée until smooth. Taste for seasoning. Serve in glass bowls, well chilled. *Serves 4–6.*

If there is any left over, it's delicious cold.

Green Pea Soup

4 tablespoons butter
1 onion, chopped
4 cups fresh peas
1 small head Boston lettuce
2–3 tablespoons chopped mint
2–3 tablespoons flour

4 cups chicken stock
2 cups light cream
Salt and fresh pepper to taste
2 egg yolks
½ cup heavy cream
2 tablespoons chopped parsley

Melt butter in saucepan. Add onion and cook 2–3 minutes. Add peas, lettuce, and mint. Cook 3 minutes. Sprinkle on flour and cook 2–3 minutes. Pour on stock and cream. Bring to boil. Cook until vegetables are tender. Purée in blender, food processor, or food mill. Reheat. Season with salt and pepper. Beat egg yolks and heavy cream together in a little bowl and add to soup. Whisk until soup barely thickens. Garnish with chopped parsley.   *Serves 4–6.*

This soup is fantastic cold.

Thick and Hearty Potato and Carrot Soup

3 lbs. potatoes, peeled and
   cubed
4 carrots, peeled and cubed
2 large onions, peeled and cut
   into chunks

2½ cups milk, or more
1 cup light cream
Salt and fresh pepper to taste
¼ cup minced parsley

Place potatoes, carrots, and onions in a large saucepan in boiling water. Cover. Cook for 20 minutes or until tender. Drain. Mash vegetables or purée in food processor. Stir in milk and cream. Season to taste. Heat soup just to boiling. Sprinkle with chopped parsley. If a thinner soup is desired, add additional milk. This soup contains no butter. If a richer soup is desired, place 1 tablespoon butter on each serving.   *Makes about 2 quarts or 4–6 servings as main dish.*

The delightful and talented French chef in charge of food at the Shreveport Club in Louisiana created this soup for a luncheon in my honor while I was visiting that charming city conducting several cooking demonstrations. The soup is simplicity itself, but keep in mind that the crab and shrimp in that area are outstanding, since Shreveport is directly on the Gulf. I wouldn't use pasteurized crabmeat and canned shrimp in this recipe.

Shreveport Club Shrimp and Crabmeat Soup

4 tablespoons butter
2 onions, finely chopped
2 leeks, finely chopped
1½ pounds medium shrimp, shells removed

4–6 cups chicken stock to cover
Salt and fresh pepper to taste
1 pound crabmeat
½ teaspoon saffron
Green onion tops, slivered

Melt the butter in a saucepan. Sauté the onions and leeks until limp, 5 minutes. Add shrimp and sauté without browning for 5 minutes. Do not overcook. Add the chicken stock, salt, and pepper. Add the crabmeat and saffron. You may need to add additional stock. Simmer 10 minutes. Add the green onion tops and serve.

Serves 6–8.

Carrot and Mushroom Soup

¼ cup butter
1½ pounds mushrooms, sliced
2 cups thinly sliced carrots
½ cup chopped onion
Chicken stock to cover vegetables (3–4 cups)

¼ cup Madeira or sherry
Salt and fresh pepper to taste
1–2 tablespoons finely chopped fresh dill

In large saucepan, melt the butter. When hot, add mushrooms, carrots, and onion. Cook 5 minutes. Add stock; bring to boil. Reduce heat, cover, and simmer 15 to 20 minutes until carrots are tender. Add Madeira or sherry, salt, pepper, and dill. Reheat and serve.

Serves 6–8.

Instead of a bacon, lettuce, and tomato sandwich, have soup instead.

Bacon, Lettuce, and Tomato Soup

6 slices of bacon, diced
1 medium onion, chopped
½ cup chopped celery
8 tomatoes, peeled, seeded, and chopped
Salt and fresh pepper to taste

1 tablespoon freshly chopped basil
4 cups chicken stock
2 teaspoons potato starch
1 cup shredded romaine lettuce

Cook diced bacon in medium-size kettle until brown; remove from kettle. Add chopped onion and celery to bacon fat and cook over medium heat until translucent. *Do not brown.* Add chopped tomatoes, cooked bacon, salt, pepper, basil, and chicken stock. Simmer without lid, for 30–35 minutes, or until all is well cooked. Purée mixture through food mill, processor, or blender. Return soup to kettle. Add potato starch blended with a little cold water. Cook over medium heat until slightly thickened. Taste for flavor. Just before serving, add shredded lettuce.

Serves 6.

"One-of-Each" Soup

1 large potato, peeled and roughly chopped
1 large onion, peeled and roughly chopped
1 large apple, cored and roughly chopped
1 large banana, peeled and roughly chopped

1 celery heart with leaves, roughly chopped
2 cups chicken stock
1 cup light cream
1 tablespoon butter, melted
½ teaspoon curry powder
Salt and fresh pepper to taste
Chopped chives

Place potato, onion, apple, banana, and celery in a saucepan and add chicken stock. Simmer them until soft. Purée in food mill, processor, or blender. Stir cream, melted butter, curry, salt, and pepper into smooth purée. Do not cook any more. Serve hot or cold. Sprinkle with chopped chives before serving. *Serves 4–6.*

Avocado Soup with Golden Caviar

4 tablespoons butter
¾ cup chopped green onions
2 ripe avocados, peeled, seeded, and chopped
3–4 cups chicken stock
Juice of 1 lemon or lime

Salt and fresh pepper to taste
1 cup heavy cream, barely whipped
Golden caviar (a few grains for each serving).

Melt the butter in a saucepan. Sauté the green onions 3 to 4 minutes. Add the avocados and stir around. Add the stock and lemon or lime juice; bring to a boil. Cook 5 minutes. Purée in blender, food processor, or food mill. Season with salt and pepper. Fold in the whipped cream. Reheat slowly. Garnish with the caviar.

Serves 4-6.

VARIATIONS:

This soup is excellent served cold. To chill rapidly, set bowl of soup over another bowl filled with ice. Stir until soup chills.

If golden caviar seems an affectation to you, omit it or use a bit of red caviar.

This is an adaptation of a wild rice soup I enjoyed in Minneapolis. Food editor Eleanor Oestman of the paper in that city happily sent me a recipe. This is quite different from hers but equally good.

Wild Rice Soup

1 medium onion, chopped
¼ pound mushrooms, chopped
2 tablespoons butter
½ cup uncooked wild rice
5 cups chicken stock

Salt and white pepper to taste
2 tablespoons flour
¼ cup water
½ cup light cream
2–4 tablespoons sherry

Cook onion and mushrooms in butter in a large kettle until tender. Add rice, chicken stock, salt, and pepper. Bring to boil, then reduce heat. Cover and cook over medium heat 35 minutes or until rice is tender. Combine flour and water until smooth. Gradually add to soup, stirring constantly, until mixture thickens slightly. Add cream and sherry; heat.

Serves 4-6.

Chicken Broth with Poached Eggs

6–8 cups strong chicken broth
4–6 eggs
1 cup heavy cream

2 tablespoons chopped chervil
Salt and fresh pepper to taste
¼ cup grated Parmesan cheese

Place broth in a saucepan and bring to simmer. Poach eggs while broth is simmering. Place an egg in each serving bowl or cup. Add cream to broth. Bring to a boil. Gently spoon the broth and cream over the eggs. Sprinkle each serving with chervil, salt and pepper, and Parmesan cheese.   *Serves 4–6.*

I personally am not fond of cold fruit soups. It seems to me they should be served for dessert. However, when hot weather arrives and fresh fruit is plentiful, these soups are certainly refreshing.

Cold Blueberry Soup

4 cups blueberries (save 4–6 large
    berries for garnish)
1 tablespoon cornstarch
½ cup sugar

Ground cardamom to taste
3 cloves
Juice of ½ lemon
½ cup sour cream

Place blueberries in a pan with water to cover. Bring to a boil on high heat, lower heat, and simmer berries until very soft, 5–10 minutes. Put berries and liquid through food mill, using the finest disk, or do in blender or processor. Pour berry juice through finest sieve, allowing it to strain through without pressing (there are many very tiny seeds in blueberries, so the clearer this soup is, the nicer result when it is served). Return strained juice to pan, add cornstarch mixed with a little water, sugar, spices, and lemon juice, and cook for 5 minutes. Remove. Cool. Chill very well in refrigerator. Serve in glass bowls. Garnish with sour cream and a blueberry on top.   *Serves 4–6.*

Note: Cornstarch gives body to soup. Omit if you desire.

Cold Cherry Soup

4 cups sour cherries, pitted	A little freshly grated nutmeg
2 cups water	1 tablespoon cornstarch
1½ cups red wine	1 lemon
½ cup sugar	½ cup sour cream
3 cloves	Thin lemon slices
1 stick cinnamon, crumbled	

Chop cherries in food processor or blender until just chopped. Place in bowl and refrigerate. Into a saucepan put water, wine, sugar, cloves, cinnamon, and nutmeg. Cook while stirring for 5 minutes, then strain.

Mix together cornstarch and the juice of ½ lemon to make a paste. Whisk it into the strained mixture. Bring to a boil to thicken slightly. Cool by stirring over a bowl of ice. Add the chopped cherries. Mix well.

To serve cherry soup, place sour cream in chilled bowl and slowly whisk cherry soup into sour cream. Serve in chilled glass serving bowls with slices of lemon.

Serves 4–6.

Note: Cornstarch gives body to soup. Omit if you desire.

Recipes in this chapter:

MINI MEAT LOAVES
BASIC ONE-HOUR STEW
BROILED CANADIAN BACON SLICES
HAM FRITTERS
GROUND LAMB KABOBS
SPICY SHOULDER OF LAMB
CURRY-GLAZED PORK BUTT
HAM SALAD ROLLED IN LETTUCE
   LEAVES
LAMB IN RHUBARB SAUCE WITH
   CORIANDER
PHILADELPHIA SCRAPPLE
SAVORY PORK STEAKS
BEEF BIRDS
HAM BALLS WITH MUSTARD SAUCE
MEDALLIONS OF PORK
VEAL SCALOPPINE MARSALA
PARMESAN VEAL
VEAL SCALLOPS WITH ASPARAGUS
BUTTERFLIED LEG OF LAMB
PORK MEDALLIONS AND APPLE RINGS
STUFFED PORK CHOPS WITH
   WATERCRESS
PARMESAN BACON
PORK PATTIES WITH SAGE AND
   ORANGE
BAKED SAUSAGE WITH ZUCCHINI
VEAL PAPRIKA
LAMB WITH EGGPLANT
CHICKEN LIVERS AND MUSHROOMS
   ON SKEWERS
SIRLOIN STEAK ON SKEWERS
BAKED WHOLE CALF'S LIVER
CHICKEN LIVERS WITH PEARS
ORANGE HAM SLICE
SLIVERS OF LIVER WITH ORANGE
LAMB CHOPS WITH PARSLEY AND
   GARLIC
STUFFED VEAL CHOPS
LAMB PATTIES WITH MINT
MINUTE STEAKS
ORIENTAL PORK CHOPS
CHILI LIVER STRIPS
TWENTY MEATBALLS
PICADILLO
BAKED LAMB CHOPS IN ZINGY SAUCE
CURRIED MUSTARD PORK CHOPS
CHILI PORK PATTIES
FAST BEEF STROGANOFF

MEATS

In my collection of old cookbooks, most of them purchased for a dollar or two at thrift shops and garage sales, there is one published back in 1932, with a special section devoted to "Recipes for Working Wives." I don't think 1932 was a vintage year for American cookbooks, and none of those old recipes are usable today. All the vegetables are cooked at least half an hour, to make sure they turn flabby and gray and tasteless, and to make it easier to pour all the vitamins and food value down the sink with the cooking water. But what makes those old recipes seem even stranger, and more old-fashioned, is that the meat section is filled with recipes for beef: pan-fried (and breaded!) steaks; lots of hamburger casseroles, with and without carrots, potatoes, rice, or noodles.

Beef seems to be disappearing from the American diet. Even on restaurant menus you see nothing more than a steak, in lonely splendor, priced at least five dollars higher than any other entrée; sometimes a filet, too, at three dollars more than the steak. The steak is always sirloin or New York strip. I can't remember when I last saw a porterhouse—the famous old T-bone steak that was the American restaurant standard. Apparently even the people willing to pay beef prices refuse to pay them for bones. Even if you are willing to pay for the best possible beef, you don't always get the best possible beef. Lowered federal standards for prime have all but driven real prime beef from the market.

Although I've included a few recipes for beef, I've concentrated in this section on recipes for other meats. Both veal and liver are cooked quickly, and they offer more consistent value for your money. Chicken and turkey breast can be substituted for veal in any recipe in this or any other cookbook and is a delicious and versatile low-cost convenience meat.

Getting consistently good meat can be a problem. The best way to solve it is to find a butcher you can trust and buy all your meat from him. Actually, that's the second-best way. The best way is my way: my gal Friday, Rose Guarrera, who contributed three of the veal recipes in this book. Rose is married to Vito Guarrera, who owns the best butcher shop in Philadelphia—and every time I order meat, she acts as if her job, and her husband's business, were on the line. Every piece of meat I get has been inspected for the slightest blemish or hint of toughness by an Italian-American housewife—the world's fussiest food shopper. So I thought I should take the time at the beginning of this section to say: Thanks, Rose.

These loaves are excellent cold with horseradish or hot with fresh tomato sauce.

Mini Meat Loaves

1 pound ground beef	1 small green pepper, chopped
½ pound ground pork	1 tablespoon chopped basil
½ pound ground veal	Salt and fresh pepper to taste
1 small onion, chopped	2 eggs, beaten
1 clove garlic, chopped	¼ cup red wine or water
1 small carrot, grated	Six 1½-inch cubes sharp Cheddar
1 medium potato, grated	cheese

Place all ingredients except cheese in a large bowl. Mix together lightly but thoroughly. Divide and shape mixture into 6 small loaves. Place loaves on a baking pan or in individual loaf molds. Press a piece of cheese into the top of each loaf. Bake at 375° F. for 30 minutes. Serve warm or cold.   *Serves 6.*

How many times I have come home late from work and desired the taste of a good old-fashioned stew, but time was against me. I usually prepare those kinds of dishes on weekends.

However, after some experimenting, I came up with this solution. I must be honest and say that it doesn't have that flavor of being cooked over a long period of time, but it does satisfy. It is important to have a good quality of meat so stew cooks rapidly. Do not cut meat in larger chunks, as it takes too long to cook.

Basic One-Hour Stew

2 cloves garlic, chopped
2 shallots, chopped
2 medium onions, chopped
1 large tomato, peeled, seeded, and chopped
5 tablespoons butter
2 tablespoons vegetable oil
2½ pounds beef round or sirloin, cut into small, 3/4-inch cubes, or cut into strips, size of index finger (see note below)
1/4 cup brandy

1 teaspoon chopped fresh thyme
1 bay leaf
1 tablespoon roughly chopped parsley
Salt and fresh pepper to taste
2 cups chicken stock
1 cup dry red wine
1½ cups sliced carrots
1½ cups sliced mushrooms
2 teaspoons potato starch (optional)

Chop garlic, shallots, onions, and tomato in food processor. Heat 4 tablespoons butter with oil in a casserole and sauté beef pieces a few at a time on both sides. Pour off fat. Return meat to pan.

Flame with brandy (see instructions p.298). Add garlic, shallots, tomato, onions, thyme, bay leaf, parsley, salt, and pepper. Stir well to mix. Add the stock and wine. Bring to a boil. Turn to a simmer. Cover with heavy lid. Cook for 45 minutes. While meat is cooking, place carrots in boiling water; cook 5–10 minutes until tender-crisp. Drain and add to stew. Melt 1 tablespoon butter in a pan. When hot, sauté mushrooms for 2–3 minutes. Add to stew. The entire cooking time for the stew is 45 minutes. If sauce is too thin, dissolve potato flour in 1 tablespoon cold water. Whisk into stew.

VARIATIONS:

1. Substitute lamb or veal for the beef and use either red or white wine. Use lamb and veal from the leg or shoulder.

2. A cut-up chicken may be used. Cook until leg juices run clear.

3. If time allows, add 1 cup peas, shelled and boiled for 3–5 minutes.

(continued)

To Flame Meat for Stews

For a gas stove: Always pour off fat from pan before flaming. Return meat to pan, add brandy and tilt pan into gas flame to ignite. (Don't forget to tilt your head back and away from the flame!) Shake pan until flame dies out.

For an electric stove: Heat brandy in a small pipkin or little pan over electric burner until just finger warm. Strike a match and ignite. Pour flaming brandy over meat in pan. Shake pan till flame dies down.

Brush these bacon slices with honey or brown sugar for a flavor change.

Broiled Canadian Bacon Slices

1–1½ pounds Canadian bacon, sliced ¼ inch thick

Lay bacon slices on broiler rack 3 inches from unit. Broil 3 minutes on one side, turn, and broil 3 minutes on other side.   *Serves 4–6.*

For the best flavor use a ham with a rich, smoky flavor. I favor country hams.

Ham Fritters

2 cups flour	4 large eggs
1 tablespoon curry powder	1½ cups ground country-style
2 cups boiling water	smoked ham

Combine flour and curry in a saucepan. Add boiling water all at once; stir until mixture leaves sides of pan. Beat in eggs one at a time, beating well after each addition. Add ham. In deep fryer, heat fat to 375° F. Drop ham mixture by tablespoonfuls into hot fat. If desired, drop by teaspoonfuls and use as snacks. Fry 4–5 minutes or until golden brown.   *Makes 36 fritters.*

Ground Lamb Kabobs

Kabobs

1 pound lamb, ground
½ cup grated carrots
1 egg
1 medium onion, finely chopped
¼ cup Parmesan cheese
   Salt and fresh pepper to taste

Marinade

½ cup olive oil or salad oil
   Juice of 1 lemon
1 clove garlic, finely chopped
   Salt and fresh pepper to taste

Mix all ingredients of kabob mixture in a bowl until well blended. Scoop out a rounded tablespoon of the meat mixture and make balls, pressing the meat firmly together with your fingers. Spear lamb balls in the center with wooden kabob sticks—3 on a stick. Place in a shallow dish. Combine marinade ingredients and pour over kabobs. Place baking dish 4–5 inches from top of meat to heat, turning kabobs until brown on all sides. Brush with the marinade as you turn the kabobs.

Serves 6.

Spicy Shoulder of Lamb

6 medium onions, finely chopped
5 tablespoons butter
1½ pounds lamb, shoulder cut, in ¾-inch cubes
1½ tablespoons finely chopped fresh coriander
¾ tablespoon turmeric
½ tablespoon cumin
1 teaspoon grated fresh ginger

   Red chilies to taste
   Salt and fresh pepper to taste
½ cup yogurt
¼ cup white seedless raisins
1 small tart apple, chopped
3 tomatoes, peeled, seeded, and chopped
½ cup red wine
   Rice Pilaf

In a deep 10-inch pan that has a lid, cook onions in butter until well browned. This takes 8–10 minutes, as a lot of moisture is given off by the onions. Add lamb, coriander, turmeric, cumin, and ginger. Cook over medium heat, stirring constantly, 10–12 minutes. Add chili, salt, pepper, yogurt, raisins, apple, and tomatoes. Stir well with wooden spoon and cook without a lid until all moisture has been absorbed, which takes 25–30 minutes (there is a lot of moisture). Add wine, cover, cook until meat is tender, 20–30 minutes. Serve with rice pilaf.

Serves 8.

Don't be put off by this strange combination. It works!

Lamb in Rhubarb Sauce with Coriander

2½ cups sliced fresh rhubarb
¾ cup sugar
¾ cup water
¼ cup butter
1 large onion, chopped
1½ pounds shoulder of lamb, cut in ¾-inch cubes
Salt and pepper to taste

½ teaspoon cinnamon
Freshly grated nutmeg
1 cup chopped parsley
1 tablespoon cornstarch
Rice Pilaf
Chopped fresh coriander

Place rhubarb in a bowl, add sugar and water, and set aside. In a 10-inch skillet with a lid, melt butter, add onion, cook 3 minutes, then remove. Sauté lamb on all sides until golden brown, replace onion, and add seasonings, parsley, and rhubarb. Continue simmering, covered, 20–30 minutes or until meat is tender. Combine cornstarch with a tablespoon of water and stir into mixture until slightly thickened. Serve over rice pilaf. Sprinkle with fresh coriander, to taste.   *Serves 4–6.*

Scrapple has long been a Philadelphia favorite. It is a mixture of ground pork scraps and cornmeal, usually sold in bricks, loaves, or thick slices. It is usually fried or sautéed for breakfast. I like broiling it, as it then does not cook in its own fat. Scrapple is very popular in the Pennsylvania Dutch country and often served with apple butter.

Philadelphia Scrapple

1 pound scrapple

Cut scrapple in six pieces and place on rack of broiler pan. Place pan on oven rack so top of scrapple is 4–5 inches from broiler heat. Brown on first side, then turn and brown on second side. Surface will be brown and slightly crisp. Apple rings that have been dipped in melted butter and brown sugar may be cooked at the same time on the broiler pan as a nice complement to scrapple.

Serves 4–6.

Curry-Glazed Pork Butt

1½ – pound boneless pork butt
¼ cup packed brown sugar
1 teaspoon curry powder

1 tablespoon orange juice
2 tablespoons orange rind

Place pork butt in large pan with water to cover. Bring to boil, reduce heat, cover, and simmer 45 minutes. Remove from pan. Make 4 or 5 slashes about 1 inch apart almost three-quarters through meat. Place in baking pan. Make a curry glaze by mixing together the brown sugar, curry powder, orange juice, and orange rind. Spread it over the pork. Bake at 350° F. for 15 minutes.　　　　*Serves 4–6.*

This is good finger food, especially to carry on a picnic.

Ham Salad Rolled in Lettuce Leaves

2 cups ground ham (preferably smoked country-style to get good flavor)
3 tablespoons finely chopped onion
1 tablespoon capers, chopped

3–4 tablespoons mayonnaise, preferably homemade
2 teaspoons Dijon mustard
6 lettuce leaves, blanched if desired

Combine all ingredients except lettuce leaves; mix well. Place about ⅓ cup ham salad mixture on each lettuce leaf; roll up. Chill.　　　　*Serves 6.*

Savory Pork Steaks

6 pork steaks (about ½ inch thick)
¼ cup flour
2 tablespoons butter
¼ cup water
¼ cup packed brown sugar

½ teaspoon ground cinnamon
Dash of ground cloves
2 tablespoons vinegar
Salt and fresh pepper to taste
2 large cooking apples, thinly sliced

Coat pork well with flour. In a 10-inch skillet, brown steaks in butter. Add water; cover and cook over medium heat 15 minutes. Combine brown sugar, spices, and vinegar. Pour over meat; salt and pepper; top with apples. Cover and simmer 15 minutes more.   *Serves 4–6.*

These are sometimes called beef roll-ups or rouladen. Don't forget to remove the picks or string before serving.

Beef Birds

Birds

1 pound round steak, cut very thin in ovals about 4 by 8 inches, then each cut in half
1 tablespoon vegetable oil
1 tablespoon butter
2 tablespoons brandy
1½ cups chicken stock
½ cup water

Stuffing

1 tablespoon butter
¼ pound sweet Italian sausage, casing removed
1 small rib celery, chopped fine
1 medium onion, chopped fine
1 small apple, chopped fine
1 tablespoon finely chopped parsley
1½ cups fresh bread crumbs
Salt and fresh pepper to taste

Preheat oven to 350° F. For the stuffing, melt butter and sauté pieces of sausage, broken fine, with the celery, onion, apple, and parsley, stirring constantly. Place lid on to cook for 2–3 minutes on medium-high heat. This will give some moisture to mixture. Add this mixture to the bread crumbs and season with salt and pepper. Stir around lightly with fork.

To prepare the birds, lay all pieces of beef out on board. Pound once or twice with a wet cleaver. Add a rounded tablespoon of filling on top of each piece. Roll birds over and stick with a couple of toothpicks or tie. Heat oil and butter in large sauté pan and brown birds on all sides over medium-high heat. Place in baking dish. Deglaze sauté pan with brandy, stirring around to loosen the brown bits. Pour into casserole. Add chicken stock and water, cover, and cook in oven at 350° F. for 45 minutes or until birds are fork-tender. Test meat at end of 30 minutes.

Remove birds to serving dish. Reduce juices to half. Pour over birds and serve.

Serves 6.

Ham Balls with Mustard Sauce

Ham Balls

- 1 pound precooked well-flavored ham, ground
- 1 egg, beaten
- 1 medium onion, finely chopped
- 2 teaspoons Dijon mustard
- ½ cup dry bread crumbs
- 2 tablespoons chopped parsley
- 1 teaspoon Worcestershire

Salt and fresh pepper to taste
- 6 tablespoons milk
- 4 tablespoons vegetable oil

Mustard Sauce

- ½ cup white vinegar
- ¾ cup light brown sugar
- 1 tablespoon horseradish mustard
- 2 teaspoons potato starch

Have the butcher grind precooked ham or use processor to grind or finely chop pieces of ham or leftover ham from a previous menu. Add egg, onion, mustard, bread crumbs, parsley, Worcestershire, salt, and pepper and combine thoroughly. Add milk, a little at a time, until the ham mixture feels that it will hold together when making the ham balls. Use a rounded tablespoon of meat mixture and roll balls firmly with the fingers.

In a 10-inch sauté pan over medium heat, heat 2 tablespoons of vegetable oil and brown half the balls carefully, moving them around with a wooden paddle. Don't crowd the balls. Remove ham balls from pan, scrape and clean the pan thoroughly, then start a second frying with remaining 2 tablespoons of oil and sauté remaining balls. Cook vinegar, brown sugar, and horseradish mustard together, allowing vinegar fumes to cook off. Mix the potato starch with a little cold water and stir it into the sauce while it simmers 3–5 minutes. Serve the warm sauce with the ham balls.

Serves 6.

Veal can be substituted for pork in this recipe.

Medallions of Pork

3 tablespoons butter
6 medallions of pork (rib chops, boned and tied) 1½ inches thick
Juice of ½ lemon

½ cup chicken stock
½ teaspoon chopped fresh thyme
½ cup heavy cream
Salt and fresh pepper to taste

Melt butter in a skillet. Sauté the medallions until brown, about 3 minutes on each side. Remove from pan. Add the lemon juice, chicken stock, and thyme and boil 3 minutes. Add the cream and bring to a boil. Turn burner to medium. When the mixture coats a spoon (3 to 5 minutes), put back medallions. Season with salt and pepper. Cover. Simmer for 20 minutes until tender. Remove lid. If there is too much sauce, reduce. Remove strings from meat and pour sauce over medallions. *Serves 4–6.*

This recipe—plus Parmesan Veal and Veal Scallops with Asparagus—is an adaptation of those prepared by my gal Friday, Rose Guarrera.

Veal Scaloppine Marsala

8–12 veal scallops
Salt and fresh pepper to taste
½ cup flour

6 tablespoons butter
½ cup chicken stock
1 cup dry Marsala

Pound veal slices as thin as possible between sheets of wax paper. Season with salt and pepper. Pat with flour. Shake off excess. Brown in 4 tablespoons butter in large frying pan over high heat until golden brown. Transfer to a hot serving platter and keep warm. Add stock and Marsala to pan and reduce over high heat to half. Remove from heat and stir in 2 tablespoons of butter. Pour sauce over veal and serve. *Serves 4–6.*

Parmesan Veal

1½ cups fresh bread crumbs
½ cup freshly grated Parmesan
   cheese
2 tablespoons chopped parsley
   Salt and fresh pepper to
   taste

8–12 veal scallops (3 by 5 inches),
     cut very thin
2 eggs, slightly beaten
½ cup oil

Mix together bread crumbs, Parmesan cheese, parsley, salt, and pepper. Dip veal in egg and cover thoroughly with bread crumb mixture. Heat oil in a large frying pan over medium-high heat. Cook veal slices for about 2 minutes on each side until golden brown.

Serves 4–6.

Veal Scallops with Asparagus

16–24 thin or 8–12 large asparagus
     spears
8–12 veal scallops (3 by 5 inches)
     Salt and fresh pepper to
     taste
½ cup flour

3 tablespoons butter
3 tablespoons oil
⅓ cup dry white wine
⅓ cup chicken stock
8–12 thin slices of fontina cheese

Cook asparagus in boiling water until tender-crisp, 5–7 minutes for thin and 7–12 minutes for thick. Refresh in cold water. Pat dry. If using large spears, cut in half lengthwise. Set aside.

Pound veal scallops as thin as possible between sheets of wax paper. Season with salt and pepper. Pat with flour, shaking off excess. Brown over high heat in hot butter and oil for 1 minute on each side. Transfer veal to a large shallow baking pan that can accommodate it in a single layer.

Pour out fat from fry pan, add wine, stock, and any juices that have dripped into baking pan, and reduce to half. Top each slice of veal with asparagus, dividing it evenly, and 1 slice of cheese. Spoon a little sauce over each scallop. Seal baking pan with foil, making sure it is airtight. Bake in upper part of 425° F. preheated oven for 10 minutes.

Serves 4–6.

This lamb is superb as is but even better if there is time to marinate it for at least an hour. Lamb haters devour this with relish.

Butterflied Leg of Lamb

½ cup olive oil
   Juice of 2 lemons
2 cloves garlic, chopped
   Salt and fresh pepper

1 tablespoon chopped rosemary
6- pound leg of lamb, boned and butterflied

Mix olive oil, lemon juice, garlic, salt, pepper, and rosemary in a bowl. Lay meat flat on a rack over a baking pan. Brush with the oil mixture. Place meat 4 inches from broiler. Broil 10 minutes, baste, and broil 10 minutes longer. Turn over, brush with oil mixture, and broil until done, basting every 10 minutes. It takes 25–35 minutes to broil. The meat is uneven and will give rare, medium, and well-done servings. Carve on the diagonal into very thin slices.   *Serves 6.*

Pork Medallions and Apple Rings

1 pork tenderloin, cut into medallions ½ inch thick
¼ cup flour
   Salt and fresh pepper to taste
3 tablespoons butter
   Juice of ½ lemon

2 tablespoons finely chopped parsley
1 large apple, cored and cut across into thin rings
2 tablespoons sugar

Pound medallions with flat side of a wet cleaver to make them thin. Pat the medallions on both sides with flour, salt, and pepper. Melt 2 tablespoons butter in a large skillet and, when hot, sauté medallions to lightly brown on each side. Make certain that they are cooked all the way through, about 5–10 minutes. Sprinkle them with lemon juice and parsley. For the apple rings, melt 1 tablespoon butter in another pan. When hot, add apples, carefully! Sprinkle half the sugar over, turn apples, and sprinkle with remaining sugar. Cover with lid. Cook 2–3 minutes. Apples should be tender, crisp, and caramelized.   *Serves 4-6.*

Stuffed Pork Chops with Watercress

6 loin pork chops, 1 inch thick
4 tablespoons butter
1 medium onion, finely chopped
¾ cup soft bread crumbs
½ teaspoon chopped fresh thyme
½ cup finely chopped watercress
  leaves

Salt and fresh pepper to taste
1 egg, beaten
½ cup dry sherry
½ cup chicken stock

Slit each chop to make a pocket. Melt the butter in a skillet. Sauté onion 2–3 minutes, add the crumbs, and stir to mix. Add thyme and mix in. Remove to a bowl. Add watercress, salt, pepper, and egg. Mix well with spatula or hand. Stuff mixture into pork chops and close slits with toothpicks. Place chops in baking pan. Add sherry to pan, cover, and bake at 350° F. for 30 minutes. Remove cover, turn chops over, and continue to cook until done, another 10 minutes. Remove chops. Remove fat from baking pan, add the chicken stock, and boil for 2–3 minutes. Pour over chops.

Serves 6.

Note: You may use whole wheat or rye crumbs.

VARIATION:

You may substitute veal chops for pork, in which case reduce cooking time to 30 minutes total.

Parmesan Bacon

1 tablespoon olive oil
1 tablespoon butter
12 slices of Canadian bacon, ¼
  inch thick

2 eggs beaten with 1 tablespoon
  milk
1 cup dry bread crumbs
2 tablespoons freshly grated Parmesan cheese

In large 10-inch sauté pan, heat oil and butter. Dip bacon in egg mixture, then drop in bread crumbs mixed with Parmesan cheese. Firmly pat each side. When fats are foaming, add bacon, cooking on medium heat to brown—2–3 minutes on each side. Use a pancake turner so as not to break up coating. Bacon should be golden crisp.

Serves 4–6.

Pork Patties with Sage and Orange

1½ pounds ground pork
2 eggs, beaten
　Salt and fresh pepper to taste
½ teaspoon chopped fresh sage
　(or more)

1 tablespoon grated orange rind
1 tablespoon oil (optional)
2 tablespoons butter
1 medium onion, chopped
1 cup red wine

Put ground pork into bowl. Add eggs, salt, pepper, sage, and orange rind. Form into 6 patties. Sauté in dry, heavy pan (fat will come out of patties) and cook 3 minutes on each side. If pork is extra lean, add 1 tablespoon oil. Remove patties from pan and add butter. Sauté onion until limp, 2–3 minutes. Add wine and bring to a boil. Boil 3 minutes. Add the patties, cover, and simmer 10 minutes. Remove cover, raise heat, and cook 3 minutes longer. Serve with the juices and onion in pan.

Serves 4–6.

This is a meal in itself.

Baked Sausage with Zucchini

4 tablespoons butter
2 pounds zucchini, sliced
½ cup finely chopped onion
1 pound bulk sausage
1 teaspoon chopped fresh thyme

Salt and fresh pepper to taste
½ cup fine dry bread crumbs
2 eggs, beaten
½ cup freshly grated Parmesan
cheese

Heat butter in skillet. When hot and foamy, add zucchini. Toss for 2–3 minutes. Remove zucchini and add onion. Cook 2–3 minutes. Add sausage, thyme, salt, and pepper. Stir to break up meat. Put back zucchini. Mix well. Add bread crumbs, eggs, and ¼ cup cheese. Mix. Pour into 1½-quart shallow casserole or baking dish. Sprinkle with remaining cheese. Bake at 350° F. for 15–20 minutes.

Serves 4–6.

Veal Paprika

1 large onion, thinly sliced	2 tablespoons paprika
4 tablespoons butter	¼ cup dry white wine
2 pounds leg veal cut in thin strips	1½ cups chicken stock
	1 cup sour cream
¼ cup flour	Cooked noodles

In a 10-inch skillet, cook onion in 1 tablespoon butter until tender but not browned. Remove from pan. Coat veal well with flour. Add some of remaining butter to skillet and brown veal, a small amount at a time, until all butter is used and all meat browned. Remove meat as each portion is browned. Add paprika and cook 1–2 minutes stirring well. Add wine to skillet; cook until reduced to syrup. Add chicken stock, onions, and veal. Bring to boil, reduce heat and cook, covered, over low heat about 25 minutes. Uncover; reduce liquid by cooking 10 minutes more. Just before serving, add sour cream. Serve over noodles. *Serves 4–6.*

VARIATION:

Substitute chicken strips for veal.

Lamb with Eggplant

1 large onion, thinly sliced	chopped
4 tablespoons butter	2 cloves garlic, chopped
1½ pounds ground lamb	Salt and fresh pepper to taste
1 medium eggplant, peeled and cut in ½-inch cubes	½ cup dry white wine
3 large tomatoes, peeled and	1 teaspoon potato flour (optional)

In a 10-inch heavy skillet, sauté onion in 3 tablespoons butter; push to one side. Add remaining 1 tablespoon butter and the lamb. Cook until pink color disappears, stirring to break up meat. Add remaining ingredients except potato flour. Cover, then cook over medium heat, stirring occasionally, 15 to 20 minutes or until eggplant is done. Combine potato flour and 1 tablespoon water; add to skillet. (The liquid in pan depends upon how much juice there is in the tomatoes and eggplant. If there is none, do not thicken.) Heat, stirring, until liquid thickens slightly.

Serves 4–6.

Chicken Livers and Mushrooms on Skewers

8 pieces of bacon, partially
  cooked, cut into thirds
24 chicken livers

24 mushrooms, stems removed
Salt and fresh pepper
¼ cup (½ stick) butter, melted

Wrap the bacon pieces around the livers. Thread the livers alternately with the mushrooms on each of 6 skewers. Salt and pepper to taste. Roll the skewers in the melted butter. Place on rack over baking pan and broil 2 inches from unit for 5–10 minutes or until nice and brown. Turn once or twice to broil evenly. For outdoor grill, cook 4 inches from hot coals, turning and basting frequently, for 5–10 minutes. Salt and pepper to taste. Some people think salt in bacon is enough.

Serves 4–6.

VARIATIONS:

1. Thread parboiled peeled baby onions on each skewer.

2. Thread pieces of parboiled green pepper on each.

3. Thread slices of apple between each liver.

Sirloin Steak on Skewers

1½ pounds sirloin steak, cut in
  1-inch cubes
1 clove garlic, peeled and
  mashed

¼ cup (½ stick) butter, melted
24 mushrooms, stems removed
Salt and fresh pepper to taste

Rub meat cubes with garlic. Add remaining garlic to melted butter in a small pan. Thread meat and mushrooms alternately on 6 skewers. Salt and pepper them. Roll them in the butter or brush the butter on them. Place on rack 3 inches from broiler unit. Turn to brown all sides, 5–10 minutes. Pour any remaining butter over skewers and serve.

Serves 6.

VARIATION:

For lamb on skewers, substitute 1½ pounds lamb cubes cut from shoulder.

Baked Whole Calf's Liver

1 whole calf's liver, 1½–2 pounds	Few sprigs of fresh thyme
4 tablespoons olive oil	Salt and fresh pepper
¼ cup lemon juice	3 slices of bacon
¼ cup orange juice	1 medium onion, sliced

Place liver in a roasting pan. Brush or rub well with oil, lemon and orange juice, and thyme. Salt and pepper to taste. Lay the bacon on top, and slice the onion over the bacon. Bake in a 375° F. oven for 30 minutes. If too pink for your taste at this stage, continue to cook for another 15–20 minutes. Baste every 10 minutes with pan juices. Serve in very thin slices.

Serves 4–6.

Chicken Livers with Pears

4 tablespoons butter	Salt and fresh pepper
1½ pounds chicken livers, cleaned and dried well	2–3 tablespoons pear vinegar or other vinegar (such as cider vinegar)
1 large pear, peeled, cored, and sliced	2 tablespoons finely chopped parsley
1 medium onion, finely chopped	

Melt butter in a skillet. When hot, add the livers. Do not move them around. Cook 3 minutes. Turn over and cook 3 minutes longer or until no longer red. They should be just pink. Remove to a platter and keep warm. Add the pear and onion and cook until barely tender, 3–5 minutes. Add the livers to the onion-pear mixture and season to taste. Stir to mix well. Add the vinegar, bring to a boil, sprinkle the parsley on top, and serve.

Serves 4–6.

Orange Ham Slice

4 tablespoons butter
2 center slices ham, ½ inch thick
4 oranges: 3 sectioned and 1
   juiced (½ cup juice)

1 tablespoon Dijon mustard
1 tablespoon brown sugar
¼ cup vinegar
Salt and fresh pepper

Melt butter in a large skillet. When hot, sauté ham on both sides until brown. Remove and keep warm on a platter. Add orange sections to fat in the pan and heat for 2 minutes. Remove to platter with ham. Mix together the orange juice, mustard, brown sugar, and vinegar. Add to pan and cook until reduced to half. Season to taste. Arrange oranges on top of ham, and pour the few tablespoons of sauce over.
Serves 4–6.

Note: Please use a ham slice of good smoky flavor.

Slivers of Liver with Orange

Flour
1½–2 pounds calf's liver, cut into
   finger-size strips
4 tablespoons butter

Salt and fresh pepper to taste
Juice and rind of ½ orange
2 tablespoons chopped chives
¼ cup chicken stock

Flour the liver strips. Melt the butter. Sauté the liver for 3–5 minutes. Season with salt and pepper. Remove liver strips to serving dish. Add the orange juice and rind, chives, and chicken stock. Reduce to half while scraping any brown bits. Pour over liver.
Serves 4–6.

Lamb Chops with Parsley and Garlic

4 tablespoons butter
6 loin lamb chops, 1 inch thick
Salt and fresh pepper

½ cup chopped parsley
2 cloves garlic, chopped
Juice of ½ lemon

Melt 3 tablespoons butter in pan. When hot, add chops and brown on both sides (3–4 minutes each side). Salt and pepper to taste. Remove chops. Add remaining tablespoon of butter to pan. Add parsley, garlic, and lemon juice and stir around. Pour over chops.

Serves 4–6.

Stuffed Veal Chops

¼ cup diced prosciutto ham (or other ham)
¼ pound mushrooms, sliced
¼ cup diced Swiss cheese
   Salt and fresh pepper to taste
1 tablespoon chopped tarragon

6 veal chops, 1 inch thick
4 tablespoons butter
4 tablespoons chopped shallots
¾ cup heavy cream
2 tablespoons port wine

Mix the ham, mushrooms, cheese, salt, pepper, and tarragon in a bowl. Make a slit in each chop for a pocket. Stuff mixture into chops. Pinch open edges together. Melt butter in a large skillet. When hot, brown the chops, about 3 minutes on each side. Season with salt and pepper. Remove chops and keep warm. Add the shallots to the pan and cook a minute or two. Add the cream and port and stir. Put back the chops, cover, and cook 10–15 minutes on medium heat. Remove cover. Turn chops and cook 10 minutes longer or until they are tender. *Serves 4–6.*

Lamb Patties with Mint

1½ pounds ground lamb
1 teaspoon chopped garlic
1 egg, slightly beaten
   Salt and fresh pepper to taste

4 tablespoons fresh bread crumbs
2 tablespoons chopped mint
2 tablespoons butter

Put all ingredients except butter into a bowl. Mix thoroughly but lightly. Form into 6 patties. Melt butter in skillet. Sauté the patties 3–5 minutes on each side.

Serves 4–6.

Minute Steaks

4–6 minute steaks (I use N.Y. strip
    steak ½ inch thick)
1 clove garlic, mashed

2 tablespoons oil
Salt and fresh pepper to taste
Watercress for garnish

Rub each steak with garlic. Brush each steak on both sides with oil. Salt and pepper steaks. Cook 2 minutes on each side in very hot pan. (I use a black iron frying pan, well seasoned and no fat for frying steaks.) Serve immediately with watercress.   *Serves 4–6.*

Note: You can substitute steaks 1 inch thick. Cook exactly the same, but count 3–4 minutes on each side for rare, longer for medium. Rather than ruin a good steak by cooking it well done, I would eat pot roast instead.

Oriental Pork Chops

6 thin loin pork chops (about
    1½ pounds)
2 tablespoons butter
1 large onion, thinly sliced
½ pound mushrooms, sliced
1 green pepper, cut into thin
    strips
6 thin slices of lemon

Fresh pepper to taste
¼ cup soy sauce
¼ cup sherry
Juice of ½ lemon
1 teaspoon chopped or grated
    fresh ginger
2 cloves garlic, chopped

In 12-inch heavy skillet, brown chops on both sides in 1 tablespoon butter; remove from skillet. Add remaining 1 tablespoon butter; sauté onion, mushrooms, and green pepper. Remove from skillet. Return chops to skillet; top with onion, mushrooms, peppers, and sliced lemon. Combine remaining ingredients; pour over chops. Cover and cook over medium heat 20–30 minutes or until chops are tender.   *Serves 4–6.*

Chili Liver Strips

1½ pounds beef or calf's liver
¼ cup butter
1 large onion, sliced

Salt and fresh pepper to taste
½ teaspoon chili powder (or
    more)

Cut liver into 4-inch pieces and then into ¼-inch strips. Melt butter in large skillet until hot. Add onion slices and sauté until soft and golden, about 3–4 minutes. Add liver. Sprinkle with salt, pepper, and chili powder. Cook over medium heat, stirring, until liver is cooked through but still pink, about 5 minutes. *Serves 4–6.*

Twenty Meatballs

1 pound ground beef
1 clove garlic, chopped
¼ cup grated Parmesan cheese
½ cup finely grated bread crumbs
1 egg
1 small onion, finely chopped

2 tablespoons sour cream
1 tablespoon roughly chopped parsley
Pinch of fresh oregano
Salt and fresh pepper to taste
2 cups Tomato Sauce

Put all ingredients except sauce into a mixing bowl. Combine and mix well. Wet hands with cold water. Form mixture into walnut-size balls. Drop them into the tomato sauce. Cook, covered, 25–30 minutes.

Serves 4–6 (or more if you make them smaller).

Note: You can also sauté the balls in olive oil until nicely browned.

Picadillo

1 medium onion, chopped
1 small green pepper, seeded and chopped
1 small clove garlic, chopped
2 tablespoons oil
1½ pounds ground beef
¼ cup raisins

2 large tomatoes, peeled, seeded, and chopped
1 tablespoon capers
½ cup dry red wine
¼ cup chopped green olives
Salt and fresh pepper
Hot cooked rice

Sauté onion, green pepper, and garlic in hot oil in a large skillet. Stir in ground beef. Cook until beef loses its color, stirring to break up meat. Drain off fat. Stir in tomatoes, raisins, capers, wine, and olives. Reduce heat. Simmer for about 30 minutes. Season to taste. Serve over hot cooked rice. *Serves 4–6.*

Baked Lamb Chops in Zingy Sauce

6 lamb shoulder chops (about
  2½ pounds)
  Salt and fresh pepper to taste
¼ cup cooking oil
¼ cup chopped shallots
2 tomatoes, peeled, seeded, and
  chopped

2 tablespoons red wine vinegar
1 tablespoon chopped basil
2 teaspoons freshly grated ginger
¼ cup dry vermouth

Season chops with salt and pepper. Place oil in a large skillet. Brown chops in hot oil, 2–3 minutes on each side. Remove and place in 13-by-9-by-2-inch baking pan. Meanwhile, combine remaining ingredients in the same skillet. Stir around with a wooden spatula for 2 minutes. Pour over chops. Bake at 375° F. for 30–40 minutes or until chops are tender, basting meat with sauce occasionally.   *Serves 4–6.*

Note: Thicken sauce, if desired, with 1 teaspoon potato flour dissolved in 1 tablespoon cold water. Whisk into juices. Or instead of using starch to thicken the sauce, remove the chops, keep warm, raise heat, and reduce any excess liquid.

Curried Mustard Pork Chops

6 pork chops, ¾–1 inch thick
2 tablespoons Dijon mustard
¾ cup bread crumbs

2 teaspoons curry powder
2 tablespoons butter, melted
  Salt and fresh pepper to taste

Brush chops with mustard. In a shallow dish, combine bread crumbs, curry powder, and butter. Coat pork chops with crumb mixture. Arrange chops on a well-greased shallow baking pan. Season with salt and pepper. Bake at 400° F. for about 30 to 40 minutes or until chops are tender.   *Serves 4–6.*

VARIATION:

Substitute chicken pieces for the pork. Adjust cooking time: bake at 350° F. for 45 minutes.

Chili Pork Patties

1½ pounds lean ground pork	2 tablespoons oil
¼ cup chopped shallots	½ cup dry white wine
½ teaspoon chili powder	Salt and fresh pepper to taste
1 teaspoon dry mustard	

Combine pork, shallots, chili powder, and mustard. Shape into 6 patties. Heat oil in large skillet. Add patties to hot oil. Brown slowly on both sides on low heat, about 10 minutes. Drain. Add white wine, cover, and simmer 15 minutes (make certain that the pork is thoroughly cooked). Remove patties. Reduce wine, season with salt and pepper, and pour over patties.

Serves 6.

Fast Beef Stroganoff

½ cup flour, or as needed	¾ pound mushrooms, sliced
2½–3 pounds filet of beef, cut into finger-size strips	1 tablespoon flour
4 tablespoons butter, or as needed	1½ cups sour cream
1 medium onion, finely chopped	Salt and fresh pepper to taste

Lightly flour each piece of meat. Melt butter in a large skillet. Quickly sauté the meat for 1–2 minutes. Remove meat and set aside. Add onion and mushrooms to pan (you may need more butter). Cook until onion is soft and mushrooms are cooked, about 5 minutes. Sprinkle over 1 tablespoon flour and rub in with a wooden spatula until flour disappears. Add the sour cream and bring to a boil, stirring. Put back beef strips. Season with salt and pepper. Reheat meat and serve.

Serves 4–6.

Note: Stroganoff usually looks like dog food when it is served on a buffet table. That's because the sour cream separated. To eliminate this the flour is added to the pan and rubbed in.

Recipes in this chapter:

CHICKEN IN RED OR WHITE WINE
WALNUT CHICKEN
CHICKEN THIGHS WITH ROSEMARY
CHICKEN THIGHS WITH VERMOUTH
BROILED DUCK
GINGER-GLAZED CHICKEN
ROAST SQUAB WITH MUSTARD
EASY BROILED CHICKEN
CHICKEN WITH APPLE CREAM
ROAST TARRAGON CHICKEN
FRIED DUCK
CHICKEN IN SAFFRON CREAM
CHICKEN WITH MUSHROOMS
GINGERED CHICKEN WITH YOGURT
DELICIOUS DRUMSTICKS
CRISPY CHICKEN WINGS
CHICKEN BREASTS WITH BASIL
    BUTTER
MINT JULEP CHICKEN
TEPID CHICKEN SALAD WITH SAFFRON
QUICK CHICKEN SUPREMES
CORNISH HENS WITH LIME

POULTRY

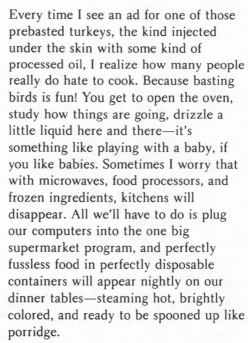

Every time I see an ad for one of those prebasted turkeys, the kind injected under the skin with some kind of processed oil, I realize how many people really do hate to cook. Because basting birds is fun! You get to open the oven, study how things are going, drizzle a little liquid here and there—it's something like playing with a baby, if you like babies. Sometimes I worry that with microwaves, food processors, and frozen ingredients, kitchens will disappear. All we'll have to do is plug our computers into the one big supermarket program, and perfectly fussless food in perfectly disposable containers will appear nightly on our dinner tables—steaming hot, brightly colored, and ready to be spooned up like porridge.

But then I remember the students in my classes who seem eager to make everything from scratch—from classic sauces to chili sauce and chocolate syrup. There seem to be more and more of them every year—and more and more of those prebasted birds, too. That seems to mean that we're dividing up into two camps: the cooks and the anticooks, with absolutely nothing in common. Even our children are going to be divided. Imagine a marriage between a man raised on homemade blueberry muffins and a woman who grew up on Pop Tarts. It's worse than Romeo and Juliet. No matter how polite the families tried to be, the kids would hate each other every time they sat down to a meal.

So stay away from the prebasted birds. Otherwise you'll be sentencing your children to a lifetime of TV dinners.

Chicken in Red or White Wine

6 tablespoons butter
4 pounds chicken pieces (breasts, legs, or thighs)
2 cloves garlic, chopped
2 onions, sliced
1 tablespoon flour
3 tomatoes, peeled, seeded, and chopped

1 cup red or white wine
½ cup sour cream
Salt and fresh pepper to taste
1½ cups sliced mushrooms
Juice of ½ lemon
2 tablespoons chopped parsley

Melt 4 tablespoons butter in a large skillet. When hot and foamy, add the chicken (in batches if necessary) and sauté until brown on all sides—about 8–10 minutes. Remove chicken from pan and put into a casserole. Add garlic and onions to fat remaining in pan and cook 2–3 minutes while stirring. Add the flour and rub it in with a wooden spatula. Add the tomatoes and wine. Mix well. Let cook, uncovered, 5 minutes, while stirring. Whisk in the sour cream. Season with salt and pepper. Pour mixture over chicken in the casserole. Melt the remaining 2 tablespoons butter in a small skillet. Add mushrooms and sauté for 2–3 minutes. Sprinkle with lemon juice. Scatter on top of chicken. Cover casserole. Place in 350°F. oven and cook 20–30 minutes, or until juices of chicken run clear. Garnish with parsley.

Serves 4–6.

VARIATION:

For a different texture, purée the sauce in blender or food processor, pour over the chicken, add the mushrooms, cover, and bake.

Walnut Chicken

2 cups walnut halves
1½ cups peanut or vegetable oil
1 tablespoon cornstarch
2 tablespoons water
2 teaspoons soy sauce

3 whole raw chicken breasts,
  cut into 3/4-inch cubes
½ cup chicken stock
Salt (optional)

Fry walnuts in hot oil, but don't brown. Drain and reserve oil. Combine cornstarch, water, and soy sauce. Place 3 tablespoons of the hot oil in a skillet. Sauté chicken cubes until browned. Add stock. Cover. Cook over high heat 5 minutes. Stir in cornstarch mixture and stir until thickened. Taste and add salt if needed. Add walnuts.

Serves 4–6.

Chicken Thighs with Rosemary

8 chicken thighs
2 cloves garlic, chopped
  Salt and fresh pepper to taste
8 tablespoons butter

8 sprigs fresh rosemary, crushed (1
  tablespoon or more)
8 thin slices onion
8 mushrooms, stems removed

Take 8 pieces of aluminum foil. Lay a chicken thigh on each. Sprinkle garlic over each. Season with salt and pepper. Dot each thigh with 1 tablespoon butter. Sprinkle on the rosemary. Lay a thin onion slice on each and top with a mushroom. Fold packages tightly and lay them on a baking sheet. Place in a 375° F. oven for 35–40 minutes to bake. Serve the chicken in its own juices. *Serves 4–6.*

Chicken Thighs with Vermouth

8 chicken thighs
2 tablespoons butter
1 medium onion, sliced
½ pound mushrooms, sliced

½ cup vermouth or sherry
Juice of ½ lemon
Salt and fresh pepper to taste
2 tablespoons chopped parsley

In skillet, brown chicken in butter; remove and set aside. Add onion and mushrooms; cook until lightly brown and tender. Add vermouth or sherry and lemon juice; cook over high heat to reduce liquid. Return chicken to skillet. Cover; cook over low heat 30 minutes or until done. Season with salt and pepper if desired. Garnish with parsley.   *Serves 4–6.*

You can grill these ducks over charcoal for an outdoor dinner.

Broiled Duck

2 ducks (3½–4 pounds each), at room temperature
2 large cloves garlic, peeled and mashed

Juice of 2 lemons
Salt and fresh pepper to taste

Wash and dry ducks thoroughly. Remove any visible interior fat. Remove tail and backbone by cutting on either side of backbone from neck to vent. Cut on other side from breast to vent. Cut each duck into 4 pieces. Rub pieces on each side with garlic. Place ducks, bone side up, on broiler rack over roasting pan to catch the grease. Squeeze lemon juice on ducks. Sprinkle with salt and pepper. Place 4–6 inches from broiler unit and broil 15 minutes. Remove pan from oven, pour off fat, and turn pieces skin side up. Squeeze lemon juice over duck, sprinkle with salt and pepper, and return to oven. Continue to broil for 20–25 minutes. If duck is getting too brown or charred, move to a lower position in oven. *Serves 4–6.*

Ginger-Glazed Chicken

2–2½ pounds frying chickens, cut up
½ cup ginger marmalade
2 tablespoons ginger-flavored brandy

2 tablespoons oil
Juice of 1 or 2 limes

Arrange chicken pieces in a large, shallow baking pan. Combine marmalade, brandy, oil, and lime juice in a small bowl. Brush on chicken pieces. Bake at 375° F. for 30–40 minutes or until tender and glazed, basting frequently.   *Serves 4–6.*

VARIATION:

Substitute quarters of duck, whole game hens, or squabs for the chicken and adjust cooking times accordingly.

Roast Squab with Mustard

6 squabs
6 tablespoons butter
  Salt and pepper to taste
2 tablespoons mustard

¾ cup dry red wine
¾ cup heavy cream
2 tablespoons chopped parsley

Rub each squab with butter. Place breast side up on rack in roasting pan. Salt and pepper birds to taste. Place in 425° F. oven and roast 25–30 minutes or to desired doneness. Remove from oven and keep warm. Remove rack from pan. Add to pan mustard, wine, cream, and parsley. Bring to a boil. Reduce a few minutes, to thicken. Place squabs on serving platter. Pour sauce over birds.   *Serves 6.*

Note: You can also roast the birds by simply rubbing them with soft butter, salt, and pepper. Just before serving, place on each hot bird a spoonful of flavored butter.

Easy Broiled Chicken

2 2½–3-pound chickens
  Juice of 1 lemon
8 tablespoons butter, softened

Coarse salt and fresh pepper to
taste
Watercress

Cut chicken into serving pieces. Rub pieces with lemon juice, then with butter. Sprinkle with salt and pepper. Place skin side down on broiler pan and place 3–4 inches from broiler unit. Broil 15 minutes. Turn pieces skin side up. Broil 10–15 minutes longer. Baste with juices frequently. Serve with watercress.   *Serves 4–6.*

VARIATION:

Mix 1 clove garlic, chopped, with the butter if a garlic flavor is desired.

Chicken with Apple Cream

2 frying chickens (2½ pounds each), quartered
¼ cup butter
¼ cup Calvados
1 cup dry white wine

1 pound mushrooms, sliced
1 large cooking apple, peeled, cored, and cubed
1 cup heavy cream
Salt and fresh pepper to taste

Partially bone chicken breasts and remove backbone from leg quarters. In a 12–14-inch skillet, brown chicken in butter. Heat Calvados, ignite, and pour over chicken in a large skillet or use 2 skillets. When flame dies down, add wine. Cover; cook over medium heat until chicken is tender (about 20 minutes). Remove chicken to platter and keep warm. Add mushrooms and apple to skillet. Cook over high heat until most of liquid evaporates. Add cream; heat. Season with salt and pepper. Serve chicken with sauce.   *Serves 4–6.*

Roast Tarragon Chicken

1 chicken (3½ pounds), visible fat removed
1 lemon
3 tablespoons butter, softened

2 tablespoons chopped fresh tarragon
Salt and fresh pepper to taste
¼ cup dry white wine

Rub chicken all over with the lemon juice. Put the lemon pieces in the cavity along with 1 tablespoon each of butter and tarragon. Gently separate the chicken skin from the breast meat, using your fingers to loosen the skin without tearing.

Distribute the remaining 1 tablespoon of tarragon mixed with 1 tablespoon of butter between the breast and skin. Rub outer skin with remaining 1 tablespoon of butter. Salt and pepper bird, if desired.

Place chicken in a snug casserole, just to fit, and put ¼ cup wine in bottom. Roast at 375°, uncovered, for 45 minutes or until juices run clear. Remove chicken to carving board and pour juices into a pan. Spoon off fat and boil the juices vigorously to reduce; there should be about 2-3 tablespoons rich juices.

To carve, remove legs and cut across at joints to separate drumsticks and thighs. Remove breast with wing on one side and cut crosswise into 2 pieces. Repeat with other side. You will have 8 pieces of chicken plus the carcass for the cook. Drizzle a bit of juices over the pieces before serving.   *Serves 4–6.*

Note: Turn chicken from side to side every 15 minutes, if desired.

VARIATION:

Rosemary and/or thyme are good substitutes for tarragon, which is sometimes hard to find.

Most of us never think of frying duck because it is so full of fat to begin with. Here the fat comes out of the duck, the skin becomes crispy, and the meat remains moist.

Fried Duck

Oil or shortening	2 ducks (3½–4 pounds), cut into
1 cup flour	pieces
Salt and fresh pepper to taste	Watercress

Place oil or shortening in heavy skillet to depth of ¼ inch. Put the flour, salt, and pepper in a brown paper bag. Shake the pieces of duck, a few at a time, in the flour. When fat in pan is very hot, carefully add the duck. (For 2 ducks, it will probably be necessary to use 2 pans.) Brown on one side for 15 minutes. Turn over and brown other side 15 minutes. Pour off half the fat from skillet. Add ¼ cup water to skillet. Cover, reduce heat, and cook until duck is tender, about 20 minutes, turning twice. Uncover duck last 5–10 minutes to crisp it. Serve with crisp watercress.   *Serves 4–6.*

Chicken in Saffron Cream

6 tablespoons butter
2–2½ pounds frying chickens, cut up
Salt and fresh pepper to taste
1 large tomato, peeled, seeded, and finely chopped

½–1 teaspoon saffron
1½ cups heavy cream
2 tablespoons finely chopped parsley

Melt the butter in a skillet. When hot and foaming, brown the pieces of chicken, 5 minutes on each side. Season with salt and pepper. Pour off the fat. Add the tomato. Add the saffron to the cream and pour over the chicken. Cover and simmer 20 minutes. Stir frequently. Sprinkle with parsley.   *Serves 4–6.*

VARIATIONS:

1. Substitute 1 tablespoon chopped fresh tarragon for the saffron.

2. Substitute 1 tablespoon fresh thyme for the saffron.

Chicken with Mushrooms

4 tablespoons butter
4 chicken breasts, split, skinned, and boned
½ pound large mushrooms, sliced
1 tablespoon flour

¾ cup chicken stock
½ cup light cream
1 teaspoon chopped fresh tarragon leaves
Salt and fresh pepper to taste

In large skillet, melt the butter. When hot, add the chicken and brown quickly on both sides; remove. Add mushrooms and cook 3 minutes; remove. Add flour to drippings. Stir in stock, cream, and tarragon. Cook, stirring, until mixture thickens. Return chicken and mushrooms to pan. Cover; simmer 10 minutes or until chicken is done. Season with salt and pepper.   *Serves 4–6.*

Gingered Chicken with Yogurt

1 cup plain yogurt
1 teaspoon chopped or grated fresh ginger
Salt and fresh pepper to taste
1 small onion, chopped

1 medium clove garlic, chopped
4 chicken breasts, split, skinned, and boned
1 cup fine dry bread crumbs
½ cup melted butter

Preheat oven to 350° F. In a flat dish combine yogurt, ginger, salt, pepper, onion, and garlic. Add chicken and coat well. Dip chicken in crumbs to coat. Place in 3-quart baking dish. Drizzle with butter. Bake 10–15 minutes or until chicken is done.

Serves 4–6.

Delicious Drumsticks

4 tablespoons butter
8 chicken drumsticks
2 cloves garlic, chopped
1 large onion, chopped
4 tomatoes, peeled, seeded, and chopped
1 tablespoon flour
½ cup sherry or Madeira
1 cup chicken stock

Salt and fresh pepper to taste
4 tablespoons freshly grated Parmesan cheese
½ cup almonds, browned and slivered
½ cup sour cream
2 tablespoons chopped parsley

Melt the butter in a skillet. When hot and foamy, add the drumsticks and brown well on all sides. Turn them frequently. This should take about 8 minutes. Remove chicken and set aside. Add garlic and onion to pan and sauté 2–3 minutes. Add tomatoes and stir well. Add the flour and rub it in with a wooden spatula. Add the wine and stock. Bring to a boil. Cook 2–3 minutes. Return chicken to pan and season with salt and pepper. Cover and simmer 15–20 minutes. When drumsticks are tender, remove them from the pan. Add cheese and almonds to the sauce. Whisk in sour cream. Reheat, and return chicken to sauce. Sprinkle with chopped parsley.

Serves 4–6.

VARIATION:

For a somewhat different texture, purée the sauce in a blender or food processor, return to pan, and add chicken, parsley, and almonds.

For my taste, the wings are the best part of the chicken. The wing tips may be removed, but it's not necessary.

Crispy Chicken Wings

2 eggs, beaten
1 cup flour
Salt and pepper to taste
¾ cup milk

12–16 chicken wings
1 cup fine bread crumbs
Fat for frying
Lemon wedges

Beat together eggs, flour, salt, pepper, and milk. Dip chicken wings in batter and roll in crumbs. Heat fat 2 inches deep in pan to point of smoking. Fry wings, 2 at a time, 5–7 minutes. Serve with lemon wedges.   *Serves 4–6.*

Both the basil butter and béarnaise are adaptations for the chicken served at the restaurant next to my school. The chef, Billy Weaver, has had great success with these chicken dishes. For other butters that combine well with chicken.

Chicken Breasts with Basil Butter

4 tablespoons butter
3 whole chicken breasts, split, skinned, and boned

Salt and fresh pepper to taste
Basil Butter (see below)

Melt the butter in a skillet. When hot, add the chicken breasts, a couple at a time, and sauté 3–5 minutes on each side, or until no longer pink. Season with salt and pepper. Serve with a spoonful of basil butter on top of each breast. *Serves 4–6.*

Basil Butter

8 tablespoons butter, softened
1 clove garlic, chopped

2 tablespoons chopped basil leaves
Few drops of lemon juice

Combine all ingredients in a bowl and beat with wooden spatula until smooth.

Place on wax paper or foil and form into a roll. Refrigerate until serving time.

Makes ½ cup.

VARIATIONS:

Chicken Breasts Béarnaise Cook chicken breasts as above. Serve with a spoonful of Béarnaise Sauce.

Chicken Breasts Piccata Cook chicken breasts as above. Squeeze juice of 1 lemon in butter in pan and pour over chicken. Serve with a thin lemon slice on each breast.

Chicken Breasts with Ham and Cheese Cook chicken breasts as above. Place a thin slice of prosciutto ham on each breast and top each with thin slice of fontina cheese. Place directly under broiler until cheese melts.

Mint Julep Chicken

6 tablespoons butter	Salt and fresh pepper to taste
4 whole chicken breasts, skinned and boned	¼ cup bourbon
¼ cup chopped shallots	1 cup heavy cream
½ pound mushrooms, sliced	2 tablespoons finely chopped mint
Juice of ½ lemon	

Melt 4 tablespoons butter in pan. When hot, sauté chicken breasts 1 minute on each side. Remove chicken and keep warm. Add shallots and cook 3 minutes. Add 2 tablespoons butter and sauté mushrooms with lemon juice, salt, and pepper for 3 minutes. Add bourbon and heavy cream and bring to a boil. Put chicken back, cover, and cook 10 minutes. If sauce is too thin, remove chicken and reduce sauce, stirring, until it coats a spoon. Garnish with chopped mint. *Serves 4–6.*

Tepid Chicken Salad with Saffron

3 whole chicken breasts, boned
    and split
2 cups chicken stock
2 ribs of celery, julienned
1 medium cucumber, peeled,
    seeded, and julienned
1 tablespoon very finely chopped
    onion

Juice of ½ lemon
½ teaspoon chopped fresh thyme
2 tablespoons finely chopped
    parsley
½ teaspoon saffron dissolved in a
    bit of chicken stock
Salt and fresh pepper to taste
¼ cup heavy cream

Poach chicken breasts in stock 10 minutes or until fork tender. Drain. Cut chicken in julienne and place in a bowl with celery, cucumber, onion, lemon juice, thyme, parsley, and dissolved saffron. Season, toss lightly, then add cream to just coat salad mixture.

Serves 4–6.

Quick Chicken Supremes

1½ cups fresh bread crumbs
4 tablespoons finely chopped
    parsley
4 cloves garlic, finely chopped
    Grated rind of 1 lemon

Salt and fresh pepper to taste
4 tablespoons butter, melted
4 whole chicken breasts,
    skinned and boned
4 tablespoons Dijon mustard

Preheat oven to 375° F. Mix bread crumbs, parsley, garlic, grated lemon rind, salt, and pepper. Toss lightly with fingers. Add 2 tablespoons melted butter and continue to toss. Hold a chicken breast in palm of hand while spreading a teaspoonful of mustard on top of its smooth side. Drop it on the crumb coating. Spread mustard on facing side and turn breast over. Pat coating firmly but carefully. Lay in shallow baking dish or pan. Follow same procedure for remaining pieces. Drizzle the remaining 2 tablespoons of melted butter over the chicken. Bake at 375° F. 15–20 minutes, or until done.

Serves 4–6.

Cornish Hens with Lime

4–6 Cornish hens (about 1 pound each)
Salt and fresh pepper to taste
2–3 tablespoons butter, melted

½ cup honey or more
4 tablespoons soy sauce
Juice of 2 limes

Preheat oven to 350° F. Season hens with salt and pepper; brush with butter. Place on rack in roasting pan. Combine remaining ingredients for basting sauce. Roast hens 20 minutes; remove from oven. Brush with basting sauce. Return to oven. Continue to roast 30 minutes or longer, basting several times. *Serves 4–6.*

Recipes in this chapter:

SOFT-SHELL CRABS WITH CAPERS
STEAMED FLOUNDER FILETS
BROILED SHRIMP
SHRIMP IN BEER I
SHRIMP IN BEER II
MARINATED SHRIMP
SPEEDY BAKED CRABMEAT
FLOUNDER SICILIAN STYLE
JAMBALAYA
POACHED SALMON STEAKS
FRESH CRAB CAKES
SWORDFISH AND CUCUMBER KABOBS
BROILED BONELESS SHAD
BAKED OYSTERS IN CREAM
CLAMS CASINO
SAUTÉED SCALLOPS
CRÊPES BOMBAY
CREOLE SHRIMP
HELEN'S BAKED SHRIMP
BAKED FLOUNDER FILETS WITH
   HERBS
BAKED FISH STEAKS WITH ANCHOVY
   BUTTER
FISH IN PARCHMENT
OVEN-BAKED SCALLOPS WITH SPINACH
BUTTERFISH WITH MUSTARD
FISH BAKED WITH SOUR CREAM
FRIED CATFISH
ALMOND FISH FILETS
BROILED SHRIMP AND SCALLOPS
SHRIMP TEMPURA

SEAFOOD

Where I grew up in central Pennsylvania in a family who loved to fish, I had plenty of fresh trout and catfish. These fresh-water fish were delicious. But I'll never forget coming to Philadelphia and for the first time seeing a whole fish in a market. It was a big silver and black striped bass, and I'd never seen a fish that fat and funny-looking. I bought it, cooked it that night in lemon and butter, and couldn't believe that anything could taste so wonderful. I've been in love with the taste of fresh seafood ever since.

Now, even if you are land-locked a thousand miles from the coast, fresh seafood is available in quantity. Just be sure you know from whom you are buying it. Fresh fish poaches beautifully. Fish that is not fresh or is frozen will not poach properly. It will fall apart into pieces. This happened to me when I decided to have a party to pay back friends. I decided to poach trout, curl it up with a string through the tail and eye, cover it with aspic, and knock everybody's socks off. I needed twenty-eight trout. I poached them two at a time and every other one disintegrated. I realized some had been over the hill and frozen and some not. I marched over to my brand-new fish seller and told him he was about to become my brand-new ex-fish seller. He couldn't understand how anyone could sell him bad fish—or so he said—but he did scour the market and came up with enough really fresh fish for my party. And we never had any more trouble. Your fish dealer is even more important than your butcher. If you get a tough piece of meat you can always stew it until it is tender. All you get from bad frozen fish is watery shreds.

In New Orleans, soft-shell crabs are called buster crabs. I always thought they were somehow named after the old movie actor Buster Crabbe. But it turns out that they are called busters because they bust out of their shells when they shed. And they have been called busters for over a century—much longer than the movie star has been alive. So, by coincidence or by design, Buster Crabbe is a movie star named after a crustacean.

Soft-Shell Crabs with Capers

8–12 **medium soft-shell crabs**
½ **cup flour**
    Salt and fresh pepper to taste
8 **tablespoons butter**

2–4 **tablespoons capers, or more, washed and drained**
    Juice of ½–1 lemon
    Lemon wedges

Lay crabs on back shell and pull shell from point on back about halfway to remove spongy matter and lungs. Repeat on other side. Remove apron. Rinse and pat dry. (Since this is a *fast* book, it would be easier to have fishmonger clean the crabs.) Flour the crabs and pat off excess. Season with salt and pepper. Heat butter in pan until foamy. Add the crabs and sauté on both sides until brown, 2–3 minutes on each side. Remove crabs and add capers and lemon juice to pan. Stir 1 minute and pour over the crabs. Serve with lemon wedges.   *Serves 4–6.*

VARIATION:

Sauté ½ cup slivered almonds in butter left in pan and sprinkle over crabs.

This recipe is an adaptation of one taught by my assistant Will Kratz. Will has studied with me for years and now teaches classes.

Steamed Flounder Filets

4–5 carrots, peeled and julienned   Salt and fresh pepper to taste
  6 leeks, trimmed and julienned   8 whole thin filets of flounder
  3 tablespoons butter, melted   Fish stock

Lightly butter a shallow baking dish and place in it the carrots, leeks, butter, salt, and pepper. Cover with a piece of foil. Place in a 350° oven and cook for 20–25 minutes, stirring frequently. (If preferred, the vegetables may be sautéed on top of stove.)

Lay filets on a work surface with the skin side down. Place a spoonful of vegetables in the center of each filet and fold over lengthwise. Fold the ends under to keep the vegetables inside. Place remaining vegetables in a layer on bottom of a steamer basket. Lay filled filets on top of vegetables. Pour fish stock (reserving ½ cup for sauce) in bottom of steamer. Place the steamer basket containing fish and vegetables in the steamer. Cover and steam 8–10 minutes, until just done.

Serve with the following sauce:

1 tablespoon butter   8 tablespoons butter, softened
1 shallot, finely chopped   Salt and fresh pepper to taste
½ cup fish stock   Juice of ½ lemon
½ cup dry white wine   2 tablespoons finely chopped
2 tablespoons heavy cream   parsley

Heat butter in small saucepan and add shallots. Cook 1 minute, add fish stock, and reduce until 3 tablespoons remain. Add wine and reduce by half. Add cream. Heat. Beat in butter, 1 tablespoon at a time. Add salt and pepper, lemon juice, and parsley. Reheat any remaining vegetables. Transfer to serving dish. Lay steamed filets on top. Top with a small amount of sauce. Serve remaining sauce on side.

Serves 4–6.

Broiled Shrimp

2 pounds shrimp, peeled
3 cloves garlic, chopped
½ cup olive oil

Juice of 2 lemons
Salt and fresh pepper to taste
2 tablespoons chopped parsley

Lay shrimp in 1½-quart baking dish. Combine garlic, oil, and lemon juice. Pour over shrimp. Salt and pepper, if desired. Place 4 inches from broiler unit. Broil 2 minutes on each side. Sprinkle parsley over.

Serves 4–6.

Shrimp in Beer I

2½–3 pounds shrimp, unpeeled   Beer to cover

Place shrimp in pan. Cover with beer. Bring to boil. Cook 5 minutes. Turn off and let shrimp stay in beer 5 more minutes. Serve warm. Each guest should peel his own. Dip in Cucumber Sauce (see page 444) or melted butter with lemon or eat plain.

Serves 4–6.

Shrimp in Beer II

6 peppercorns
Salt to taste
Juice of 1 lemon
1 bay leaf, crumbled
Leaves from 3 ribs celery
1 tablespoon parsley sprigs,
stems removed

2 tablespoons horseradish
Cayenne pepper to taste
Two 12-ounce cans beer
1½–2 pounds shrimp

Combine all ingredients except shrimp in a saucepan. Bring to a boil. Add shrimp. Return to boil and cook 3 minutes. Turn off heat. Let stand 10–15 minutes. Serve from liquid or strain, as desired.

Serves 4–6.

Marinated Shrimp

Prepare Shrimp in Beer II (see above)
1 cup vinaigrette
Lettuce leaves

Lemon wedges
2 tablespoons chopped parsley, dill, or chives

Peel shrimp. Place in bowl. Add vinaigrette and toss well. Serve on lettuce with a lemon wedge. Sprinkle tops with parsley, dill, or chives. *Serves 4–6.*

For crabmeat lovers this method of cooking is the best. Nothing in the recipe adulterates the sweet flavor of the crab.

Speedy Baked Crabmeat

2 pounds crabmeat, membranes removed
½ cup butter, melted
Salt and fresh pepper to taste

Juice of 1 lemon
1 tablespoon chopped parsley
4 tablespoons brandy

Place crabmeat in shallow baking dish. Pour melted butter over. Season with salt and pepper. Squeeze lemon juice over crab. Sprinkle with parsley and brandy. Bake at 375° F. for 10 minutes, until hot. *Serves 4–6.*

Flounder Sicilian Style

3 sweet red peppers
3 medium zucchini, sliced
8 tablespoons butter
Salt and fresh pepper to taste
4 tomatoes, peeled, seeded, and chopped

1 tablespoon chopped fresh basil
4–6 filets of flounder
½ cup flour
1 tablespoon chopped parsley

Roast peppers under broiler or place on long fork and hold over flame. Keep turning until charred, about 10 minutes. Peel, seed, and cut into strips. Sauté zucchini in 2 tablespoons hot butter until tender-crisp, about 3–4 minutes. Salt and pepper to taste. Sauté chopped tomatoes in 3 tablespoons hot butter for 10 minutes. Add basil, salt, and pepper. Pat the filets with flour on both sides. Sauté in remaining hot butter for 3 minutes on each side over medium-high heat. Arrange vegetables on a heated platter and top with filets. Sprinkle with parsley.

Serves 4–6.

Jambalaya

1 pound cubed cooked ham	½ cup chopped parsley
1 large onion, sliced	½ teaspoon crushed thyme
1 large clove garlic, chopped	leaves
3 tablespoons butter	1 large bay leaf
½ pound thinly sliced peperoni	4 cups chicken stock
4 large tomatoes, peeled and	2 cups rice
chopped	1½ pounds shrimp, cooked and
1 large green pepper, diced	cleaned
½ cup chopped celery leaves	Salt and fresh pepper to taste

In large heavy kettle, brown ham and cook onion with garlic in butter until onion is transparent. Add peperoni, tomatoes, green pepper, celery leaves, parsley, thyme and bay. Bring to boil; reduce heat. Cover; simmer 10 minutes. Add chicken stock; bring to boil. Add rice, reduce heat, cover, and cook 20 minutes or until rice is tender. Add shrimp, salt, and pepper; heat.

Serves 6–8.

If there is no time to make court bouillon, poach the salmon steaks in a mixture of 8 cups of water and 1 cup of vinegar.

Poached Salmon Steaks

6 salmon steaks, 1 inch thick   Court Bouillon

Arrange salmon steaks in a pan. Pour court bouillon over to cover. Bring to a boil. Reduce heat to simmer. Cover and simmer 7 minutes. Serve with Béarnaise (page 446) or a Flavored Butter (page 439).

Serves 6.

Fresh Crab Cakes

1½ pounds fresh crabmeat,
    membranes removed
1 tablespoon finely chopped
    parsley
¼ cup chopped chives
1 tablespoon Dijon mustard
    Juice of ½ lemon

2 eggs, beaten
1–1½ cups fresh bread crumbs,
    lightly packed
¼ cup heavy cream
    Salt and red pepper to taste
4 tablespoons butter

Put crabmeat in a bowl. Add the parsley, chives, mustard, lemon juice, and eggs. Blend well. Add the bread crumbs and mix, adding the heavy cream, salt, and red pepper. If mixture is too dry to form cakes, add a little more cream. Form into about 8 cakes. Melt butter in skillet. When hot and foamy, sauté crab cakes 1–2 minutes on each side or until heated through. Serve with Tartar Sauce.

Serves 4–6.

Note: You can also put all these ingredients into a shallow baking dish and bake in the oven for 10–15 minutes at 375° F.

Any other firm fish can be used in this recipe. Try salmon, halibut, monkfish, lobster, shrimp, or scallops.

Swordfish and Cucumber Kabobs

2½ pounds swordfish, cut in 1-
    inch cubes
2 cucumbers, peeled, seeds re-
    moved, cut in 1-inch pieces

Salt and fresh pepper to taste
½ cup olive oil
    Juice of ½ lemon
1 bay leaf, crushed

Thread fish and cucumbers alternately on each of 6 skewers. Season with salt and pepper. Mix together the oil, lemon juice, and bay leaf. Brush each serving with the mixture. Broil kabobs 4 inches from heating unit (or over charcoal) for 5–10 minutes, turning skewers and basting frequently.

Serves 6.

Broiled Boneless Shad

Shad is and always has been my favorite fish. I remember when my mother baked it in milk for hours to dissolve the bones. Now I buy it boned and broil it for maximum flavor.

1½–2 pounds boneless shad
Salt and fresh pepper to
taste
Juice of 1 large lemon

2 tablespoons butter, in small
pieces
2 lemons, cut into wedges

Generously butter an ovenproof dish and lay shad in dish skin side down. Salt and pepper the shad to taste and sprinkle lemon juice over. Dot with pieces of butter and place in a preheated broiler 4 inches from source of heat. Broil for approximately 5 minutes. Serve with lemon wedges. *Serves 4–6.*

I have my fishmonger open the oysters for this recipe.

Baked Oysters in Cream

24 oysters on the half shell
1¼ cups heavy cream
¾ cup freshly grated Parmesan
cheese

Fresh pepper (optional)
½ cup butter, melted

Place oysters on heated rack or salt, or lay them on a baking sheet. Pour the cream over them. Sprinkle the cheese evenly over them, and sprinkle on fresh pepper if desired. Drizzle the butter over the cheese. Place in oven and broil 5 minutes, 2 inches from unit, or bake at 400° F. for 7–10 minutes. *Serves 4–6.*

I have my fishmonger open the clams. Be certain not to overcook clams, as they will become rubbery.

Clams Casino

8 slices bacon
24 cherrystone clams on the half shell
Salt and pepper (optional)
½ large green pepper, very finely chopped

4 tablespoons fresh bread crumbs
1 tablespoon finely chopped parsley
¼ cup butter, melted
Lemon wedges

Partially cook the bacon—it should still be limp. Cut into 3 pieces each. Arrange clams on heated rack, or lay them on a baking sheet. Salt and pepper if desired. Mix together the green pepper, bread crumbs, parsley, and butter. It should resemble a paste. If too thick, add the bacon fat. Place a bit of this mixture on each clam. Place piece of bacon on each. Broil 5 minutes 2 inches from unit or bake at 400° F. for 7–10 minutes. Do not overcook or clams will be tough. Serve with lemon wedges.   *Serves 4–6.*

Sautéed Scallops

1½ pounds bay scallops
½ cup flour
6 tablespoons butter

Salt and fresh pepper to taste
2 tablespoons chopped parsley
Lemon wedges

Roll the scallops in flour. Pat off excess. Melt butter in skillet. When hot and foaming, add scallops, salt, pepper, and parsley. Toss over high heat 5 minutes. Serve with lemon wedges.   *Serves 4–6.*

Note: If using sea scallops, sauté longer—about 7 minutes.

VARIATION:

Sometimes I add fresh ginger to taste and toss it with the scallops. This combination was served to me by Richard Nelson in Portland, Oregon.

This dish will take you right down to the wire of one hour with not much time to spare!

Crêpes Bombay

Batter for Crêpes (see page 444)
3 tablespoons butter
3 tablespoons flour
2 teaspoons curry powder
1 cup chicken stock

Salt and fresh pepper to taste
½ cup sour cream
1 pound crabmeat
Melted butter
Chutney

Make crêpe batter.

Meanwhile, to make filling: In saucepan, melt butter; blend in flour and curry and cook for 2 minutes. Gradually add chicken stock. Cook, stirring constantly, until mixture comes to a boil and thickens. Season with salt and pepper; blend in sour cream until smooth. Gently fold in crabmeat, being careful not to break into flakes. Keep warm over very low heat.

To make crêpes: Heat 6-inch omelet pan over high heat; add a small amount of butter. Pour in about 2 tablespoons crêpe batter, tilting pan to coat bottom evenly. Brown quickly on each side; stack on wire racks. Repeat until all batter is used.

To assemble: Preheat oven to 375° F. Place about ⅓ cup crab filling on center of each crêpe. Roll and place seam side down in individual baking dishes (or 1 large dish). Repeat until all crêpes are filled. Brush with melted butter. Bake on shelf near top of oven about 15 minutes or until hot and bubbly. Serve with chutney. Makes 9 crêpes.

Serves 4–6.

Creole Shrimp

1 large onion, chopped
1 small green pepper, chopped
2 celery ribs, chopped
1 large clove garlic, chopped
Few sprigs of fresh thyme
3 tablespoons butter
2 tablespoons flour
1 cup chicken stock

6 large ripe tomatoes, peeled and chopped
1 teaspoon chili powder
Salt to taste
2 dashes hot pepper sauce
2 pounds raw shrimp
Salt
Cooked rice

In 10-inch skillet, cook onion, green pepper, celery, garlic, and thyme in butter until vegetables are tender. Blend in flour, then gradually add chicken broth, stirring constantly. Add remaining ingredients except shrimp and rice; simmer 20 minutes. Meanwhile, shell and devein shrimp. Add shrimp to skillet and cook 5–10 minutes or until shrimp are done. Salt to taste. Serve over rice.   *Serves 4–6.*

Helen's Baked Shrimp

12 raw jumbo shrimp
 1 cup butter, melted
 1 cup fine dry bread crumbs
 1 tablespoon finely chopped parsley

1 tablespoon finely chopped fresh dill
¼ cup dry white wine
 Salt and fresh pepper to taste

Remove little legs from shrimp. With sharp knife, split shrimp in half through top shell, being careful not to cut through membrane on lower side. Remove intestinal vein. Preheat oven to 350° F. To make stuffing, combine ½ cup melted butter with remaining ingredients; mix well. Stuff each shrimp with about 2 tablespoons mixture. Place in individual baking dishes; drizzle with remaining butter. Bake in 350° F. oven for 15–20 minutes.   *Serves 4–6.*

Baked Flounder Filets with Herbs

1½–2 pounds filets of flounder, fluke, or other white fish
 8 tablespoons butter
 Juice of 1 lemon
 Salt and fresh pepper to taste

1 small onion, chopped
4 tablespoons chopped parsley
2 tablespoons chopped chives

Put the butter into a small pan. Melt, add lemon juice, salt, pepper, and onion, and cook 2 minutes. Add the parsley and chives and cook 1 minute. Take a baking dish and pour half the butter mixture in. Lay fish filets on the butter and pour rest of the mixture on top of fish. Bake at 350° F. for 10–15 minutes, depending on thickness of fish. Serve from baking dish.   *Serves 4–6.*

Baked Fish Steaks with Anchovy Butter

6 tablespoons butter
Juice of 1 lemon
2 tablespoons anchovy paste
2 tablespoons finely chopped
chives, parsley, or dill

2–3 pounds fish steaks (tuna, halibut, swordfish), 1 inch thick
Salt and fresh pepper to taste

In a small pan, melt the butter with lemon juice, anchovy paste, and chives, parsley, or dill. Lay steaks on baking pan. Brush tops with half the butter mixture. Bake at 400° F. for 10 minutes, basting once. Fish should just flake. Cook a few minutes longer if better-done fish is preferred. Pour remainder of butter over fish.

Serves 4–6.

These filets were demonstrated in my classes at the Greenbrier by my two favorite young chefs, Liz and Bob Briggs.

Fish in Parchment

Vegetable oil
6 thin fish filets: salmon, flounder, or trout
¾ cup peeled, seeded, and diced
tomato
½ cup sliced mushrooms
4 tablespoons finely chopped
shallots

4 tablespoons butter, melted
Juice of 1 lemon
4 tablespoons white wine
Salt and fresh pepper to taste
2 tablespoons chopped fresh parsley, chives, or dill

Cut 6 hearts from 6 pieces of parchment measuring 6 inches wide by 10 inches long. Lay parchment hearts out flat and brush oil on them. Lay each filet on the right side. Divide all remaining ingredients among the 6 hearts. Fold the edges together by pleating so no steam can escape. Brush outside of hearts with oil. Put on baking sheets into 350° F. oven for 7–10 minutes. Serve 1 to each guest and slit the packages at the table. They should be beautifully puffed. *Serves 6.*

VARIATIONS:

1. Use a Flavored Butter.

2. Use Fennel Butter.

3. Use aluminum foil if parchment is not available.

4. Bake a few at a time if oven is not large enough.

Oven-Baked Scallops with Spinach

9 tablespoons butter	Juice of ½ lemon
2 tablespoons finely chopped shallots	1 cup spinach leaves, stems removed, chopped
1½–2 pounds bay scallops, or sea scallops cut in rounds	2 tablespoons flour
¾ cup vermouth	1 egg yolk
½ cup water	½ cup heavy cream or more
1 pound mushrooms, sliced	½ cup bread crumbs
Salt and fresh pepper to taste	¼ cup freshly grated Parmesan cheese
	2 tablespoons butter, melted

Melt 4 tablespoons butter in saucepan. Sauté the shallots for 1 minute. Add the scallops. Stir around. Add vermouth and ½ cup water. Simmer 5 minutes or until scallops have an opaque look. Remove scallops. Reduce juices to ¾ cup.

Meanwhile, melt 3 tablespoons butter in skillet and add mushrooms, salt, pepper, and lemon juice. Add spinach. Toss mushrooms and spinach for 2–3 minutes. Add juices, if any, to reduction. Next, melt 2 tablespoons butter, stir in flour, and cook 1 minute. Add the scallop juice reduction; whisk until thick. With a fork, beat the egg yolk and heavy cream together. Warm with a bit of the sauce and whisk this mixture into the sauce. If too thick, thin with more cream, just to napping consistency. Combine scallops and mushrooms and spinach mixture with cream mixture. Place in an oval gratin dish. Sprinkle top with bread crumbs and cheese and drizzle melted butter over. Bake at 350° F. until bubbly, about 15 minutes. Place under broiler to brown, if desired. *Serves 4–6.*

Butterfish with Mustard

8–12 butterfish (2 per serving),
   cleaned
½ cup white wine
¼ cup Fish Stock (see page
   448)
   Salt and fresh pepper to
   taste

½ cup heavy cream
1 tablespoon sweet mustard
1 tablespoon strong mustard
2 tablespoons butter, softened

Lay butterfish in baking dish. Sprinkle the wine, fish stock, salt, and pepper over them. Place in a 400° F. oven. Bake 5–7 minutes. Drain juices into saucepan while keeping the fish warm. Add cream and mustards. Cook on medium high flame for 3–4 minutes. Whisk in the butter. Serve sauce over fish.   *Serves 4–6.*

Notice that there is no butter on this fish. The sour cream keeps it moist.

Fish Baked with Sour Cream

1 large onion, sliced thin
1 lemon, sliced thin
¾ cup dry white wine
6 filets of fish, 1 inch thick (halibut, swordfish, or any thick
   fish)

Salt and fresh pepper to taste
1 cup sour cream

Cover the bottom of a shallow baking dish with slices of onion. Lay the lemon slices over the onion. Add wine and stir. Put into 400° F. oven and cook 10–15 minutes to soften. Arrange fish filets on top of onion and lemon. Sprinkle with salt and pepper. Place in 400° F. oven and bake 10–15 minutes covered. Uncover. Spread the sour cream over the fish and place dish 2 inches from broiler unit. Glaze the top until cream is lightly brown. Serve from baking dish.   *Serves 4–6.*

Catfish is one of the best-tasting fish I know. I still remember when the Forpaugh Circus came to town. The owner, who was a family cousin, always came to our house for dinner. My mother served catfish more than once, as it was cousin Billy's favorite. The circus was later sold to Ringling Brothers, but we still ate catfish.

Fried Catfish

Shortening or bacon fat
4–6 medium-size catfish, skinned, heads and tails removed

1½ cups yellow and white corn-meal, mixed (equal parts)
Salt and fresh pepper to taste

Put fat in a heavy skillet to a depth of ¼ inch. Dip each fish into cornmeal mixture. When fat is hot and to the point of smoking, drop in the fish and fry until brown, crisp, and done—about 8 minutes on one side and 5 on the other. Season with salt and lots of pepper.

Serves 4–6.

Almond Fish Filets

6 fish filets (any white fish in season: flounder, fluke, sole, monk, or trout)
Juice of ½ lemon
1 egg
2 tablespoons milk

½ cup flour
¾ cup ground almonds
2 tablespoons butter
1 tablespoon vegetable oil
Salt and fresh pepper to taste
½ lemon, sliced thin

Wash filets and pat dry with paper towels. Sprinkle lemon juice over fish and pat dry again. Mix the egg and milk. Dip each filet in the mixture, then coat in a mixture of flour and ground almonds. Heat butter and oil in a 10-inch sauté pan until foaming. Add filets and brown on each side on medium-high heat or until filets are golden brown. Sprinkle with salt and pepper and serve with thin slices of lemon.

Serves 4–6.

Broiled Shrimp and Scallops

½ cup vegetable oil
½ cup Tomato Sauce (see page
   447)
¼ cup soy sauce
   Juice of 1 lime
   Salt and fresh pepper to taste

1 tablespoon finely chopped onion
1 clove garlic, chopped
1 pound large shrimp, peeled and
   deveined
1 pound scallops

Combine all ingredients except shrimp and scallops; mix well. Place shrimp and scallops in shallow dish; cover with marinade. Refrigerate until ready to broil. Stir occasionally to coat well. Place seafood on rack of broiler pan. Broil 4 inches from heat about 3 minutes. Turn; brush with remaining marinade; broil 3 minutes more until done.

Serves 4–6.

Tempura vegetables can be served with the shrimp. Use fresh asparagus tips (cook 3 minutes), green beans (3 minutes), wax beans (3 minutes), parsley (1 minute), mushrooms (2 minutes), cauliflower florets (5 minutes), carrot sticks (5 minutes). If you prefer, vegetables (but not parsley and mushrooms) can be parboiled, but all should be golden brown with a slightly crunchy texture.

Shrimp Tempura

Batter

1 egg (beaten)
1 cup ice water
1 cup flour (or more)

2 tablespoons vegetable oil
½ teaspoon salt
½ teaspoon sugar
½ teaspoon baking powder

Make batter by beating the egg and water together in a bowl. With a fork, stir in remaining ingredients. No matter if a few lumps remain. Batter should have consistency to cling to food to be fried.

Shrimp

   Fat for frying

2 pounds raw medium shrimp,
   shelled

Place fat in pan to a depth of 2 inches and heat to 375°F. Dip shrimp in tempura batter, letting excess drip off. Put a few shrimp at a time in hot fat. Cook 2–3 minutes or until golden. Serve while hot and crisp. Keep skimming batter off top of fat. Serve with equal parts of grated turnips and white radishes and dipping sauce.

Serves 4–6.

VARIATION:

Instead of shrimp, fry smelts or pieces of fish filets cut into finger strips.

Dipping Sauce

1 cup chicken stock
1 tablespoon sugar
6 tablespoons soy sauce
1 clove garlic, chopped
1 tablespoon grated fresh horse-radish
1 teaspoon grated fresh ginger

Mix all ingredients together and beat for 1 minute.

Recipes in this chapter:

MUSHROOMS WITH CREAM
SAUTÉED MUSHROOMS
KOHLRABI DAUPHINOIS
BAKED ZUCCHINI AND TOMATOES
BAKED ONIONS
BROILED TOMATOES
OKRA AND TOMATOES
CARROTS AND ZUCCHINI
FRITTERS AND VARIATIONS
GREEN BEANS AND JULIENNE CELERY
SHREDDED RED CABBAGE
PEAS FRENCH STYLE
CABBAGE TIMBALES
FRESH ASPARAGUS LOAF
SAUTÉED BELGIAN ENDIVE
ASPARAGUS WITH WALNUT BUTTER
GREEN TOMATO SAUTÉ
SUCCOTASH
BRAISED SLICED CELERY
COOKED HERBED CUCUMBERS
ACORN SQUASH WITH GLAZED APPLES
STUFFED ONIONS
PURÉED BUTTERNUT SQUASH
ACORN SQUASH WITH SESAME SEEDS
SPINACH WITH BROWN BUTTER
SOUR CREAM SPINACH
BOILED ARTICHOKES
LEMONY TURNIP STICKS
EASY SUMMER SQUASH
BAKED CAULIFLOWER
BROILED TOMATOES AND YOGURT
PARSNIPS WITH PARSLEY
BABY EGGPLANT
BABY LIMA BEANS IN CHERVIL CREAM
SAUTÉED SAUERKRAUT
PENCIL-THIN ASPARAGUS WITH
    WALNUT OIL
QUICK RATATOUILLE
STEAMED GREEN BEANS WITH LEMON
    AND OLIVE OIL
CARROTS STEAMED IN FOIL
VEGETABLE SKILLET
CARROTS WITH PISTACHIO NUTS
SUMMER SQUASH SAUTÉ

VEGETABLES

It's hard to find a recipe for fresh succotash made from scratch. Most cookbooks don't bother with it, and the few that do add a helpful hint like "Succotash is also good made with canned or frozen vegetables." That must be because cookbook writers, like most Americans, don't know anything about fresh succotash, made in the height of the season when baby limas and new corn are both available. Fresh succotash is easy to make, delicious, and a genuine American culinary invention, three good reasons why you should try it. A fourth is that sooner or later the French will discover it, the way they discovered canned corn a few years ago, and put corn in everything, even in salads. When your friends come back from Paris with the latest food fad, you'll be a whole step ahead of them if you start making succotash now!

Many of these recipes are ideal as entrées. There are still some people who think that if they don't eat meat every day their teeth or hair will fall out, but it is not really necessary, or even desirable, to eat meat every day. Corn fritters or vegetable tempura, baked acorn squash or mixed vegetable skillet—all work equally well as main courses or side dishes.

And now, a few words in praise of

roots. We all owe a debt of grat'tude to our children, who discovered how wonderful good fresh vegetables can taste. But the funny thing about these kids is that they've rediscovered the pretty vegetables. I look through shelves of vegetarian cookbooks for the kind that come out in flower-decked paperbacks, all hand lettered and with illustrations showing willowy couples in willowier caftans, and the vegetables turn out to be carrots, daikon, or leafy greens all covered with granola or sprouts. I like sprouts in salads, though if you eat too many of them you come away feeling as if you have hair caught in your teeth. But I rarely see anything about root vegetables. Beets, turnips, rutabagas, parsnips and Jerusalem artichokes are the dark secrets of the American kitchen.

The young people probably dislike root vegetables because not all of them can be cut into slivers and served on a bed of romaine lettuce with a honey walnut dip. But I think my generation dislikes root vegetables because they associate them with the Depression. Mashed rutabagas with old-fashioned uncolored margarine convinced a whole generation that root vegetables on the plate were a confession of poverty in the house.

Whenever I give a turnip recipe to my classes, I hear a soft sigh of despair: "Ohhhhh, turnips . . .

"How many hate turnips?" I ask. Almost all the hands go up.

"How many have tasted turnips in the past five or ten years?" I ask.

And almost all the hands go down.

So try some of these recipes for turnips and parsnips and other roots. Get brave and try Kohlrabi Dauphinois (on opposite page). Many people have never tasted many of the root vegetables, or have forgotten the taste long ago. They're shocked to discover what they have been missing. You can help to convince them that it's time to bring root vegetables up out of the root cellar.

Mushrooms with Cream

4 tablespoons butter
2 tablespoons chopped shallots
1½ pounds mushrooms, cleaned and sliced
¼ cup sherry
1 cup heavy cream
1 tablespoon chopped parsley
Salt and fresh pepper to taste

Melt butter in a skillet. Sauté shallots for 2–3 minutes. Add mushrooms and cook 3 minutes. Add the sherry and cook until almost evaporated. Add cream and cook, stirring, until it coats a spoon. Add parsley, salt, and pepper.   *Serves 4–6.*

Note: To speed up cooking time, add 1 tablespoon flour after sherry has reduced.

Sautéed Mushrooms

4 tablespoons butter
1–1½ pounds mushrooms,
   cleaned, stems removed
   Salt and fresh pepper to
   taste

Juice of ½ lemon
2 tablespoons finely chopped
   parsley

Melt the butter in a skillet until hot. When foamy, add the mushrooms, salt, pepper, and lemon juice. Toss over high heat for 3 minutes. Sprinkle parsley over.

Serves 4–6.

VARIATION:

To vary the flavor of mushrooms, add different herbs. Try tarragon or thyme rather than parsley.

I discovered this method of cooking kohlrabi from a restaurateur student of mine. At first it tastes like turnips or cabbage. It is an intriguing way of fooling your guests. Other vegetables may also be prepared this way, such as turnips, rutabagas, thin slices of onion, leeks, carrots, and potatoes.

Kohlrabi Dauphinois

4–6 medium-size kohlrabi
1 clove garlic, mashed
6 tablespoons butter
   Salt and fresh pepper to taste

1 cup shredded Gruyère cheese
¾ cup freshly grated Parmesan
   cheese
1½ cups heavy cream or more

Remove leaves and trim kohlrabi. Peel, if desired, and slice as thin as possible in the food processor, on a mandoline, or by hand. Rub a baking dish with the garlic and grease with 2 tablespoons butter. Arrange half the slices in the dish. Salt and pepper them. Scatter the Gruyère cheese over them. Arrange the remainder of the kohlrabi in the dish. Sprinkle with the Parmesan cheese. Dot with slivers of 4 tablespoons butter. Pour the heavy cream carefully into the dish. Shake it to let it settle. Add enough heavy cream to come halfway up the side of the baking dish. Place in a 350° F. oven and bake 45 minutes or until the kohlrabi is tender when pierced with the tip of a knife.

Serves 4–6.

This is exceptionally tasty served at room temperature.

Baked Zucchini and Tomatoes

4–6 medium zucchini, sliced on
    the diagonal, ½-inch slices
4–6 tomatoes, sliced vertically
2 medium-size red onions, sliced
2 cloves garlic, chopped
2 tablespoons chopped parsley

Salt and fresh pepper to taste
2 bay leaves, crumbled
1 tablespoon chopped fresh
    thyme
½ cup olive oil

Grease a baking dish with oil. Alternate the slices of zucchini, tomato, and onion. Pack the vegetables into the dish tightly. Sprinkle with garlic and parsley. Season with salt and pepper. Sprinkle with the bay leaf and thyme. Drizzle the olive oil over the top. Place in a 350° F. oven for 30 minutes or longer, until tender-crisp.

Serves 4–6.

Baked Onions

3 large yellow onions
    Salt and fresh pepper to taste
2 tablespoons butter

½ cup shredded Cheddar cheese
½ cup buttered fresh fine dry
    bread crumbs

Preheat oven to 350° F. Peel onions and cut in half crosswise; season with salt and pepper. Place in shallow 1-quart casserole; add enough water to reach ¼ inch up the sides of the casserole. Cover and bake 45 minutes. Combine cheese and crumbs; sprinkle over onions. Bake uncovered 15 minutes more.

Serves 4–6.

Broiled Tomatoes

3 large tomatoes
    Salt and fresh pepper to taste
1 egg, beaten

1 cup fresh fine dry bread crumbs
2 tablespoons butter
2 tablespoons brown sugar

Cut thin slices from bottom and top of tomatoes; cut in half crosswise. Sprinkle with salt and pepper. Dip in egg, then bread crumbs. Place on broiler rack with bottom or top side up. Dot each with butter; broil 4 inches from source of heat; turn and repeat on other side. Sprinkle with brown sugar; brown quickly (few seconds) under broiler.

Serves 4–6.

Note: If you do not care for sugar on tomatoes, eliminate it.

Okra and Tomatoes

¾ pound okra, sliced	2 tablespoons water
Curry powder to taste	1 clove garlic, chopped
1 medium onion, chopped	1 bay leaf, crumbled
3 tablespoons butter	1 teaspoon chopped thyme
3 medium tomatoes, peeled and chopped	Salt and fresh pepper to taste

In 10-inch skillet, cook okra, curry, and onion in butter about 10 minutes. Add remaining ingredients. Reduce heat to low and simmer about 25 minutes or until vegetables are done.

Serves 4–6.

This is a very colorful combination.

Carrots and Zucchini

1 medium onion, chopped	1 pound carrots, thinly sliced
1 tablespoon chopped marjoram	1 pound zucchini, thinly sliced
4 tablespoons butter	Salt and fresh pepper to taste

In 10-inch skillet, cook onion with marjoram in butter until tender. Add carrots and cook 5 minutes, stirring occasionally. Push carrots to one side, add zucchini, and cook 5 minutes more or until vegetables are crisp-tender. Mix or toss cooked vegetables together. Season with salt and pepper.

Serves 4–6.

Fritters and Variations

2 eggs	1 teaspoon salt
½ cup milk	1 tablespoon melted shortening
1 cup all-purpose flour	Vegetable oil for deep frying
1 teaspoon baking powder	

Beat eggs on medium speed of electric mixer for at least 1 minute. Add milk. Mix together flour, baking powder, and salt and add to milk mixture. Add shortening. Beat on medium speed until well blended. You can mix in bowl with a whisk if an electric mixer is not available; or use a processor or blender. Stir in desired fruit or vegetable (see variations below). Heat vegetable oil to 375° F. Allow about 3 minutes for frying time of fruits or vegetables. Makes about 1 dozen.   *Serves 4–6.*

VARIATIONS:

Corn Fritters Add 2 cups fresh uncooked corn to standard fritter batter. Drop by spoonfuls into preheated shortening. Serve with maple syrup.

Fruit Fritters Add 1 tablespoon sugar to fritter batter. Mix 1 cup of any fresh fruit—pears, peaches, or slices of oranges—into batter and fry as above. If using apple or banana slices, dip in lemon juice first to prevent discoloration. Drain fritters on brown paper. Sprinkle with confectioners' sugar.

Vegetable Fritters Any cooked or blanched vegetable, such as cauliflower, asparagus, eggplant, may be cut up and added to standard fritter batter. Use about 1 cup. A good way to use leftovers.

Note: For a thinner batter, increase the milk to create a consistency that will just cling to food to be fried.

Green Beans and Julienne Celery

1½ pounds young green beans	2 tablespoons butter
2 large ribs of celery, about 10 inches long	Juice of ½ lemon
	Salt and fresh pepper to taste

Cut off ends of beans. Cut ribs of celery in 2-inch lengths and julienne. Bring a large pot of water to a boil and drop beans in to cook for about 7–8 minutes. Remove and refresh in cold water. Add julienne celery and cook for 5–7 minutes.

Taste for tender-crunch vegetables. Drain vegetables. Mix together. Add butter and squeeze on lemon juice. Season with salt and pepper. Reheat.   *Serves 4–6.*

Shredded Red Cabbage

2½-pound head red cabbage
2 tablespoons butter
½ cup chicken stock
1 cup red wine
¼ cup sugar
Grated rind of 1 orange
Salt and fresh pepper to taste

Remove any bruised outer leaves of cabbage. Cut cabbage in quarters and shred it into a bowl. Melt butter in large saucepan on high heat. Add cabbage and chicken stock. Cover with lid. Cook on high heat until steamed almost tender— 15–20 minutes. Add wine, sugar, orange rind, salt, and pepper. Continue cooking on low heat 10–20 minutes.   *Serves 6.*

Note: To keep cabbage from turning color, add a few drops of vinegar or juice of half a lemon to it after shredding.

It is definitely worth the effort it takes to shell the peas and peel the onions for this dish.

Peas French Style

8 baby white onions, peeled
2 pounds peas, shelled
2 tablespoons butter
Pinch of sugar
1 small head Boston lettuce, shredded
1 tablespoon flour
Salt and fresh pepper to taste

Bring 1½ cups water to a boil. Add the onions and parboil them for 5 minutes. Add the peas, 1 tablespoon of butter, and a pinch of sugar. Cover with the lettuce and cook, covered, over low heat until the peas are tender, about 15 minutes. While the peas are cooking, make a beurre manié by blending together 1 tablespoon of butter and the flour. When the peas are tender, add the beurre manié in small bits and stir until the liquid has thickened. Season with salt and pepper.   *Serves 4–6.*

These timbales dress up a dinner. Serve them plain, or with melted butter and lemon juice, or reduce 1½ cups heavy cream to 1 cup and add 2 tablespoons chopped fresh dill to serve as a sauce.

Cabbage Timbales

5 tablespoons butter, melted
½ pound cabbage, shredded
¼ cup chopped onion
½ teaspoon caraway seed
Salt and fresh pepper to taste

4 eggs, beaten
1½ cups light cream
2 tablespoons finely chopped
    parsley

Preheat oven to 350° F. Generously grease eight ½-cup timbale molds with 2 tablespoons melted butter. Cook cabbage with onion and caraway in covered skillet until barely tender, 15–20 minutes. Stir frequently. Purée in food processor with 3 tablespoons melted butter until smooth. Combine with remaining ingredients. Spoon into prepared molds; set molds in a pan of hot water. Bake 25 minutes or until knife inserted near center comes out clean; unmold.   *Serves 8.*

This loaf is not very high, as it would take too long to cook. If there is time, bake in a smaller loaf pan. Or bake in individual timbale molds or custard cups.

Fresh Asparagus Loaf

1 tablespoon butter for greasing
    baking dish
1 pound fresh asparagus
2 tablespoons finely chopped
    onion
2 tablespoons chopped parsley

¼ cup butter
1 cup fine fresh bread crumbs
    Salt and fresh pepper to taste
3 eggs, beaten
2 cups light cream
½ cup Cheddar cheese, grated

Preheat oven to 375° F. Generously butter a 9-by-5-by-3-inch loaf pan. Clean asparagus and cut into 1-inch pieces (there should be about 2 cups). Cook; drain well. Meanwhile, in skillet, cook onion and parsley in butter; add crumbs, salt, and pepper. In bowl, combine eggs, cream, asparagus, and crumb mixture. Pour

into prepared pan. Bake 25 minutes or until set. Let stand 5 minutes before unmolding. Unmold and sprinkle with cheese. *Serves 4–6.*

*Belgian endive is one of those vegetables one either loves or loathes. I like it
cooked or uncooked.*

Sautéed Belgian Endive

8 Belgian endive	1 cup heavy cream
8 tablespoons butter	2 tablespoons chopped fresh
½ cup chopped shallots	chervil
Juice of ½ lemon	1 lemon, thinly sliced, slices
Salt and fresh pepper to taste	halved

Trim endive. Remove tough cores. Cut across into small pieces. Melt butter in
skillet. When hot, add shallots. Sauté 3–4 minutes. Add endive. Squeeze lemon
juice over. Season with salt and pepper. Cook, covered, 20 minutes, stirring occasionally. Remove lid and add cream. Continue to cook 10–15 minutes longer. Stir
in chervil. Serve with halves of thin lemon slices around edge of serving dish.
Serves 4–6.

*The word "asparagus" evokes springtime, and when it is in season I eat it every
day. You can also serve it with hollandaise (page 452), vinaigrette (page 456), or
polonaise sauce (page 459).*

Asparagus with Walnut Butter

24 stalks medium-size asparagus,	½ cup butter
trimmed and peeled, if desired	2 tablespoons black walnuts,
2 tablespoons butter	chopped
Salt and fresh pepper to taste	

Bring water to boil in a skillet to barely cover asparagus. Add asparagus and cook,
uncovered, 7–10 minutes, or until tender-crisp. Drain and plunge into ice water to

stop the cooking and refresh the color. To reheat, melt 2 tablespoons butter in skillet. Add drained asparagus and roll in the hot butter. Add salt and pepper. Melt ½ cup butter and add walnuts. Pour over asparagus.   *Serves 4–6.*

Green Tomato Sauté

6 green tomatoes   8 tablespoons butter
¾ cup bread crumbs   Salt and fresh pepper to taste
½ cup brown sugar

Cut tomatoes in half. Trim bottoms and tops. Mix together the bread crumbs and brown sugar. Coat the tomato slices on both sides with the bread crumb–sugar mixture. Melt the butter in a large heavy skillet. When hot, add tomatoes and cook *slowly* for 3 minutes on each side. Season with salt and pepper. Tomatoes should be cooked through, crisp on outside.   *Serves 6.*

VARIATION:

Add ½ cup heavy cream to juices remaining in pan, raise heat, boil, and scrape for 3 minutes. Pour over tomatoes.

In the summer when the corn and limas are at their peak, this combination is the best. They are the two vegetables I miss when in Europe in the summer.

Succotash

2½ pounds fresh lima beans,   Salt and fresh pepper to taste
  shelled   4–5 ears corn on cob, scraped
½ cup milk   2 tablespoons butter

Drop lima beans in boiling water to cover. Cook until tender, 10–15 minutes, depending on size. Drain. Return to pan. Add milk, salt, pepper, and corn. Simmer 5 minutes. Add butter and stir well.   *Serves 4–6.*

Braised Sliced Celery

2 tablespoons butter	1 cup chicken stock
2 tablespoons chopped shallots	Salt and fresh pepper to taste
4–5 cups sliced celery	¾ cup Parmesan cheese
1 green pepper, diced	

Melt butter in skillet. When hot, add shallots. Cook 1–2 minutes. Add celery and green pepper and sauté 2–3 minutes. Add the chicken stock; bring to a boil. Cover. Cook 10 minutes. Remove cover, add salt and pepper, and reduce the liquid in the pan. Add the Parmesan cheese. Stir well.

Serves 4–6.

Cooked Herbed Cucumbers

8 cucumbers	2 tablespoons chopped fresh dill,
4 tablespoons butter	mint, or parsley
Salt and fresh pepper to taste	

Peel and cut cucumbers lengthwise. Remove seeds with tip of spoon. Cut into 2-inch pieces crosswise. Parboil them for 4–5 minutes. Drain them, refresh in cold water, and dry thoroughly. Melt the butter in a fry pan. Add cucumbers and toss them until heated through. Season with salt, pepper, and chopped herb.

Serves 4–6.

Acorn Squash with Glazed Apples

3 small acorn squash (about ½ pound each)	2 tablespoons butter
¼ cup sugar	2 medium apples, peeled, cored, and chopped

Preheat oven to 400° F. Cut squash in half lengthwise; scoop out seeds and stringy pulp. Place cut side down in baking pan; add just enough water to barely cover bottom of pan. Bake 30–40 minutes. Meanwhile, to make glazed apples, in a 6-inch skillet melt sugar over medium heat (do not stir until completely melted). Add butter and apples; continue cooking and stirring until apples are glazed but still hold their shape. To serve, spoon glazed apples and syrup into each squash cavity.

Serves 4–6.

Stuffed Onions

4–6 medium-size sweet Spanish onions	4 tablespoons freshly grated Parmesan cheese
1 pound fresh broccoli	4 tablespoons light cream
4 tablespoons butter	Salt and fresh pepper to taste

Preheat oven to 400° F. Cut about ½ inch off top of onion and thin slice off bottom; peel. Scoop out center of onion, leaving about ½-inch shell (about 2 layers of onion). Cook, covered, in boiling salted water 10–15 minutes or until tender; drain. Wash broccoli well. Trim so flowerets have about 1 inch of stem attached. Cook in boiling salted water until *just* tender (7 minutes). Drain and chop. Meanwhile, chop scooped-out onion. In skillet, cook onion in butter until tender. Add broccoli, Parmesan, and cream; mix well. Season with salt and pepper. Stuff into cooked onion shells, mounding slightly. (Bake extra stuffing, if any, in custard cup.) Place in baking pan with water to just film bottom of pan. Bake 25–30 minutes.

Serves 4–6.

Puréed Butternut Squash

3 pounds butternut squash	Salt and fresh pepper to taste
1 tablespoon brown sugar	1 tablespoon finely chopped parsley
Freshly grated nutmeg to taste	

Preheat oven to 375° F. Line baking pan with foil; oil lightly. Cut squash in half lengthwise; place cut side down in baking pan. Bake 30–45 minutes (depending upon size of squash) or until you can easily pierce the flesh with a knife or skewer.

Remove seeds. Scoop out pulp; place in blender or food processor with brown sugar, nutmeg, salt, and pepper. Purée until smooth. Serve garnished with chopped parsley.

Serves 4–6.

Acorn Squash with Sesame Seeds

3 small acorn squash (about ½ pound each)
¼ cup melted butter

Salt and fresh pepper to taste
Sesame seeds

Preheat oven to 400° F. Cut squash in half lengthwise; scoop out seeds and stringy pulp. Place cut side down in baking pan; add just enough water to barely cover bottom of pan. Bake 30 minutes; turn cut side up. Meanwhile toast sesame seeds: Place seeds in a shallow pan. Bake until golden, about 10 minutes. Brush squash with melted butter; season with salt and pepper to taste. Sprinkle with sesame seeds. Bake 10 minutes more or until squash is done.

Serves 4–6.

You can do beet greens, collard greens, mustard greens, kale, Swiss chard, turnip greens, radish greens, and dandelion greens by this same method. Spinach wilts in a couple of minutes. Other greens will vary timewise. Serve with lemon juice and olive oil to taste, if preferred.

Spinach with Brown Butter

2 pounds spinach, well washed and tough stems removed
½ cup butter

Freshly grated nutmeg
Salt and fresh pepper to taste

Place spinach in pan with water that clings to it. Stir over medium heat with a wooden spoon until it wilts. Melt the butter in a pan and cook until brown but not burned. Add to spinach with nutmeg, salt, and pepper. Stir well and serve.

Serves 4–6.

Sour Cream Spinach

2 tablespoons butter
¼ cup finely chopped onion
2 pounds fresh spinach, well
  washed and tough stems removed

½ cup sour cream
Juice of ½ lemon
Salt and fresh pepper to taste

In large kettle, heat butter on high heat until melted. Add chopped onion, and sauté until cooked but not brown, about 2 minutes. Add spinach to pan, allowing the water that clings to the leaves to remain. Cook spinach on high heat with lid until it steams. Remove lid, and continue to cook on high heat while stirring to reduce some of the liquid. Transfer to smaller pan. Add sour cream and lemon juice. Stir with wooden spatula to combine with the spinach. Add salt and pepper. Keep warm over hot water until ready to serve.   *Serves 4–6.*

Boiled Artichokes

4–6 artichokes, 1 inch cut off top,
  leaves trimmed with scissors,
  and stem removed

1 tablespoon salt

Put artichokes in kettle and cover with 4–6 quarts water. Add salt to water. Bring to a boil and cook for 30–45 minutes, depending on size. If a leaf can be pulled off easily, the artichokes are done. Drain upside down and serve one to a person. Serve these with almond mayonnaise (page 451), vinaigrette (page 446), or hollandaise (page 452).   *Serves 4–6.*

Lemony Turnip Sticks

1½ pounds turnips
3 tablespoons butter
Juice of ½ lemon

2 tablespoons chopped parsley
Salt and fresh pepper to taste

Peel turnips. Cut into slices ¼ inch thick. Cut into ¼ inch sticks. Drop in boiling salted water and cook 15 minutes or until tender. Drain. Toss with butter, lemon juice, parsley, salt, and pepper.   *Serves 4–6.*

This is good cold the next day. Zucchini may be used instead of summer squash.

Easy Summer Squash

4 medium onions, thinly sliced
6–8 small yellow summer squash, thinly sliced (2–2½ pounds)
Salt and fresh pepper to taste

2–3 tablespoons butter
Chopped fresh marjoram to taste
½ cup heavy cream

Grease an 8- to 9-inch baking dish with a little of the butter. Arrange onions and squash alternately in dish. Sprinkle with salt, pepper, and marjoram between layers and on top. Drizzle heavy cream over top. Place in 375° F. oven for 20 minutes until tender.

Serves 4–6.

Baked Cauliflower

1 cauliflower, trimmed and cut into florets (2-2½ pounds)
2–3 tablespoons freshly grated Parmesan cheese

2–3 tablespoons bread crumbs
Salt and fresh pepper to taste
2–3 tablespoons butter, melted

Steam the florets for 7 minutes, until barely tender. Lay in baking dish, mounding the florets to resemble a whole head of cauliflower. Sprinkle the crumbs and cheese over the cauliflower, sprinkle with salt and pepper, and drizzle the melted butter over. Bake at 350° F. for 5–10 minutes.

Serves 4–6

VARIATION:

This recipe is also good with broccoli instead of cauliflower.

Broiled Tomatoes and Yogurt

3–4 large tomatoes
  1 cup plain yogurt
  2 tablespoons chopped parsley
  2 tablespoons chopped dill

1 cup fresh bread crumbs
  Salt and fresh pepper to taste
1 clove garlic, chopped

Cut tomatoes in half crosswise. Lay them in a baking dish. Mix remaining ingredients and divide among the tomato halves. Spread evenly. Broil 4 inches from unit for 5 minutes.

Serves 4–6

Parsnips with Parsley

1½ pounds parsnips, peeled
  1 cup water
    Salt and fresh pepper to taste

1 teaspoon sugar
4 tablespoons butter
2 tablespoons chopped parsley

Shred the parsnips in the food processor or with a hand grater. Put parsnips in a saucepan. Add the water and sugar and bring to a boil. Cover. Cook until tender, about 10–12 minutes. Drain and add butter, salt and pepper; stir until melted. Place in serving dish. Garnish with chopped parsley.

Serves 4–6.

Serve this hot as a vegetable or serve at room temperature for a first course. It might seem to be an inordinate amount of oil, but it's necessary, as eggplant actually devours oil.

Baby Eggplant

8 baby eggplants (size of your fist)
 ¾ cup good olive oil
   Salt and fresh pepper to taste

1–2 tablespoons chopped mint
  2 cloves garlic, chopped
    Few sprigs of fresh thyme

Trim the eggplants. Make 4–5 slits, on an angle, top to bottom, and fan them out flat. Film the bottom of a baking dish with ¼ cup of the olive oil. Lay the eggplant in the dish. Sprinkle over ¼ cup of the oil. Salt and pepper the eggplant. Sprinkle over the garlic, mint, and thyme. Place in 350° F. oven 15 minutes. Remove eggplant and sprinkle over the rest of the oil. Return to oven and bake until barely tender.

Serves 8.

I still have the old slaw cutter that my mother used to make sauerkraut. Most of us don't have the time to make our own sauerkraut today, and it is possible to buy delicious sauerkraut in delicatessens and in farmers' markets. I buy mine from a farmer who sells it directly from a barrel. There are excellent brands available in plastic bags.

Sautéed Sauerkraut

1–2 pounds sauerkraut
  4 tablespoons duck fat, vegetable oil, bacon fat, or butter
  1 medium onion, peeled and chopped
1 clove garlic, chopped
1 small apple, peeled, cored and chopped
Fresh pepper

Heat fat and add onion, garlic, and apple. Cook 2 minutes and add the sauerkraut (do not drain or wash). Grind some pepper over kraut and stir to mix well. Turn to medium heat and cover. Cook 30–35 minutes. Sauerkraut will be crunchy.

Serves 4–6.

VARIATION:

Sauté ¼ pound finely diced bacon until crisp and add just before serving.

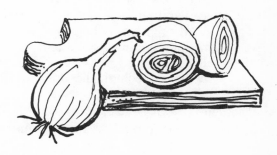

Baby Lima Beans in Chervil Cream

3 pounds baby lima beans, shelled   1 cup heavy cream
Salt and fresh pepper to taste   2 tablespoons finely chopped chervil

Put the shelled beans in a saucepan. Cover with water. Bring to a boil. Cook at a simmer for 10–15 minutes until beans are tender. Don't overcook, as they will split. Drain. Salt and pepper them to taste. Heat the cream and chervil together for 2 minutes while stirring. Pour over beans and serve.   *Serves 4–6.*

Pencil-Thin Asparagus with Walnut Oil

1½ pounds pencil-thin asparagus   Salt and fresh pepper to taste
Walnut oil

Trim any tough ends from the asparagus. Lay them in a large skillet. Cover with boiling water. Bring to a boil and cook 2–3 minutes. Turn off heat. Test one piece to make certain it is tender. Pour off hot water and serve asparagus while very hot. Drizzle with walnut oil, and sprinkle with salt and pepper.   *Serves 4–6.*

Quick Ratatouille

½ cup olive oil
6 medium tomatoes, peeled, seeded, and chopped
1 small eggplant, cubed
2 medium onions, peeled and sliced
3 medium zucchini, sliced

2 garlic cloves, chopped
A few fresh basil leaves, chopped
2 or 3 sprigs of fresh thyme
A little summer savory, if available
Salt and fresh pepper to taste

Place olive oil in large saucepan and heat. Add all ingredients and stir to thoroughly mix. Bring to a boil, turn to simmer, cover, and cook, stirring occasionally, for 30 minutes. Remove cover. If too much liquid remains, remove with a bulb baster, place in a small pan, and reduce to half over medium heat. Return liquid to vegetable mixture. Complete cooking time should be about 45 minutes.

Serves 4–6 generously.

Note: Good hot or tepid. Also good baked in a pastry shell. Leftovers keep well for 3–4 days.

Steamed Green Beans with Lemon and Olive Oil

1½–2 pounds green beans, topped
    and tailed
    Lemon quarters

Olive oil
Salt and fresh pepper to
    taste

Place water in large saucepan (2–3 inches deep in 2-quart saucepan) and insert collapsible steamer in place. Put beans in steamer. Put on lid and bring to a boil. Steam 5–7 minutes, until tender-crisp. Serve with lemon wedges and olive oil in a cruet. Salt and fresh pepper can be available, if desired.

Serves 4–6.

VARIATION:

Yellow wax beans may be substituted for the green beans. Add 1 tablespoon chopped fresh dill to the yellow beans and toss.

Carrots Steamed in Foil

12–16 thin carrots, peeled and
    trimmed
    1 tablespoon butter

1 tablespoon chopped pars-
    ley, dill, or mint
Salt and fresh pepper to taste

Lay carrots on a piece of aluminum foil and put butter on top. Sprinkle over the parsley, dill, or mint. Season with salt and pepper. Fold foil into a tight package. Put package on rack in oven preheated to 375° F. Bake 15 minutes. Open package and pierce a carrot with tip of knife. The carrots should be tender-crisp.

Serves 4–6.

VARIATION:

Try doing other vegetables in foil; I do parsnips, turnips, baby white onions, and small potatoes.

Serve this as a vegetable dinner.

Vegetable Skillet

4 tablespoons cooking oil or enough to film bottom of pan
3 cups chopped cabbage
1 cup chopped celery
1 cup chopped green pepper
½ cup chopped onion
2 cups chopped seeded tomatoes
1 tablespoon chopped fresh basil
Salt and fresh pepper to taste
1 cup shredded Cheddar cheese

Heat oil in a large skillet. Add cabbage, celery, green pepper, onion, tomatoes, basil, salt, and pepper. Mix well. Cover. Cook over medium heat for about 15 minutes or longer until cabbage is tender but crisp. Remove from heat. Sprinkle with cheese. Toss 2 minutes to melt cheese.   *Serves 4–6.*

This recipe comes from a friend in Egypt.

Carrots with Pistachio Nuts

1½–2 pounds carrots, peeled and thinly sliced
1½ cups water
Juice of ½ lemon
3 tablespoons butter
¼ cup shelled pistachio nuts
3 tablespoons Grand Marnier
Salt and fresh pepper to taste

Combine carrots with water and lemon juice in a large skillet. Bring to a boil. Cover. Cook 10–15 minutes or until tender. Drain. Meanwhile, melt butter in a small skillet. Add pistachio nuts. Sauté for 3 minutes. Pour over cooked carrots along with Grand Marnier. Sauté, tossing gently for 5 minutes, or until carrots are glazed. Season with salt and pepper.   *Serves 4–6.*

Summer Squash Sauté

1½ pound small summer squash
  or zucchini
2 eggs plus 1 tablespoon water,
  beaten
¾ cup yellow cornmeal

1 tablespoon chopped fresh
  basil
½ cup oil
Salt and fresh pepper to taste
Lemon wedges

Cut squash into 1-inch slices. Pour egg mixture into a shallow dish. Pour cornmeal and basil into another dish. Dip squash slices into egg mixture and then in cornmeal, coating well. Heat ¼ cup oil in a large skillet. Fry zucchini in hot oil, adding more oil if necessary, until golden brown. Drain on paper towels and season with salt and pepper. Serve with lemon wedges. *Serves 4–6.*

Recipes in this chapter:

POTATOES AND RICE

Everyone in my family eats and likes potatoes and rice. But we are evenly divided fifty-fifty—half of us, given the choice, will take potatoes every time, and half of us will take rice. It's potatoes for me. When I tested the recipe for potato pancakes in this book I wanted to know how many pancakes the batter would yield. But I ate the pancakes right out of the pan as I went along and completely forgot to count. So I made a second batch, carefully putting them on a big platter, and counted every one—then ate up the second batch, too. Cooks should always profit from their mistakes.

The rice recipes start with foolproof basic white rice. Anyone can make good white rice, and no one should buy instant or minute rice. I had to buy instant rice one time, of course—because in my cooking classes I can't ever say, "I've never tried that." And besides, I always feel that I might hit on something good one day. But I haven't so far. Instant rice is expensive and it tastes like boiled spitballs.

Plain Rice

1½ cups rice
3 cups water

Salt and fresh pepper to taste

Put rice into 6–8-cup casserole and add water and salt and pepper. Bring to a boil. Turn to a simmer. Cover. Simmer 23 minutes. Remove cover. Fluff up with two forks.

Serves 6.

Brown Rice

4 tablespoons butter
1 medium finely chopped onion
1 cup brown rice

2 cups chicken stock or water
Salt and fresh pepper to taste

Melt butter in small heavy casserole. Add onion and stir until wilted. Add rice. Stir for 2 or 3 minutes. Pour on liquid, salt, and fresh pepper. Bring to a boil. Turn to simmer. Put on lid and simmer for approximately 40–50 minutes. Fluff with two forks.

Serves 4–6.

Note: You can add ¼ cup sautéed almonds, chopped, and/or ¼ cup raisins or currants soaked in red wine to cover for a few minutes.

Rice with Mushrooms

1 cup chopped onions
1 cup raw rice
½ teaspoon crushed marjoram
leaves

¼ cup butter
½ pound mushrooms, chopped
2 cups chicken stock
Salt and fresh pepper to taste

In a 10-inch skillet, cook onion and rice with marjoram in butter until onions are tender, about 5 minutes. Add remaining ingredients. Cover and cook over low heat until rice is tender and all liquid is absorbed (about 25 minutes).   *Serves 4–6.*

Rice Pilaf

½ cup butter or other fat
1 medium finely chopped onion
1 cup long-grain rice
2 cups chicken stock, brown
   stock, or water

Salt and fresh pepper to taste
2 tablespoons finely chopped
   fresh parsley

Melt ¼ cup butter or fat in a heavy casserole (one with a tight-fitting lid) and sauté the onion over high heat. When onion is translucent but not brown (about 2 minutes), add the rice. Stir it around to coat the grains with butter. Add stock or water, salt, and pepper. Bring mixture to a full boil over high heat, then cover it tightly and reduce heat to simmer. Cook exactly 23 minutes (use a timer, if possible), and do not lift the lid during this time. Then lift the lid, fluff up the rice with two forks, sprinkle with the remaining ¼ cup butter, which you have melted, and border with chopped parsley.

Serves 6.

VARIATION:

Pack rice into buttered timbale molds or custard cups, pack down with back of spoon, and invert. Or pack into a ring mold or charlotte mold.

Rice Pilaf with Noodles

4 tablespoons butter
1 cup fine noodles, uncooked
1 cup rice
2 cups chicken stock

Salt and fresh pepper to taste
½ cup freshly grated Parmesan
   cheese
¼ cup chopped parsley

Melt butter in 2-quart saucepan. Add noodles and rice. Sauté until golden brown. Stir in chicken stock, salt, and pepper. Bring to a boil. Cover. Simmer for about 25 minutes or until rice and noodles are tender and stock is absorbed. Add Parmesan cheese and parsley; toss lightly.

Serves 4–6.

Rice Pilaf with Crystallized Ginger

Rice Pilaf
¼ cup finely chopped crystallized
ginger

Stir crystallized ginger into cooked pilaf and fluff up with two forks.   *Serves 6.*

Rice Pilaf with Grated Raw Carrots

½ cup carrots peeled and shredded by hand or in food processor
Rice Pilaf

Stir carrots into cooked pilaf and fluff with two forks.   *Serves 6.*

Rice Pilaf with Bouquet Garni

1 celery rib	Few sprigs of fresh thyme
1 tablespoon parsley sprigs, stems removed	Bay leaf
	Rice Pilaf

Make bouquet garni by laying celery rib on counter. Into its hollow put parsley, thyme, and bay. Fold in half by breaking celery. Tie tightly, leaving string on end for easy removal. Place on rice to cook. Remove before serving.   *Serves 6.*

Pink Rice Pilaf

Rice Pilaf
2 medium tomatoes, peeled, seeded and finely chopped

Add tomatoes along with the rice.   *Serves 6.*

Rice Pilaf with Green and Red Peppers

Rice Pilaf
4 tablespoons finely chopped red
pepper

4 tablespoons finely chopped
green pepper

Add peppers with onion.

Serves 6.

Rice Pilaf with Orange

Rice Pilaf
½ cup orange juice

1 tablespoon grated orange rind

Substitute ½ cup orange juice for some of stock and add 1 tablespoon grated orange rind.

Serves 6.

Rice Pilaf with Parsley

½ cup chopped parsley
Rice Pilaf

Add parsley to pilaf before serving.

Serves 6.

Wild Pecan Rice Pilaf

Substitute wild pecan rice for white rice in basic pilaf recipe. Wild pecan rice grows under pecan trees in Louisiana and Mississippi. It takes on the flavor of pecans and is delicious.

Rice Pilaf with Saffron and Peas

2 tablespoons butter
2 tablespoons olive oil
1 medium onion, finely
  chopped
½ teaspoon chopped garlic
1½ cups long-grain rice

½ cup shelled fresh peas
1 teaspoon saffron threads
3 cups chicken stock
  Salt and freshly cracked white
  pepper to taste

Using a heavy casserole that has a tight-fitting lid, heat the butter and oil. Sauté, but do not brown, the onion and garlic (this will take about 3 minutes). Add the rice and peas, stirring around to coat the grains and peas with butter and oil. Dissolve saffron in 1 tablespoon of the stock. Pour remaining stock into the casserole and add the dissolved saffron, salt, and pepper. Bring to a full boil over high heat; immediately cover tightly and reduce heat to simmer. Without lifting lid, cook for 23 minutes. Then remove lid and fluff the rice with two forks.   *Serves 6.*

Fried Potato Ribbons

2 or 3 large Idaho potatoes,
  washed but not peeled

Fat for frying
Salt to taste

Place potatoes in a Benriner slicer. Turn the handle and watch the potatoes emerge from the other end in long ribbons. Fill a deep frying pan with fat to a depth of 2 inches. When hot, 375° F., drop ribbons in fat and fry 3–4 minutes. Drain on paper towel. Salt just before serving.   *Serves 4–6.*

Note: I purchased the Benriner slicer from a mail order catalog. It's a plastic device with 3 blades; it looks like a large pencil sharpener. If you don't have one, these potatoes can be cut on a mandoline, sliced paper-thin, and then julienned. They are good but not as much fun as the ribbons. A new gadget for doing this job has recently appeared on the market. It is made by Daisy.

Small Potatoes in Stock and Saffron

½–1 teaspoon saffron
1½ cups chicken stock
16–20 small new potatoes, washed

Salt and fresh pepper to taste
2 tablespoons butter, melted

Dissolve the saffron in the stock. Place potatoes in a saucepan and pour the stock over. Add salt and pepper. Bring to a boil, cover, and turn to simmer. Cook until potatoes are barely tender, about 8–10 minutes. Pierce each potato with the point of a knife to absorb stock, and continue to cook another 5 minutes. Remove potatoes to a serving dish. Pour melted butter over them. Reduce the saffron stock, if any is left, in the pan and pour over potatoes.   *Serves 4–6.*

VARIATION:

Cook the potatoes in water to cover for 10–15 minutes, more or less. Serve warm, adding ¼ cup olive oil and 3 tablespoons finely chopped chives. Toss with salt and fresh pepper to taste. These are unusually good served with Basil Butter

If you prefer, serve baked potatoes with 1 cup yogurt combined with 4 table-spoons chopped chives. Or serve with 1 cup yogurt or cottage cheese combined with ½ cup sliced radishes. Or try a Flavored Butter (see page 439). When I am dieting, I frequently eat a baked potato with nothing on it: I have it as a main course with a salad.

Baked Potatoes with Basil Butter

4–6 Idaho potatoes   Basil Butter

Thoroughly scrub potatoes and place on a rack in a 425° F. preheated oven. Bake 40–55 minutes. Remove, cut a cross on top, and fluff up each potato. Spoon basil sauce over potato.   *Serves 4–6.*

Broiled Potato Slices

5 Idaho potatoes
⅓ cup oil

Coarse salt
Freshly cracked pepper

Preheat broiler. Scrub potatoes well. Cut into ¼-inch slices. Place on a baking sheet. Brush potatoes with oil. Broil 6 inches from heat for 7 minutes. Turn and brush with oil. Broil 8 minutes. Drain on paper towels. Sprinkle with coarse salt, and freshly cracked pepper.

Serves 4–6.

Red-Skin Potatoes

2–3 red-skin walnut-size potatoes
   per person
4 tablespoons butter, melted

Salt and fresh pepper to taste
1–2 tablespoons chives, parsley, or
   dill

Put potatoes in saucepan. Cover with water. Bring to a boil. Boil 10–15 minutes, just until tender. Drain. Return to pan. Add butter, salt, pepper, and herb. Toss.

Serve 2–3 to each person.

Broiled Grated Potatoes

4 medium baking potatoes
⅔ cup half-and-half cream
   Salt and fresh pepper to taste
½ teaspoon finely chopped fresh
   thyme

2 tablespoons butter, melted
Paprika

Peel, dice, and cook potatoes until fork tender. Place in food processor with just quick off-and-on turns to give grated appearance. Or grate by hand. Add cream, salt, pepper, and thyme, stirring potatoes lightly. Use some melted butter to cover bottom of baking dish. Add potato mixture and drizzle on remaining butter. Sprin-

Rice and Potatoes **381**

kle paprika on top. Place under broiler 5–6 inches from top of potatoes to lightly brown—12–15 minutes.

Serves 4–6.

VARIATION:

Bake, instead of broiling, 18–20 minutes at 375° F.

Cheddar Cheese Potatoes

6 tablespoons melted butter
3 large Idaho potatoes, scrubbed and thinly sliced (about 1½ pounds)

Salt and fresh pepper to taste
¾ cup grated Cheddar cheese

Cover bottom of 6-inch skillet with some butter. Layer potatoes in bottom of skillet, overlapping slightly; drizzle with more butter; season with salt and pepper. Repeat layers until all potatoes are used. Place over medium heat until butter is hot and sizzles. Reduce heat to low and cook, covered, about 30 minutes or until potatoes are tender and bottom layer is browned. Sprinkle with cheese; cover and heat a few minutes until cheese melts. Invert onto serving platter.

Serves 4–6.

Note: It's not necessary to peel the potatoes.

Stuffed Baked Potato Halves

¾ pound mild or sweet Italian sausage, casing removed
1 large shallot, finely chopped

4 tablespoons butter, melted
4–6 small baking potatoes

Preheat oven to 375° F. Mix sausage and chopped shallot. Melt butter in small sauté pan. Peel potatoes; cut in half lengthwise. Carefully hollow out centers with melon ball cutter, allowing ½-inch-thick edge (potato halves look like a baked potato shell before stuffing). Rinse potatoes in cold water, pat dry with paper towels, roll each potato in melted butter, and place in a small baking dish or pan. Add remainder of melted butter to baking dish. Stuff sausage mix in each potato half. Cover with aluminum foil or wrap each potato in foil and place on small baking sheet. Bake at 375° F. for 30–35 minutes or until fork tender.   *Serves 4–6.*

These potatoes have been a family favorite for years.

Red Pepper Potatoes

6 medium-size potatoes
1 onion, chopped
¾ cup diced sweet red pepper

4 tablespoons butter
Salt and fresh pepper to taste

Peel and cut potatoes into small cubes. Cook in boiling salted water in a medium saucepan until tender, about 15 minutes. Drain. Sauté onion and red peppers in butter in a 10-inch skillet until soft but not brown. Stir in drained potatoes, salt, and pepper. Toss lightly. Sauté, stirring occasionally, for about 5 minutes or until potatoes are golden brown.   *Serves 6–8.*

These pancakes are great served with any of the fruit toppings in this book or with applesauce.

Potato Pancakes with Sour Cream and Chives

2 potatoes, scrubbed, cut into pieces (do not peel)
1 small onion, peeled and cut in quarters
1 egg, beaten

1–2 tablespoons flour
Salt and fresh pepper to taste
Oil for frying
1 cup sour cream
¼ cup chopped chives

Place the potatoes and onion in blender or food processor, and process until potatoes are finely chopped. Place in a bowl and spoon off any liquid. Add the egg, flour, salt, and pepper and mix well. In an 8-inch frying pan or skillet, place oil to come ¼ inch up sides of pan. When hot, drop the potato mixture in with a tablespoon. Flatten each with the back of the spoon. Fry 4 at a time. Cook 2–3 minutes on one side until brown, turn once, and brown other side, 2–3 minutes. Mix the sour cream and chives together in a bowl and spoon over the pancakes at the table.

Makes 14–16 three-inch pancakes.

Wine-Laced Potatoes

1 tablespoon butter	Salt and fresh pepper to taste
2 tablespoons oil	½ cup chopped chives
3 cups potatoes sliced ¼ inch thick	¼ cup white wine

Melt butter with oil in large skillet. Add potatoes, salt, pepper, and chives. Sauté about 15 minutes or until golden brown, turning occasionally. Stir in wine. Cover. Cook 5 minutes.

Serves 4–6.

Potatoes Simmered in Chicken Broth

½ cup chopped onion	1 tablespoon chopped fresh basil
½ cup chopped celery	Salt and fresh pepper to taste
½ cup shredded carrots	¼ cup freshly grated Parmesan cheese
1 clove garlic, chopped	¼ cup chopped parsley
2 tablespoons butter	
1½ cups chicken stock	
2 pounds potatoes, peeled and cut in quarters	

Sauté onion, celery, carrots, and garlic in hot butter in a large skillet until tender. Add chicken stock, potatoes, basil, salt, and pepper. Cover. Simmer for 10 minutes. Remove cover. Simmer for 10 minutes or until potatoes are tender and broth is reduced. Sprinkle with Parmesan cheese and parsley.

Serves 4–6.

Fried Potato and Apple Cake

As served to me several years ago at the Restaurant D'Olympe in Paris.

1 pound potatoes, cut in chunks and boiled 10 minutes   Freshly grated nutmeg to taste
1 apple (½ pound), cored and cut in chunks   6 tablespoons butter

Roughly grate the potatoes in food processor or by hand. Put into a bowl. Grate the apple and combine. Season with nutmeg. Melt 4 tablespoons butter in non-stick 8-inch fry pan. Add apple-potato mixture and press down into a cake. Put on a lid. Cook on medium heat until bottom is brown, about 20 minutes. Keep the cake loose by sliding a spatula underneath. Remove lid and add butter to pan, putting pieces around the edge of the cake to keep it from sticking too much. Continue cooking slowly a few minutes more until brown and crispy on the bottom. To serve, carefully invert potato cake onto a round platter. Cut into pie-shaped wedges to serve.   *Serves 4–6.*

Note: Season with salt and fresh pepper if you like, but I do not find it necessary.

These can be eaten out of hand or with knife and fork. Place potatoes in paper napkin. No need for butter or salt.

Baked Potatoes, Cheese, and Salami

6 Idaho potatoes   Chopped parsley
6 strips of salami or ham (4 inches long by ½ inch wide)
6 strips of Muenster or Cheddar cheese (4 inches long by ½ inch wide)

Scrub potatoes thoroughly. Bake at 450° F. for 40–45 minutes or until done. Remove from oven. Cut a long vertical gash in each potato. Squeeze potatoes. Insert a strip of salami and cheese into each potato. Sprinkle with parsley.

Serves 4–6.

Baked Ham and Cheese Potatoes

6 medium-sized baking potatoes
1 cup diced ham
¼ cup chopped green pepper
2 tablespoons chopped shallots

Salt and fresh pepper to taste
1½ cups sour cream
½ cup shredded Swiss cheese

Bake potatoes in a hot oven (450° F.) for 40–45 minutes or until done. Make a cross on top of each potato. Squeeze gently to split open. Combine ham, green pepper, shallots, salt, pepper, and sour cream in a small saucepan. Heat gently; do not boil. Spoon hot sour cream mixture over potatoes. Sprinkle each with shredded Swiss cheese.

Serves 6.

Serve these potatoes out of the shell as mashed sherried yams. The deep orange color of the yams looks attractive on the plate, and the rich moist flavor enhances almost any entrée, especially ham.

Sherried Yams with Nuts

6 medium yams
¼ cup softened butter
¼ cup sherry

¼ cup light cream
⅓ cup coarsely chopped nuts:
   peanuts, cashews, pecans, etc.

Preheat oven to 400° F. Bake yams about 40 minutes or until tender. Cut slice off top of potato. Scoop out potato, keeping skin intact. Combine in bowl with butter and sherry; mix well with electric mixer or by hand. Add enough cream to make potatoes light and fluffy. Add nuts; stuff mixture back into shells. If necessary, just before serving heat for 5 minutes.

Serves 4–6.

Recipes in this chapter:

SALADS AND DRESSINGS

Every once in a while I see an article about make-ahead salads for the busy cook—complete with the information that iceberg lettuce is the best make-ahead ingredient because it never wilts, and warning us never to cut lettuce with a knife, or with anything but a stainless steel knife, because the lettuce will rust or bruise or crinkle and look hideous on the salad plate. All nonsense. I've been cutting lettuce with a knife for years. Cutting does not bruise romaine or even the soft buttery lettuces. The cut edges do not rust or wilt in the short time it takes lettuce to go from the knife to the salad bowl.

No salad needs make-ahead preparation—salads are quick and easy, and they give a quick meal a feeling of completeness and elegance. If you are really rushed, it's better to skip the vegetables rather than the salad—the meal will look less bare.

Cabbage is one of the longest-keeping vegetables, and it can be shredded almost instantly to make Gorgonzola coleslaw or crunchy winter salad. Try to keep some on hand for emergencies.

You can vary your salads easily by switching from romaine to Boston to Bibb to curly endive to red leaf lettuce. Vary vinaigrettes by changing to walnut oil or different oils in combination, and use sherry vinegar, or red or white wine vinegar. When good lettuce is difficult to find and you haven't even a head of cabbage, don't use second-best lettuce; serve relishes like radishes, celery hearts, cucumber, or zucchini sticks. In summer I serve big beefsteak tomatoes as a salad, simply sliced, alone or with slices of red onion, plain or drizzled with a bit of good olive oil and a few drops of vinegar. When tomatoes are ripe and fresh and local, they taste much too good to fool with.

This old-fashioned salad is enjoying a revival. It was a company staple in our house, as my mother always served it to very special guests. Now rediscovered, it is making its way onto the menus of elegant "new cuisine" restaurants. Which only goes to show that there's nothing older than even the newest cuisine.

My Mother's Sweetbread and Cucumber Salad

2 pairs large sweetbreads
1 lemon, cut in half
3 small cucumbers, peeled, seeded, and thinly sliced
Salt and fresh pepper to taste

⅔ cup mayonnaise, preferably homemade
½ cup heavy cream, whipped
Lettuce leaves
2 tablespoons finely chopped dill

Put sweetbreads into a pan. Cover with cold water and juice of ½ lemon. Bring to a boil. Turn to simmer and cook 15–20 minutes. Drain. Plunge into ice water for 5 minutes to stiffen them. Remove and take off membranes and remove tubes. Cut sweetbreads into cubes. Add the cucumber, juice of ½ lemon, and salt and pepper. Combine the mayonnaise and whipped cream and fold into the sweetbread mixture. Line a bowl with lettuce leaves and fill with salad. Garnish with dill.

Serves 4–6.

Broiled Salad with Thyme

4 Belgian endive
2 fennel bulbs, inside part
8 large mushrooms
1 red onion
  Salt and fresh pepper to taste

2 teaspoons finely chopped fresh
  thyme, or more
4 tablespoons olive oil
  Juice of 1½ lemons

Cut all vegetables into julienne strips. Place on shallow baking pan. Sprinkle over salt and pepper, thyme, and olive oil. Mix well. Set under the broiler 4 inches from unit for about 3 minutes. Toss the vegetables and return to broiler. Cook until vegetables are done, about 5–6 minutes. Remove. Squeeze lemon juice over the vegetables and serve warm.   *Serves 4–6.*

Zucchini and Red Onion Salad

4 small zucchini, sliced (1 pound)   Vinaigrette
2 medium red onions, sliced
1 large bunch escarole, in bite-size
  pieces

Combine all ingredients in bowl. Toss and serve.   *Serves 4–6.*

Shrimp and Honeydew Salad

1½ pounds shrimp, cooked and
   deveined (if long, cut into
   thirds; if small, leave whole)
1 cup thinly sliced celery
  Juice of ½ lemon
1 honeydew melon, cut into
  melon balls

¼ cup homemade mayonnaise
¼ cup sour cream
  Salt and fresh pepper to taste
  Boston lettuce
  Watercress

Combine shrimp, celery, and lemon juice. Refrigerate. Just before serving, drain off liquid. Combine shrimp and melon balls. Add mayonnaise, sour cream, salt, and pepper. (Add enough pepper here, as it points up the melon.) Toss lightly with a fork. Serve in Boston lettuce cups with a few sprigs of watercress on the side.   *Serves 4–6.*

Grapefruit Salad with Watercress Dressing

3–4 large grapefruit
½ cup olive oil
　Juice of 1 lime
1 shallot, finely chopped
　Salt and fresh pepper to taste

1 bunch watercress, stems removed and chopped medium coarse
　Boston lettuce

Peel and section grapefruit. Chill in refrigerator while making dressing. Whisk olive oil into lime juice, chopped shallot, and seasoning. Add watercress. Chill while arranging grapefruit sections in spokelike design on Boston lettuce. When ready to serve, add a tablespoon of watercress dressing to center of salad.

Serves 4–6.

Avocado and Rice Salad

　Rice Pilaf (see page 375)
2 tablespoons lemon juice
2 tablespoons olive oil
8–10 stuffed green olives, sliced

2 tablespoons chopped chervil
3 ripe avocados
　Lettuce cups or red curly lettuce if in season

Toss rice with 1 tablespoon lemon juice, olive oil, olives, and chervil. Chill in refrigerator while cutting avocados in half lengthwise. Remove pits. Peel fruit and sprinkle with 1 tablespoon of lemon juice to keep from discoloring. Hollow out a larger hole in center of each avocado half. Fill center with a large mound of the cold rice and serve on your selection of lettuce.   *Serves 6.*

Good on cold chicken, fish, meat, or vegetables, aside from salad greens or toma-
to slices.

Creamy Salad Dressing

4 tablespoons vegetable oil
4 tablespoons heavy cream
3 tablespoons wine vinegar

1 tablespoon Dijon mustard
Salt and fresh pepper to taste

Beat all ingredients in bowl with whisk until thick.   *Makes ¾ cup.*

Bibb Lettuce with Tomato Mayonnaise

1 cup mayonnaise, preferably homemade
¼ cup heavy cream
1 tomato, peeled, seeded, and finely diced

Bibb lettuce leaves

Thin mayonnaise with heavy cream. Add the diced tomato. Taste for seasoning. Serve over Bibb lettuce leaves.   *Serves 4–6.*

Serve on raw spinach, cucumber slices, or sliced tomatoes.

Buttermilk Dressing

1 cup buttermilk
1 tablespoon horseradish

1 teaspoon Dijon mustard
Salt and fresh pepper to taste

Combine all ingredients in a bowl and whisk. Or put in a jar and shake.

Makes 1 cup.

Lemon-pepper dressing is especially good over escarole. Be sure to add all the pepper.

Cucumber Melon Salad with Lemon-Pepper Dressing

2 cucumbers, peeled, seeded, and thinly sliced
1 large cantaloupe, cut in chunks
Lettuce leaves
1 teaspoon Dijon mustard
Salt to taste

1 teaspoon coarsely cracked fresh pepper
Juice of 2 lemons
¾ cup vegetable oil
2 tablespoons finely chopped mint

Mix cucumbers and cantaloupe together. Place on lettuce leaves. Put mustard, salt, and pepper in a small bowl. Add lemon juice. Mix with whisk. Gradually whisk in the oil. Sprinkle mint over top. Spoon dressing over salad.   *Serves 4–6.*

Freshly chopped rosemary is delicious in this salad.

Orange and Red Onion Salad

2 bunches watercress, stems removed
4 oranges, peeled, seeded, and thinly sliced

2 medium-size red onions
Vinaigrette

Arrange watercress on each salad plate. Place the orange slices on the watercress. Thinly slice one onion and finely chop the other one. Sprinkle half the chopped onion on the orange slices; add the other chopped half to the vinaigrette. Arrange the sliced onion over the orange and chopped onion. Spoon dressing over each salad.   *Serves 4–6.*

Summer Fruit Salad

1 cup honey
¼ cup lime juice
1 large honeydew melon

1 medium cantaloupe
1 cup grapes

Combine honey and lime juice to make dressing. Blend well. Chill while preparing fruit. Cut honeydew into 6 wedges; seed and peel. Cut cantaloupe crosswise into slices about 1 inch thick; seed, peel, and cut in half. Place honeydew on chilled salad plate, arch cantaloupe slice over melon and garnish each serving with few grapes. Serve with dressing.   *Serves 4-6.*

Accordion Tomato and Cucumber Salad

1 tomato per person
½ medium unpeeled cucumber
   per person

2 tablespoons freshly chopped
chives
Vinaigrette (see page 446)

Peel tomatoes, if you wish. Stand each tomato on stem end. Make seven slits top to bottom, but not all the way through. Slice the cucumber into seven slices and insert them in the slits. Lay each tomato accordion on individual salad plate. Drizzle vinaigrette over each. Sprinkle with chives.

Bibb Lettuce and Cherry Tomato Salad

3-4 heads Bibb lettuce, washed
   and dried
12-16 cherry tomatoes, stemmed

2 tablespoons chopped chives
Vinaigrette (see page 446)
Salt and fresh pepper

Arrange lettuce in salad bowl. Add tomatoes. Sprinkle with chopped chives. Pour enough dressing over to coat greens. Season to taste. Toss.   *Serves 4-6.*

Bacon, Tomato, and Rice Salad

3 cups cooked rice
½ pound bacon, cooked and crumbled
2 medium tomatoes, peeled, seeded, and chopped

¼ cup chopped green onions
½ cup mayonnaise, preferably homemade
Salt and fresh pepper to taste
Salad greens

Combine all ingredients except salad greens; mix well. Pack into 5-cup mold or bowl. To serve, unmold on salad greens. Serve at room temperature.   *Serves 4–6.*

Black Walnut Salad Dressing

1 teaspoon Dijon mustard
Salt and fresh pepper to taste
¼ cup red wine vinegar

¼ cup walnut oil
¼ cup olive oil
¼ cup chopped black walnuts

Put the mustard, salt, pepper, and vinegar in a small bowl. Whisk to mix. Add the oils gradually while whisking. Fold in walnuts. Pour over salad greens.

Makes about 1 cup.

Avocados with Oil and Vinegar

½ avocado per person
Cruets of good olive oil and vinegar

Salt and fresh pepper to taste

Serve ½ avocado to each person and pass the cruets for each person to help himself. Salt and pepper should also be provided.

Cheese and Olive Tossed Salad

6 cups mixed greens
½ cup chopped green onions
¼ cup chopped red pepper
½ cup pitted ripe olives, sliced

3 tomatoes, quartered
½ cup shredded Cheddar cheese
Creamy Avocado Dressing (following recipe)

Combine greens, green onions, pepper, olives, and tomatoes in large salad bowl. Sprinkle with cheese. Top with avocado dressing. Toss lightly but thoroughly.

Serves 4–6.

Creamy Avocado Dressing

1 large ripe avocado, pitted, peeled, and mashed
Juice of ½ lemon
½ cup sour cream

¼ cup oil
½ teaspoon chili powder
Salt and fresh pepper to taste

Combine all ingredients in a bowl. Mix well.

Serves 4–6.

Avocado, Pink Grapefruit, and Orange Salad

2 ripe avocados, peeled, pitted and cut into eighths
1 large pink grapefruit, peeled and opened into 14 sections
2 oranges, peeled and opened into 16 sections

1 bunch watercress
Fresh mint (optional)
Cruets of oil and vinegar

Arrange the slices of avocado, grapefruit, and orange alternately on individual plates. Tuck watercress leaves on each. Sprinkle with mint if you like. Pass the cruets of oil and vinegar.

Serves 4–6.

Dandelion Salad

2 quarts dandelion greens, washed and dried
½ lb. bacon, diced and cooked crisp
Bacon fat
2 garlic cloves, peeled and chopped

1 tablespoon sugar
1 tablespoon dry mustard
Salt and fresh pepper to taste
¼ cup red wine vinegar

Put greens in salad bowl and sprinkle bacon on top. Into the bacon fat in fry pan, put the garlic, sugar, mustard, salt, pepper, and vinegar. Bring to a boil. Pour over salad. Toss quickly and serve. *Serves 4–6.*

VARIATIONS:

Add 1 cup sautéed croutons to salad and/or 1 onion, grated. Use curly endive when dandelion is out of season.

Curried Potato Salad in Green Pepper Shells

6 medium potatoes
¼ cup chopped green pepper
½ cup chopped celery
1 cup mayonnaise, preferably homemade, or ½ cup sour cream and ½ cup mayonnaise

2 teaspoons curry powder
3 tablespoons chopped chives
Salt and fresh pepper to taste
6 medium green peppers

Cook potatoes in boiling salted water until tender. Drain. Cool slightly. Remove skins and cube. Combine warm potatoes with chopped green pepper and celery in a large bowl. Combine mayonnaise, curry powder, chives, salt, and pepper. Stir into potatoes and toss gently to coat. Cut slices off tops of green peppers. Remove seeds and membrane. Parboil in boiling water for 5 minutes. Drain and plunge into ice water. Pat dry. Spoon potato salad into pepper shells. *Serves 6.*

VARIATION:

Try dressing the potatoes while hot with vinaigrette.

Pineapple and Green Pepper Salad

2 green peppers
1 medium pineapple, cubed
4 tablespoons sherry vinegar

8 tablespoons olive oil
Salt and fresh pepper to taste

Cut peppers in half, remove the seeds and pith, and cut into strips. Add the pineapple, vinegar, oil, salt, and pepper. Toss well before serving.   *Serves 4–6.*

Crunchy Winter Salad

1 cup coarsely grated raw turnip
3 cups shredded cabbage
2 cups diced red apples
½ cup chopped peanuts

Juice of ½ lemon
1 cup mayonnaise, preferably homemade, or ½ cup sour cream and ½ cup mayonnaise

Combine turnip, cabbage, apples, and peanuts in a large bowl. Blend together lemon juice and mayonnaise. Add to salad. Toss well.   *Serves 4–6.*

Sweet-and-Sour Greens

6 strips bacon
¼ cup cider vinegar
¼ cup water
1 tablespoon sugar

3 cups torn romaine leaves
3 cups torn fresh spinach
4 hard-cooked eggs, sliced
Salt and fresh pepper to taste

Fry bacon in a large skillet until crisp. Remove and drain on paper towels. Pour off drippings except for 2 tablespoons. Add vinegar, water, and sugar to drippings. Bring to boil. Boil 1 minute, stirring constantly. Combine romaine, spinach, and eggs in a large bowl. Pour hot dressing over them. Toss lightly but thoroughly. Add salt and fresh pepper as desired.   *Serves 4–6.*

Green Pea and Swiss Cheese Salad

1½ pounds peas in shell
    Juice of ½ lemon or lime
¼ cup olive oil
1 clove garlic, chopped
    Salt and fresh pepper to taste

1 cup thinly sliced celery
2 cups diced Swiss cheese (½-inch cubes)
1 tablespoon finely chopped dill
    Lettuce

Shell peas and place in a saucepan. Add ¼ cup water. Cook 7–10 minutes or until tender. Drain peas and refresh in cold water to set the color. Put into a bowl and add the lemon or lime juice, oil, garlic, salt, and pepper. Mix well. Add the celery, cheese, and dill. Mix again and serve from a lettuce-lined bowl. *Serves 4–6.*

Gorgonzola Cole Slaw

4 cups shredded cabbage
1 cup mayonnaise, preferably homemade
¼ cup milk
1 tablespoon grated onion

1 cup crumbled Gorgonzola cheese
1 cup shredded carrots
½ cup chopped green pepper
    Salt and fresh pepper to taste

Crisp shredded cabbage in ice water. Drain. Blend mayonnaise, milk, and onion. Stir in Gorgonzola cheese. Combine cabbage, carrots, and green pepper in large bowl. Add mayonnaise-cheese mixture. Season with salt and pepper. Toss gently but thoroughly until vegetables are well coated. *Serves 4–6.*

Turnip, Radish, and Romaine Salad

½ cup grated raw turnip
½ cup thinly sliced celery
1 cup thinly sliced radishes
4 cups shredded romaine

¼ cup oil
2 tablespoons white vinegar
    Salt and fresh pepper to taste

Combine turnips, celery, radishes, and romaine in a large bowl. Blend oil, vinegar, salt, and pepper together. Pour over salad. Toss.   *Serves 4–6.*

Cottage Cheese and Tomato Salad on Lettuce Wedges

1½ cups cottage cheese
1½ cups sour cream
1 cup peeled, seeded, and diced cucumber
1 cup sliced radishes

½ cup chopped green onions
Salt and fresh pepper to taste
Lettuce wedges
Tomato quarters

Combine cottage cheese, sour cream, cucumber, radishes, onions, salt, and pepper; mix well. For each serving, spoon over 4–6 lettuce wedges. Garnish with tomato quarters.   *Serves 4–6.*

Recipes in this chapter:

CORN BREAD

MELBA ROUNDS AND FINGERS

BUTTERFINGERS

HOMEMADE BISCUIT MIX

HOT BISCUITS

PANCAKES AND WAFFLES

FRUIT TOPPINGS FOR PANCAKES,
    WAFFLES, CRÊPES, ICE CREAM,
    CAKE

BANANA NUT BREAD

OLD-FASHIONED WHEAT BATTER
    BREAD

GOLDEN POPOVERS

COTTAGE CHEESE PANCAKES

LEMON SCONES

OPEN-FACE CHEESE RADISH
    SANDWICH

CHEDDAR CHEESE PORT WINE SPREAD

BAKED CHEESE FONDUE

CHEESE COOKIES

GRILLED CHEESE AND GREEN PEPPER
    SANDWICH

TOMATO RAREBIT SANDWICH

CHEESE CUSTARDS

STILTON CHEESE WITH CELERY

BAKED BACON AND EGGS

CHICKEN LIVERS AND EGGS

EGGS INDIENNE

STUFFED EGGS SUPREME

MAGGIE AND JIGGS SOUFFLÉ

EGG TIMBALES

BAKED EGGS IN ENGLISH MUFFIN AND
    BACON NESTS

EGG SALAD ROLLED IN LETTUCE
    LEAVES

VERMOUTH-GLAZED EGGS

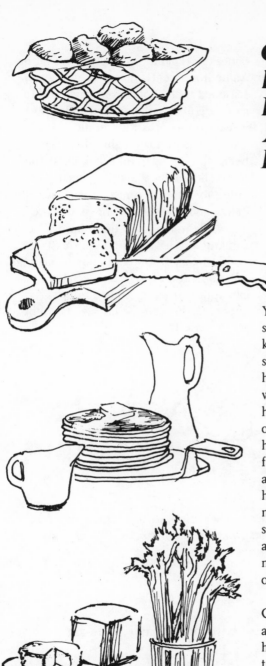

CHEESE, EGGS, BREADS, AND PANCAKES

You can make bread in one hour—from start to finish, including mixing, kneading, and baking. It will be a slightly heavier loaf than a two- or three-hour bread, because it is a batter bread with no yeast. But it keeps well and it has a wonderful taste right out of the oven. Contrary to whatever else you have heard, fresh bread is at its best hot from the oven. I think that old story about its giving you a stomachache and heartburn was started by nervous mothers who realized they had to tell us something—otherwise there wouldn't be any bread left for dinner. I always eat my bread the minute it comes out of the oven, and I never have had a problem.

Hot breads used to be a staple in Grandmother's day. Though we were always warned about bread, we always had hot biscuits or corn bread on the table. This is another of those old-fashioned ideas that need reviving. Hot biscuits make any meal look like more, and they don't take any time at all. You can even make up your own biscuit mix (see page 404) and whip up a batch in minutes. Look around a dining room in a Southern resort hotel and watch sophisticated people wolfing down hot muffins and good old cornbread. There is something about these American hot breads that brings out the appetite in everybody. It's more than food. It's more than soul food. It's soul-satisfying food.

Waffles and pancakes are the great American breakfast, as American as apple pie, and maybe a little more so. Waffles are so easy and quick—there is nothing simpler than bringing the waffle iron to the table and just cooking as you eat. A portable electric griddle makes pancake preparation simple. I've had my waffle iron twenty years and it's so well seasoned that I don't even have to throw away the first waffle anymore. But for weeks and months I forget all about it. Then some Sunday night when I've been working late and I look up at the clock and finally think: Oh, what's in the house for supper? someone will say, "How about waffles?" I break out the old waffle iron and all the toppings I can think of and have a late-night feast.

It is easy to think of cheese and eggs in combination—they are versatile and can appear in every course from appetizer through the entrée and right on to dessert.

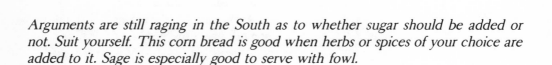

Arguments are still raging in the South as to whether sugar should be added or not. Suit yourself. This corn bread is good when herbs or spices of your choice are added to it. Sage is especially good to serve with fowl.

Corn Bread

1 cup flour	4 teaspoons baking powder
1 cup yellow cornmeal	2 eggs, beaten
½ teaspoon salt	1 cup milk
2 tablespoons sugar (optional)	⅓ cup butter, melted

Mix all dry ingredients in a large mixing bowl. Make a well in the center. Combine eggs, milk, and butter and add to the dry ingredients. Stir until smooth.

Butter an 8-inch-square baking pan. Pour in the batter. Place in a 425° F. oven and bake 25–30 minutes, or until the top is golden brown. Cut into 12–16 squares.

Melba Rounds and Fingers

12 slices thin bread   ½ cup butter, melted

For Rounds

Cut rounds from bread, using a 2-inch cutter. Lay on baking sheet. Brush with butter. Bake at 350° F. for 15–20 minutes or longer.   *Makes 24 rounds.*

For Fingers

Cut off crusts. Cut bread into thirds. Brush with the butter and bake as above.

Makes 36 fingers.

Note: Use trimmings remaining from bread for crumbs.

Serve these with soup. They are tasty sprinkled with cinnamon and sugar and served as a snack or with tea in the afternoon.

Butterfingers

1 pound loaf bread, sliced and   ½ pound butter, melted
  crusts removed

There should be 16 slices of bread. Cut each slice in 3 pieces. Dip them, one by one, into the melted butter. Lay on baking sheet and bake at 350° F. until bread is toasted, about 20 minutes.   *Makes 48 pieces.*

Homemade Biscuit Mix

6 cups flour	1 tablespoon salt
3 tablespoons baking powder	1 cup vegetable shortening

Put flour and baking powder into a bowl. Add the salt. Cut in the shortening until mixture resembles cornmeal. Store in a covered container. It is not necessary to refrigerate, but I do. To use this mix:

2½ cups mix	Flour for board
¾ cup milk	1 tablespoon butter

Blend the mix and milk together in a bowl. Knead very lightly for 2 minutes. Roll out on a lightly floured board ½ inch thick. Cut into 1½-inch rounds. Place on greased baking sheet. Bake at 425° F. for 15 minutes.   *Makes 20 biscuits.*

Note: Buttermilk can be substituted for milk, in which case add ½ teaspoon soda.

Biscuits were a staple of family meals in my grandmother's day. The secret to good biscuits is not to overmix.

Hot Biscuits

1 tablespoon butter for greasing baking pan	1 teaspoon salt
	1 teaspoon sugar
2 cups flour	4 tablespoons butter
2 teaspoons baking powder	¾ cup milk

Butter a baking sheet. Put flour, baking powder, salt, and sugar into a bowl. Rub in the 4 tablespoons butter until mixture looks like coarse cornmeal. Add milk. Mix well to make a soft dough. Turn out on lightly floured board. Pat out ¾ inch thick. Cut biscuits into 2-inch rounds or cut into 2-inch squares with a knife. Place on buttered baking pan and bake at 450° F. for 12–15 minutes or until biscuits are golden.   *Makes 12 biscuits.*

VARIATIONS:

Chive Biscuits: Add ¼ cup chopped chives to flour and shortening mixture.

Herb Biscuits: Add your favorite herb—2 tablespoons thyme or 1 tablespoon sage.

Spicy Biscuits: Add your favorite spice—1 tablespoon caraway or poppy seed or 1 teaspoon cinnamon.

Saffron Biscuits: Add ½ teaspoon saffron to milk to dissolve.

Orange Biscuits: Add 2 tablespoons grated orange rind to flour and shortening mixture. Before baking, press a tiny sugar cube dipped in orange juice into top of each biscuit.

Pancakes and Waffles

1¼ cups flour	2 eggs, beaten
2 tablespoons sugar	1 cup milk
2 teaspoons baking powder	3 tablespoons oil
½ teaspoon salt	

Pancakes

In bowl, combine dry ingredients; add remaining ingredients, beating just until smooth. Preheat griddle according to manufacturer's directions; grease lightly. Spoon about ¼ cup batter on griddle for each pancake. Cook until top is bubbly and dry; turn and cook to brown underside.   *Makes about ten 5-inch pancakes.*

VARIATIONS:

Ham and Cheese: Increase to 1¼ cups milk; add ½ cup finely chopped ham and ¼ cup grated Parmesan cheese.

Banana Nut: Add 1 cup mashed ripe bananas and ¼ cup chopped nuts.

Wheat Germ: Decrease flour to 1 cup and add ¼ cup wheat germ with dry ingredients.

Bacon: Substitute bacon drippings for oil and add 8 slices crumbled, cooked bacon.

(continued)

Waffles

In basic recipe, increase to 3 tablespoons sugar and ¼ cup oil. Preheat waffle iron according to manufacturer's directions; grease lightly. Spoon about ¼ cup batter on griddle for each waffle. Cook until steam stops during cooking. Makes 8 waffles.

Variations for pancakes can also be used for waffle batter.

You can omit the starch in the toppings, but then the fruit will be more juicy. Serve the pancakes or waffles with maple butter or honey and brandy mixed together.

FRUIT TOPPINGS

For Pancakes, Waffles, Crêpes, Ice Cream, Cake

½ cup sugar	2 cups sliced strawberries
1 teaspoon cornstarch	1 tablespoon butter
½ cup water	½ teaspoon lemon juice

In saucepan, combine sugar and cornstarch. Blend in water until smooth. Cook over medium heat, stirring constantly, until slightly thickened. Add fruit; simmer *just until* fruit begins to cook. Remove from heat; add butter and lemon juice.

Makes about 2 cups.

VARIATIONS:

Blueberries: Increase cornstarch to 2 teaspoons; substitute blueberries for strawberries.

Black Cherries: Increase cornstarch to 2 teaspoons; substitute cherries for strawberries. Omit lemon juice and add 1 tablespoon cherry liqueur.

Peach: Increase cornstarch to 2 teaspoons; substitute sliced peaches for strawberries.

Banana Nut Bread

½ cup softened butter
1 cup sugar
1 cup mashed bananas
2 eggs, well beaten
1 teaspoon lemon juice

1 teaspoon baking soda
2 tablespoons boiling water
1¾ cups flour
1 cup chopped walnuts

Preheat oven to 350° F. Generously grease 3 loaf pans (5½ by 3 by 2 inches). In bowl, cream together butter and sugar. Add bananas, eggs, and lemon juice. Dissolve baking soda in water. Add with flour to banana mixture, stirring until just blended. Add nuts. Divide batter among prepared pans. Bake 35 minutes or until done. Remove from pans to baking rack to cool. *Makes 3 loaves.*

This bread is rather heavy, but very tasty. Now there is no excuse not to have homemade bread in under an hour.

Old-Fashioned Wheat Batter Bread

2½ cups flour
2 tablespoons packed brown sugar
2 teaspoons baking powder
1 teaspoon baking soda

½ teaspoon salt
2 tablespoons butter
1 cup whole wheat flour
1½ cups buttermilk

Preheat oven to 375° F. Generously grease a 7-inch round cake pan. In bowl, combine white flour, sugar, baking powder, baking soda, and salt. Cut in butter until like coarse cornmeal. Add whole wheat flour and buttermilk; mix. Knead on lightly floured board 5–6 times. Place in prepared pan. With floured knife, cut cross almost to bottom of batter. Bake 40 minutes. If desired, brush with melted butter. Remove from pan to cool. *Makes 1 loaf.*

Golden Popovers

Oil for greasing molds
2 eggs
1 cup milk

¼ teaspoon salt, if desired
1 cup flour

Preheat oven to 450° F. Grease 10 iron popover pans or individual custard cups very well. Place pans or cups in oven while it is preheating. Place eggs, milk, and salt in blender. Cover and blend at high speed until bubbly. Add flour and blend at high speed until perfectly smooth. Remove heated popover pans and fill half full. Bake at 450° for 15 minutes. Reduce heat to 350° and bake 15–20 minutes longer.

Makes 10 popovers.

Cottage Cheese Pancakes

1 cup cottage cheese
1 cup sour cream
4 eggs

¾ cup flour
1 tablespoon sugar
¼ teaspoon salt

In bowl, combine cottage cheese, sour cream, and eggs; beat until smooth. Add dry ingredients; mix until well blended. Heat griddle according to manufacturer's directions. Drop batter onto hot griddle (¼ cup batter per pancake makes 14 four-inch pancakes; 2 tablespoons batter makes 28 three-inch pancakes). Cook until bubbles appear around edge; turn and brown on second side.

Serve these hot with jam when your Aunt Gertrude comes to tea.

Lemon Scones

3 cups flour
1 teaspoon baking powder
½ teaspoon baking soda
½ teaspoon salt
2 tablespoons sugar

⅓ cup soft butter
2 tablespoons lemon rind
¼ cup lemon juice
¾ cup buttermilk
1 egg, separated

Preheat oven to 425° F. Grease baking sheet. In bowl, combine dry ingredients. With pastry blender, cut in butter until well blended. Add lemon rind, juice, buttermilk, and egg yolk; mix well. Toss on lightly floured board; knead 30 seconds. Roll to ¼ inch thick; cut with diamond cookie cutters. Place on prepared sheet; brush with egg white and sprinkle with additional sugar. Bake 10–12 minutes. *Makes 36 scones.*

Open-Face Cheese Radish Sandwich

2 cups cottage cheese	6 slices rye or pumpernickel toast
¼ cup sour cream	1 cup thinly sliced radishes
¼ cup snipped chives	Watercress

Combine cheese, sour cream, and chives in a small bowl; mix well. Spread mixture on each slice of toast. Sprinkle radishes over cheese surface. Wreath each sandwich with watercress. *Serves 4–6.*

Serve with drinks at cocktail time, spread on crackers, melba toast or pumpernickel bread. Or serve instead of dessert.

Cheddar Cheese Port Wine Spread

½ pound sharp Cheddar cheese, grated	½ cup finely chopped pecans
3 ounces cream cheese, softened	¼ cup port wine
	¼ cup chopped parsley

Combine cheeses, pecans, and wine in a small bowl or food processor. Blend well. Shape into a 4-inch mound. Sprinkle with chopped parsley. *Makes 1 generous cup.*

Baked Cheese Fondue

1 tablespoon butter for greasing baking dish	2 teaspoons Dijon mustard
5 eggs, separated	Salt and fresh pepper to taste
1¼ cups scalded milk	2 cups soft bread cubes
	½ pound Cheddar cheese, grated

Preheat oven to 325° F. Generously butter a 1-quart casserole. In bowl, combine egg yolks, milk, mustard, salt, and pepper; mix well. Add bread cubes and cheese. Using clean bowl and beater, beat whites until soft peaks form; fold into cheese mixture. Carefully pour into prepared casserole. Set in pan of hot water; bake 30 minutes or until knife inserted near center comes out clean. *Serves 4–6.*

Cheese Cookies

2½ cups shredded sharp Cheddar cheese at room temperature	¾ cup cornmeal
½ cup butter, softened	¾ cup flour
¼ cup milk	½ teaspoon salt
1 tablespoon Dijon mustard	Chopped dill or paprika

Preheat oven to 375° F. Grease two baking sheets. In bowl, combine cheese, butter, milk and mustard. Beat well with electric mixer. Add cornmeal, flour, and salt; mix well (will be a stiff dough). Force through cookie press onto prepared baking sheet. Sprinkle with dill or paprika as desired. Bake 10 minutes or until lightly browned around edges. *Makes about 5 dozen cookies.*

Grilled Cheese and Green Pepper Sandwich

½–¾ pound cheese, grated (medium-sharp Colby melts very well)	1 tablespoon Dijon mustard
	Salt and fresh pepper to taste
¼–½ cup finely chopped green pepper	4–6 slices of bread: white, whole wheat or rye

Mix all ingredients except bread in a bowl. Toast one side of bread placed on broiler pan 4–5 inches from heat. Turn toast to other side and pile cheese mixture evenly over bread slices. Broil 4–5 minutes or until melted.   *Serves 4–6.*

Tomato Rarebit Sandwich

3 tablespoons butter
3 tablespoons flour
1 clove garlic, chopped
1 teaspoon Dijon mustard
1½ cups milk
2 cups shredded sharp Cheddar cheese

1 egg, beaten
6 slices toast
6 slices tomato
6 slices cooked bacon
Salt and fresh pepper to taste

In saucepan, melt butter; blend in flour, garlic, and mustard. Gradually stir in milk. Cook, stirring constantly, until thickened. Add cheese and stir until it melts. Pour a small amount over egg; blend well. Return to pan and cook about 1 minute. In individual serving dishes, place 1 slice toast; top with 1 slice tomato. Top with about ⅓ cup cheese mixture and 1 slice bacon, cut in half.   *Serves 6.*

These are especially good served with a fresh tomato sauce and/or sautéed mushrooms.

Cheese Custards

2¼ cups heavy cream
4 eggs
Salt and fresh pepper to taste
Freshly grated nutmeg to taste

1 cup shredded Swiss cheese
½ cup freshly grated Parmesan cheese

Preheat oven to 350° F. Grease six 6-ounce custard cups. In small bowl, combine cream, eggs, and seasonings; mix well. Stir in cheeses. Pour into prepared custard cups. Set in pan of hot water. Bake 35–40 minutes or until knife inserted near center comes out clean. Serve at once.   *Serves 6.*

Serve French bread and butter or water biscuits along with this appetizer.

Stilton Cheese with Celery

1 whole Stilton cheese   Celery hearts

Scrape top from Stilton cheese. Wrap the cheese neatly with a white napkin. Serve the cheese with a silver cheese scoop. Place crisp celery hearts in a tall glass. Eat the celery along with the cheese.

Baked Bacon and Eggs

12 slices bacon, cooked and   12 eggs
    drained   ¾ cup heavy cream
½ pound Gruyère cheese, thinly   Salt and fresh pepper to taste
    sliced

Arrange bacon in a shallow baking dish. Cover with thin slices of cheese. Break eggs over cheese. Drizzle the cream over the whites of the eggs. Put dish in a larger pan with hot water half-way up egg dish. Set into a 350° F. oven and bake 15 minutes until eggs are set. Salt and pepper eggs, if desired.   *Serves 6.*

Chicken Livers and Eggs

2 tablespoons butter   6 eggs
½ pound chicken livers   ¼ cup light cream
2 tablespoons snipped chives   Salt and fresh pepper to taste

Melt butter in large skillet. Add livers. Sauté until livers are lightly browned, about 5 minutes. Sprinkle chives over liver. Beat eggs with cream, salt, and pepper. Stir into skillet. Cook over low heat, stirring occasionally, until eggs are softly set.   *Serves 4–6.*

Eggs Indienne

¼ cup butter
¼ cup minced onion
1 clove garlic, chopped
½ teaspoon grated fresh ginger
¼ cup flour
2 teaspoons curry powder*
1½ cups chicken stock
1½ cups light cream

½ cup seedless raisins
1 medium apple, cored and chopped
8 hard-cooked eggs, chopped
4–6 English muffins, toasted
1 avocado, sliced

In saucepan melt the butter. When hot, add onion, garlic, and ginger and cook for 5 minutes. Blend in flour and curry. Cook, stirring, 1 minute. Remove from heat. Add stock and cream. Cook, stirring, until thickened. Add raisins, apple, and eggs; heat. Serve over English muffins; garnish with slices of avocado.   *Serves 6.*

*Amount of curry may vary, depending on hotness.

Stuffed Eggs Supreme

¼ pound mushrooms, chopped
1 teaspoon chopped tarragon leaves
8 tablespoons butter
3 tablespoons flour
Salt and fresh pepper to taste

2½ cups light cream
1 cup grated Swiss cheese
3 tablespoons grated Parmesan cheese
8 hard-cooked eggs
1 cup soft bread crumbs

Preheat oven to 350° F. In small skillet, cook mushrooms with tarragon in 2 tablespoons butter until all liquid evaporates. Melt 4 tablespoons butter in another saucepan. Blend in flour, salt and pepper. Cook, stirring 1 minute. Add cream; cook, stirring until mixture boils and thickens slightly. Remove from heat. Add Swiss cheese and 2 tablespoons Parmesan; stir until cheese melts. To assemble, cut eggs in half lengthwise. Place yolks in small bowl; mash. Add cooked mushrooms and ¼ cup sauce; mix well. Fill whites with yolk mixture. Pour half the sauce in a shallow 1½-quart casserole (11 by 7 by 2 inches). Arrange eggs in sauce; top with remaining sauce. Combine bread crumbs, remaining 1 tablespoon Parmesan cheese, and 2 tablespoons melted butter; toss well. Sprinkle over casserole. Bake 15–20 minutes or until bubbly.   *Serves 4–6.*

I named this after Maggie and Jiggs in the comic strips because Jiggs is fond of ham and cabbage or corned beef and cabbage.

Maggie and Jiggs Soufflé

1 cup finely chopped ham	¼ teaspoon salt
2 cups finely chopped cabbage	⅛ teaspoon freshly cracked pepper
¼ cup butter	per
¼ cup flour	4 egg yolks, slightly beaten
1 teaspoon Dijon mustard	6 egg whites
1 cup chicken stock	⅛ teaspoon cream of tartar

Preheat oven to 375° F. Butter a 6-cup soufflé dish. In saucepan, cook ham and cabbage in butter until tender. Add flour and mustard and stir with wooden spatula. Add chicken stock, salt, and pepper. Whisk until smooth and thickened. Add a small amount to egg yolks; return mixture to pan. Cook, stirring, for 1 minute. Using clean bowl and beaters, beat egg whites with cream of tartar until stiff peaks form. Mix small amount of egg whites into vegetable mixture. Gently fold in remaining whites. Spoon into soufflé dish. Bake 30 minutes.   *Serves 4–6.*

Egg Timbales

2 tablespoons butter	Few sprigs of fresh thyme
2 tablespoons chopped shallots	¾ cup light cream, scalded
1 tablespoon flour	3 eggs, separated
Salt and fresh pepper to taste	2 tablespoons chopped parsley
Freshly grated nutmeg to taste	Tomato Sauce (see page 447)

Preheat oven to 325° F. Generously butter 8 timbale molds (½–¾ cup). In saucepan melt butter and sauté the shallots. Combine flour, salt, pepper, and nutmeg. Add to butter; cook, stirring a few minutes, to cook flour. Add thyme. Gradually add cream, whisking constantly, until thickened. In large bowl, beat egg yolks until thick and lemon-colored. Gradually add sauce mixture, whisking constantly so eggs will not cook. Add parsley. Using clean bowl and beaters, beat egg whites until stiff peaks form. Fold into yolk mixture. Spoon into prepared molds, filling almost to top (mixture rises like soufflé as it bakes, then falls upon cooling). Place molds in pan of hot water. Bake 25 minutes or until knife inserted near center comes out clean. Let stand 5 minutes before removing from mold. Serve with fresh tomato sauce. (Some people will eat 1, others 2.)   *Serves 4–6.*

Baked Eggs in English Muffin and Bacon Nests

3 English muffins, split
12 slices bacon, partially cooked

6 eggs
2 tablespoons chopped parsley

Place 6 English muffin halves on a baking sheet. Shape two slices of bacon around base of each muffin. Fasten with toothpicks (if bacon slices are long enough to encircle the muffin, one slice is fine). Crack egg onto base of each muffin. Bake at 375° F. for 15 minutes or until egg is set. Sprinkle with parsley. *Serves 4–6.*

These rolls can be eaten out of hand and are excellent for a picnic.

Egg Salad Rolled in Lettuce Leaves

6 hard-cooked eggs, chopped
2 tablespoons chopped scallions
¼ cup sour cream

1 tablespoon chopped dill
Salt and pepper to taste
6 lettuce leaves

In bowl, combine all ingredients except lettuce leaves. Set aside. Blanch lettuce in boiling water; drain well. Place about ⅓ cup egg salad in each leaf; roll. *Serves 6.*

VARIATIONS:

Substitute curry powder for dill. Use as a spread on cucumber slices.

Really quick and easy.

Vermouth-Glazed Eggs

3 tablespoons butter
6 eggs
Salt and fresh pepper to taste

⅓ cup dry vermouth
¼ cup chopped parsley

Melt butter in a large skillet until hot and foamy. Break eggs into hot butter. Add salt and pepper. Cook for 2 minutes until barely set. Pour vermouth over eggs. Cover. Cook about 3 minutes or until eggs are set. Sprinkle with chopped parsley. *Serves 4–6.*

Recipes in this chapter:

DESSERTS

Stop.

Before you read any of the recipes in this section, think a minute. You are going to make a meal in one hour. That means you are going to have to spend most of the time on the entrée. Maybe you should think about keeping the dessert fairly simple.

At least check the menus in the back of the book and make sure that you are not combining the most complicated and time-consuming entrée with the most involved dessert and appetizer. You can't have dinner ready in an hour if it consists of three forty-minute dishes.

One of the simplest and one of the very best desserts is fresh fruit. You don't need a recipe for this—just see the dessert ideas on page 434 as a reminder of how varied fresh fruit can be.

Fresh Figs in Curaçao

1 cup sour cream
¼ cup curaçao

12 fresh figs, peeled and halved
1 tablespoon brandy

Combine cream and curaçao. Separately combine figs and brandy. Let stand 15 minutes. Drain figs and gently fold into cream mixture.   *Serves 4–6.*

VARIATION:

The fresh figs can also be served with cream or covered with port wine.

Almond Coffee Cake

1 cup blanched almonds
2¼ cups sugar
10 tablespoons butter, softened
2 teaspoons vanilla extract

4 eggs
4½ cups flour
1 tablespoon baking powder

Preheat oven to 350°F. In covered blender or food processor blend almonds until ground. In large bowl, cream together sugar, butter, and vanilla. Add 3 eggs; mix well. Stir in almonds. Combine flour and baking powder; gradually add to almond mixture, stirring to make a stiff dough. Turn onto lightly floured board; knead just to blend. (Can be made ahead to this point and refrigerated.) Divide dough in half. Press each half into 10-inch circle on well-greased baking sheet. Beat remaining egg; brush over top of cake. Using tines of fork, make crisscross pattern over top of cake. Bake 20 minutes; serve warm.   *Makes two 10-inch coffee cakes.*

Daiquiri Peaches

½ cup honey
Juice of 2 limes
6–8 peaches, halved, stoned, and peeled

Rum
Freshly grated nutmeg to taste
½ cup sour cream

Mix honey and lime juice together. Dip peaches in the mixture. Place the peaches cut side up in a shallow baking pan. Fill the center of each peach with 2 tablespoons rum and sprinkle with nutmeg. Place under broiler for 2 minutes or until light brown. Serve with sour cream.   *Serves 4–6.*

Fried Peaches

4 tablespoons butter
6–8 peaches, halved, stoned, and peeled
1 cup light brown sugar

½ cup heavy cream
Freshly grated nutmeg to taste

Melt the butter in a skillet. Add the peaches. Sprinkle with the sugar. Let simmer, uncovered, about 20–30 minutes, turning frequently, When just ready to serve, add the cream. Serve hot sprinkled with nutmeg.   *Serves 4–6.*

VARIATION:

Substitute nectarines, apples, or pears.

Glazed Pears

6 ripe Bosc pears
1 teaspoon grated orange rind
Freshly grated nutmeg

½ cup orange juice
¼ cup Cointreau

Halve, core, and peel pears. Place cut side up in a large, shallow, buttered baking dish. Combine orange rind, nutmeg, orange juice, and Cointreau in a small saucepan. Heat to boiling. Pour over pears. Cover with foil. Bake at 350° F. for 30 minutes or until tender, basting 3 times with orange mixture. Serve warm.
                                                                Serves 6.

VARIATION:

Substitute peaches for pears and serve with sour or heavy cream.

Very rich, not overly sweet, fudgy type.

Toasted Almond Fudgies

½ cup butter
3 squares unsweetened chocolate
¾ cup sugar
1 teaspoon vanilla extract

2 eggs
½ cup flour
¼ cup slivered toasted almonds

Grease an 8-by-8-by-2-inch baking dish. Melt ½ cup butter and chocolate in saucepan over very low heat. Remove from heat and beat in sugar and vanilla. Beat in eggs. Add flour. Mix well. Add nuts and pour into prepared pan. Bake at 350° F. for 30–40 minutes. Cut into squares. *Makes about 12–16 squares.*

Broiled Fruits with Sugar Crust

1 tablespoon butter, softened
2 oranges, diced
1 large banana, sliced
3 pears, peeled, cored, and sliced
1 apple, cored and thinly sliced
¾ cup brown sugar

½ cup finely chopped pecans
6 tablespoons melted butter
Juice of ½ lemon
1 teaspoon grated lemon rind, or more

Arrange fruits in a buttered 10-inch baking dish. Combine remaining ingredients. Sprinkle over fruit. Broil about 8 inches from heat for 8–10 minutes or until mixture is melted and bubbly. Cool 10 minutes before serving. *Serves 4–6.*

Honey-Glazed Peaches

6 large peaches, halved, stoned, and peeled
½ cup honey

2 tablespoons butter
Juice of ½ lemon
1 teaspoon grated lemon rind

Arrange peaches in a shallow greased baking dish, cut side up. Combine honey, 2 tablespoons butter, lemon juice, and rind in a small saucepan. Bring to a boil. Pour over peaches. Cover with foil. Bake at 350° F. for 20 minutes, basting with syrup several times. Serve warm.   *Serves 4–6.*

VARIATION:

Substitute pears for peaches and serve with heavy or sour cream.

This dessert separates into a wet cake with creamy sauce underneath. It's scrumptious served with coffee ice cream.

Hot Fudge Baked Pudding

1¼ cups flour	1 teaspoon vanilla extract
¾ cup sugar	¾ cup chopped pecans
¼ cup cocoa	½ cup brown sugar
3 teaspoons baking powder	3 tablespoons cocoa
½ teaspoon salt	1½ cups boiling water
¾ cup milk	Whipped cream
2 tablespoons butter, melted	

Combine flour, sugar, cocoa, baking powder, and salt in a bowl. Add milk, butter, and vanilla. Beat well. Stir in pecans. Spread batter in buttered 13-by-9-by-2-inch baking pan. Combine brown sugar and cocoa. Sprinkle over batter. Pour boiling water over mixture. Bake at 350° F. for 40 minutes. Cool 15–20 minutes. Cut in 12 squares. Serve very warm topped with whipped cream.   *Serves 12.*

Nectarines in Curaçao

6–8 nectarines, peeled, pitted, and sliced	¼ cup curaçao or more
	Mint leaves

Arrange nectarine slices in a bowl. Sprinkle over the curaçao. Toss to coat well. Let stand 15 minutes. Garnish each serving with fresh mint leaves.   *Serves 4–6.*

This is the only way I will eat rhubarb for dessert.

Stewed Rhubarb, Strawberries, and Bananas

2 pounds rhubarb, trimmed and cut into 1-inch pieces
¾ cup sugar, or less
1 cup strawberries, hulled and sliced

1–2 medium bananas, peeled and sliced
Sour cream (optional)

Put rhubarb and sugar in a saucepan. Simmer slowly until it reaches doneness desired, 10–15 minutes or less. Remove from stove. Add the berries and bananas. Mix well. Serve warm or chill. Put a tablespoon of sour cream on top of each serving if you like.   *Serves 4–6.*

Sangría Grapes

1 lemon, sliced
1 orange, sliced
2 tablespoons sugar
2 cups red wine

¼ cup brandy
3–4 cups seedless grapes, stemmed, rinsed, and dried
4–6 small cinnamon sticks

Place lemon and orange in pitcher. Add sugar, wine, and brandy. Place grapes in 4–6 stemmed glasses. Add wine mixture to each glass. Add a lemon and orange slice to each. Garnish with cinnamon stick. Chill until ready to serve.   *Serves 4–6.*

Cardamom Peaches

1 cup sugar
1 cup water
2 cups white wine
1-inch vanilla bean

1 teaspoon crushed cardamom seeds, or more
6 peaches, halved, stoned, and peeled

Bring sugar, water, wine, vanilla, and cardamom to a boil in a saucepan. Boil 5 minutes. Turn to simmer. Add the peaches, cover, and simmer 10–20 minutes, depending on ripeness of fruit. To test, pierce fruit with tip of small knife.

Serves 4–6.

VARIATION:

Pears may be substituted for peaches.

Fruit Compote

3 navel oranges, peeled and sectioned	1 tablespoon sugar Freshly grated nutmeg to taste
1 cup seedless grapes, halved	1 teaspoon grated fresh ginger
1 pint strawberries, sliced	

Combine fruits in bowl. Combine sugar and spices. Toss with fruit. Refrigerate until ready to serve.

Serves 4–6.

VARIATION:

Just before serving, blend in 1 cup plain yogurt.

South Seas Compote

1 pint strawberries, hulled and cut in half	¾ cup fresh orange juice
3 large oranges, peeled and sectioned	¼ cup honey
	2 bananas, sliced Freshly grated coconut

Place strawberries and oranges in serving bowl. Combine orange juice and honey; mix well. Pour over fruit. Refrigerate until ready to serve. Add bananas and mix. Serve garnished with coconut.

Serves 4–6.

Spiced Fall Compote

4 large cooking apples
1 cup water
¼ cup sugar
1 stick cinnamon broken in 2–3 pieces
1 tablespoon butter
Salt to taste
3 large oranges, peeled and sectioned

Grated rind of 1 lemon
¼ cup red wine
¼ cup Grand Marnier, curaçao, or Cointreau
½ cup chopped walnuts

Peel, core, and slice apples; reserve skins. In small saucepan, combine skins and water; bring to a boil. Reduce heat and cook over low heat about 10 minutes. Meanwhile, in another saucepan, combine apples, sugar, cinnamon, butter, and salt. Add liquid from skins; bring to a boil. Reduce heat and cook, stirring occasionally, over low heat until apples are *just barely* tender (about 5–8 minutes); remove cinnamon. Combine with remaining ingredients except walnuts in serving bowl; refrigerate until ready to serve. Serve garnished with walnuts.   *Serves 4–6.*

Baked Lemon Soufflé with Rum Sauce

¼ cup butter
¼ cup flour
1 cup milk
¼ cup sugar
5 egg yolks
Grated rind of 1 lemon
¼ cup lemon juice
7 egg whites

Sauce:

2 egg yolks, beaten
3 tablespoons sugar
1 cup milk
2 tablespoons rum
½ cup heavy cream, whipped

Preheat oven to 375° F. Generously butter and lightly sugar a 6-cup soufflé dish; set aside. In saucepan, melt butter; blend in flour. Gradually add milk. Cook, stirring constantly, until mixture comes to boil and thickens. Add sugar, stir, and remove from burner. Beat yolks until thick and lemon-colored. Add to flour mixture with lemon rind and juice. Place mixture in bowl. Set in freezer to chill. Meanwhile, beat egg whites until stiff but not dry. Add a small amount of egg whites to custard mixture; mix well. Gently fold egg whites into custard mixture. Pour into prepared soufflé dish. Bake 30 minutes or until browned on top.

   While soufflé is baking, prepare sauce. In saucepan, combine egg yolks and sugar; gradually add milk. Cook, stirring constantly, until mixture thickens slightly and coats metal spoon. Remove from heat; add rum. Chill in freezer. About 5 minutes before soufflé is done, fold chilled custard sauce into whipped cream. Serve over soufflé.

Serves 4–6.

Strawberries Dipped in White Chocolate

¾ pound white chocolate, cut up   30 large strawberries

Put the chocolate in a saucepan and melt slowly while stirring over direct heat. (Or do it over simmering water.) Do not scorch. Remove from stove when melted. Hold berries by stem end and dip the pointed ends into the white chocolate halfway up the berry. Twist the berry to remove excess chocolate. Place on a baking sheet lined with wax paper. Refrigerate 10–15 minutes to set.

Rich Apple Bars
Crust:

¾ cup butter, softened
¼ cup sugar
1 egg, beaten
1 teaspoon vanilla extract
2 cups flour
¼ teaspoon salt

Topping:

½ cup flour
⅓ cup sugar
½ cup butter, softened

Filling:

5 cups peeled and thinly sliced tart cooking apples
Juice of ½ lemon
¼ cup sugar
3 tablespoons flour
2 teaspoons grated lemon rind
About 1 teaspoon freshly grated nutmeg, or less
1½ cups grated sharp Cheddar cheese

Preheat oven to 425° F. Grease jelly-roll pan (15 by 10 by 1 inch). Combine all ingredients for crust; mix well. Press firmly into prepared pan. Combine apples with lemon juice; toss to coat well with remaining filling ingredients. Arrange over crust. Combine flour and sugar for topping; cut in butter until mixture is crumbly. Sprinkle over apples. Bake 25 minutes or until apples are tender and top is brown. Cut into squares.   *Makes fifteen 3-inch squares.*

Fruit Crunch

1 pound plums, pitted and quartered
1 pound nectarines or peaches, pitted, peeled, and sliced
¼ cup packed brown sugar
1 teaspoon ground cinnamon
1 cup plus 1 tablespoon flour

1 cup sugar
1 teaspoon baking powder
½ teaspoon salt
½ teaspoon freshly grated nutmeg
1 egg, well beaten
¼ cup melted butter

Preheat oven to 375° F. Combine fruit, brown sugar, cinnamon, and 1 tablespoon flour in a medium-size baking dish. Combine remaining ingredients except butter; mix until crumbly. Sprinkle over fruit; drizzle with butter. Bake 40 minutes or until top is brown.   *Serves 4–6.*

Grand Marnier Soufflé

4 tablespoons butter
4 tablespoons flour
1 cup milk
2 tablespoons sugar
4 egg yolks

1 teaspoon grated orange rind
¼ cup orange juice
¼ cup Grand Marnier
5 egg whites

Preheat oven to 375° F. In saucepan, melt butter; blend in flour. Gradually add milk. Cook, stirring constantly, until mixture comes to a boil and thickens. Add sugar. Cook 1 minute. Pour into bowl, and add egg yolks one at a time, beating well after each addition. Add orange rind and juice and Grand Marnier. Chill in freezer 10 minutes. Meanwhile, beat egg whites until stiff but not dry. Beat a small amount of whites into custard mixture, then gently fold in remaining egg whites. Spoon the mixture into a 1½-quart soufflé dish. Bake 25–30 minutes. Remove and serve at once. *Serves 4–6.*

Sour Cream Cookies

1 cup sugar
2 tablespoons butter, softened
¼ cup sour cream
1 egg
1 teaspoon vanilla extract

1¼ cups flour
¼ teaspoon baking powder
¼ teaspoon baking soda
½ teaspoon salt

In bowl, cream together sugar and butter; add sour cream, egg, and vanilla. Combine remaining ingredients. With wooden spoon (do not use mixer) add to creamed mixture. Drop by level teaspoons, about 2 inches apart, onto well-greased baking sheet. Sprinkle with additional sugar. Bake 6–8 minutes, until lightly browned. Let stand 1 minute before removing to baking rack to cool.

Makes about 4 dozen 2-inch cookies.

Pecan Balls

½ cup butter, at room temperature
2 tablespoons sugar
1 teaspoon vanilla extract

1 cup flour
1 cup chopped pecans
About ½ cup confectioners' sugar

Preheat oven to 350° F. In small mixer bowl, cream together butter, sugar, and vanilla with electric beater. Gradually add flour; mix well. With wooden spoon, stir in nuts (it may be necessary to mix with hands at this point). Shape into ¾-inch balls (about 1 level teaspoon); place on ungreased baking sheet about 1 inch apart. Bake 15 minutes. While still warm, roll in confectioners' sugar; cool on wire rack.

Makes 36–40 cookies.

Marble Cookies

1 square (1 ounce) semisweet chocolate (or use unsweetened chocolate for darker color)
½ cup butter, at room temperature
½ cup sugar

1 egg yolk
1 teaspoon vanilla extract
1½ cups flour
½ teaspoon baking powder
¼ teaspoon salt
3 tablespoons milk

Preheat oven to 350° F. Melt chocolate. Meanwhile, in small mixer bowl, cream together butter, sugar, egg yolk, and vanilla with electric beater until light and fluffy. Combine flour, baking powder, and salt. Add with milk to creamed mixture. With wooden spoon, blend in melted chocolate to make a marbled mixture. Place on waxed paper; form into 1½-inch roll. Wrap tightly and place in freezer about 20 minutes or until firm. Cut into ¼-inch slices; place 2 inches apart on ungreased baking sheet (cookies spread slightly when baked). Bake 10 minutes; cool on cake rack. *Makes thirty 2-inch cookies.*

Honeydew Melon with Seedless Grapes

1 honeydew melon
2–3 pounds green seedless grapes

¼ cup port wine
½ cup honey

Cut melon in half and remove the seeds. Take out the fruit with a melon baller. Put into a bowl. Remove grapes from stems. Combine with melon. Scrape remaining flesh from melon shell and place in food processor or blender. Add port and honey. Purée and pour over fruit. Serve in stem glasses. *Serves 4–6.*

Melon Balls with Sparkling Cider

1 medium watermelon or honeydew or Persian melon

1 bottle sparkling cider

Scoop out balls from the melon. Divide among dessert dishes. Just before serving, put ½ cup of iced sparkling cider over each. *Serves 4–6.*

Crushed Peaches with Vanilla Cream

6–8 ripe peaches, pitted and   1 teaspoon vanilla extract
    peeled   1 cup heavy cream
½ cup confectioners' sugar

Crush or mash peaches in a bowl. Add sugar. Mix. Add vanilla to heavy cream. Add to peaches and chill for 10 minutes. Spoon into dessert dishes.   *Serves 4–6.*

VARIATION:

Substitute 1 quart strawberries, washed, hulled, and mashed, for the peaches.

Broiled Oranges with Brown Sugar

3–4 large California oranges   ½ cup light brown sugar
¼ cup Grand Marnier

Peel and slice oranges about ¼ inch thick. Place slices in a flat dish with sides to marinate with the Grand Marnier for 30 minutes or longer. Place orange slices on broiler rack of pan and sieve light brown sugar over them. Broil 4–5 inches from top of fruit to heat. Pour any juice in bottom of broiler pan over each serving on dessert plate.   *Serves 4–6.*

Fresh Fruit Compote for Winter

2–3 grapefruits, sectioned   2 tablespoons sugar
  4 oranges, sectioned   2 tablespoons Kirsch
½ pound red grapes, halved and
    seeded

Mix all fruit together in a bowl. Sprinkle sugar and Kirsch over fruit and chill 10–15 minutes. Spoon into dessert dishes.   *Serves 4–6.*

Top-of-the-Stove Blueberry Pudding

Blueberries

   2 tablespoons butter
 ½ cup sugar
   1 teaspoon cornstarch
 ⅛ teaspoon salt
 ½ teaspoon cinnamon
   2 cups hot water
     Juice of ½ lemon
   2 cups blueberries

Dumplings

   1 cup flour
 1½ teaspoons baking powder
 ½ teaspoon salt
 ¼ cup sugar
   3 tablespoons shortening
 ⅓ cup milk
   1 egg, beaten
     Freshly grated nutmeg
     Cream or milk

Melt butter in deep 10-inch, straight-sided skillet that has a tight-fitting lid. Combine ½ cup sugar, cornstarch, ⅛ teaspoon salt, and cinnamon and stir into butter. Add water and cook until clear, stirring constantly. Add lemon juice and berries. Bring to a boil and top with dumplings.

For dumplings, put flour, baking powder, salt, and sugar into a bowl. Cut in shortening until mixture is crumbly. Add milk to beaten egg; stir into flour mixture until flour is well moistened. Drop by tablespoons on top of boiling berry mixture, or drop dumpling mixture with an ice-cream scoop. Sprinkle top of dumplings with nutmeg. Cover tightly. Reduce heat to low and cook for 20 minutes. Serve warm with cream or milk. *Makes 8 good-size dumplings; serves 4–6.*

All hard sauce should be cold, served on a hot dessert. Also, hard sauce can be made into rosettes from a pastry tube and stored in freezer.

Quick Sautéed Apples

Apples

   4 large Golden Delicious apples or
     baking apples in season
     Juice of ½ lemon
   6 tablespoons butter
     Freshly grated nutmeg

Hard Sauce

   5 tablespoons butter (softened)
 1¼ cups confectioners' sugar
   2 tablespoons Calvados (apple
     brandy)

Wash and peel apples, cut in quarters, and core. Cut each quarter in thirds into a bowl with lemon juice. Toss around to keep apples from discoloring. Melt butter in 10-inch sauté pan on high. When butter is foaming, add apple wedges so they all lie flat in bottom of pan. Place lid on pan. When apples steam, turn heat to low. Cook for about 10 minutes, turning apples halfway through the cooking time. Test apples for fork tender (not mushy). While apples are cooking, make hard sauce.

Cream butter until softened, add sugar, and beat until fluffy, adding Calvados a little at a time. For quick chill, place in freezer. Serve hot apples in low fruit dishes with hard sauce. *Serves 4–6.*

These easy, pretty babas are light and delicate even though they are made with no yeast.

Rum Babas

Fine bread crumbs	¼ cup lukewarm milk
2 eggs	1 tablespoon orange juice
1¼ cups sugar	Grated rind of 1 orange
½ cup plus 2 tablespoons flour	1 cup water
2 teaspoons baking powder	2 tablespoons rum or brandy
3 tablespoons butter, melted	1 cup heavy cream, whipped

Preheat oven to 375° F. Butter 6 custard cups and dust with fine bread crumbs. Set on a trivet or place in a small shallow oblong pan. Beat eggs until fluffy. Add ¼ cup sugar and continue beating on high speed of mixer until sugar is dissolved. Sift flour and baking powder together and add them. Add melted butter, warm milk, orange juice, and orange rind. Mix vigorously. Pour the same amount into each custard cup. Bake at 375° F. for 25 minutes. Remove from oven and loosen from molds after 2–3 minutes.

Boil 1 cup sugar and water for a few minutes until it forms a thin syrup. Cool slightly. Flavor with rum or brandy. Pour syrup over molds—a tablespoon at a time—so the babas will absorb it. Each will take 3 tablespoons of syrup. When cool, serve with whipped cream. *Serves 6.*

Lemon Ladyfingers

4 eggs, separated, at room temperature
⅛ teaspoon salt
¾ cups granulated sugar

Rind of 1 lemon, grated fine
⅔ cup flour (measured lightly)
Confectioners' sugar

Grease and flour ladyfinger pans or a large cookie sheet. In large bowl of electric mixer, at high speed, beat egg whites and salt until soft peaks form. Gradually sprinkle in ¼ cup granulated sugar; continue to beat until sugar is dissolved and egg whites form stiff, glossy peaks. In another mixer bowl with mixer at medium speed and then high, beat egg yolks, lemon rind, and ½ cup granulated sugar. It will be a stiff batter. Fold flour into egg yolks by hand. Fold egg yolk mixture into beaten egg whites. Batter will be light and well mixed. Use level tablespoon of batter spread into each mold. This takes time and batter is thick. If you only have two ladyfinger pans, a repeated baking can be done with no fear of not rising. Or, using a pastry bag with ½-inch tip tube, pipe batter in 3-inch lengths about 1 inch apart on cookie sheet. Sprinkle cakes with confectioners' sugar before placing in the oven. Bake at 350° F. for 15 minutes.   *Makes 40–50 cakes, depending on size.*

Sinfully rich, fairly wet pudding.

Apple Nut Pudding

1½ cups sugar
2 eggs
½ cup oil
1 teaspoon vanilla extract
2 cups flour
1 teaspoon baking powder
1 teaspoon baking soda
1 teaspoon cinnamon
½ teaspoon freshly grated nutmeg
½ teaspoon salt
⅓ cup buttermilk

¾ cup chopped pecans
2 cups thinly sliced cooking apples

Sauce

¾ cup sugar
⅓ cup buttermilk
1 teaspoon vanilla extract
1 tablespoon corn syrup
¼ pound butter
2 tablespoons grated lemon rind

Preheat oven to 350° F. Butter a 2½-quart (13-by-9-by-2-inch) baking dish. In large bowl, mix together 1½ cups sugar, eggs, oil, and 1 teaspoon vanilla. Combine flour, baking powder, baking soda, spices, and salt. Add alternately with buttermilk to creamed mixture. Fold in nuts and apples. Spread in prepared pan. Bake 30 minutes. Meanwhile, combine all ingredients for sauce in saucepan; heat just to a boil. With fork, poke holes over top of cake; top with warm sauce.

Serves 12.

Orange Sour Cream Cake

¾ cup softened butter
1½ cups sugar
1 tablespoon orange rind
2 eggs
2 cups flour
1 teaspoon baking soda

1 cup sour cream
1 cup orange juice
1 cup raisins
¼ cup chopped dates
½ cups chopped nuts
2 tablespoons honey

Preheat oven to 350° F. Generously grease a 1½-quart (12-by-9-by-2-inch) shallow baking pan. Cream together butter and sugar. Add orange rind and eggs, one at a time, beating well after each addition. Combine flour and baking soda. Add alternately to creamed mixture with sour cream and ½ cup orange juice. Fold in raisins, dates, and nuts. Spoon into prepared pan. Bake 35 minutes. Combine remaining ½ cup orange juice and honey. Pour over cake; return to oven for 5 minutes.

Serves 12.

Baked Apples with Bourbon

4–6 medium Winesap apples, McIntosh, Roman Beauty, or any baking apples in season
Juice of ½ lemon
1 cup light brown sugar, packed

4 tablespoons butter, melted
4–6 tablespoons bourbon
Cream, whipped cream, or sour cream

Preheat oven to 375° F. Core each apple and peel around top about one-third of the way down from stem. Dip tops in lemon juice. Place in shallow baking dish or pan. Mix sugar and melted butter. Pour 1 tablespoon bourbon into each apple cavity. Bake at 375° F. for 45–50 minutes. Halfway through baking, spoon glaze over apples. Test apples with fork for tenderness in 45–50 minutes. Serve apples in low dessert dishes with cream, whipped cream, or sour cream.

Serves 4–6.

Peaches in Honey

6–8 peaches, pitted and sliced thin   ¼ cup honey

Slice peaches into a bowl and add the honey. Mix well. Chill before serving in stem glasses.   *Serves 4–6.*

Pears and Raspberries

4–6 pears, peeled, cored, and   1 pint raspberries
  sliced across in circles   4–6 tablespoons sour cream

Arrange pear circles on dessert plates. Mound a few of the berries in the center of each pear. Spoon sour cream over each serving.   *Serves 4–6.*

Other Dessert Ideas

Apples, Cheese, and Nuts

Apples, polished, in a bowl, served along with Roquefort cheese, softened, and walnuts in the shell.

Grapes

A bowl of grapes, bunches of different types: red, purple, green.

Cheeses

Present three kinds of cheese on a marble slab—one hard, one semisoft, and one soft. Serve French bread, butter in a crock, and unsalted crackers.

Melons

Slice into chunks, or balls if there is time, a selection of various melons in season: cantaloupe, honeydew, watermelon, Persian, cranshaw.

Fresh Fruits

Fill a bowl with fresh fruit to be eaten out of hand: apples, oranges, plums, apricots, cherries, bananas, pears, grapes, and figs.

Cut-up Fresh Fruits

• Add lemon or orange juice to mixed cut-up fresh fruit.
• Sprinkle cut-up fresh fruit with white or brown sugar to taste, or add honey.
• For fresh fruit combinations, mix and match what is in season, such as oranges, grapefruit, strawberries, blueberries, blackberries, pineapple, apples, pears, nectarines, peaches, bananas, kiwis.
• Serve cut-up fruit or berries with sour cream, whipped cream, or yogurt.
• Select exotic fruits when they are in season—mangoes, persimmons, kiwis, and papaya—and serve with wedges of lime.
• Sprinkle fresh fruits with chopped fresh mint or ginger.
• Douse cut-up fruits with rum or brandy or a fruit liqueur such as curaçao.

Recipes in this chapter:

FLAVORED BUTTERS
FENNEL BUTTER
MAPLE BUTTER
SUGARED PECANS
CHOCOLATE SYRUP FOR DRINKS
DEPRESSION CANDY
HOMEMADE HORSERADISH
DUCK STOCK
DILLED MUSHROOMS AND CARROTS
PICKLED GARDEN RELISH
HORSERADISH CREAM
CUCUMBER SAUCE
CRÊPES
CRANBERRIES WITH SHERRY
LEMON SAUCE
VINEGAR MINT SAUCE
BRANDIED HONEY
VINAIGRETTE
BÉARNAISE SAUCE
TOMATO SAUCE
CHICKEN STOCK
BOUQUET GARNI
FISH STOCK
DEVILED WALNUTS
POLONAISE SAUCE
COURT BOUILLON
TARTAR SAUCE
CUSTARD SAUCE
MAYONNAISE AND VARIATIONS
ALMOND MAYONNAISE
BLENDER MAYONNAISE
HOLLANDAISE SAUCE
BLENDER HOLLANDAISE

MISCELLANY

Gifts from the Kitchen

What can you give the host or hostess who has everything? Easy. A jar of homemade mayonnaise. Or herb butter made with home-grown herbs and packed into a crock. Homemade horseradish, basil sauce, and tartar sauce will delight and astonish friends who have tried only commercial versions. Pickled garden relishes, depression candy, deviled walnuts, and sugared pecans are all quick, easy to make, and genuinely personal gifts. If your hosts have small children, be sure to bring along a jar of homemade chocolate syrup. There is nothing like it on the market anymore.

Picnics

For years I've been telling myself that I loved picnics, but then one morning I took a long look in the mirror and decided to admit the truth to myself and everyone else. Sometimes picnics are fun. And sometimes picnics are a pain in the basket.

Picnics are fun when they're grown-up picnics and you can bring real food. Things like mini meat loaf, hot soup in a thermos, and cold fruit soup in another thermos. Fried duck, ham, egg salad rolled up in lettuce leaves, and ginger-glazed chicken are grown-up dishes that pack well in a picnic basket and will get you lots of compliments.

Picnics are also fun when they are kid picnics, and you bring simple sandwiches and plain old American standbys like potato salad and watermelon. Kid food doesn't have to be junk food. But when you try to mix the two, picnics are a pain. You unpack a basket of grown-up delights, you pass them around, and the kids mope and sigh over their plates because it tastes just like company dinner. So remember, one kid makes it a kids' picnic, and all the adults will have to sneak their fried duck and fruit soup on the sly.

Covered dish parties don't have to be picnics, but they are a lot of fun—if you organize things so that everybody doesn't bring the same favorite recipe for chili, with lots and lots of beans. I keep hoping we'll all discover covered dish parties and make them popular again. They began to disappear around the time when the ladies discovered that tuna fish casserole was even cheaper than chili and beans. I remember going to covered dish dinners with my mother when I was very young. I used to look under every cover very carefully, and

then nine out of ten times refuse to eat anything but what we brought from home. My mother said I was impolite, but even then I knew better than to trust to luck in a crowd of cooks. Know your dish makers when you throw your covered dish party, and never judge a covered dish by its cover.

Cocktails

Have a little pity on your guests at cocktail parties. They are going to be carrying a glass in one hand almost constantly, and since they are going to empty that glass one or three times, hand-eye coordination will suffer slightly. Not so much that you will have to take their keys away and refuse to let them drive home—as we are all advised in those safety ads put out by insurance companies. But enough so that balancing a plate full of juicy food, or manipulating little sticks of vegetables from loose and clotty dips to the mouth, is an invitation to minor personal tragedy. Some hosts never seem to give thought to the fact that they are, in one short afternoon, responsible for hundreds and hundreds of dollars in cleaning bills.

I like to serve almonds and olives at cocktail time. You can use one kind of olive, mix and match green and black, Italian, Greek, and Spanish. Buy freshly roasted almonds from a nut store, or put them on a baking sheet with a bit of oil and toast them in a slow oven for a few minutes, salting them just before serving.

If a cocktail party is late in the afternoon, or going to last more than a couple of hours, you may want more substantial food. This book is filled with ideas easy to prepare and more or less safe to eat.

Flavored Butters

12 tablespoons butter, softened

Place butter in food processor or bowl.

FOR HERB BUTTER:
Add 2 tablespoons chopped rosemary
add 2 tablespoons chopped basil
add 2 tablespoons chopped chervil
add 2 tablespoons chopped tarragon
add 2 tablespoons chopped parsley
add 2 tablespoons chopped dill
add 2 tablespoons finely chopped mint

FOR SHALLOT BUTTER:
Add 2 tablespoons chopped shallots

FOR GARLIC BUTTER:
Add 1 tablespoon chopped garlic

FOR LEMON BUTTER:
Add 1 tablespoon lemon juice
and 1 teaspoon grated lemon rind

FOR CAPER BUTTER:
Add 1–2 tablespoons capers, drained

FOR MAÎTRE D'HÔTEL BUTTER:
Add 2 tablespoons chopped parsley,
and 2 tablespoons lemon juice

Fennel Butter

8 tablespoons butter, softened	1 tablespoon freshly chopped
2–3 tablespoons finely chopped fresh fennel leaves	parsley

Place butter in a bowl. Add fennel and parsley. Beat until well mixed. Serve on broiled fish or in fish baked in parchment.   *Makes ½ cup.*

Great on pancakes and French toast

Maple Butter

12 tablespoons butter	1 cup maple syrup

Place butter in food processor or mixer bowl and cream until very light. Add syrup in a thin stream and continue beating until fluffy and pale.

Makes about 2 cups.

This recipe is an adaptation of one used by a cousin in the family. She would never give the exact recipe, as she sold these nuts commercially to support herself and her father, whom she kept in a pint of whiskey a day.

Sugared Pecans

2¼ cups sugar	2 teaspoons vanilla extract
1 cup sour cream	5 cups pecans
Salt to taste	

Brush a baking sheet with melted butter and set aside. In a saucepan, mix together the sugar, sour cream, and salt. Bring slowly to a boil and stir until soft ball stage is reached, 236° F. on a candy thermometer. Remove from burner and add vanilla. With a wooden spatula, beat until the mixture loses its gloss. It should begin to thicken at this point. Add the pecans. Stir to coat well. Place on baking sheet and separate the nuts, using two forks. *Makes 1½ pounds or more.*

Chocolate Syrup for Drinks

2 cups cocoa
1½ cups sugar
2 cups hot water

1 cup corn syrup
1 tablespoon vanilla extract

In a saucepan mix together cocoa, sugar, and hot water. Add corn syrup. Boil 3 minutes, stirring. Add vanilla. Cool. Store in jar in refrigerator. *Makes 1 quart.*

Note: For hot chocolate, stir 1–2 tablespoons chocolate syrup into 1 cup hot milk. For chocolate milk, add 1–2 tablespoons chocolate syrup to 1 cup cold milk. Use also for chocolate sodas and milkshakes.

We used to make this when I was a small girl. I had to crack the walnuts and remember the stains they left on my small fingers. The sugar was always melted in a black iron skillet.

Depression Candy

Butter
2 cups sugar

1½ cups black walnuts or other nuts

Heavily butter a baking sheet. Put sugar in heavy fry pan and cook while stirring over medium flame until sugar melts and turns an amber color. This will take about 15 minutes. Strew the nuts over the baking sheet and carefully pour the sugar evenly over nuts. Let stand in a cool place until hard. Break into pieces and eat! *Makes a little over 1 pound.*

Wear goggles when making this or you surely will cry.

Homemade Horseradish

½ pound fresh horseradish,
   peeled and cut into chunks
3 tablespoons heavy cream

3 tablespoons vinegar
1 tablespoon Dijon mustard
Salt and fresh pepper to taste

Drop the horseradish through feed tube of food processor and chop, using the steel blade. Remove horseradish to a bowl. Combine cream, vinegar, and mustard. Add the cream mixture to the horseradish. Add salt and pepper, if desired.

Makes about 1 cup.

Duck Stock

Trimmings and giblets from
   ducks, backs hacked into pieces
1 small carrot, cut into chunks
1 onion, quartered

1 celery rib, chopped
Salt and fresh pepper to taste
Few sprigs of thyme
Few sprigs of parsley

Put all ingredients into saucepan. Cover with water. Bring to a boil, half cover, and turn to medium heat. Boil 30 minutes or longer. Strain. Reduce to half.

Makes 1 cup or less.

Note: This stock is great to add to rice or soup or to moisten vegetables.
   For duck soup, add this stock to 5–6 cups chicken stock. Add 1 cup julienned vegetables if desired. Cook 3–5 minutes.

Serves 4–6.

Dilled Mushrooms and Carrots

3 pounds small mushrooms
1 pound carrots, cut in ½-inch
   pieces
2 cups water
2 cups white vinegar

½ cup sugar
¼ cup salt
¼ cup chopped fresh dill
2 teaspoons whole peppercorns
6–12 cloves garlic

Place enough water in water bath to cover 6 pint jars or 12 half-pint jars by 1–2 inches; cover and bring to boil. Combine mushrooms and carrots in boiling water; simmer 5 minutes. Drain well. Meanwhile, combine water, vinegar, sugar, salt, dill, and peppercorns; bring to boil. Pack sterilized jars with carrots and mushrooms; top with clove of garlic (if using half-pint jars, use 12 cloves garlic). Pour vinegar mixture over vegetables to cover. Wipe jars clean; seal. Process 20 minutes; cool.   *Makes 6 pints or 12 half-pints.*

Pickled Garden Relish

1 small cauliflower, broken in tiny flowerets
4 carrots, peeled, cut in 2-inch strips or julienned
4 large long ribs of celery, in 1-inch pieces
2 green peppers, cut in 2-inch strips
2 small white onions, thinly sliced
½ cup wine vinegar
½ cup salad oil
¼ cup sugar
Salt and fresh pepper to taste
1 tablespoon chopped oregano leaves
½ cup water

In large kettle, combine all ingredients. Bring vegetables to a boil, stirring occasionally. Reduce heat to simmer. Cover pan and cook for 5 minutes. Cool. Store in refrigerator.   *Makes 5 pints.*

Serve this over fish.

Horseradish Cream

2 cups heavy cream
¼ cup freshly grated horseradish

Reduce 2 cups heavy cream to 1 cup over medium heat. Add the horseradish. Stir and serve hot or cold.   *Makes 1 cup.*

Use this as a sauce for fish.

Cucumber Sauce

1 cup sour cream
1 cup mayonnaise, preferably
  homemade
1 tablespoon Dijon mustard

2 medium cucumbers, peeled,
  seeded, and chopped
2 tablespoons finely chopped dill
Salt and fresh pepper to taste

Put the sour cream, mayonnaise, and mustard in a bowl. Add the cucumbers, dill, salt, and pepper and fold together gently.   *Makes about 3 cups.*

Crêpes

½ cup flour
2 eggs
2 egg yolks
¼ cup vegetable oil or melted

butter
½ cup milk
Oil for crêpe pan

Put all ingredients except oil into a blender or food processor. Blend well. Or put all ingredients into a bowl and whisk. Strain if lumpy. Batter should be the consistency of heavy cream. Film a seasoned crêpe pan with a bit of oil. Add 2–3 tablespoons batter and swirl pan in all directions. Fry one side until edges are brown, about 1 minute. Turn over and fry second side about 30 seconds.

Makes 5–6 twelve-inch crêpes or 8–10 seven-inch crêpes.

Cranberries with Sherry

1 cup sugar
1 cup dry sherry

2–3 cups fresh cranberries
½ cup roughly chopped walnuts

Dissolve sugar and sherry in pan over medium heat. Add the cranberries and cook, while stirring, about 5–8 minutes or until the berries pop. Cool 10 minutes and add the walnuts. Store in refrigerator.   *Makes 3–4 cups.*

Serve this with fish or vegetables.

Lemon Sauce

2 eggs
2 egg yolks
Juice of 1 lemon
Salt and fresh pepper to taste
1 cup milk

2 tablespoons finely chopped parsley, chives, or dill, or 2–3 tablespoons capers, rinsed and drained

Put the eggs, egg yolks, lemon juice, salt and pepper, in a small heavy pan. Whisk, off the heat, until well blended. Add milk and place on low heat. Whisk constantly until mixture thickens, about 5 minutes. When thick, remove from heat and add desired herb or capers. Check seasoning.   *Makes 1½ cups.*

Excellent with broiled lamb chops.

Vinegar Mint Sauce

¾ cup vinegar
2 tablespoons sugar

2 tablespoons water
½ cup chopped mint leaves

Combine all ingredients in a pan. Bring to a boil; boil for 1–2 minutes. Let stand 10–15 minutes.   *Makes about ¾ cup.*

Serve on pancakes or waffles.

Brandied Honey

1 cup honey

2 tablespoons brandy

Combine honey and brandy in a bowl. Serve warm or cold.   *Makes 1 cup.*

Vinaigrette

1 teaspoon salt
½ teaspoon freshly cracked black pepper

2 tablespoons vinegar or lemon juice
6 tablespoons oil

Whisk all ingredients together in a bowl. Pour over salad just before serving.

Makes ½ cup.

This makes enough dressing for any one of the following: 3–4 Belgian endives; 3–4 Bibb lettuces; 1 Romaine lettuce; 2–3 bunches of watercress; or 10 ounces spinach.

Béarnaise is recommended for use with steak, poached salmon and chicken supremes. I also like it with lamb. Make certain that the sauce is served on hot *food.*

Béarnaise Sauce

1 tablespoon chopped shallots
½ cup tarragon vinegar
3 tablespoons finely chopped fresh tarragon
3 egg yolks

½ cup melted butter, very hot but not browned
Salt and fresh pepper to taste
2 tablespoons chopped fresh parsley (optional)

In a small heavy pan, over moderately high heat, put shallots, vinegar, and tarragon. Cook, stirring with a wooden spatula, for about 5 minutes or until almost all the liquid evaporates. (Be careful not to let it burn.)

Remove pan from heat. Add the egg yolks and 2 tablespoons of cold water; whisk together until well blended. Return pan to heat and, raising and lowering the pan to keep mixture from becoming hot, whisk until mixture is the consistency of heavy cream.

Remove pan from heat and whisk in 4 tablespoons of the hot melted butter, 1 tablespoon at a time. Again returning the pan to the heat, keep whisking as you add the remaining hot melted butter in a thin stream. Whisk until the mixture is thick. Season with salt and pepper. If you want to stir in the parsley, you might want to strain the béarnaise sauce first.

Makes ¾–1 cup.

Tomato Sauce

4 pounds plum tomatoes
2 tablespoons butter
2 tablespoons oil
1 onion, finely chopped
2 large cloves garlic, or more or less, according to your taste
Tiny pinch of sugar (not much, but do use more sugar than salt here)

Salt and freshly cracked black pepper to taste
4–6 fresh basil leaves, finely chopped
¼ cup chicken stock

Slice off the tips of the tomatoes. Drop them into boiling water for 10 seconds, then plunge into cold water with ice cubes. Squeeze each tomato in your hand and skin will slip off in one piece. Finely chop the tomatoes. Heat the butter and oil in a noncorrosive pan. Sauté onion and garlic together for 5 minutes—do not brown. Add tomatoes, sugar, salt, pepper, basil, and stock. Simmer 25 minutes or until sauce gives up liquid. *Makes 5–6 cups.*

Chicken Stock

4 pounds chicken backs, wings, necks, or a 4-pound whole chicken
1 cup sliced carrots
1 cup sliced celery, with leaves
4 medium onions, peeled
4 whole cloves
1 cup dry white wine

1 clove garlic, mashed
1½ teaspoons chopped thyme
1 bay leaf
3 sprigs parsley
2 tablespoons tomato paste
1 tablespoon salt
Freshly cracked black pepper

Place all ingredients and 4 quarts of cold water in a deep kettle or stock pot. Slowly bring to a boil. Skim; reduce heat and half-cover the kettle. Simmer gently for 1½ hours. Remove the chicken and strip the meat from the bones (use it in any recipe that calls for cooked chicken). Return bones to the kettle and simmer for another 2½ hours. Wring out a cheesecloth of double thickness in cold water, and use it as a lining for a sieve. Strain the stock through this. Stock can be stored in refrigerator for up to a week, if boiled every day, or in the freezer for up to 2 months. If a recipe calls for extra-strong stock, boil, uncovered, over moderately high heat, to reduce by one-third. *Makes 2–3 quarts.*

Bouquet garni is indispensable for flavoring soups, rice, stews, and ragouts.

Bouquet Garni

1 rib celery	3–4 sprigs of parsley
1 bay leaf	Few sprigs of fresh thyme

Make a sandwich of the celery; lay herbs on half the rib, fold the other half over, and tie with a string. Leave one end of the string long enough to tie to the handle of the pot or casserole so it will be easy to remove.

Fish Stock

1 cup sliced onion	1 cup dry white wine
½ cup sliced celery	Bouquet garni
½ cup sliced carrot	Salt and freshly cracked white
2 pounds fish bones and trimmings, all from lean fish	pepper to taste

Put all ingredients and 1 quart of cold water into a kettle or stock pot and bring to a boil. Skim. Reduce heat, half-cover the pot, and simmer 30 minutes. Strain through a fine sieve.   *Makes 3–4 cups.*

Deviled Walnuts

2 tablespoons butter	⅛ teaspoon salt
½ teaspoon dry mustard	2 cups walnut halves or pieces
½ teaspoon chili powder	2 tablespoons grated Parmesan
½ teaspoon Worcestershire	cheese

Preheat oven to 300° F. In saucepan, combine butter and seasonings; heat to melt butter. Add walnuts, toss to coat evenly. Spread nuts on baking sheet. Bake 15 minutes or until toasted; remove from oven. While still warm, sprinkle with cheese.   *Makes 2 cups.*

Polonaise Sauce

½ cup butter
½ cup soft bread crumbs

2 hard-boiled eggs, finely
  chopped

Melt the butter in a small skillet. Add the crumbs and toss until lightly browned. Add the chopped egg. Stir and serve over hot asparagus, cauliflower, or broccoli.

Enough for 4–6 servings.

Court Bouillon

2 cups dry vermouth or other dry white wine, or 1 cup cider vinegar
½ cup chopped onion
½ cup chopped carrot
½ cup chopped celery

2 teaspoons salt
8 peppercorns
3 sprigs of parsley
1 bay leaf
1 clove
½ teaspoon dried thyme

Put all ingredients and 2 quarts cold water into a large saucepan or kettle. Bring to a boil and boil rapidly for 30 minutes. Strain and cool. *Makes 9–10 cups.*

Serve this with fish, crab cakes, and soft-shell crabs.

Tartar Sauce

1 cup homemade mayonnaise
1 small white onion, peeled and grated
1 tablespoon chopped parsley
1 tablespoon chopped tarragon or chervil

2 tablespoons chopped dill pickle
1 tablespoon chopped olives
2 teaspoons horseradish
1 tablespoon capers
Salt and fresh pepper to taste

Mix all ingredients together in bowl.

Makes 1 generous cup.

Use this sauce on berries, fruits, stale cake, babas, and fruit soufflés.

Custard Sauce

2 cups light cream
4 egg yolks
½ cup sugar
2–3 tablespoons liqueur (Grand Marnier or other), or 2 tablespoons rum or cognac, or ¼ cup orange or lemon juice plus 1 tablespoon grated rind,
or 1 tablespoon vanilla extract, or for spicy sauce, add cinnamon, ginger, or nutmeg to taste.

Scald the cream. Beat egg yolks with sugar until thick. Add hot cream slowly, stirring. Cook until mixture coats the back of a spoon. Flavor as desired.

Makes 2½ cups.

Mayonnaise and Variations

Salt and fresh pepper to taste
3 egg yolks
1 teaspoon mustard, Dijon style or dry
1½ cups oil (any kind you select)
1–2 tablespoons vinegar or lemon juice

In a bowl, mix the salt, pepper, egg yolks, and mustard. Whisk well. Begin adding the oil a teaspoonful at a time. Continue to whisk until the mixture emulsifies (thickens). Add the oil, a little more rapidly, in a thin stream, as you whisk. Finish with 1–2 tablespoons vinegar or lemon juice, depending on consistency desired.

Makes 1½ cups.

VARIATIONS:

Add to basic mayonnaise any of the following puréed vegetables: the white part of cooked leeks; a carrot, peeled and cooked; a little cooked fresh spinach or sorrel (this is quite good with fish).

For fruit salad, add 1 tablespoon chopped mint.
For shrimp or fish, add 1 teaspoon saffron.
For fish or shrimp, add 1 tablespoon dill.
For fish, add 1 or more tablespoons capers.

Serve almond mayonnaise as a dip for artichokes.

Almond Mayonnaise

Mayonnaise (preceding recipe) made with juice of ½ lemon   ½ cup chopped toasted almonds

Fold almonds into mayonnaise just before serving.   *Makes about 2 cups.*

Blender Mayonnaise

Using ingredients listed for mayonnaise on page 450 blend salt, pepper, egg yolks, mustard, and vinegar or lemon juice with 2 tablespoons of the oil for a few seconds to mix. With blender on high speed, add the remaining oil in a thin stream. Stop blender as soon as mayonnaise thickens.

Hollandaise Sauce

½ cup butter
3 egg yolks
2 tablespoons lemon juice
Salt and fresh pepper to taste

Melt the butter, but be careful not to brown it. In a small heavy pan that is not aluminum, place the egg yolks and 3 tablespoons of cold water. Over high heat, raising and lowering the pan constantly so as not to let it overheat, whisk together the yolks and water. If the outside of the pan gets too hot, the sauce will curdle. If necessary, remove the pan from the heat entirely—but don't stop whisking. Do this for about 10 minutes or until the mixture begins to mound. It should have the consistency of heavy cream.

Remove the pan from the heat and whisk in ¼ cup of the hot melted butter, a tablespoon at a time (4 tablespoons in all). Return the pan to high heat, keep whisking, and add the remaining hot melted butter in a thin stream. Whisk until the mixture is thick and creamy—this should take about 5 minutes—and continue to move the pan on and off the heat.

Add lemon juice, salt, and pepper. If necessary to wait a while before serving, place the pan over a pan of warm water and whisk now and then. If the sauce seems too thin, return it to the stove—still moving pan to keep it from overheating—and whisk until it thickens. *Makes ¾–1 cup.*

Note: If the sauce should curdle, you can rectify it by whisking in 1 tablespoon of cold water or 1 tablespoon of boiling water. Another method is to whisk an egg yolk in a bowl, then whisk the sauce into it very slowly.

VARIATIONS:

Add 1 tablespoon chopped mint for serving with lamb; add 1 teaspoon saffron for fish or shrimp; add 1 tablespoon dill for fish or shrimp.

Blender Hollandaise

Using the same ingredients, same measures, as preceding hollandaise sauce, blend the egg yolks, lemon juice, salt, and pepper for 1 minute. Turn blender to high speed and pour in the very hot melted butter in a thin stream. The sauce will thicken and it will hold over warm water until serving time—but whisk it now and then.

MENUS

The part I like best about writing cookbooks is designing menus—imagining, experimenting, and testing to decide what goes with what is the most fascinating and the most fun of any of the work that goes into my books.

For this book, for the first time, I have divided the recipes into kinds of food, and left the menus for last. I thought long and hard before I did it—and finally decided that presenting recipes in menu form can be limiting. Some readers think they can't serve roast lamb because they don't have fresh peas to go with it. Other readers never notice a recipe for kohlrabi because it may be listed on a menu with chicken and they don't like chicken.

So I changed the form of the book, just slightly. The work that went into this section was still the most exciting and satisfying of all. And I emphasize again, as I always have before, that these menus are merely suggestions, not orders. If you find good fresh spinach instead of peas, please make the spinach instead. As long as you are using fresh ingredients, you will never go far wrong in taste combinations.

When I began putting this section together I tried grouping meals by time: hour meals, half-hour meals, and fifteen-minute meals. But that eventually got silly. There are, no matter what anybody says, no fifteen-minute meals. You can cook a Chinese stir-fry in seconds, but it still takes time cutting and slicing all those ingredients, with or without a food processor. It takes fifteen minutes to merely wash the vegetables. For some cooks all these recipes will be half-hour or forty-five-minute recipes; for others an hour, or even more. That shouldn't matter. All these menus can be prepared quickly and easily—more so than any other kind of cooking you do. So you don't have to rush. If you are slow, practice will make you faster. If your practice doesn't make you faster, well, nobody ever starved in five or ten minutes. My mother told me that just as your mother told you that. And it's a little bit of wisdom we should pass along, whenever we have the chance, to our own families and friends. A little consideration for the cook, please.

Breakfast, Brunch, and Lunch

"What's lunch?" my daughter says. "Unless you mean the meal I eat every week-day on my lunch hour, I don't ever have lunch. And breakfast is the quickest and craziest meal of the day; the one I most often skip."

For many of us, breakfast, brunch, and lunch are weekend or vacation meals. But that doesn't mean that they are unimportant. For those long lazy mornings when there's no work to worry about, a breakfast slides comfortably into brunch and can be one of the most delightful meals of the week. Don't spend too much time and effort on these meals—the food is important, but it tastes better if you have the feeling that you've loafed through the preparation as well as the eating.

My favorite drink for brunch is a mimosa, a combination of champagne and orange juice. Use a decent champagne and take time to squeeze fresh orange juice. Mimosas are such good drinks that you can suddenly discover you're sitting around the house in your night clothes with only half the Sunday paper read, too giddy on champagne to do anything but go back to bed. Not always a bad idea on a lazy day, but be forewarned: it's easier to arrange your schedule around mimosas than it is to arrange mimosas around your schedule.

Blueberry Soup 292

Baked Eggs in English
Muffin and Bacon
Nests 415

Egg Timbales 414

Fresh Tomato Sauce 447

Fruit Compote with
Yogurt 423

Chicken Livers with
Eggs 412

Broiled Tomatoes 354

Melba Fingers 403

Peaches in Honey 434

Vermouth-Glazed Eggs 415

Broiled Tomatoes with
Yogurt 366

*Breakfast
and Brunch
Menus*

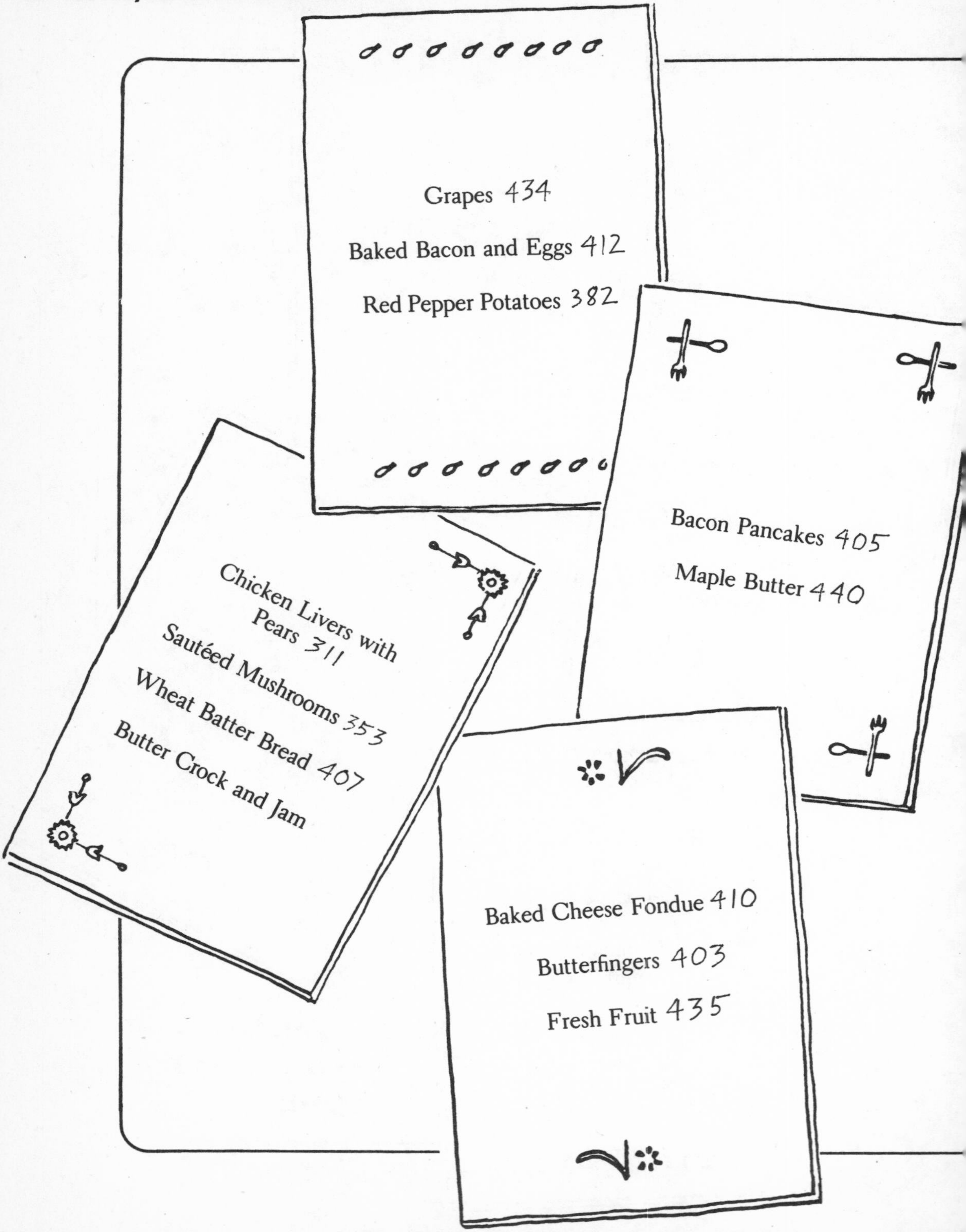

Grapes 434

Baked Bacon and Eggs 412

Red Pepper Potatoes 382

Bacon Pancakes 405

Maple Butter 440

Chicken Livers with Pears 311

Sautéed Mushrooms 353

Wheat Batter Bread 407

Butter Crock and Jam

Baked Cheese Fondue 410

Butterfingers 403

Fresh Fruit 435

Broiled Canadian
Bacon *298*

Banana Nut Bread *407*

Fresh Fruit *435*

Broiled Philadelphia
Scrapple *300*

Quick Sautéed Apples *430*

Broiled Potato Slices *380*

Chicken Livers on
Skewers *310*

Toasted English
Muffins

Broiled Sliced Oranges
with Grand Marnier *416*

Glazed Pears *419*

Pork Patties with Sage
and Orange *308*

Golden Popovers *408*

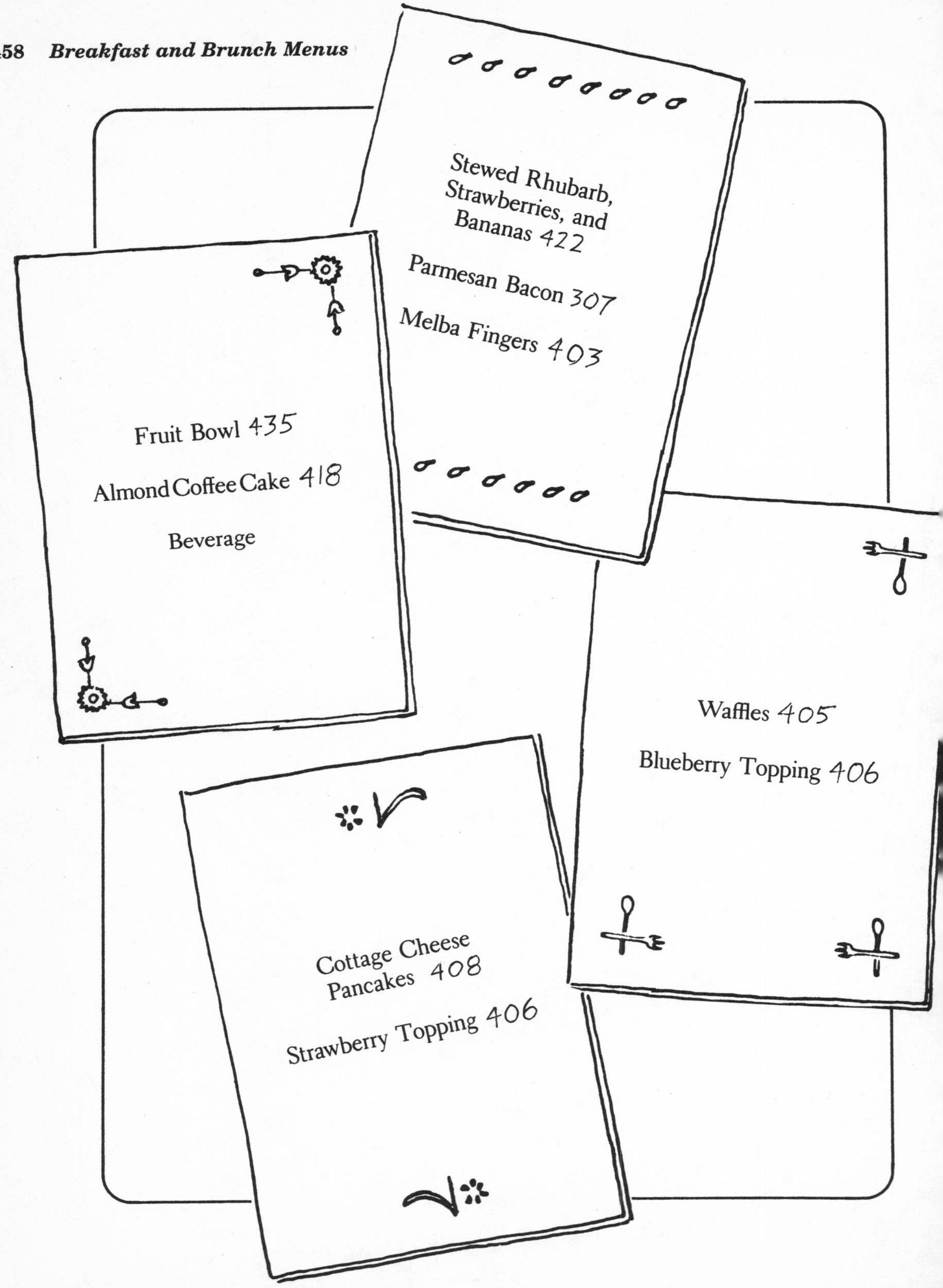

Stewed Rhubarb,
Strawberries, and
Bananas 422

Parmesan Bacon 307

Melba Fingers 403

Fruit Bowl 435

Almond Coffee Cake 418

Beverage

Waffles 405

Blueberry Topping 406

Cottage Cheese
Pancakes 408

Strawberry Topping 406

Zucchini and Potato
Soup *281*

Dandelion Salad *396*

Fruit *435*

Gingered Chicken with
Yogurt *327*

Brown Rice *374*

Escarole with Black
Walnut Dressing *394*

Plums *435*

Walnut Chicken *321*

Plain Rice *374*

Honey-Glazed Peaches *420*

Summer Vegetable Soup
with Basil Sauce *282*

Top-of-the-Stove
Blueberry Pudding *430*

Lunch
Menus

Crêpes Bombay 342

Sliced Tomatoes,
Vinaigrette 446

Sliced Oranges with
Grand Marnier 435

Stuffed Eggs
Supreme 413

Crunchy Winter Salad 396

Polished Apples and
Roquefort Cheese 434

Eggs Indienne 413

Rice Pilaf with
Crystallized Ginger 376

Melon Balls with
Sparkling Cider 428

Egg Drop Soup 285

Shrimp Tempura,
Dipping Sauce 348

Fresh Fruit in Season 435

Julienne of Vegetable
Soup 284

Baked Ham and Cheese
Potatoes 385

Fresh Raspberries 435

Zucchini and Red Onion
Salad 389

Soft-Shell Crabs with
Capers 334

Crushed Peaches with
Vanilla Cream 429

Pineapple and Green
Pepper Salad 397

Baked Potatoes Stuffed
with Sausage 381

Cheese and Crackers 434

Baked Fish Steaks with
Anchovy Butter 344

Red-Skin Potatoes 380

Sour Cream Spinach 364

Fresh Strawberries 435

Chicken Broth with
Poached Eggs 292

Avocado, Pink
Grapefruit, and Orange
Salad 395

Egg or Ham Salad Rolled
in Lettuce Leaf 415

Marble Cookies 428

Maggie and Jiggs
Soufflé 414

Fresh Fruit Compote for
Winter 429

Asparagus Tip
Consommé 280

Green Pea and Swiss
Cheese Salad 398

Fresh Blueberries with
Rum 435

Bacon, Tomato, and Rice
Salad *394*

Toasted Wheat Batter
Bread *407*

Sliced Peaches with
White Port *435*

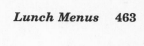

Bacon, Lettuce, and
Tomato Soup *290*

Summer Fruit Salad *393*

Cheese Board *434*

Curried Potato Salad in
Green Pepper Shells *396*

Sliced Grapefruit *435*

Mushroom Consommé *281*

Shrimp and Honeydew
Salad *389*

Butterfingers *403*

Stilton Cheese and
Celery *412*

Almond Fish Filets *347*

Green Beans and
Julienne Celery *356*

Cucumber Melon Salad,
Lemon-Pepper
Dressing *392*

Cheese *434*

Sweetbread and
Cucumber Salad *388*

Fruit Crunch *426*

Corn and Crabmeat
Chowder *282*

Lettuce with Vinaigrette
Dressing *446*

Baked Apples with
Bourbon *433*

Tomato Rarebit
Sandwich *411*

Fruit *435*

Cream of Cauliflower
Soup 285

Melba Rounds 403

Sangría Grapes 422

Cheese Custards 411

Fresh Tomato Sauce 447

Lettuce Leaves,
Vinaigrette Dressing 446

Sautéed Apples 306

Open-Face Cheese
Radish Sandwich or
Grilled Cheese and
Green Pepper
Sandwich 409-10

Bunch of Grapes 434

Dinners

Only a few short years ago, cookbooks and food columnists were worrying that the family dinner was becoming a thing of the past—a victim of television and busy schedules.

But for the working couple, dinner has become much more than a meal. It is the time that they have to spend together, comparing their working days, enjoying each other, and rewarding themselves for getting through one more day of career-building.

Families with teen-agers do have a special problem with dinner. If there are two teen-agers in the family, one always seems to be out of the house when the other one is home. If both are by some strange coincidence home at the same time, one is always asleep when the other is awake. One is always hungry while the other is on a crash diet to lose one pound, or in training and unable to eat anything except raw eggs in milk. The best way to deal with teen-age taste in food, and teen-age eccentricities about food, is to lure them to the table. No matter how severe the diet, no matter how rigorous the training schedule, your teen-ager makes one or two stops at the local fast-food emporium a week. If you haven't seen them at the table for a while, announce casually that tomorrow night is crispy chicken wing night or promise them baked hot fudge pudding for dessert. Promise them good food. Your only competition is mass-produced hamburgers and freeze-dried potato shreds masquerading as French fries. You can beat the fast-food shop on the corner, once a week at least, by giving the kids what they want. Almost any teen-ager will find time to eat good home cooking.

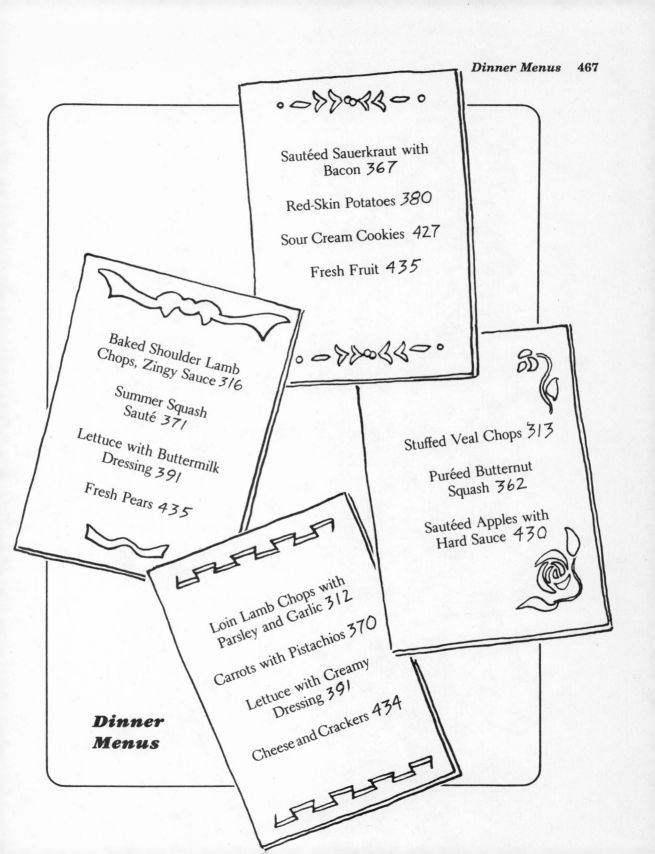

Sautéed Sauerkraut with
Bacon *367*

Red-Skin Potatoes *380*

Sour Cream Cookies *427*

Fresh Fruit *435*

Baked Shoulder Lamb
Chops, Zingy Sauce *316*

Summer Squash
Sauté *371*

Lettuce with Buttermilk
Dressing *391*

Fresh Pears *435*

Stuffed Veal Chops *313*

Puréed Butternut
Squash *362*

Sautéed Apples with
Hard Sauce *430*

Loin Lamb Chops with
Parsley and Garlic *312*

Carrots with Pistachios *370*

Lettuce with Creamy
Dressing *391*

Cheese and Crackers *434*

*Dinner
Menus*

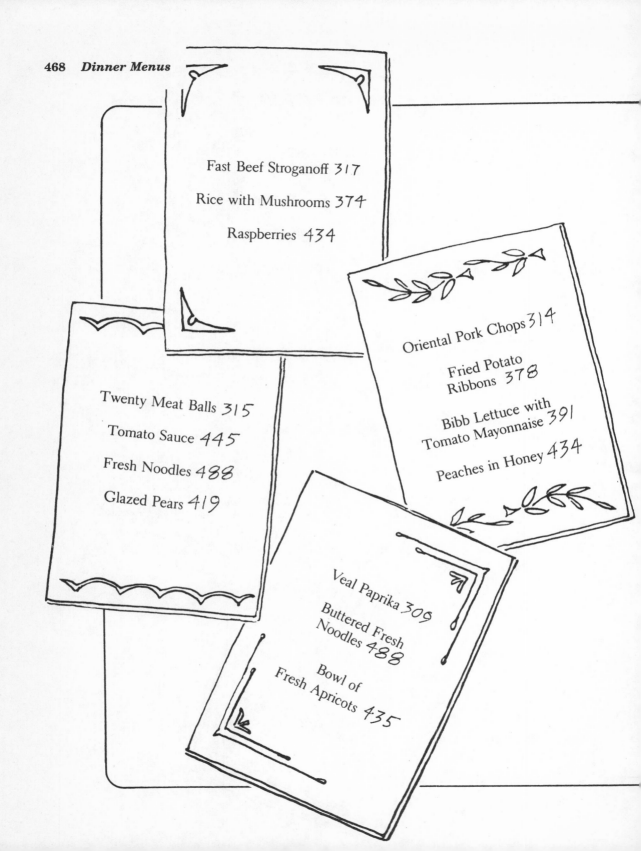

Fast Beef Stroganoff 317

Rice with Mushrooms 374

Raspberries 434

Oriental Pork Chops 314

Fried Potato
Ribbons 378

Bibb Lettuce with
Tomato Mayonnaise 391

Peaches in Honey 434

Twenty Meat Balls 315

Tomato Sauce 445

Fresh Noodles 488

Glazed Pears 419

Veal Paprika 309

Buttered Fresh
Noodles 488

Bowl of
Fresh Apricots 435

Carrot and Mushroom
Soup *289*

Lamb on Skewers *310*

Brown Rice *374*

Baked Apples with
Bourbon *433*

Grapefruit Salad,
Watercress Dressing *390*

Quick Baked Chicken
Supremes *330*

Carrots Steamed in
Foil *369*

Cheese *434*

Mini Meat Loaves *296*

Quick Ratatouille *368*

Fresh Fruit Compote for
Winter *429*

Curry Soup *283*

Lamb Patties with
Mint *313*

Carrots Steamed in
Foil *369*

Honeydew with Seedless
Grapes *428*

Chili Pork Patties 317

Wine-Laced Potatoes 383

Bibb Lettuce with
Creamy Salad Dressing 391

Sliced Oranges with
Cointreau 435

Sweet Potato Bisque 286

Orange Ham Slice 312

Sliced Tomatoes with
Buttermilk Dressing 391

Sliced Pineapple with
Rum 435

Lamb with Eggplant 309

Brown Rice with
Almonds 374

Sweet and Sour Greens 397

Fresh Figs 435

Picadillo 315

Rice 374

Fruit Compote with
Yogurt 423

Baked Whole Calf's
Liver *311*

Mixed Vegetable
Skillet *370*

Lettuce with Vinaigrette
Dressing *446*

Figs in Cream *435*

Curried Mustard Pork
Chops *316*

Acorn Squash with
Sesame Seeds *363*

Artichokes with Melted
Butter *364*

Sliced Bananas with
Orange Juice *435*

Chili Liver Strips *314*

Cheddar Cheese
Potatoes *381*

Zucchini and Red Onion
Salad *389*

Purple Grapes *434*

Sirloin Steak on
Skewers *310*

Baked Potatoes with Basil
Butter *379*

Sliced Tomatoes and Red
Onion *387*

Wedge of Melon* *435*

*Cantaloupe, Honeydew,
Watermelon, Cassaba, Persian

Green Pea Soup *288*

Veal Scallops with
Asparagus *305*

Broiled Salad with
Thyme *389*

Fresh Raspberries and
Strawberries *435*

Jerusalem Artichoke
Soup *284*

Minute Steaks, Herb
Butter *314*

Pencil-Thin Asparagus
with Walnut Oil *368*

Watermelon Wedges *435*

Thick Hearty Potato and
Carrot Soup *288*

Tempura Vegetables,
Dipping Sauce *348*

Sliced Kiwi Fruit *435*

Parmesan Veal *305*

Spinach with Brown
Butter *363*

Bowl of Radishes

Blueberries *435*

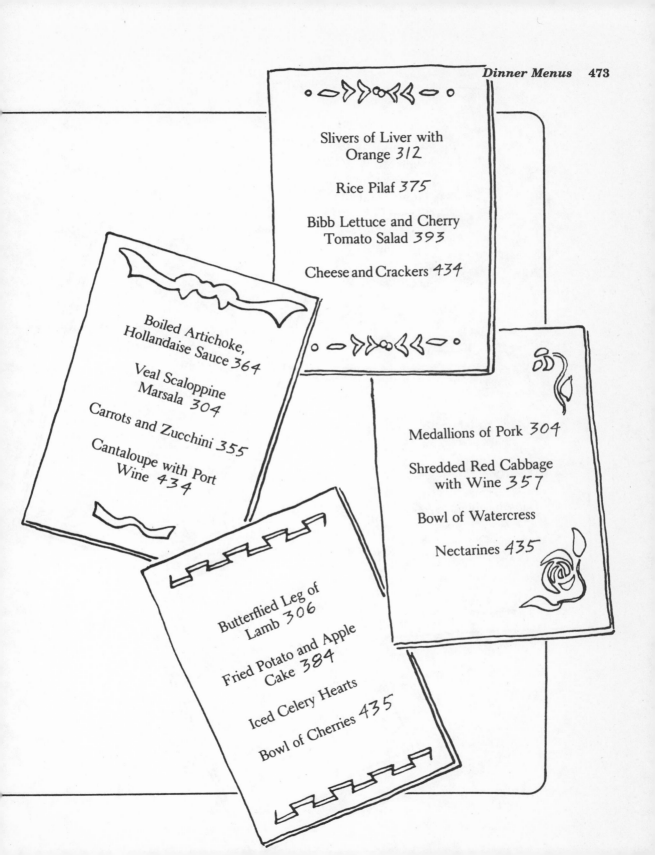

Slivers of Liver with Orange *312*

Rice Pilaf *375*

Bibb Lettuce and Cherry Tomato Salad *393*

Cheese and Crackers *434*

Boiled Artichoke, Hollandaise Sauce *364*

Veal Scaloppine Marsala *304*

Carrots and Zucchini *355*

Cantaloupe with Port Wine *434*

Medallions of Pork *304*

Shredded Red Cabbage with Wine *357*

Bowl of Watercress

Nectarines *435*

Butterflied Leg of Lamb *306*

Fried Potato and Apple Cake *384*

Iced Celery Hearts

Bowl of Cherries *435*

Stuffed Pork Chops with
Watercress *307*

Potatoes Simmered in
Chicken Stock *383*

Iced Cucumber Sticks

Sliced Peaches *435*

Spicy Shoulder of
Lamb *299*

Rice Pilaf with Bouquet
Garni *376*

Top-of-the-Stove
Blueberry Pudding *430*

Lamb in Rhubarb
Sauce *301*

Rice *374*

Baby Eggplant *366*

Cheese and Crackers *434*

Baked Sausage with
Zucchini *308*

Sherried Yams with
Nuts *385*

Celery Sticks

Grapefruit Halves *435*

Beef Birds *302*

Glazed Acorn Squash *361*

Escarole with Creamy
Dressing *391*

Apples, Roquefort
Cheese, and Walnuts in
the Shell *435*

Avocado Soup with
Golden Caviar *291*

Roast Squab with
Mustard *323*

Brown Rice with
Currants *374*

Strawberries with Custard
Sauce *450*

Pumpkin Soup *286*

Ham Balls with Mustard
Sauce *303*

Spiced Fall Compote *424*

Ground Lamb Kabobs *299*

Rice with Mushrooms *374*

Lemony Turnip Sticks *364*

Sangría Grapes *422*

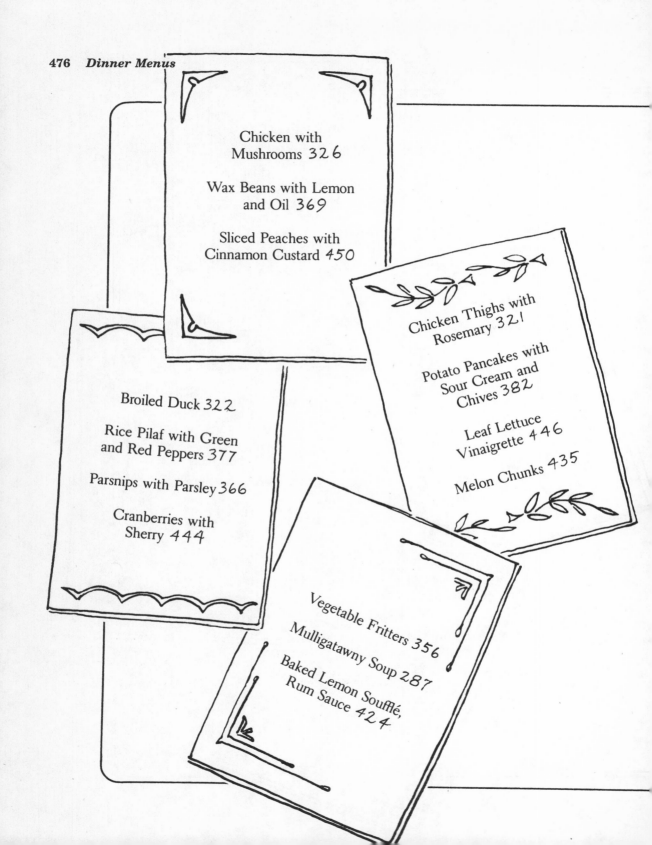

Chicken with
Mushrooms 326

Wax Beans with Lemon
and Oil 369

Sliced Peaches with
Cinnamon Custard 450

Chicken Thighs with
Rosemary 321

Potato Pancakes with
Sour Cream and
Chives 382

Leaf Lettuce
Vinaigrette 446

Melon Chunks 435

Broiled Duck 322

Rice Pilaf with Green
and Red Peppers 377

Parsnips with Parsley 366

Cranberries with
Sherry 444

Vegetable Fritters 356

Mulligatawny Soup 287

Baked Lemon Soufflé,
Rum Sauce 424

Chicken in Saffron
Cream 326

Buttered Noodles 488

Lettuce with Vinaigrette
Dressing 446

Blueberries 435

Roast Tarragon
Chicken 324

Mushrooms in Cream 352

Baked Zucchini and
Tomatoes 354

Crushed Strawberries in
Vanilla Cream 429

Wild Rice Soup 291

Fried Duck 325

Bowl of Relishes

Baked Apples with
Bourbon 433

Ginger-Glazed Chicken
322

Brown Rice with
Almonds 374

Stuffed Onions 362

Raspberries with
Whipped Cream 435

Chicken with Apple
Cream 324

Cabbage Timbales 358

Zucchini and Red Onion
Salad 389

Tangerines 435

Chicken Breasts with
Béarnaise or Basil
Butter 329

Braised Sliced Celery 361

Rice Pilaf with Parsley 377

Grand Marnier Soufflé 426

Chicken Thighs with
Vermouth 321

Green Beans with Lemon
and Oil 369

Pink Rice Pilaf 376

Sliced Oranges and
Grapefruit with Rum 435

Mint Julep Chicken 329

Rice Pilaf with Grated
Carrots 376

Orange and Onion
Salad 392

Cheese 435

Greek Lemon Soup 285

Chicken Breasts with
Ham and Cheese 329

Buttered Noodles 488

Honeydew Slices with
Mint 435

Cream of Broccoli
Soup 285

Quick Chicken Supremes,
Baked 330

Rice Pilaf with Orange 377

Fresh Figs 435

Shreveport Crab Soup 289

Easy Broiled Chicken 323

Okra and Tomatoes 355

Cardamom Peaches 422

Crispy Chicken
Wings 328

Easy Summer Squash 365

Wild Pecan Rice 376

Fresh Fruit with Spiced
Custard Sauce 450

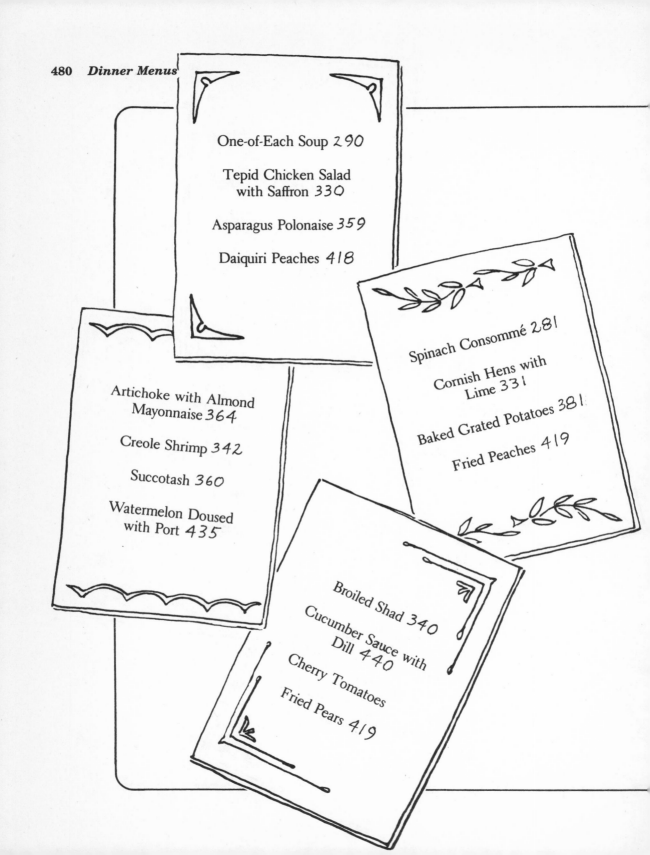

One-of-Each Soup *290*

Tepid Chicken Salad
with Saffron *330*

Asparagus Polonaise *359*

Daiquiri Peaches *418*

Spinach Consommé *281*

Cornish Hens with
Lime *331*

Baked Grated Potatoes *381*

Fried Peaches *419*

Artichoke with Almond
Mayonnaise *364*

Creole Shrimp *342*

Succotash *360*

Watermelon Doused
with Port *435*

Broiled Shad *340*

Cucumber Sauce with
Dill *440*

Cherry Tomatoes

Fried Pears *419*

Cold Cherry Soup 293

Chicken Piccata 329

Baked Cauliflower 365

Cheese 435

Baked Oysters in Cream 340

Small Potatoes in Stock and Saffron 379

Bowl of Watercress

Nectarines and Peaches in Cointreau 435

Shrimp in Beer 336

Gorgonzola Coleslaw 398

Apple Bars 425

Flounder Sicilian Style 337

Artichoke with Vinaigrette 364

Relish Dish

Pears with Gorgonzola 435

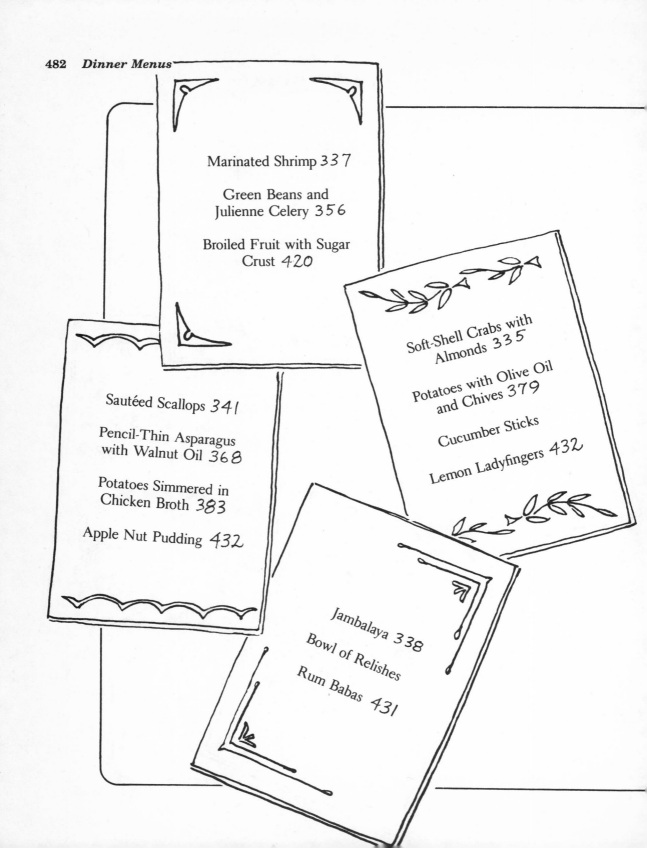

Marinated Shrimp 337

Green Beans and
Julienne Celery 356

Broiled Fruit with Sugar
Crust 420

Sautéed Scallops 341

Pencil-Thin Asparagus
with Walnut Oil 368

Potatoes Simmered in
Chicken Broth 383

Apple Nut Pudding 432

Soft-Shell Crabs with
Almonds 335

Potatoes with Olive Oil
and Chives 379

Cucumber Sticks

Lemon Ladyfingers 432

Jambalaya 338

Bowl of Relishes

Rum Babas 431

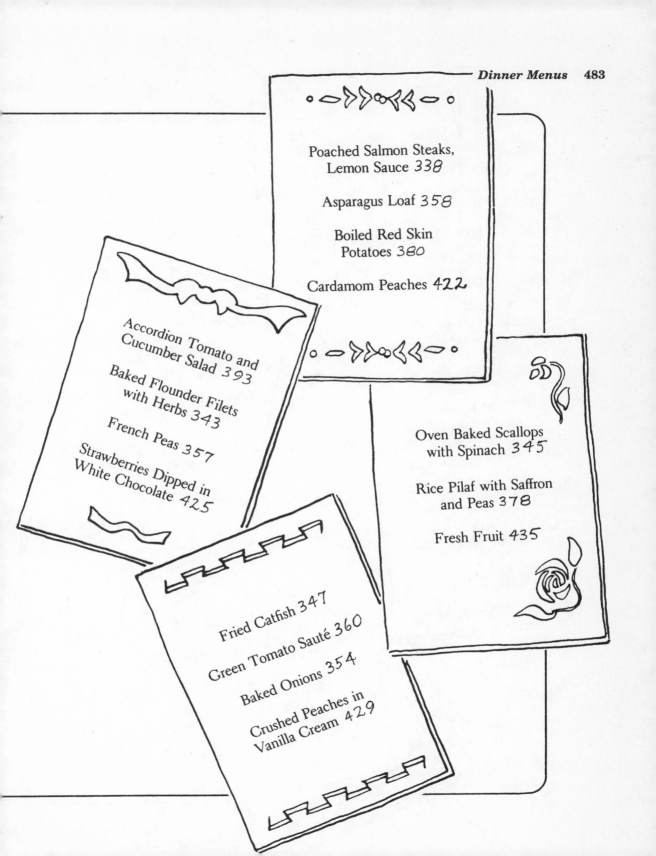

Poached Salmon Steaks,
Lemon Sauce *338*

Asparagus Loaf *358*

Boiled Red Skin
Potatoes *380*

Cardamom Peaches *422*

Accordion Tomato and
Cucumber Salad *393*

Baked Flounder Filets
with Herbs *343*

French Peas *357*

Strawberries Dipped in
White Chocolate *425*

Oven Baked Scallops
with Spinach *345*

Rice Pilaf with Saffron
and Peas *378*

Fresh Fruit *435*

Fried Catfish *347*

Green Tomato Sauté *360*

Baked Onions *354*

Crushed Peaches in
Vanilla Cream *429*

Fish in Parchment 344

Asparagus with Walnut
Butter 359

Boiled Red Skin
Potatoes 380

Stewed Rhubarb,
Strawberries, and
Bananas 422

Fresh Crab Cakes, Tartar
Sauce 339

Cheese and Olive Tossed
Salad 395

Orange Sour Cream
Cake 433

Fish Filets Baked with
Sour Cream 346

Sautéed Belgian Endive 359

Rice Pilaf with Ginger 376

Papaya with Lime
Wedges 435

Broiled Shrimp 336

Buttered Noodles 488

Dandelion Salad 396

Mangoes 435

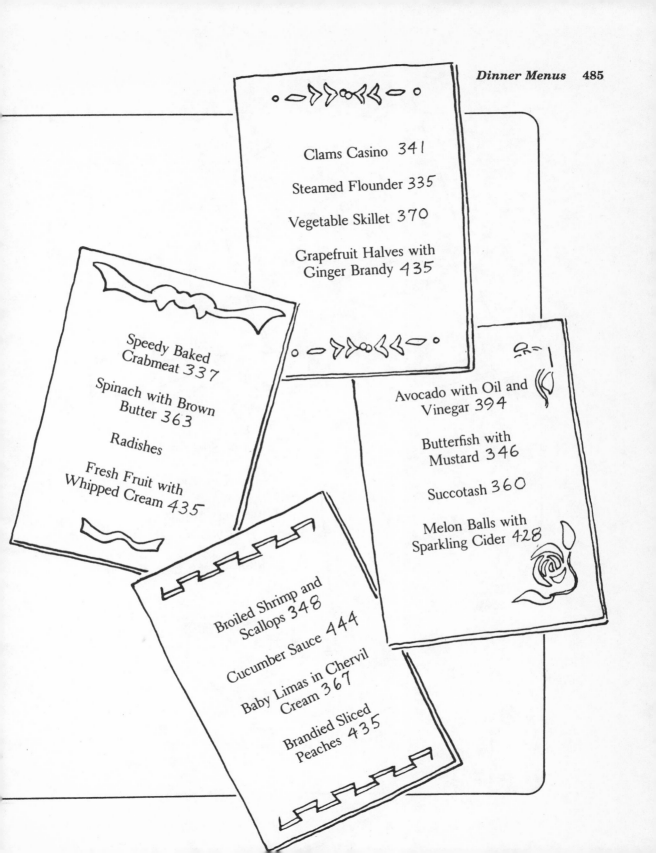

Clams Casino 341

Steamed Flounder 335

Vegetable Skillet 370

Grapefruit Halves with
Ginger Brandy 435

Speedy Baked
Crabmeat 337

Spinach with Brown
Butter 363

Radishes

Fresh Fruit with
Whipped Cream 435

Avocado with Oil and
Vinegar 394

Butterfish with
Mustard 346

Succotash 360

Melon Balls with
Sparkling Cider 428

Broiled Shrimp and
Scallops 348

Cucumber Sauce 444

Baby Limas in Chervil
Cream 367

Brandied Sliced
Peaches 435

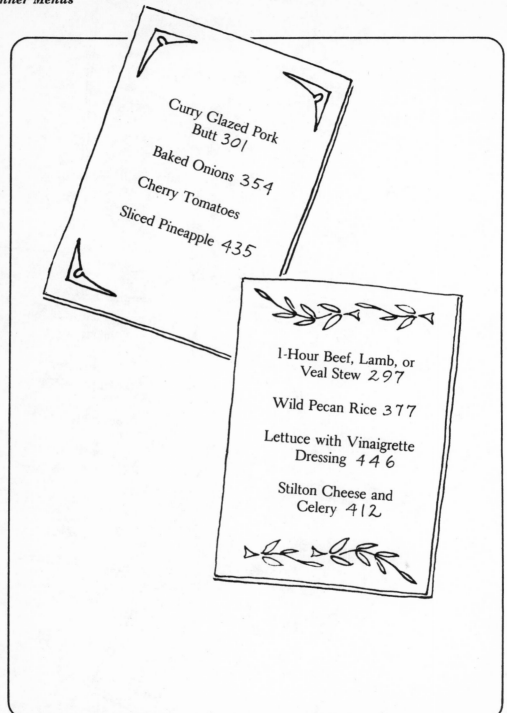

Curry Glazed Pork
Butt 301

Baked Onions 354

Cherry Tomatoes

Sliced Pineapple 435

1-Hour Beef, Lamb, or
Veal Stew 297

Wild Pecan Rice 377

Lettuce with Vinaigrette
Dressing 446

Stilton Cheese and
Celery 412

QUICK TIPS

You bought this book because your schedule demands that you not spend too much time cooking—and because you like good food. So try a few tips to make food easier to fit into your schedule.

Whenever you are hard-boiling eggs, boil a few extra. Mark them with an x and put them in the refrigerator. You can always make a quick first course by deviling or stuffing them, or following the recipes on pages 412–415.

Whenever you roast a chicken, roast two. Cold roast chicken makes a delicious summer meal served with salad and a fresh vegetable. Or make the chicken salad on page 330.

When you make mini meat loaves (page 96), make enough to put some away in the fridge. Cold meat loaf is quite the same as pâté; it will do for a first course or snack and for a delicious sandwich.

Take the time to cut or have your butcher cut meat into finger-size pieces or very small pieces—the meat will cook faster, stay tender, and develop good flavor. See the basic one-hour stew on page 97.

Learn to use the julienne disk on your food processor. Or practice on a mandoline until you get fast. Buy one of those julienne contraptions made by

Mouli—they work fine, too. If nothing else, grate vegetables on your hand grater and they will cook faster.

If you are cooking in an hour and have only one oven, don't worry if you're faced with two different foods that call for two different temperatures. If you don't have the time to cook things separately, just average things out, and set the oven to 350°F. That's a good round number which will not really hurt anything (soufflés excepted). This simple tip has saved many students many long and anxious moments in the kitchen.

In a very big hurry? Wash the vegetables carefully and forget about peeling them. I mash potatoes and turnips now with the skins on. It doesn't look as elegant, but it does taste delicious. Somewhere in America there are cooks who still string celery, but I stopped that long ago. Your family and guests will never notice.

If you are trying to cool something quickly, place it over a bowl of ice and stir until cold. This is quicker than the freezer and anyway if you put it in the freezer there is a law that says you will always spill bright red sour cherry soup on the box of vanilla ice cream in the freezer and some of it will leak through.

Plan ahead and have plenty of ice on hand—there is another law that says if you try to use the same ice for the guests' drinks, you'll discover that the soup spilled on the ice, too. After you've filled the glass.

If you have time to cook an entrée and nothing else, you can fool yourself and your dinner companions into thinking it's a full-course meal. Smoked salmon, served alone or with dill mayonnaise, is a no-work first course that can be eaten while you are waiting for the rest of the dinner to be cooked. Prosciutto, served with melon, pears, figs, or pineapple, is a ready-made appetizer, garnished with a wedge of lime.

Fresh noodles—either homemade or bought from a specialty store that makes fresh pasta daily—fill up the plate and can be tossed with the pan juices of the entrée or with butter and cheese, fresh basil, or fresh tomato sauce.

Herb butters, always a great idea to keep on hand, can be added to steak, fish, or chicken—anything broiled, poached, or sautéed will look better and taste better with a little medallion of herb butter on top. And it even seems more elegant.

WHAT HAS HAPPENED TO AMERICAN FOOD?

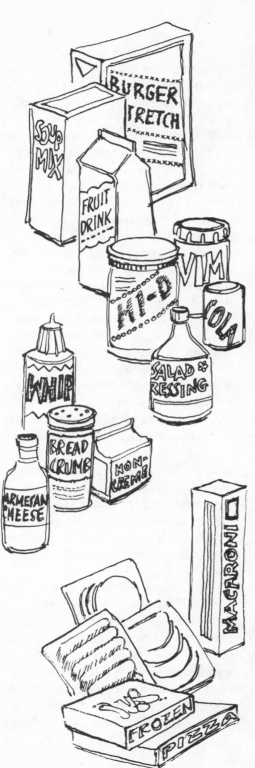

For years I rubbed a well-known brand of cooking oil on ring molds to keep cakes from sticking. I started demonstrating this trick in class one day and—the cake stuck. I thought that someone must have scoured the ring with steel wool or Brillo, which will sometimes take off the cure if it's done long and persistently enough. So I gave the ring mold another coat of oil and tried again. Still stuck. I had to go on with the class, but when I went home later, for my own peace of mind I tried the same recipe with another ring mold. Stuck. Oiled it and tried again. Tried all my ring molds. Cakes stuck to every one of them. Finally my family came home and asked me, "What's for dinner?"

"Nothing much," I said, "unless you're hungry for a lot of broken cakes. Something's wrong with all my ring molds."

But I was soon to find out. It wasn't the molds. It was the oil. During the oil crisis and the rapid inflation of food prices, many cooking oils went so high that manufacturers simply changed their formulas. They put in more or less cotton or peanut or linseed oil—without bothering to mention the fact, and without caring that it made the oil a little less usable. I was blaming my ring pans when I had merely stumbled on one more example of the deterioration of American food.

Sometimes I think too much is made of that deterioration. Some people seem to have eaten their last decent meal when they were five or six years old. And I suspect that's because they wouldn't have it any other way—they seem to enjoy the fact that everything is lousier, enjoy it so much that it's hard to believe they're not exaggerating just a little bit.

But I spend a lot of time cooking for my classes, and some food has definitely changed, for the worse. Cream cheese, which I used to love straight from the supermarket package, is now so heavily loaded with stabilizers and emulsifiers that it has the consistency of bubble gum. I get my cream cheese from a cheese shop now, the kind that comes with a label saying "All Natural, No Additives." It tastes like cream cheese and, oddly enough, it doesn't cost any more than emulsified cheese. Actually, I suppose, it should cost less. It costs money to put additives in, not leave them out.

Unsalted butter, which I used to buy in the supermarket, also has to come from a specialty store now. It costs a little more, but at least it hasn't been frozen. Frozen butter picks up ice

crystals and the water stays in the butter after it thaws. Put a lump of frozen butter in the pan and it starts to sizzle as the water boils out—and goes on sizzling and sizzling. Eventually you can get the water out if you cook it long enough, but you can't do that if you're cutting the butter into flour to make pastry. I had a few pastry disasters until I switched to specialty store butter.

My cream comes from a nearby dairy, a tiny independent one that still sells cream in glass bottles. It is not stabilized, so it won't keep for months in the refrigerator—and it doesn't taste stabilized. It is also so thick that I have trouble pouring it out of the bottle—it is so heavy that I actually have to add a little water to whip it. And it costs $2 a quart instead of the 89¢ a pint that stabilized cream costs.

Mushrooms used to get dark if they were exposed to light. Now, unless you buy them at a farmer's market, they've been treated with sodium bicarbonate and wrapped in plastic. So they stay bone white and turn slimy. That is, they stay white until you wipe them off with a damp cloth, when they turn pink! One more item on the specialty shopping lists.

No wonder supermarkets are in trouble. The only things you can buy there with any confidence are tissue paper and plastic garbage bags. Cheese comes shrink-wrapped in plastic; it's waxy, cardboardy, and tasteless; and it costs more than real cheese in a cheese store. Whatever they've done to cottage cheese has made it both gummy *and* full of runny white liquid—plus increased the calories.

I never buy meat except at a butcher store nowadays—even the pork in those big open refrigerated trays has a weird reddish or pinkish cast to it. Some meat packer decided to soak everything in blood to make it look "appetizing" (though there's nothing appetizing to me in a pork roast the color of a raw beet). And all the blood in those meats—which we pay for, since it adds weight—makes roasts so wet that they don't roast at all. They just boil in the oven. They taste tough and they simply will not brown properly. If you get a roast like this, tell the butcher it's his fault; and if he can't get you better meat, find a butcher who will.

Packaged yeast has changed. A few years ago, it just got weaker. I don't know how the manufacturer managed that; but I do know that you have to let the yeast work a little longer in warm water now, to make sure it grows up to the old strength.

I check the labels on all the imported products I buy. German beers, French mustards, Italian pasta, olive oil, and vinegar—the only thing imported about many of those things is the name. And as soon as I find out that they're made in America, I switch brands. Something happens to food mass produced in this country. Emulsifiers happen. The formula is changed so that it can be more easily turned out by a machine, or something is added to make sure that it will have a shelf life of five or six years. You're much better off

getting fresh pasta from one of those specialty stores where it is made fresh daily than you are buying "imported" spaghetti packed in Brooklyn.

The last ham I ever bought from a major packing house was three years ago. I sliced the leftovers to make myself a sandwich for lunch and sat down eating at the typewriter, working on a recipe. It was two bites before I realized: All I'm tasting is the whole wheat bread. Why spend money on something without any real taste? I buy country hams now, or locally produced hams from my butcher. They cost a lot more. But at least I'm paying for ham, not water; and I don't have to use white bread to know what kind of meat is in the sandwich.

Packaged bacon must be stretched on a rack before it's wrapped up in all that plastic—it feels like rubber when it's raw, and when it cooks it shrivels up to nothing. I buy slab bacon instead, have the butcher cut it half an inch thick, and cook it by starting in a cold iron skillet, on low flame, so it cooks slowly and gets crisp and crunchy all the way through.

Sausages have turned a horrible flesh color, so that they look pinkish gray raw, and they won't brown no matter how they're cooked.

Sometimes it seems as if nobody cares about food in America.

And sometimes it seems as if everybody cares about food. Though mass-produced food is getting worse and worse, there is more good food available in specialty stores than there ever was before. Pistachios are now grown in California—better than any of the pistachios we used to get from Iran. When I first started teaching my classes, I could never find greens like arugula or roquette; now they're available every summer. After years of nothing but big potatoey Delicious apples, I find tiny tart Granny Smith and McIntosh everywhere now. In my area there is a farm that produces fresh herbs year around—in a greenhouse in winter. There are other farms that raise pheasant and duck and partridge in big open-air cages hundreds of yards long filled with the bushes and greens that give those birds their natural taste. My butcher is able to get meat that is every bit as good as meat used to be years ago—and sometimes even better. My daughter and her friends have turned their backyards into gardens—they club together, spade up one plot at a time, and raise their own fresh fruit and vegetables.

We seem to be separating into two entirely different food cultures: one all natural, one all artificial. And strangely enough, the stores that stock the artificial preserved food, the stuff designed so that they can keep it on the shelves forever and never throw anything away, are having the most trouble. Another chain of supermarkets has just gone broke in my home town—and the little stores that supply the home-grown spices and carefully raised poultry have never been busier.

Maybe that's the secret. The rapid rise in food prices has made it possible for little local producers and small stores to compete with the big chains. Compete—and beat their prices. So maybe what's happening to American food is something good. Maybe we're discovering that food that can't go bad can never be very good. And that locally produced food is often the very best we can eat—especially if you buy it fast, and cook it while it's fresh.

INDEX